The Believers' Church
In Canada

THE BELIEVERS' CHURCH IN CANADA

Addresses and Papers from the Study Conference
in Winnipeg, May 15-18, 1978

Edited by
Jarold K. Zeman and Walter Klaassen
with the assistance of
John D. Rempel

Published by
The Baptist Federation of Canada
and
Mennonite Central Committee (Canada)
1979

Typeset by Mennonite Publishing Service Inc.
Printed by Waterloo Printing Company, Waterloo, Ontario

ISBN 0-9690066-0-8

Additional copies may be ordered from

The Baptist Federation of Canada,
    P.O. Box 1298, Brantford, Ont. N3T 5T6
or
Mennonite Central Committee (Canada),
    201-1483 Pembina Highway, Winnipeg, Man. R3T 2C8

STUDY
CONFERENCE
on
the
Believers Church
in
Canada

TABLE OF CONTENTS

PREFACE

The term "Believers' Church" appears to have been coined by the German sociologist Max Weber in his important work **The Protestant Ethic and the Spirit of Capitalism**. Weber introduced the English expression, rather than a German equivalent, in the original German edition of his book in 1904. He defined the Believers' Church as "a community of personal believers of the reborn and only these."[1]

For half a century, English-speaking historians and theologians ignored Weber's term and used "Free Church" instead to describe the concept of the gathered church, "a voluntary association of convinced believers."[2] With its many connotations of meaning,[3] the term "Free Church" lacks precision and has lost much of its original significance in the contemporary context of separation of church and state in North America and elsewhere.

The concept of the Believers' Church implies the vision of a church which strives to practise regenerate church membership. It is "the gathered church of committed disciples living in fellowship of mutual correction, support, and abiding hope" (George H. Williams).[4] Those who subscribe to such a concept reject the idea of territorial or national churches as exemplified for centuries in most European countries. In such cases, church membership and citizenship in a country overlap.

However, the advocates of the Believers' Church principle also find unacceptable the concept of the church as "a mixed multitude" based on the Old Testament model of the children of Israel (Exodus 12:38). Denominations which subscribe to such inclusivistic ecclesiology acknowledge as a matter of principle the reality of a church which is made up of committed Christians as well as of many members with only nominal relationship to Christ and the church.[5]

Baptists, Mennonites and other Christians in the Believers' Church tradition, admit that in practice many of their congregations fall short of the ideal of regenerate church membership. Nevertheless, they refuse to endorse their failure as the normative principle. Rather, the vision of the Believers' Church is upheld as a call to repentance and renewal as well as a summons to uncompromising obedience. Believer's baptism has served as the symbolic mark of their ecclesiological identity.

To some, the designation of a church or denomination as a Believers' Church is offensive since it can be misunderstood as an expression of "Pharisaic pride" and contemptuous exclusivism in an age of ecumenicity.[6] Similar if not stronger objections may be raised against many other denominational labels. To call one church "Catholic" (universal, global) suggests that all others are fragmentary in jurisdiction and incomplete in their understanding of Christian truth. The labels "Orthodox," "Reformed," or "Christian," when appropriated as official names of denominations, can imply condemnation of others as unorthodox, unreformed and non-Christian. Several spokesmen for the current Believers' Church thrust have expressed reservations about the term but a better designation is yet to be proposed.

Rather than being separatist and isolationist, the "movement" has provided a fresh impetus for dialogue and fellowship among Christians of many traditions. For Canadian Baptists, at least for those who are linked with the Baptist Federation of Canada (BFC), the Believers' Church thrust has served as a necessary and healthy corrective to their somewhat lopsided ecumenicity in the past. As a member body of the Canadian Council of Churches, the BFC Baptists have tended to limit their interchurch contacts to the "mainline" Protestant bodies (Anglican, Presbyterian and United).

The Believers' Church initiative has opened opportunities for fellowship with other communions, such as the Mennonites, with whom the Baptists shared common roots in the Radical Reformation but from whom they were later alienated due to ethnic and other barriers. The Mennonites in Canada have lived in relative religious and cultural isolation for several generations. For them, the Believers' Church movement has erected roadsigns to wider fellowship and to new areas in which to bear their distinctive witness.

Several conferences on the history, theology and contemporary implications of the Believers' Church vision were convened in the U.S.A. and prepared the way for the 1978 conference in Winnipeg. A few Canadian Baptists and Mennonites participated in the 1967 conference at the Southern Baptist Theological Seminary in Louisville, Kentucky; the 1970 conference at the Chicago Theological Seminary in Chicago; and the 1975 conference at Pepperdine University, Malibu, California.[7] A Committee on Continuing Conversations serves as a link between conferences and encourages sponsorship of additional meetings. There is no other organization or office.

In contrast to the American conferences which were convened by more heterogeneous interdenominational committees, related mostly to seminaries and without any official mandate from denominational bodies, The Study Conference on the Believers' Church in Canada was sponsored and subsidized by the Baptist Federation of Canada (BFC) and the Mennonite Central Committee (Canada). The MCC serves as a cooperative agency for most Mennonite bodies in Canada. The combined BFC and MCC constituency represents a majority of congregations which can be classified as Believers' Churches in Canada.

A Planning Committee was appointed initially by the BFC and MCC, and was responsible for the programme and all other conference arrangements. Once constituted, the committee sought to involve representatives of other major Believers' Churches in the planning process and in the conference itself but succeeded only in a modest way.

Letters of invitation asking for the nomination of conference participants were sent to the head offices of Canadian denominations identified as Believers' Churches, and to seminaries and Bible colleges linked with them. Representatives of several other (paedobaptist) denominations, the Canadian Council of Churches and the Evangelical Fellowship of Canada were invited as observers. The conference was also announced in several papers. Interested persons were encouraged to obtain invitation from the conference office in Winnipeg. Thus, conference participation was "by invitation," interpreted in a broad sense.

In choosing this procedure, the Planning Committee deliberately sought to safeguard a reasonable balance of representation at the conference, with respect to denominational affiliation and geographical distribution across Canada. Whereas the preceding conferences in the U.S.A. were conceived primarily as symposia of scholars, the Canadian conference was envisaged as a fellowship of well-informed semi-official representatives of the different Believers' Church traditions, many of whom would be bearers of institutional responsibilities, denominational and educational. The conference would therefore provide a reasonably accurate mirror of the present identity of the Believers' Church tradition in Canada. It was hoped as well that the conference would speak with a prophetic voice to the conscience of the people within the tradition and those without.

Four conference objectives were set:

1. To evaluate the major contributions of the Free Church tradition in Canada.

2. To examine the present state of the communions representing the Believers' Church vision in Canada, and their impact upon society.

3. To consider the future witness of the Believers' Church community in Canada.

4. To worship and fellowship together as brothers and sisters in Christ.

The conference met during May 15-18 on the campus of the Canadian Mennonite Bible College in Winnipeg, with additional accommodation and services provided by the Mennonite Brethren Bible College. One hundred and fifty persons took part in the proceedings as registered participants. Many others attended two evening public rallies held in the Portage Avenue Mennonite Brethren Church.

In its composition, the conference met the expectations of the Planning Committee only partially. There was a good balance in the proportion of laity and ordained ministers. All but two provinces (Newfoundland and Prince Edward Island) were represented.[8] Eleven persons from the U.S.A. attended the conference. There was only a token presence of women participants, with no women listed on the programme. The Planning Committee sought in vain to rectify this shortcoming. Nomination of women participants was underscored in the letters of invitation. The failure to secure such nominations indicates the predominantly male leadership in the existing denominational and educational institutions.

With the exception of the Rev. Maurice C. Boillat, General Secretary of the Union of French Baptist Churches of Canada, French Canadian Christians were not represented at the conference. The Planning Committee had considered the format of a bilingual conference as well as a substantial emphasis on the growing Believers' Church movement in French Canada. It finally decided against it in view of the long agenda for the conference and of the different set of issues faced by the Believers' Churches in Quebec and in other French-speaking areas of Canada. A special conference on the Believers' Church in French Canada should be considered.

The guidelines followed in the selection of participants determined, to a large extent, the educational and age profile of the conference.[9] Eighty per cent of the persons in attendance reported graduate degrees.

The most serious shortcoming of the conference was the lack of representation from Believers' Churches other than Baptists and Mennonites. The two denominational families supplied, in balanced proportions, ninety per cent of conference participants and included persons from most groups within the divided Baptist and Mennonite camps.[10] BFC Baptists and Mennonites were represented by their top leadership: denominational executives, professors, editors and pastors of "key" churches. There was only token representation from the following groups: The Brethren in Christ Church, the Christian Church (Disciples of Christ), The Christian and Missionary Alliance, The Evangelical Church in Canada, The Free Methodist Church and the Pentecostal Assemblies of Canada.

In spite of such shortcomings, the conference was a unique event in the history of Christianity in Canada and was recognized as such in press reports.[11] The conference issued "A Message to Christians and Churches in Canada" (see the Appendix) and passed a resolution calling for the appointment of a Task Force on Believers' Church Witness in Canada "to continue the interest which has been engendered at this study conference" (see the Appendix). Recommendations and resolutions formulated by seminar groups will be considered by the Task Force. There was an enthusiastic consensus of opinion that follow-up conferences should be held, perhaps on a regional rather than national level, and with more limited agendas.

With the exception of the Bible Studies presented by David Ewert, and addresses delivered at public rallies by Franklin H. Littell and Frank C. Peters, this volume makes available, in edited form, all addresses and seminar papers presented at the conference. We regret that economic considerations precluded the printing of all but three responses.

Professor Walter Klaassen of Conrad Grebel College, Waterloo, Ontario, was responsible for the first phase of the editorial process, prior to his departure for a sabbatical study leave in Oxford, England. Mr. C. Alvin Armstrong, a professional journalist and contributing editor to several papers in Ontario, served as the copy editor. Mr. John D. Rempel of Conrad Grebel College assumed responsibility for the final preparation of the manuscript and the supervision of the publication process. Without the personal interest and sustained support of Dr. R. Fred Bullen and Mr. Daniel Zehr, secretaries respectively of the BFC and MCC (Canada), co-publishers of the book, the publication of this volume would not have been possible.

To all of them, and to many others whose names must remain unmentioned, I wish to express my personal gratitude as well as the appreciation of all who will benefit from the reading of the book. It is our prayer that the study of this volume will enrich the lives of the readers, stimulate fruitful discussion of vital issues among members of the Believers' Churches and with Christians of other traditions, and thus contribute to the clarification and strengthening of Christian witness and Christ's church in Canada.

Acadia Divinity College
Acadia University
Wolfville, N.S.   **Jarold K. Zeman**

I

The Believers' Church
In General Perspectives

Plenary Addresses

THE BELIEVERS' CHURCH: GLOBAL PERSPECTIVES

John H. Yoder

First, let me affirm: The Church of tomorrow cannot but be a Believers' Church.

What historians of the last generation have agreed to designate as the Believers' Church vision arose, in all of the major episodes of which we are informed, not out of any conscious calculation of the timeliness, the popularity or the relevance of the particular point being made. Yet by a strange reversal of circumstance, the convictions which for Cheltchitski and Hubmaier, Sattler and Smythe, Helwys and Fox were adopted simply on the grounds of revealed imperative are turning out in our age to be the coming thing. The major items of the Believers' Churches' distinctive agenda of witness are now being seen even by uncommitted observers and by people who would still not accept them as biblically imperative, to be fitting when one looks at the social possibilities of modern times.

We may ask about the numbers of people belonging to churches committed to a Believers' Church polity and the rate of numeric growth of those communities, or we may ask about the social structures within which the work and witness of the church needs to be carried forward: the reading is the same. The future of the church of Jesus Christ on earth, East, West, and South is the future of a voluntarily confessing community of committed adults.

Thinkers in many schools of thought have been brought to make this statement on grounds of systematic theological integrity. Karl Rahner has been saying for a decade that the future form of existence of the community of Christian belief will be that of a church in the diaspora. His Protestant countryman Juergen Moltmann, in other language speaks as well of the community of faith as intrinsically voluntary. Juan-Luis Segundo, the most theologically sophisticated of the Latin liberation theologians, has long been saying that while God's saving purposes are far broader than the church, the confessing community should expect to be a minority. What in the 1930s was a rare hypothetical reopening of the question of infant baptism, when Karl Barth first challenged the biblical foundations for infant baptism, has now become a growing movement in Reformed, and then Lutheran, and now increasingly even in Catholic ecclesiology. The church thus has no longer a strong hold upon the loyalties of the children of her members. Even with regard to adult birthright members, it is not always sure with what degree of conscious commitment they continue to belong to the body. It is thus becoming increasingly functional to think about the church as community in terms most like the classical Believers' Church vision.

A third line of causation, prior to the other two in both chronology and importance, leads to this new affirmation from the perspective of the rediscovery of world mission. The very idea of sending missionaries, which was within Protestant experience an initiative of pietists and free church people, predisposes one for the rediscovery of the naturalness of being the church in a world whose sovereigns are not friends or members of the body. The inherited habits of national church thinking were so powerful that in the early days of world missions one did not perceive in the overseas missionary experience the potential for a reversal of the self-understanding of the churches back home. Even all the way through the nineteenth century, the Christian world mission was a specialty for uniquely called people who left the "Christian world" for the "non-Christian world." Thus what they did "out there" was understood as an affirmation and in no sense a critique of, or an alternative to, the Christendom base from which they were sent out. Yet, the authenticity of what came into being in the response to their witness burst the limits of the efforts to keep the missionary self-understanding of the church restricted to overseas. Therefore, when later analysts of the European situation woke up to the fact that western Europe is mission territory, there existed already a reservoir of understanding among missiologists and overseas Christians, to reinforce our sense of the rightness of that reading.

The theme already identified is in one sense central to all the others: If the church were not a voluntary minority community none of the other things we say about her nature and mission would have any foundation. It is, however, not only this particular quality of the church as voluntary which is coming into its own as we take stock in global perspective.

One major derivative mark which for some is more definitional than voluntariness or mission is the insistence on religious liberty and church-state separation. More than ever it is visible that the Christian faith demands this restraint upon government, and by analogy the same restraint by each church on her own temptation to heighten conformity or gain security by appeal to civil supports and sanctions. There are still those who do not really believe that church-state separation is universally ideal and normative, but the number of those advocating any renewal of the classical partnership of throne and altar is diminishing radically. With the Roman Catholic communion now committed explicitly to religious liberty, with most major Protestant bodies having made the same move in the course of the nineteenth century, and with the Orthodox who historically had been most committed to the other model, largely under the control of Marxist and Muslim governments, the case for religious liberty on the level of theoretical proclamations no longer needs to be made. What in Michael Sattler was a heresy and in Roger Williams still a civil offence is now normative Christian political theory. This observation does not however call for a victory celebration. As the number of those in churches and in modern governments stating verbally that every citizen is free for his/her own religious practice is growing, the number of societies in which that stated liberty is concretely experienced by religious dissenters is rather decreasing than increasing. This pessimistic observation is due to be heightened to the degree to which "theologies of liberation" will increasingly bring church people to link their freedom to celebrate their faith in the God of the Jews and the father of Jesus with a new form of conviction and action in the political realm. Religious liberty has always been by implication political dissent, but most of the governments affirming religious liberty as a social desideratum do not see it that way. Thus on the level of implementation our world is no freer than in earlier ages: yet the observation stands that theologically this case has been won.

A further element of the Believers' Church identity is the distinctive quality of community which is made possible by the fact that adhesion is voluntary and is often made indispensable by the fact that Christian faith is persecuted. The concept of the church as brotherhood was identified by H.S. Bender as one of the three marks of the "Anabaptist vision."[1] We locate the reality we call the "church" not so much in a personage executing sacramental acts or in the hierarchy administering canonical structures, as in the people themselves who gather around Jesus and celebrate their unity by belonging to one another as well as to the same Lord. This value too is coming into its own; only now do we see more completely its importance.

In pre-industrial village cultures, the clan and the neighbourhood provided for many a sense of personhood-in-community. You did not need to join a voluntary community to be recognized and accepted as a person mattering to other persons, having access to esteem, attention and material welfare. So it is no surprise that then, over against the backdrop of unitary village culture, what was striking about the early Believers' Church format was the individual freedom it created: the idea and the reality of one person making his own decision about faith and obedience. Since, however, industry and the city have destroyed for most of us the sense of a natural home, it becomes fitting to observe that here is another complementary point where the voluntary community speaks to a vacuum in our culture and in our soul. The popular **Ersatz** faith communities, some of them developed around synthetic psychological disciplines, some of them around modifications of eastern religious vision, some derived from a more or less recognizable Christian root, are sufficient demonstration of the hunger for belonging to God's people. It is only regrettable that in some times and places congregations of our Believers' Church family have failed to respond to that hunger, being still captive of the age (or class) within which individual liberation seemed more urgent than reaffirmed community.

The point at which traditional Believers' Church order affirmed this new gift was the special respect given to the "Rule of Christ" in Matthew

18: 15-18. The meaning of that guidance from the Lord was however, not, as it later was often thought to be, a ritual form for admonition and if necessary excommunication, nor a charter for authoritarianism, but rather the foundation of mutual moral responsibility in voluntary covenant. If my duty to my brother or sister includes restoration when there has been sin, it cannot but include all the other needs of body and spirit in the family of faith.

If it were my purpose to extend this first address with some claim to completeness, the dimensions of the claim that the world is ready for the message could be expanded considerably: egalitarianism, servanthood as a life-style, non-authoritarian decision-making, simplicity in ritual. But for our purpose these specimens should suffice. The position which once was so unpopular as to be taken only by those for whom the clear word of God overturned all considerations of popularity is now a message whose time has come.

My second affirmation: We are unworthy servants of this timely cause.

For reasons only partly understandable, the power and attraction of the Believers' Church vision are not matched by the conviction with which Mennonites and Baptists, Brethren and Disciples are advocating this witness in their inter-church relations, whether locally or in broader ecumenical contexts.

If it be the case that the needs of our age invite a resounding reaffirmation of the proclamation of the gospel in the form for which "Believers' Church" has become a code, then we must confess as a particular problem our own confusion and directionlessness, as denominations traditionally committed to these accents, yet singularly quiet and in fact somehow embarrassed when it comes to representing them on the ecumenical scene. I have had to demonstrate the relevance of the Believers' Church vision by showing that, on their own, Catholics and Lutherans are rediscovering it without the label, without being helped (or hindered) by much awareness of the fact that the new vision they discover in the late twentieth century is the old vision of Cheltchitski and Marpeck, of Fox and Mack, of Campbell and Uchimura.

Why is it that this new discovery has not been more creatively fostered by the midwifery of an articulate Free Church ecumenical witness?

Is it because of a feeling that a new age of ecumenical politeness makes it uncouth to state truth-claims that imply criticism of other traditions? Is it because the standards of intellectual respectability are set even for theologians in our communities by the universities and the writers of the mainstream? Is it that in some inescapable way this position cannot be held with conviction by the children or the grandchildren or the descendants of the Nth generation? Certainly part of the reason is the discovery, which would not have surprised Hubmaier or Fox, that over against the things "we" are right about, there are also other things which "they" are right about, which we need to learn or to affirm together. Certainly, as well, we have been properly humbled by discovering that some of the qualities of any position bring with them a special susceptibility to certain related vices.

There are elements of explanation to be drawn from the fact that some of us have experienced survival, only thanks to having taken refuge in ethnic enclaves and selective migration, so that our children in the second and third generation have come to feel that the distinctive identity is the result of a cultural fluke, meaningful to ourselves but hardly something to commend to people of other origins. For others, the rapid growth of membership has outstripped the capacity of our own theology and catechetical process to integrate fully into our thought-world people educated in other kinds of Christendom, so that people may be Baptists by form and still multitudinist with regard to social ethics or spiritualists with regard to piety. For some, the experience of isolation and oppression within a defensive minority has been a source of doubt as to whether the inherited witness can stand the encounter with intelligent exponents of the majority traditions. For some of us, the very notion of affirming confessional identity is undercut by the dangers of self-righteousness and provincialism, documented so firmly in our experience with bigots and ignoramuses.

So much for the first address that had to be given. The Believers' Church vision is not only biblically mandated, it is of increasingly visible contemporary relevance around the world, and our only regret should be our feebleness in finding for it in every age a new worthy incarnation.

But the profound challenge of the second address, the one that we need more, would reach beyond the struggle with our sense of inferiority. The profound challenge is not whether we can demonstrate, when we get a chance, that the right answers of our common past are still the right answers to those questions, nor that those questions are still indispensable questions. What matters more deeply is that other as yet unanswered questions be wrestled with and resolved in the context of the same commitment to scriptural and contemporary accountability, and in the same confidence that the Spirit leads into unity. What are those still unanswered questions? Forgive me if my effort to state them appears too vicariously repentant, or too cheaply prophetic.

We have yet to find how it is that our Lord wants us to respond to fundamentally repressive political regimes. We are accustomed to being "Free Churches" in the sense that in the face of repression our fathers have often accepted sacrifice and risk in order to seek out another freer place. It has been demonstrated especially in the Anglo-Saxon experience that when we get a chance to speak within a post-reformation society, the very fact of free speech itself and the gospel content of which we speak tend to produce a democratizing effect upon the wider society, even though many of its members be of other persuasions. Where the issue of religious liberty has surfaced clearly, especially in the face of the claims of the state, we have been competent. Our Baptist and Adventist friends have been effective in establishing safeguards against any infringement, and in making of religious liberty a distinctive object of intellectual and institutional concern. But what we have not done with any great depth or clarity (or success) is think together about whether there is anything for Christians to do, and if so what it might be, in the face of a fundamentally repressive civil order. In South Korea and in South Brazil it is the Presbyterians (some of them) and more recently the Roman Catholics who have had what it takes to talk back to the pressures of authoritarian regimes desiring unconditional moral support from the churches: it has not been Baptists and Mennonites. In the Soviet Union, some Mennonites and Baptists register properly with the civil authorities, and others do not. A common ecclesiology and a common gospel message have not yet enabled unity on this major issue.

In the past, suffering at the hands of authoritarian regimes could be dealt with as at worst a passing test, since one could emigrate, or the period of persecution would be replaced by progress toward toleration. The Anglo-Saxon experience of progress toward toleration, the North American experience of the open frontier to which one could always move if necessary, have ill-prepared us to wrestle with the status of oppressed believing communities in a world from which emigration is every year less possible.

Nor is the other kind of escape as promising as it used to be. Until just a generation ago it was possible to look at world history in the perspective of increasing democratization. The old nations of the old world were themselves becoming progressively more tolerant, the new peoples of the new worlds were increasingly becoming independent, and democratization was just as definite a progressive self-starting process as industrialization and education. But something strange happened on the way to freedom land. In one set of nations the revolutionary vision of greater righteousness to be achieved through new structures more committed to the welfare of the common people has resulted in a chain of dictatorships all across the world in which the state structure is by no means ready to wither away. Most of the young independent nations and an embarrassing number of the older ones have discovered that democracy is a very fragile organism when the people the structure seeks to serve are deeply divided. On the global scale the evolution of national governments is proceeding, not toward democracy and assured rights, but in the direction of the so-called national security state, in which repression has a good conscience in the face of the worse things it claims to be warding off. Repression in the service of peace and order, enforced conformity in the interest of western spiritual values, represent a vision which numerous free church people find more acceptable than the chaos which it promises to avoid. Old ethnic Mennonite communities with Russian experience, now living under dictatorships in Brazil and Paraguay, young evangelistic communities of Baptists and Pentecostals in Chile and Argentina, sister communities in eastern Europe and southeast Asia can hardly be reproached for feeling more at home with separatistic and spiritualistic versions of free church identity which leave them free for mission, rather than with the anti-authoritarian proclamation of a Hut or a Sattler, a Winstanley or a Milton or a Roger Williams. How, in the face of the modern police state, whether the ideology justifying that state be the socialist humanism of eastern Europe or the occidental humanism of Christendom's law and order, to go on being a Free Church, is a challenge we have not up-dated for a long time.

From Tertullian to Campbell the Free Church witness has never been satisfied with religious liberty on the level of authorization for the individual to practise his own religiosity without hindrance. It has always asked for more: namely for the renunciation of all governmental absolutism and every claim of any state to promise any kind of salvation. **That** message today would be more costly than a century ago, as the lands of asylum become rare and the tools of oppression become efficient.

What we Anglo-Saxon Free Churches have experienced by way of good solutions to the church-state relationship problem has been the complementary separation which in the Anglo-Saxon context turns out to be the best arrangement for both parties, and thereby in a sense the most refined form of establishment, the easiest form of religious liberty. It has not equipped us even to continue the debate about church-state relations in North America (witness the recurrent borderline skirmishes on abortion and support to schools) to say nothing of providing us a springboard from which to leap into the challenges of defining religious liberty and anti-authoritarianism under the national security state.

The challenge thus stated may be in terms of scale and intensity the best specimen, in the perspective of global outreach, of my general claim that unresolved challenges lie before us for which the rightness of our past identity definitions provides a launching pad but no security. Another perhaps less evident specimen is more inwardly ecclesiological. In our western experience, Believers' Churches have been responses to and extensions of debates whose terms had already been fixed by some minority movement: by Hus coming out of late medieval Catholic renewal, by Zwingli coming out of Catholic humanism by way of Erasmus, by Puritanism coming out of the Anglican establishment, by radical Pietism coming out of the Lutheran **Volkskirche**. The distinctiveness of the Believers' Church agenda was thus almost always formulated as corrective or as extension or supplement to a structure, both ecclesiastical and intellectual, which was already operational and which the Free Church critic did not seek to replace integrally. But what then do you do if there does not exist an incomplete reformation to radicalize? Can the position we call Believers' Church stand on its own? Or must it always be only a corrective?

At the first conference of this series, George Huntston Williams suggested that we might make of this historically documented symbiosis or dependency a norm.[2] The Radical Reformation not only corrects and completes less thorough efforts, but is dependent upon both the unreformed mother church and the incomplete beginning reformation, in a regularly recurrent complementarity. It would then follow for some, that in a missionary situation, with no fallen church to reform, what we would need first would be to plant a fallen church and then to renew it, i.e. to propagate the faith in a popular and effective way without asking immediate questions about faithfulness, trusting that, with time, renewal would come and the more "graduate level agenda" of Christian faithfulness would then have a fitting terrain. Then the "hard sayings" of Jesus would come into play. This view grants that the voluntary community of committed disciples is in one sense what the Lord wants for his whole church but only in a derivative way. First He wants a more accessible and more easily propagated, less rigourous church for all the people.

By no means is such relativizing of the Free Church thrust a mere intellectual playfulness calculated to cool the self-righteousness of Baptist or Mennonite apologetics. It has been carefully propounded as a vision for the overarching dynamics of church history by Emile G. Leonard, the first accredited church historian of French Protestantism to give serious recognition to the Free Church phenomenon, which he had first encountered in contemporary Brazil before becoming attentive to it in earlier Europe. Something of the same churchmanship underlies, as well, the currently very popular focus upon "church growth" derived in part from a popularization of the analytical tools developed especially by Donald McGavran, according to which sweeping disciples into an initial Christian commitment whose total form has not been spelled out, and for which no ultimate level of intensity has been set as a criterion, will then later be followed by experiences and processes of education and renewal. Such intensification could never happen if we were not first of all satisfied with a more minimal initial loyalty made accessible to and accepted by a greater number of hearers.

If our concern here were missiology or churchmanship, several lines of dialogues would be needed. On how many counts of doctrine, ethics and church order is it fitting to be "patient" or "more accommodating" in order to facilitate the initial faith commitment of more people? But for the purposes of this address that defensive debate must be set aside. It is true that the circumstances of our fathers' pilgrimages often enabled them to avoid the demanding challenges of being either theologians or churchmen with a global responsibility for the whole job. It is true that we have piggybacked intellectually and institutionally on the "Great Church" traditions we have criticized. There is no reason to be ashamed of that fact: it demonstrates the cultural flexibility and contextual relevance of a witness which can be put in terms of almost any wider system, so that there can be Lutheran and Calvinist, predestinarian and Arminian, pietist and orthodox exemplars of the pertinence of the Free Church critique. But we must not let the readiness and the rightness of those past corrective syntheses excuse us from the duty of working at what would represent a non-dependent, non-piggybacking, non-post-establishment form of Believers' Church community.

One place where this always has to happen is obviously the planting of Christian communities in societies under non-Christian domination, whether they be post-Christendom Marxist or pre-Constantinian animist. Too often in these contexts we have accepted being the bearers of too much of the pre-Believers' Church pre-renewal forms of our home culture. We have carried to the Third World something of the Calvinism or Anglicanism which we were reacting against rather than the more contextually relevant creativity which our claimed New Testament rootage should have freed us for. We have not profited from the absence of Christendom to seize the freedom to move less indirectly from the Bible to the missionary context. Why did it have to be an Anglican Roland Allen who tried to free missionary methods from establishment patterns of ministry? Why did it have to be the Reformed Hromadka rather than Baptists or Pentecostals who could first pioneer in freeing Christians in eastern Europe from the reproach of being a western fifth column dependent on resources of piety parachuted or radioed or smuggled in from the West, and looking forward to the liberation promised by John Foster Dulles and Radio Free Europe? Yet despite the limits which plague our effort to let first generation Christianity be recreated in a first generation context, there are forces at work to assist in that project. Persecution, the implacable discipline of poverty in persons and education (greater handicaps than poverty in money) and the continuing miracle of community discovered under pressure will continue as they have in the past to push Third World churches into a posture of renewal and restoration, even if the missiologists, the mission states persons, and the roving ecumenical consultants do not carry a very large share of resources to encourage its happening.

But the greater challenge "to do" Believers' Church theology on its own feet instead of piggyback may well be the one we shall need to face in the modern West as we rapidly move beyond that kind of post-Christian culture where the memories of establishment were still alive, where Shakespeare and Milton were still in the syllabi and the momentum of the establishment still present in our reflexes, into the age of neo-paganism in which voodoo and pornography, fundamentalist neo-fascism and characterless media pietism will literally have more than equal time in the common culture, and when the maintenance of some awareness of who Moses and Amos and Jesus and Paul were will have to be provided from within the resources of the minority community. Now what in the post-secular mix will we insist on as defining the believing community? Which fragments of a theology will we now put together as a unity in their own right, when the ground floor is no longer dictated for us by a big sister church whose language we use in order to tell her that she is not radical enough in her reformation? Will we make common cause with older Christian traditions, now that they are no longer in the saddle, reappropriating elements of trinitarianism in thought or sacramentalism in practice because in the situation where we are all Free Churches those elements are a part of maintaining identity and are no longer linked with oppression? Will we aggressively buy into the thought moods of the time (historicism, secularism, new religiosity) because their distance from tradition correlates with our traditional low view of tradition? What would we teach our own children if nobody else taught them anything? Would we be less or more apologetic about our own Southern Baptist or Russian Mennonite folklore?

Within this overarching challenge of doing theology on its own feet, two sub-segments demand special attention. We have always claimed to be in some sense more biblical than the majority churches. Sometimes we said this by rejecting creeds, letting the task of synthesizing a message out of the Bible be occasionalistic and unself-conscious. Sometimes we did it by obeying specific biblical texts more simply and with fewer footnotes than the mainstream traditions. Sometimes we did it by trying to let the church experience of the early centuries be more thoroughly a guide (or even "pattern") to us than it was to the established churches. Sometimes we stated our biblical loyalty backhandedly by challenging the authority of those other models and other wisdoms which were important for the established churches. But what now shall we make of the Bible or the Bible of us, in the fact of historical relativism and historicist skepticism about the accessibility of any relevatory authority in any ancient text, in the face of the embarrassment with which we have to look at the naive trust with which some of our fathers claimed they could discern the only "biblical pattern" and let the canonical text settle every question for them? Does the Believers' Church identity leave us any less at sea than other moderns in the effort to define what authority a "canon" has, or any less guilty than other tradition-bound groups of reading our own confessions unfairly into an ancient text, or any less guilty than other larger churches of letting a teaching tradition assure us of what the Bible must mean, in such a way that our own identities and biases are reinforced and we are as safe as the orthodox against any "new light and truth breaking forth from the Holy Word?"

I have stated this challenge first in terms of what our fathers thought was their strength. It has a counterpart where they saw one of their adversaries: What does it mean in our day to keep from using one's own wisdom? The counterpart to the authoritative Bible was the idolatry of human wisdom, its arbitrariness and unaccountability. The Radical Reformers were suspicious not only of ideas but of institutions and people at every point where a claimed autonomy could dilute the call to simple trust and obedience. That polemic suspicion of anti-biblical wisdom had an undeniable validity in the context of reformation, where it was often or usually such "wisdom" which was appealed to to explain why we cannot afford to follow the Bible after all. The other churches needed to leave room for traditions and practices warranted on other grounds. But does not the space occupied by other sources of insight than special revelation have to be different once the spectre of defending apostasy has been replaced with the challenge of elaborating a self-sustaining theological culture? The Free Churches have not in the past been anti-scientific, anti-technological, anti-philosophical when those human cultural resources were not appealed to in the defense of an unfaithful church. On the contrary, it has been argued by some that there is a particular readiness on the part of the Free Church to contribute to the development of a free culture, a free school, a free state, and in other words to bring to some genuine self-fulfillment the several strands of human wisdom which despite our falleness still reflect something of the created and creative goodness entrusted by God to those He placed in His garden. What is the Free Church vision for culture when it is not warped by the prior imperative of saying "no" to apostate culture? Is there a distinctive Believers' Church apologetic? Is there some mark by which we might identify a distinctive Believers' Church graphic art, as some of our conservative Calvinist friends believe there is a Christian pattern of painting and pottery? Is there, as some of our fathers thought, a Mennonite way to farm? Is there, as some management consultants today think, a team ministry way to operate a business? Is there, as Robert Greenleaf claims, a servanthood way to administer?[3] Is there, as some interpreters of the extensive investment of Mennonite resources in private mental health services have suggested, a particular peace church stake in community therapy?

The next-to-last major challenge I must not avoid naming is likewise one of inward-looking ecclesiology. According to the concurrent witness of express statements in Galatians, Ephesians, and Colossians, **the** standard mark of the "New Humanity" (what we used to translate the "new man") or of the "New Creation" is that the differences between insider and outsider, Jew and Greek, male and female, slave and free, cease to divide people. The need for inter-ethnic, inter-sexual, inter-generational reconciliation is not a peculiar problem of Believers' Churches. It plagues other churches and societies no less. Yet it is a peculiar failing if in Believers' Churches the record is no better, for these Pauline phrases describing the new humanity are derived from baptism formulae. They state specifically a dimension of the very nature of a society of the regenerate, that "henceforth human standards do not count in our estimate of a person." It is, then, a far greater failure for a self-styled Believers' Church than a **Volkskirche** if in a congregation or in denominational leadership, or in a study conference on the Believers' Church, the presence and the voice of women, and of our day's Greeks, barbarians, Scythians, are not regularly part of the experience of fellowship.

It may be that the relative racial and sexual homogeneity of the participants in this week's program do not represent a specific mistake in the planning of the program: but then they must be the proof of a general mistake in the life of our churches, if the only people with free time, interest, recognized competence, travel budget, and something to say on our themes are males of northern European extraction.

Behind our other unresolved uncertainties, I must lastly name one wider unfinished debate separating Believers' Churches from one another. In the sixteenth century this debate separated the theologically most competent Anabaptist teacher, Balthasar Hubmaier, from many of his other Anabaptist brethren. In the seventeenth century it separated the radical Puritans called Quakers from the radical Puritans called Baptists. Since a part of what constitutes "Believers' Church" is the insistence that the church-state relationship problem is important and must be resolved in ways different from the heritage of Christendom, it is very representative and a fitting challenge that we should recognize, on our current agenda, the violence of the state as a continuing item of unfinished business and a peculiar responsibility. We cannot keep saying that we believe that scripture and prophecy will lead the community to growing commonality and then leave the question of war and peace, as inclusive ecumenism would, under the mantle of a charitable pluralism where everyone is right in his own way.

This matter is not my assignment. It appears on our program elsewhere. Others will discuss how progress might be made on that ancient issue, but that we hope and trust for progression toward a common witness needs to be said at this point. When Balthasar Hubmaier said that the otherwise normally non-resistant Christian will for the sake of the peace of the civil order be willing to use defensive violence, nothing of what he said could possibly be extended to cover modern war, the deterrence of mutual reciprocal atom threats, or the restriction of liberties in the name of national security. When Michael Sattler said of the rulers of this world that their style of sovereignty is "outside the perfection of Christ" and incompatible with discipleship, he was making a specific empirical statement about the governments which gave him no right to free religious expression and were in a few weeks to take his life: it is not fair to his intent to project a vision of civil absenteeism in contexts where significant public involvement without moral disobedience can be contemplated.

In an age in which the escalation of violence has gone beyond anything Hubmaier could have imagined or taken responsibility for, and in which room for citizen involvement has opened worlds which did not exist for Sattler, it is most illegitimate to let our thinking on social ethics continue to be constrained within the straight-jacket of the axiomatic either/or decision between "involvement" and "withdrawal." Today, commitment to peace-making and civil involvement belong together rather than being alternatives. Were Hubmaier alive today he would be working to ban the bomb. Is there any reason the Baptists should not be as much a peace church tomorrow as the Brethren? Is there any reason the Pentecostals and the Disciples should not again be peace churches as they were in their respective first generations?

I have set aside in this survey another broad range of challenge which we face together with other kinds of churches and with other people of good will: ecology and energy, redefining sexuality and the family, economic decolonialization and more. That they do not **prima facie** correlate with Believers' Church distinctives, and that we must all work together on them with many others, justifies my neglecting them tonight. Yet we cannot be sure that we would not discover distinctive and fruitful angles on some of these issues, as well, if with new confidence and discipline we gathered our wits in the light of what we know about the call to be a community of prophetic discernment. It has happened before.

I have taken my assignment as directed toward the beginning of a serious working session among colleagues in the serious task of church leadership. For that purpose I have, without apology, picked up the agenda right where it lay, identifying the gifts and the challenges of a distinctive identity as constituting a task for our work together. I should however, in conclusion, acknowledge that, in the pressure of our brief time together, this very bluntness and professionalism with which I have spoken to theologians and leaders about the challenges which theology and leadership represent is a diversion from the standard balance which would be more fitting if our gathering could afford the leisure of regular encounters. We have bent our format, without resentment, to be more a studying conference than a worshiping congregation; and for the limited purposes of our gathering that is justified. Yet even as I reiterate its justification it is fitting to acknowledge that by moving into this format we have slipped just an inch toward a more "established" vision of fellowship and witness, one in which by the grace of God we will never feel completely at home.

THE BELIEVERS' CHURCH: CANADIAN FOCUS

Jarold K. Zeman

A keynote address is a risky venture. A speaker who accepts such an assignment is tempted either to blow his own horn, or to prepare a "key hole" address instead. I have tried to resist both temptations, but particularly the latter. I do not think that anyone here would wish me "to peek through the key hole," so to say, in order to give you a preview of the main topics of the conference. It would not be fair to encroach upon the territories assigned to other speakers.

Rather I shall attempt to clarify three aspects of the conference under the following headings: the character of the conference, the theological focus of the conference, and the goals of the conference.

THE CHARACTER OF THE CONFERENCE

I can find no better word by which to describe the character of the conference than the term **dialectic**. It refers to the method originally developed by the ancient Greek philosophers, which employs the art of discussion or dialogue to discover and define truth. In modern philosophical usage the method usually implies the sequel of thesis, antithesis and synthesis. If this conference is to fulfill the expectations of the planning committee, and of the people we represent, it must follow the dialectical approach at several levels.

First, there is the dialectic of continuity and discontinuity. This is not the first conference on the Believers' Church. At least three similar conferences were held in the U.S.A.: in Louisville (1967), Chicago (1970) and Malibu, Cal. (1975). The papers presented and discussed there have been published. This conference will build on their findings and insights. It is the duty of those in our midst who took part in these earlier conferences to be spokesmen for the continuity.

At the same time, this is the first Believers' Church (BC) conference in Canada, and therefore, without precedent. For the first time in the history of Christianity in this country, spokesmen for the denominations in the BC tradition meet to explore, in an intensive and comprehensive manner, the place and role of the Believers' Church in Canadian society, past, present and future. The conference, therefore, should produce insights which are peculiar to the Canadian scene. At the same time, it should lead to fresh departures in the interpretation of the BC movement in its general characteristics. I therefore plead for a genuine dialectic between elements of continuity and those of discontinuity.

Second, we should be engaged in the dialectic of several BC traditions. The Canadian denominations and groups which today uphold the concept of regenerate church membership, can trace their roots to at least four different streams in history: the Evangelical Anabaptist tradition during the sixteenth-century Reformation in Europe; the Radical Puritan Separatist tradition in England; several movements of Evangelical Awakenings or Revivals, both in Europe and in America; the recent and indeed current renewal thrust represented by denominationally unattached and unlabelled house churches and other experimental groups committed to the BC style.[1]

Unfortunately, the representation of the different segments of the BC thrust in Canada is quite uneven at our conference. The vast majority of the participants come from Baptist and Mennonite circles. This imbalance places a heavy burden of responsibility on those who come from the other streams of the BC tradition. The issues faced by the older BC traditions are different from those typical of the newer groups. A lively dialogue will be beneficial to both sides.

Third, any conference which seeks to be truly Canadian should provide for proportionate representation of English and French Canadians as well as Canadians of other ethnic origins. A glance at the names of conference leaders listed on the program should convince everybody about the adequate presence of the so-called third ethnic element. The BC denominations in Canada—not only the Mennonites—have a much higher proportion of persons with non-English and non-French background than the population as a whole. But the representatives from French Canada, few in numbers—much to our regret—must be encouraged to be involved in the conference dialectic at every opportunity.

Fourth, the designation of the conference as a study conference, and the plan to have all, or most papers published in a conference volume, inevitably led to a strong accent on academic input. Of the sixty-six leaders listed on the program, exactly one half are professors, deans, principals and presidents of universities, colleges, seminaries and Bible colleges. The other half is made up of pastors, denominational executives and lay persons. With embarrassment, we confess that the list is an all-male gallery of saints. A comparable vocational profile of the rest of the participants is not available at this time. Even though all of us are active churchmen, the dialectic between the academics and the ecclesiasts should add to the fruitful dimensions of the conference.

Fifth, we cannot bypass yet another aspect of the conference dialectic. BC conferences are not intended to become new ecumenical institutions. We are **not** seeking to create alternative ecumenical structures to compete with the Canadian Council of Churches, or the Evangelical Fellowship of Canada. Since attendance at this conference was by invitation, letters were sent to the headquarters of all denominations in the BC tradition as well as to schools affiliated with such bodies, asking them to suggest suitable participants. Press releases and advertisements were placed in several church papers so that interested individuals might express their wish to participate in the conference. Observers from other Christian traditions were invited as well.

In one sense, therefore, we do not come to this meeting with an official mandate to speak on behalf of our denominations or institutions. Nor do we have, as a conference, any conciliar authority to make decisions. Nevertheless, with a few exceptions, most of us do represent, ideologically even if not constitutionally, the heritage, hopes and convictions of our local churches, denominational groups and institutions. Since no Christian lives unto himself but is a member of the body of Christ, each of us has the right, and indeed the duty, to contribute insights to this conference as a responsible representative of his or her group. Therein lies the final dimension of the conference dialectic. Each of us should seek to exercise both the freedom of personal opinion, and the responsibility of mirroring the stance of his ecclesial fellowship.

THE THEOLOGICAL FOCUS OF THE CONFERENCE

It may seem superfluous to include in a keynote address a reminder that the theological focus of the conference is on the concept of the church (ecclesiology). What else could it be if the conference is designated as a study conference on the Believers' Church? The reiteration of the central theme is desirable for several reasons. The ecclesiological focus must be considered in the broad context of the contemporary Canadian—and North American—attitudes to, and ideas about the church. We may distinguish three major camps.

First, the increasing unchurched portion of Canadian population ignores the church as an irrelevant relic of the past.

Second, many evangelical Christians, especially those who were introduced to Christ through the witness of non-denominational agencies and groups, often fail to appreciate the role of the church fellowship with proper order and discipline. Personal relationship to Jesus Christ is all that matters to them. The place of the church in God's plan of redemption is either misunderstood or deliberately dismissed.

The one-sided emphasis on religious individualism, if not subjectivism, must be linked, in part, with the heritage of evangelical revivals and revivalism. The trend has been further strengthened by evangelical cooperative ventures such as the Evangelical Fellowship in Canada. No common ecclesiological basis which would be expressed in a mutually acceptable understanding of the standards of admission into church membership, of sacraments and church polity, can be agreed upon by evangelical Anglicans, Presbyterians, Lutherans, United Churchmen, Baptists, Mennonites, Pentecostals, and members of the Christian and Missionary Alliance or Salvation Army. Thus the ecclesiological issues are avoided and attention is directed to other questions.

Third, the official ecumenical agencies, such as the Canadian Council of Churches, exist for the avowed purpose of furthering Christian unity and ultimately organizational church reunion. Due to the distribution of religious affiliation in Canada, paedobaptist church bodies control the ecumenical consensus. In the ecumenical assemblies, councils and committees the dissenting position of the Believers' Churches which insist on regenerate church membership and believers' baptism, has been presented again and again but inevitably remains a weak voice of a small minority, which is tolerated with a sort of charitable benevolence by the ecumenical establishment in Canada.

Meeting in the context of such conflicting interpretations of the nature of the church, we dare not fail to keep, in our deliberations, the theological focus on ecclesiology. The particular subjects of the twelve seminars should in all cases be discussed from the ecclesiological perspective, as indicated on the program: The BC in the congregational context, in the Canadian context, and in the global context. The great gospel text of John 3: 16 ("For God so loved **the world** that He gave His only begotten Son, that **whosoever** believes in Him, should not perish but have everlasting life") must be balanced by the equally significant statement in Ephesians 5: 25ff.: "Christ loved the church, and gave Himself for it, that He might sanctify and cleanse it...and present it to Himself a glorious church, without spot, or wrinkle...."

THE GOALS OF THE CONFERENCE

Early in the planning process, the following four objectives were set for the conference: (1) To evaluate the major contributions of the Free Church tradition in Canada; (2) To examine the present state of the communions representing the BC vision in Canada, and their impact upon society; (3) To consider the future witness of the BC community in Canada; and (4) To worship and fellowship together as brothers and sisters in Christ. May I be permitted to amplify these objectives by a brief discussion of the goals for the conference, as I see them.

In the early chapters of the Book of Acts, five Greek words are used to describe the characteristic marks of the early church: **koinonia** (fellowship), **dynamis** (the power of the Holy Spirit), **didache** (teaching), **kerygma** (witness or proclamation), and **diakonia** (service). Since all Believers' Churches in the modern era have sought to restore the primitive church, it is appropriate to use these five terms in the definition of the goals of our conference.

1. **The Didactic Goal.** The conference has been designated as a study conference. The preparation of eight addresses, twenty-four seminar papers and twenty-four responses, all to be presented in three days, may well set a record in research input for any conference held under church auspices in Canada. We owe a debt of gratitude to all leaders who have invested a great deal of time in disciplined study. But the second, and in some respects more crucial phase of the learning process, begins tonight. Any one admitted to this conference has committed himself to three days of active participation in an intensive experience of **didache**. No seats have been reserved for mere listeners. We are here to study, to think critically, to speak up freely, to raise questions, and together to search for adequate answers. The study of the Bible, our norm, comes first on the agenda for every day. Let us make sure that we hear the voice of God through the day. The discussions which follow the presentations of papers in the plenary sessions and in the seminars, constitute the brain of the conference.

2. The Koinonic Goal. Denominations in the BC stream assign priority to fellowship over concerns for liturgy and priestly orders. Fellowship in Christ means, among other things, the breaking down of barriers to communication. "Christ is our peace...He has broken down the wall of partition between us" (Ephesians 2: 14). At this conference, we have an opportunity to experience the peacemaking power of Christ in new ways. Let His presence break down the barriers due to lack of information, to prejudice, or personal shyness. We are here to get to know one another. All of us like to spend time with old friends. Let's break the tradition and deliberately make many new friends, reaching across denominational, regional and vocational lines.

3. The Kerygmatic Goal. In the May 1st issue of **Time** magazine, the following statement by the Russian Orthodox priest Dmitri Dudko, banned from Moscow, was quoted by a reporter: "There is a spiritual crisis in this country (Soviet Union), a vacuum that has to be filled." His words may well be applied to Canada. We are passing through a crisis which has spiritual roots and causes, whether in French or English Canada. In ancient Israel, the people used to ask their prophet: Is there any word from the Lord? We must ask the same question again and again during our conference discussions. What is the word from the Lord that we should hear in order to pass it on as our message (**kerygma**), first, to our churches, and then, to our nation? The conference was not convened as an end in itself. Rather, it is a means to an end: to hear the living God speak to us while we are here, so that we may have a clear message to bear when we leave this place. The conference may wish to formulate an appeal to the churches, and perhaps also a message to the people of Canada.

4. The Diakonic Goal. We are known to be the people "under the Word" (as the Louisville BC conference expressed it). But words are not a substitute for deeds. The Divine Word "became flesh and dwelt among us." Our words must also become incarnate in obedient service. The focus on the Lordship of Christ and on our obedient servanthood has been one of, if not **the** central emphasis in our respective traditions.

Roland H. Bainton wrote: "When Christianity takes itself seriously, it must either forsake or master the world, and at times may try to do both at once." In the past, under the influence of Continental Anabaptism or English Puritanism, we have interpreted the Lordship of Christ, as it affects the relations between church and society, in varying degrees of withdrawal from society, or theocratic domination of society. Is it not high time for all of us to re-examine our traditional positions and to risk new departures in obedience to God's leading today? Will any practical actions follow the flood of words uttered during the conference?

5. The Dynamic Goal. The four marks of the apostolic church — **didache**, **koinonia**, **kerygma**, and **diakonia**—were the fruit of the power (**dynamis**) of the Holy Spirit at work in and through the early Christians. They faced a hostile world subject to demonic powers. Only by the divine power of the Spirit could they bear witness, conquer the hearts of men and change conditions in society.

Our sick North American society suffers from a tyranny of evil which is super-human in its origins and effects. No human effort, however dedicated, well intentioned, or even religiously motivated, can reverse the trend to decadence and self-destruction which is apparent all around us. Malcolm Muggeridge said three years ago:

> The barbarians who overran Rome came from without. Ours are home products, trained and suitably brain washed and conditioned at public expense. It is difficult to resist the conclusion that Western man, wearied of the struggle, has decided to abolish himself. Creating boredom out of his own affluence, impotence out of his own erotomania, vulnerability out of his own strength, he himself blows the trumpet that brings the walls of his own city tumbling down. Until at last, having educated himself into imbecility, and drugged and polluted himself into stupefaction, he keels over, a weary, battered old brontosaurus, and becomes extinct.[2]

We have met on the day following the Sunday of Pentecost. Is it a mere coincidence, or is it a pointer to the only source of vitality for the BC and its mission in the world? Many of us have been involved in a prolonged search for denominational identity, Baptist, Mennonite, or whatever. We have been excavating the hidden roots of our respective traditions. There are considerable varieties in the **horizontal** (i.e. human) identity of the different BC groups since such identity is derived, at least in part, from cultural and ethnic factors. But all of us share a common **vertical** identity which is essentially pneumatic, i.e. determined by the work of the Holy Spirit **(pneuma)**. Unless He continues His gracious ministry of conviction and regeneration, a BC faces extinction in one generation. Under normal circumstances, a paedobaptist denomination can predict its numerical growth on the basis of vital statistics of the population it serves. We have no such humanly predictable future. As a BC, we exist by the grace of God. From such perspective, the times spent in prayer during the conference may well determine the effectiveness, or feebleness, of our gathering.

CONCLUSION

At the time when Adolf Hitler and his party were launching their conquest of Germany, and eventually of Europe, Edmund Husserl, the founder of the phenomenological school in philosophy, said (1935): "The greatest danger which threatens Europe, is fatigue." How well he assessed the demoralized state of the Western democratic societies ready for a political and moral capitulation before Nazism.

His observation may be applied, **mutatis mutandis,** to the present state of the major religious bodies, including several denominations in the BC tradition, in Canada. The symptoms of their general state of fatigue are obvious to any perceptive observer of the Canadian religious scene.

Whenever I reflect upon the thirty years of my life in Canada, I find it difficult and disturbing to admit the full dimensions of the changes which have occurred in the spiritual climate of this country. When I arrived in Toronto in 1948 I witnessed the final years of the Protestant cultural establishment in English Canada, and of the Roman Catholic establishment in French Canada.

At the risk of oversimplification, we may suggest that the Canadian society as a whole, English and French, has passed, or is passing, from the final phase of the Constantinian era to a post-Constantinian age. The cultural establishment of Christianity, whether in its Protestant or Catholic forms, will soon be a matter of history. To go to church, or at least, to send one's children to Sunday school, is no longer the expected and accepted social norm. In many areas of Canada, and particularly in the large urban centres, the Christian churches now find themselves in the context of a frontier society which calls for basic evangelization comparable to mission fields abroad.

In the U.S.A., the churches faced such a situation in the early nineteenth century when—according to estimates—less than ten per cent of the population had any active church affiliation. In Canada, a comparable missionary challenge has never existed up to now. I find myself torn between sentiments of nostalgia for "the good old days" when Canadian society displayed the traditional Christian veneer, however thin and superficial, and an attitude of thanksgiving for the change, as well as of hope for much healthier and more genuine manifestations of the Christian presence in the Canada of tomorrow.

About one thing there can be no doubt. The next ten to twenty years will decide the future shape of Christianity in our land. Will Canada follow the path of Western European countries and Great Britain, toward nearly complete secularization of life? If the Believers' Churches bear a clear and convincing witness, they will face an unparallelled opportunity for growth. With the passing of the Constantinian era, the appeal of superficial traditional "churchianity" will be gone. In the future, Canadians, like people in other missionary situations, will be choosing between genuine Christian commitment, no religion at all, or some pseudo-religious substitutes.

If our analysis of the Canadian religious scene is reliable, then the timing of this conference is providential. As we meet, we stand on the threshold of a new era, without precedent in Canadian history.

We do not face the unknown future alone. Our risen, living Lord "goes before us" as He promised when He conquered death (Matthew 28:7). With eschatological urgency, each of us personally, and all of us together, must deal with the most pressing, albeit unprinted, question on the agenda of this conference: In what sense are we—am I— prepared and ready to follow Him?

In Psalm 86:11 we find a perfect prayer for this occasion. Let it be offered again and again during our conference:

Teach me Thy way, O Lord,
that I may walk in Thy truth.
Unite my heart to fear Thy name.

THE BELIEVERS' CHURCH IN CANADA: THE PAST

Cornelius J. Dyck

The story of the church in early Canada is essentially a description of the settlement and missionary activity of Roman Catholics. Though not without its Gallican elements, the Catholicism that came to New France was an anti-Protestant, post-Tridentine Catholicism relying much on the Recollet, Sulpician and Jesuit orders for both its missionary and pastoral work. Some Huguenot traders initially managed to gain a foothold in Nova Scotia and up the St. Lawrence River, but they were soon banished. From approximately 1605 to the Seven Years' War (1756-63), which brought New France under British rule, ultra-montanism, while often vitiated by policital exigencies, shaped ecclesiastical policies in the land — a period of 150 years! Contact with the colonies to the south could, of course, not be avoided, and led to some fear of these Calvinist mercantile wizards, but seldom had Catholicism possessed a more significant, if largely unrecognized, opportunity to establish itself.

There were exceptions to this hegemony. The Hudson's Bay Company began its trading activities after 1670. Newfoundland had been an early exception to the French Catholic settlement patterns in that both the fishing industry and the Society for the Propagation of the Gospel brought active Anglican influence to that land by 1583, but especially after 1700. A church building had been erected by 1706. Most significant, perhaps, was the acquisition of Nova Scotia by the British through the Treaty of Utrecht in 1713. This was to lead to the settling of a group of Reformed Protestants from the Upper Rhine by 1750-51, and the building of St. Paul's Church in Halifax in 1750. New Brunswick was entered in 1755, and the first Anglican service held in Montreal in 1760.[1] Nevertheless, except for native Canadians, the population of New France numbered some 60,000 at the end of the French era, of which the majority were French and Roman Catholic.

During the British colonial era in Canada, 1763-1867, Anglicanism was the dominant, but by no means exclusive, religious force added to established Roman Catholicism. Under Bishop Charles Inglis, schools were established, ecclesiastical appointments expedited, and an administrative network created which greatly facilitated the growth of the Church of England. The founding of the Protestant Episcopal Church of the United States following the War of Independence of the thirteen colonies hastened the autonomy of Anglicanism in the Atlantic Provinces and Upper Canada. Yet this new church was part of the civil colonial establishment, and the appointment of Inglis as bishop was as much a civil-political one as ecclesiastical. He was not a friend of religious dissent: "Whoever is sincerely religious towards God...will also...be loyal to his earthly Sovereign....Fanatics are impatient under civil restraint, and run into the democratic system...."[2] These comments must be seen against the background of his negative experiences with republicanism in New York, from where he had returned in 1777. Yet on his appointment as bishop of Canada a decade later, he resolved "to avoid in my conduct what would give dissenters disgust and shock their prejudices."[3] This, of course, did not prevent him from keeping largely for his own disposal the vast resources of the clergy reserves, nor from opposing the granting of authorization for other religious traditions to perform marriages. It may well be, however, that the privileges of establishment and concomitant financial security placed Anglicanism at a disadvantage in relation to the aggressive dissenters who were arriving on the scene. It is with these that we come to the history of Believers' Church tradition in Canada. In pursuing this history, however, it is important to remember the pervasive influence of these twin authorities, papacy and monarchy, and their ecclesiastical counterparts, upon social and religious developments.

The attempt to lay some of the historical groundwork through a discussion of the participating traditions led quickly to an awareness of the impossibility of discussing them all, or any one, in sufficient depth to really do justice to them, and also to the question of parameters, i.e., who is to be included in the story? Is this latter question to be answered on the basis of doctrine, of self-identity, or of practice? Taking the preliminary list which the planning committee has been using, I arrived at the following membership tabulation with the help of the **Yearbook of American and Canadian Churches**:[4] Baptists, ca. 200,000; Mennonites and Amish, ca. 80,000; Hutterites, ca. 16,000; Pentecostal Assemblies and other Pentecostal groups, ca. 195,000; Brethren in Christ, ca. 1,700; Christian and Missionary Alliance, ca. 13,000; Church of God, ca. 9,000; Christian Church (Disciples of Christ), ca. 3,000; Evangelical Covenant Church of Canada, ca. 1,100; Society of Friends, ca. 1,000; Church of the Nazarene, ca. 8,000; Free Methodist Church, ca. 4,000; for a combined total of "communicant members": 504,200.

It is not possible to discuss the history of each of these traditions in the brief space allotted to this paper. It seems best, therefore, to limit the discussion to the history of the Baptists affiliated with the Baptist Federation of Canada and of the Mennonites as the two sponsoring bodies in this conference, but to precede this with general background considerations and a brief reference to two groups — the Pentecostal Assemblies because of their numerical strength, and the Christian and Missionary Alliance because of their origin in Canada. Some attempt will then be made at a broader statement by comparing the historical experience of all of these traditions with Believers' Church categories and definitions.

BACKGROUNDS IN CONGREGATIONALISM

The Separatist tradition of Robert Browne and John Robinson in late sixteenth century England is well known. Browne's followers have usually been identified as "Independents," while those of Robinson, who found their way back from Leiden and to New England, came to be known as Congregationalists.[5] The Independents were not far behind the latter. When the call went forth in England in 1749 for settlers to establish Nova Scotia as an English colony, a substantial number of volunteers were recruited immediately, of whom it was said that seven-eighths were Independents.[6] While the new St. Paul's Church in Halifax was open to them, a chapel known as the Mather's Meeting-house was soon built by them for their own use.

The response of New England Congregationalists to the Nova Scotia settlement invitation of 1749 had been slow because of the dominant presence of establishment Anglicanism, until the invitation was repeated by Governor Charles Lawrence in 1758, together with the assurance of full religious toleration for all Protestants. This assurance led to an immediate increase in the flow of immigrants from New England, 1,800 settlers arriving in 1760, for example, and including clergymen who were in particularly short supply.[7] The first provincial census of 1776 showed 6,913 Americans out of a total population of 13,374 and did not include those who had returned to New England when southern independence was established. Most of the Congregationalists, in fact, in keeping with their theological separatist convictions, seemed to be republican at heart and maintained their neutrality with some difficulty in the midst of Toryism. Their ministers were eyed with particular suspicion. Soon all but two had returned to New England. Coupled with the usual hardships of pioneer life this environment caused the ten congregations of 1761 to dwindle to two by 1799.[8]

These comments about the struggles of Congregationalism in Nova Scotia would be very incomplete, however, without reference to the New Light revival and to Henry Alline (1748-1784), often referred to as "The Apostle of Nova Scotia." His ministry was brief and divisive; so divisive, in fact, that it is frequently cited as being the primary cause for the demise of Congregationalism in the Maritime Provinces. Many of the newly forming groups eventually became Baptists. Alline's revivalist methods were regarded with despair and disgust by his opponents, who included Congregational clergy. The Reverend Jonathan Scott of Jebogue Church knew what was coming when Alline asked for ordination to an **itinerant** ministry, a request quite out of harmony with Congregationalist polity. Scott resented the disruption caused in his church by the "disorderly practices and wild enthusiasm of one whom the Anabaptists at Horton have been concerned in approbating as an Itinerant Preacher."[9]

Alline's revivals, carried on by others after his death, were an extension to the Maritime Provinces of the Great Awakening in New England. The historiography of his life and work has often been unusually hostile. Yet as a major defender has pointed out, his ministry met a deep need:

> While Nova Scotians on the whole remained neutral during the
> American Revolution, they were in open revolt against the old order
> and the old doctrines of Congregationalism. Through his preaching,
> his hymns, and his theological writings, Henry Alline made this revolt
> vocal, and gave it coherence. It is true that the path of mystical
> speculation which he proposed ran for the most part through waste
> places; but it did provide an escape and facilitated the transition from
> the New England way to the evangelicalism of the newer churches.[10]

It is time to consider seriously the possibility that Henry Alline may well
have been the earliest and clearest voice of the Believers' Church in
Canada. His mystical theology would, for the most part, hardly be in
harmony with Believers' Church emphases, but his stress upon the
importance of the new birth, of obedience to the will of God as revealed
in Christ, and his conviction about the importance of the fellowship of
believers have been central Believers' Church emphases from the
sixteenth century to the present.

The end of Congregationalism in the Maritime Provinces did not
mean the end of this tradition in Canada. When the lines of
communication to New England were disrupted by political conditions
after 1776, and by antipathy to the work of Alline, help came from
England. Under sponsorship of the Canada Education and Home
Missionary Society, which was made up of Presbyterian, Baptist, and
Congregational representatives, Henry Wilkes not only secured much
needed help from abroad, but was himself enabled to facilitate the
founding of no fewer than twenty-five congregations in Upper and
Lower Canada by mid-nineteenth century.[11] The eventual blending of
influences from both England and New England, strengthened through
continuing immigration to Canada, gave shape to a Congregationalism
that was to be uniquely Canadian in polity and, at points, in theology.

Developments in western Canada were to take a form still different
from those in the Maritimes, as well as those in Upper and Lower
Canada. Because of the sparse population of the prairies and the
competitive presence of Anglicanism, the merger which was to become
the United Church of Canada in 1925 was anticipated long before through
the forming of small union congregations among the Congregationalists, Presbyterians and Methodists. When the merger of 1925
came, "no less than three thousand such congregations joined in the
union."[12] While the cherished Congregational principle of local
autonomy became a casualty of this merger, other traditional
emphases contributed in a major way to the shape of the new United
Church.

THE PENTECOSTAL ASSEMBLIES

The roots of Canadian Pentecostal groups, including the **Assemblies**,
go back to the well-known 1901 experience in Topeka, Kansas, and the
subsequent events in Los Angeles in 1906. R.E. McAlister of Ontario was
in Los Angeles at that time, became a part of the movement, and
returned to Ontario as a faithful witness to the time of his death in 1953.

The first Pentecostal convention in Canada was held in Toronto in 1908. From Ontario the movement spread to other parts of Canada: Winnipeg in 1907, Saskatchewan in 1910, Alberta in 1917, and on to British Columbia. A federal charter was granted to the Pentecostal Assemblies in 1919.

The Pentecostal Assemblies include most of the Pentecostal groups in Canada and must be seen as a movement rather than as a traditional denomination. They do share a familiar denominational concern for education, supporting four Bible colleges and numerous non-English language Bible schools. Extensive missionary work is today being carried on in many countries of Africa, Asia and Latin America. The official monthly journal is entitled **The Pentecostal Testimony**.[13]

THE CHRISTIAN AND MISSIONARY ALLIANCE

Albert Benjamin Simpson, a Presbyterian minister from Prince Edward Island, with pastoral experience in Kentucky and New York, founded the International Missionary Alliance in 1887, and in 1889 the Christian Alliance. In 1890 the two organizations were merged under the present name. Since the initial alliances were founded in Maine and New York respectively, the claim that this denomination is indigenous to Canada may be challenged. Theologically its roots must be seen in the Pentecostal tradition, but with less emphasis upon speaking in tongues, replaced possibly by a strong emphasis upon healing, holiness and mission. There are presently three CMA regions in Canada, with a fourth in process of being created. Canadian Bible College and Canadian Theological Seminary, both in Regina, serve the graduate and post-graduate educational needs of the denomination. A volume recording the history of the denomination is in preparation. **The Alliance Witness** is a bi-weekly publication serving the worldwide denomination. The earlier cited membership figure of 13,000 does not include an approximately equal number of adherents. A close working relationship exists with the denominational regions in the United States, which include a membership of approximately 100,000 plus some 60,000 adherents.[14]

THE BAPTISTS

The Baptists today constitute the largest body of the Believers' Church tradition in Canada both in terms of individual members and numbers of congregations. Their influence on many aspects of church and national life in the past has been significant. In the brief space available here it is not possible to report more than a few of the high points of this more than two-hundred-year experience of faith and prayer, defeat and victory. It has, however, been my good fortune to have available to me a number of excellent articles and books of recent vintage, as well as earlier writings by Baptist authors themselves, and my references to these in the notes may encourage others to become familiar with them also.

Not all Baptist historians begin their account of origins with the Separatists and Nonconformists in sixteenth and seventeenth century Europe, but few would reject this history. Where discussion about this issue has been carried on in the past it has been over connections with sixteenth century continental Anabaptism and early seventeenth century English Puritanism,[15] but most Canadian Baptist writers have been careful to identify both the Arminian and Puritan motifs in their history and the institutional representation of these emphases in the Free Will Baptists and the Regular (Calvinist) Baptists. Roger Williams, who is often identified as the first Baptist in America and who established the church at Providence in 1639, obviously stood in the English Nonconformist tradition. Speaking in terms of direct historical antecedents, Stuart Ivison has commented that "The Baptist body in Canada today still shows to the careful observer these three main strata, American, Scottish and English, however they may have been welded together by the pressure of forces peculiar to our Canadian environment."[16] The influence of these traditions will become clear as we move along.

The initial Baptist presence in the Maritimes came from New England in the persons of Ebenezer Moulton and Nathan Mason. Moulton came to Yarmouth in 1760, but later visited Horton (present-day Wolfville) and founded a congregation there in 1765. Most of the new members were probably converts from Congregationalism. Mason and the small group of twelve members accompanying him settled in Sackville, New Brunswick in 1763. They were part of the larger movement from New England to Nova Scotia, taking advantage of the lands made available by the expulsion of the Acadians in 1755. Moulton, however, returned to New England, which led one Baptist leader to say that "the Lord sent Mr. Moulton to Horton; the devil sent him away."[17] The Mason group was also back in Massachussetts by 1771. Nevertheless, others continued the work at Horton (Wolfville). The church was reconstituted in 1778 and is recognized as the oldest continuing Baptist church in Canada.

The most significant roots of this early period go back to the work of New Light Henry Alline and the religious ferment he created. While he was not a Baptist himself, the revival he began in 1776 benefited the Baptists most in terms of church growth but also brought troubling questions about membership and communion. Since his converts were usually received into the church without believer's baptism, not to speak of immersion, were they full members or was a split-level membership developing, and could unimmersed believers participate at the Lord's Table?[18] A major step towards solving these problems was taken with the formation of an "Association" of churches, in 1798, including eighteen congregations, of which several were Congregationalist. Within a decade the decision was made to withdraw "fellowship from all churches who admit unbaptized persons to what is called occasional communion and consider themselves a regular close communion Baptist Association."[19]

These early heterogeneous beginnings received strong impetus in the first half of the nineteenth century through the founding of home mission societies and the raising of funds for foreign missions. Heterogeneity, a true mark of being the church of Christ, was furthered in the mid 1820s when a group of influential Anglicans joined the Baptists because of a schism in their congregation in Halifax. They brought with them a strong concern for education which, through their able leadership, soon led to the founding of Horton Academy, now Acadia University. Soon the Free Will Baptist influence entered into this area through immigration and other contacts, but the Regular Baptist orientation remained dominant.

A Baptist presence in what is now Ontario and Quebec began with the coming of the Loyalists in the last decades of the nineteenth century. Congregations were formed mainly in three areas: one south of the St. Lawrence River and known as "the eastern townships," a second in the Niagara and adjacent area, and a third along the north shore of lake Ontario, including what is now Toronto.[20] These settlements were in close contact with Baptist mission societies in New York and Boston and stood largely in the Regular Baptist tradition. Great value was placed upon congregations belonging to an association, either in Canada or the United States. With the growth of autonomy among Canadian congregations and associations, as well as the communication and emotional impediments caused by the war of 1812, all associational ties with United States associations had been terminated, by mutual consent, by 1819.[21]

About the year 1816 the so-called "Scottish Baptists," products of the Haldane revivals in Scotland, arrived to settle in the Ottawa Valley between Ottawa and Montreal. These immigrants carried a particular concern for the education of ministers, and by 1838 had founded Canada Baptist College in Montreal.[22]

Furthering the heterogeneous Baptist mix still more was the coming of Henrietta Feller from Switzerland to Quebec in 1835, to carry on evangelistic work among the French Canadians. That her work bore fruit is evidenced by the formation of the Union of French Baptist Churches in Canada by ten congregations in 1969.[23] In southwestern Ontario, as well as in Nova Scotia, congregations were established during the nineteenth century by fugitive Blacks from the United States, growing in number to over 20,000 by mid twentieth century.[24]

With the westward expansion of the population, the Ontario Baptists sent two men to scout out the Northwest in 1869. In due course they arrived in Winnipeg, which they described as "...a small town, consisting of about thirty log buildings, and one small brick structure. The town is situated on the west bank of the Red River...."[25] Roman Catholic, Anglican, Presbyterian and Methodist missionaries had long been at work in this area. By 1873 Alexander McDonald was at work in Winnipeg, where the first Baptist church in the west was organized in 1875. Other congregations followed in rapid succession across the plains and into the foothills, with the Baptist Convention of Manitoba and the Northwest Territories being organized in 1884. At its first meeting, in 1885 in Brandon, it agreed typically, among other things, to also establish a college. The college at that location was the ultimate result of that decision.[26]

Finally, Baptist work in British Columbia came about independently of prairie or eastern activities. Alexander Clyde of Ontario came to Victoria in 1874, apparently on his own initiative, and began cottage prayer meetings with other Baptists he managed to find. This led to the founding of a congregation by 1876. Other Baptists, possibly from Washington state, were meanwhile beginning their own work in the Vancouver area, where a church was organized in 1887. The Baptist Convention of British Columbia was formed in 1897 with eleven congregations in membership. Merger negotiations with the prairies convention led to the forming of the Baptist Convention of Western Canada in 1907, and a change to the Baptist Union of Western Canada in the interests of greater provincial independence, two years later.[27]

The geography of Canada which stretches its population in a rather narrow band across the continent does not facilitate easy communication. The Baptist polity stressing local autonomy and regional association is ideal for this kind of situation. Still, it has been possible since 1944 to have a Baptist Federation of Canada (BFC). While the regional conventions have retained their relationships, the BFC makes it possible for all of its members (128,000 in 1976) to speak with one voice on important church or national issues, to pursue projects which only the combined resources of the BFC make possible, to channel funds through the Baptist World Alliance (BWA) for relief, educational or other purposes around the world, and other projects.[28] The Canadian Baptist Overseas Mission Board is the only major national agency with full executive powers.

This quick summary of Baptist history in Canada would by missing an important aspect if it did not underscore the many cultural traditions which have become a part of the Baptist family. We referred earlier to Baptist roots in England, Scotland and New England. It is equally important to see the branching out of those roots, through the identification with immigrant groups as well as through direct missionary effort, until some twenty different national and cultural groups are included in this part of the Body of Christ. Included among these are not only Anglo-Saxon types and the Blacks already referred to, but also many European and Oriental groups, and others who have either simply joined existing English congregations as individuals, or who have formed ethnic congregations and associations, sometimes within the context of a regional convention, at other times separate from it, such as the Baptist General Conference or the North American Baptist Conference.

Equally significant is the apparently strong commitment to mission throughout this Baptist history, and particularly to home mission. While Richard E. Burpee and his wife went to Burma already in 1845, to be followed by many others to other lands including India, Bolivia and Angola, what impresses the reader of this history is the evangelistic zeal with which many Baptists lived and worked. Perhaps Alexander Grant (d.1897) was not as exceptional as we think when, on arriving in

Calgary, he asked the building contractor of the new Baptist Church to take him out where they could shoot prairie chicken, and by evening another Baptist was safely in the fold. It was said of Grant that "It was his ambition to see a Baptist church established in every hamlet in Western Canada."[29]

In the 1920s, Baptists in Ontario and Quebec as well as in the Western provinces passed through a protracted controversy over fundamentalist-liberal interpretation of basic theological issues. A major division led to the formation of several rival organizations. Since 1953, most of these have been united in The Fellowship of Evangelical Baptist Churches in Canada, the second largest Baptist body in the country.

THE MENNONITES

Although Mennonites and Baptists share some common historical roots and significant theological agreement, their differing histories and emphases have made them quite different in some respects in the past. Chief among these differences may well have been Mennonite ethnicity, which shaped and was shaped by a unique sense of identity, which in turn was brought about, in part, by convictions about nonconformity, including nonresistance. A variety of external and internal factors, such as isolated community settlements, in-group language and an implicit theology of the faithful remnant have contributed to relative isolation of most Mennonite settlements in the past. In Canada, however, the cultural mosaic notwithstanding, Mennonites appear to be assimilating very rapidly to the prevailing culture. One may assume that this will facilitate cross-cultural and theological dialogue, particularly also with other members of the Believers' Church tradition.

It has frequently been the case in Mennonite migrations that the coming of a large group is preceded by some hardy individuals or small groups pioneering on their own, and about which later historians are unable to discover much. This was apparently also true about Canadian Mennonites, for as early as 1754 an Anglican rector in Lunenburg, Nova Scotia made mention of Anabaptists in that area, but these may in fact have been the **avant garde** of Baptists from New England or England! There is also a 1783 reference at St. John's River in Nova Scotia to an "Anabaptist Company of 47 persons of which 20 were adult men, 11 women, and 16 children."[30] Others will undoubtedly be found.

The first major Mennonite immigration to Canada came with the United Empire Loyalists after 1783, likely beginning with a group who came from Pennsylvania to the Niagara area in 1786. At the same time settlements were established in what became Waterloo County. These migrations into Ontario continued until the War of 1812. The Mennonite settlers were of Swiss or South German stock, their fathers or grandfathers having come to Pennsylvania mostly after 1715. Their motives for coming to Canada were loyalist, coupled with concern for continuing religious liberty, but they also felt the need for more land and the availability of good cheap land. By 1841, the year in which Upper and Lower Canada became the Province of Canada, the census indicates a total Mennonite population of 5,382 in the province, of which 3,022 were in the Niagara district. These included Amish settlers who began arriving from south Germany and from Pennsylvania after 1822.[31]

The second migration of Mennonites to Canada was to the prairies from Russia, beginning in 1873. Because of socio-economic developments in Russia which were making the lot of the serfs more bearable, some Mennonites began to fear cultural assimilation and the loss of their special religious privileges, including nonresistance, and looked to Canada as a new haven. Approximately 18,000 left Russia at that time, of which some 8,000 settled on the East and West Reserves in Manitoba, while the others settled in the US Midwest. In 1877, after only a few years of pioneering, Governor General Lord Dufferin wrote about these settlements:

> Although I have witnessed many sights to cause me pleasure during my various progresses through the Dominion, seldom have I beheld any spectacle more pregnant with prophecy, more fraught with promise of a successful future than the Mennonite settlement. When I visited these interesting people they had been only two years in the province, and yet in a long ride I took across many miles of prairie, which but yesterday was absolutely bare, desolate, untenanted, the home of the wolf, the badger, and the eagle, I passed village after village, homestead after homestead, furnished with all the conveniences and incidents of European comfort, and of a scientific agriculture; while on either side of the road, cornfields ripe for harvest, and pastures populous with herds of cattle stretched away to the horizon. Even on this continent — the peculiar theatre of rapid change and progress — there has nowhere, I imagine, taken place so marvelous a transformation.[32]

The third immigration of Mennonites from Russia to Canada began in 1922 and continued until 1930, bringing over 20,000 persons to all parts of the Dominion, but especially to the prairie provinces. Some of them were able to buy the farms of those who felt their faith threatened in Canada and were on their way to Mexico and Paraguay. Mennonite urbanization in Canada began with the coming of this movement from Russia, since many could not find, or finance, large block settlements.

A fourth major migration to Canada came after World War II when the Mennonites became part of the several millions of immigrants which this nation received from Europe. Initially perhaps some 7,000 may have come, but the movement of families and small groups has continued to the present, including some who first went to South America from Europe, but later came to Canada. Most of these immigrants were quickly assimilated into the urban communities of their friends and relatives. By 1970 their number likely exceeded 10,000 immigrants.

Summarizing these statistically, it is likely that no fewer than 45,000 Mennonites and Amish came to Canada as immigrants, some from the United States and other regions, but most of them from Europe. The heaviest settlement concentrations have been Ontario, the prairie provinces and British Columbia, with very few choosing any of the other provinces. There has been considerable internal migration, but the location pattern has not changed much, except for urbanization. At the present time the number of baptized members in all Mennonite, Amish, and Brethren in Christ congregations totals approximately 80,000, plus approximately 16,000 Hutterites for a combined membership quickly approaching 100,000.[33]

Mennonites and Brethren in Christ in Canada are grouped either into conferences, or maintain loose associations for fellowship. The fraternal ties of a number of the conferences to their counterpart bodies in the United States are as close or closer than they are to their co-religionists of other conferences in Canada. The Ontario Conference was the first to be organized, in 1825, followed years later by the Conference of Mennonites in Canada in 1903. The former, with several regroupings, and representing primarily the (Old) Mennonite and some Amish membership, today comprises 9,448 members, the latter 22,621. The Mennonite Brethren Conference includes 18,663 members. The other conferences are smaller, but the unaffiliated, loose associations include some 15,000 members. These, together with the Hutterites, and a few Amish, participate little in Mennonite relief or missionary activity. Some have been strongly opposed to higher education. For these, being Mennonite carries more of an ethnic than religious connotation, though the two are admittedly difficult to separate. The Brethren in Christ, to whom reference has been made, arose in Pennsylvania in the second half of the eighteenth century, through Mennonite interaction with revivalism in Reformed and other traditions.[34]

For many years the Mennonites pursued an agricultural way of life. They were known as people of the soil and took pride in their agricultural achievements. While this may still be part of their self-image the twentieth century has, in fact, seen a vast proliferation into most of the professions and skills of the Canadian economy. Recent studies have confirmed, however, that there are proportionately few blue collar workers among Mennonites. Education has been very much a part of the upward mobility of Mennonites, and they have founded many schools — Bible schools, high schools and colleges — often at great sacrifice. In contrast to the literary dearth among them in Russia, the Mennonites have found Canada conducive to literary production, including several excellent denominational papers. They have also excelled in the arts, particularly in music. During the past several decades many became affluent participants in the aspirations of the Canadian middle class. It remained to be seen how these developments influenced their identity and sense of values.

Like Baptists, Mennonites have carried a deep sense of mission to all people, but they came later to the task of overseas mission and only in recent decades have they developed a dynamic concern for people around them, including the poor and oppressed. A rather unique ministry in behalf of the needy around the world has been carried on through the Mennonite Central Committee (MCC) which has provided unlimited service opportunities for young and old volunteers and has helped Mennonites, in the process of helping others, to find themselves closer to one another at home. For many, the giving of themselves and their means for others became a way of life much more than a compensatory alternative to participation in war.

These concerns, activities and attitudes helped to modify the ethnicity, to which earlier reference was made, in the direction of a mild ecumenicity. There were no historic attempts to participate in ecclesiastical mergers of any kind, but out of the experiences of the past came a mild benevolence towards others and a new willingness to talk about differences. This was a promising sign of growth.

NORMS AND ACHIEVEMENTS

In the first chapter of his classic book **The Believers' Church**, Donald F. Durnbaugh cites Martin Luther's well-known "truly evangelical order" for those "who want to be Christian in earnest and who profess the gospel with hand and mouth," and uses Luther's categories to propose a definition of the Believers' Church. Except for the requirement of performing Christian works and giving to the poor, Luther's proposal is completely inner-directed: meeting alone in a house, excommunication, proper baptism, centreing everything in the Word, prayer and love — a kind of blending of his early monastic and mystical commitments. In contrast to this, Durnbaugh shares his own proposal by giving all of Part Three of his book to a discussion of "The Character of Believers' Churches." Here the five primary categories, each with sub-headings, are: discipleship and apostolicity; mission and evangelism; church and state; mutual aid and service; sectarian and ecumenical. These two profiles can well be taken as supplementary, rather than mutually exclusive. Even so, they do not together exhaust the range of profiles we think of in connection with the nature of the Believers' Church.

If we use these criteria as a grid for testing the life and thought of the Believers' Church tradition in Canada in the past, we run into several problems, including the subjectivity involved in measuring performance norms, but also the simple lack of adequate information about most of the groups outside of Baptists and Mennonites, and which account for nearly one-half of the totals indicated. We do, however, have some records about a good number of Baptists and Mennonites, and some others, which can be the basis of a preliminary reading of the record.

In relation to the inner-directed emphases of Luther's profile, it is clear that conversion and personal experience were central to Baptist life in Canada, even before the revivals brought about by Henry Alline. The close communion question which plagued them for so many years may have been primarily a question about the meaning of baptism, but it also included regeneration and the visible marks of dying and rising with Christ. This same concern was central to the early history of the Brethren in Christ, the Christian and Missionary Alliance, and certainly to those in the Pentecostal movement.

On this issue Mennonites in Canada might be classified historically as ranging from revivalism and crisis conversion expectations to something close to birth-right Mennonitism. Many have seen their heritage as embodying both cultural and doctrinal motifs interwoven so inextricably that only God could know the difference between them, and they have been willing to leave it at that. For example, to speak of assurance of salvation seemed presumptuous, if not blasphemous to some, while its denial smacked of apostasy to others. Some among the former have placed great emphasis on adherence to specific traditional codes of conduct, often legalistically enforced, while antinomianism has been a temptation for the latter. The Mennonite Brethren were familiar with revivalism from the impact of pietism upon them in Russia in mid-nineteenth century. An hypothesis worth testing might be whether this pattern of membership recruitment led to less ethnic self-consciousness and greater identification with the dominant culture than the others experienced. The Evangelical Mennonite Mission Conference grew out of a revival among conservative Mennonites in the 1930s. In the past the variety of Mennonite church and community expectations have had a significant influence upon the religious response of young people. At times baptism became a traditional rite of passage not unlike confirmation in sacramental traditions. This is not to say that it was not meaningful to them, but that it lacked spontaneity and conscious choice. The problem of the transmission of faith, and the place of the adolescent in the Believers' Church before baptism, have remained for Mennonites in this context.

How have the Believers' Churches in Canada fared in the past in relation to Durnbaugh's grid, beginning with the categories of discipleship and apostolicity? The intention of discipleship was certainly there among both Baptists and Mennonites from the beginning, though a careful study of documents and publications would be necessary to chart the scale of achievement. Both groups clearly considered themselves unique and said so publicly, but not to each other. For the Baptists this became particularly evident during the inter-church conversations leading to the forming of the United Church of Canada in 1925. Participation does not seem to have been a viable option for Baptists. Without using the term **restitution**, both Baptists and Mennonites clearly saw themselves as being uniquely in harmony with the church in the Bible, even in congregational order, whereas the Christian Church (Disciples of Christ) tended to stress essence more.[35]

If church discipline is identified as a mark on this grid, the answer is yes, it was practised, but the story is both long and painful. Aside from individual cases, the best known of these among the Baptists was likely the Modernist-Fundamentalist controversy from 1919-1927.[36] Among the Mennonites the best available historical data are of the Conference of Mennonites in Canada for the period 1950-55, when it had a membership of approximately 15,000. During this period 143 persons were excommunicated. The scripture cited most frequently was Matthew 18:15-18. The reasons for excommunication and the number, in percentages, were: secret societies 1%, military service 2%, divorce 4%, remarriage 9%, immorality 28%, crime 3%, business ethics 1%, beliefs 29%, disobedience 17%, attendance (i.e., non-attendance of worship) 4%, other 2%. Of all these, 62% were restored to fellowship, 12% transferred their membership, 25% were lost track of, and 1% other.[37] In contrast to a cherished conviction of Believers' Church theology that discipline is carried on most effectively in the small, gathered fellowship, it was the smaller congregations which were more reluctant to practise discipline in this sampling while the congregations with membership over 300 had the most courage. There are no statistics about whether the percentage of those won back was larger in small congregations than in others.

Positive references have already been made to mission and evangelism, the next plank in the Durnbaugh grid. Suffice it to cite here the following statement from J.E. Harris's recent history of The Baptist Union of Western Canada:

> Dr. Roy Bell of First Baptist Church, Vancouver, has called Canadian Baptists to leadership in the Believers' Church Movement or otherwise to lose identity by merging with Canadian mainline churches. We fully recognize and rejoice that each denomination, as a part of Christ's church, makes its contribution to His Kingdom. But we are convinced that commitment to the Believers' Church position produces fewer nominal Christians, and a far greater percentage of committed followers of Christ. Conversion, believers' baptism and then church membership, in that order, is the New Testament pattern. It takes more than nominal Christians to make any notable impact for good upon the world at large.[38]

In relation to issues of church and state, Baptists recorded several notable achievements in the nineteenth century, particularly on the issues of clergy reserves and the establishing of nonsectarian universities by the state. Approximately one-seventh of the land in Upper Canada had been set aside by the Crown for Protestant church use, primarily Anglican. Baptists opposed this arrangement from the beginning, and carried on a relentless campaign to have these lands sold and the monies made available for public education and other uses. And they finally won. Quoting W.G. Pitman:

> The Baptists had won a real victory. In a sense they had led the way in creating a climate of opinion which would accept this solution....In spite of the resistance of every major denomination, the Baptists saw their principle of voluntarism and their ideal of the separation of church and state triumph.[39]

The university question was similar in that Anglicanism had secured a university charter in the 1830s and intended to control the institution, though financed by public funds. Meeting in Montreal in 1844, the Baptists declared:

> The great principles of Religious Liberty which they thus held have been grievously violated in the manner in which the Episcopalian sect of Christians has been allowed to divert a large portion of the funds set

apart for the education of the youth of the Province, from their original purposes, and to obtain an undue influence in the distribution of the benefits and management of the affairs of the University of King's College at Toronto.[40]

The Baptists were again successful in arousing public opinion until a new university bill in 1849 provided for the establishing of the University of Toronto on a nonsectarian basis.

It is interesting to note that Convention Baptists were part of the anti-war sentiment of the 1930s. This included the adoption of a resolution at the 1935 convention urging "the churches of the Convention in the event of war neither to bless nor give support in any way whatever as organizations to it." This resolution seems to have been superseded, however, by the events of World War II.[41]

Historically, Mennonites have been content to enjoy the exemption from military service and to have control of their own schools as granted them in the 1870s and, until recently, were not greatly concerned about what this meant for their neighbours. When state control of education threatened them, some of the most conservative groups left for Mexico and Paraguay in the 1920s, followed by a second migration to Paraguay in 1948. A substantial number of Mennonite young men served in military or non-combatant services during World War II, though the majority performed alternative service. The establishing of a Mennonite office in Ottawa to keep its constituency informed of legislative and other concerns, as well as speaking out in behalf of national and social issues were largely developments following 1945. Though some Mennonites have been politically active in every generation, an increasing number were seeking, and filling, political offices at various local, provincial and national levels in the post World War II era, at times with the strong encouragement of their own Mennonite constituencies, but not conferences or congregations.

The fourth plank of Durnbaugh's grid identifies mutual aid and service as a necessary mark of Believers' Church identity. Reference has already been made to the work of the Mennonite Central Committee, under which disaster and mental health services might be identified particularly as meeting national social needs. The temperance movement found strong support among Baptists throughout most of their history,[42] the Convention of 1912 came out strongly in favour of woman's suffrage,[43] and the Baptist Union of Western Canada has had two women presidents.[44] International relief and service activities have been carried on by Baptists through the channels of The Baptist World Alliance.

In his final section Durnbaugh proposes the criteria of "sectarian and ecumenical" as distinctive of Believers' churches. Earlier references have been made to a mild ecumenism among Mennonites and to Baptist responses to discussions about church union prior to 1925. These attitudes have shaped even more recent history. Both groups have normally worked actively with ministerial alliances and other inter-church projects at the local level, but have been reluctant to participate in larger alliances. The strong historic congregational polity continued to prevail. This became apparent again in the Baptist attitudes towards the **Plan of Union** discussions among the Anglicans and United Church and Disciples during the present decade. In a perceptive article on "Baptists in Canada and Co-operative Christianity," Jarold K. Zeman summarizes the Baptist consensus as follows: "Christian unity in free fellowship for the furtherance of the gospel — YES! Organic church union — NO! "[45] In discussing the conflict between denominational and national loyalties, Zeman saw a new leadership role for Baptists in ecumenical discussions and cited Roy Bell, president of the Baptist Union of Western Canada in 1969, as follows:

> The choice that we have from a practical point of view is either to offer leadership of the Believers' Church Movement or to lose identity in the merger with the United and Anglican Churches. Our slogan cannot be isolation but must be cooperation.[46]

CONCLUSION

The history of the Believers' Church in Canada now spans more than two centuries. These centuries brought both difficult and glorious moments to those in this tradition, forcing them again and again to "look to the rock from which [they] were hewn, and to the quarry from which [they] were digged" (Isaiah 51: 1). All odds notwithstanding, they would seem to have a good future to look forward to if they continue doing this.

THE BELIEVERS' CHURCH IN CANADA THE PRESENT[1]

Samuel J. Mikolaski

CHRISTIANITY IN CANADA

Christianity in Canada strongly reflects its British and European heritage. In recent decades it also reflects the distinct though parallel religious influences of the United States. Certain generalizations can be made about Canadian Christianity. The Roman Catholic Church is the largest Christian body, not only in Quebec but also in several other provinces. Judged on an international scale, the formation of the United Church of Canada in 1925, which was a union of the Methodists, Congregationalists and about half the Presbyterians, is the largest ecumenical merger in this century. Since World War II there has developed in Canada a growing emotional detachment from British religious influence and increased religious influence from the United States, which parallels cultural influence as well. While the Canadian social model rejects an established church there persists an establishment or elitist mentality as to the role of the Roman Catholic Church in Quebec and of the United and Anglican churches in other parts of Canada. Important changes have been going on in the way the churches are viewed in Canada and these changes probably outweigh the importance of statistics of membership.

Available statistical data are adequate only in general terms to assess the strength and vitality of the churches, including the evangelical churches and Believers' Churches. A comparative summary of data appears on page 42.

Since 1921, Anglicans have suffered the sharpest decline of any religious body in Canada. Trends within the United Church are more difficult to assess because of the union of 1925. Composite figures (1901) show that prior to union they amounted to 33 per cent of the population (this figure includes the Methodists and Presbyterians, but not the smaller Congregationalists) and 29.3 per cent in 1921. Since union in 1925 the United Church and the continuing Presbyterians held 26.3 per cent in 1941, 24.6 per cent in 1961, and 21.5 per cent in 1971. The decline of the Protestant churches in Canada as a percentage of population has been of longstanding duration and is dramatic. Baptists have declined in this period as a percentage of the population, despite the growth of Baptist bodies outside the Baptist Federation of Canada. The evangelical churches have grown, but the exact figures are uncertain. Some

---

[1] Abridged version of the author's paper as presented. Omitted are extensive sociological and statistical data about Canada and religion in Canada.

POPULATION BY RELIGIOUS AFFILIATION
Source: Statistics Canada
Adapted as a percentage of population

Religious denomination	1941	%	1951	%	1961	%	1971	%
CANADA (1)	11,506,655		14,009,429		18,238,247		21,568,310	
Adventist	18,485		21,398		25,999		28,590	
Anglican	1,754,368	15.20	2,060,720	14.70	2,409,068	13.20	2,543,180	11.00
Baptist	484,465	4.20	519,585	3.70	593,553	3.30	667,245	3.10
Buddhist	15,676		8,184		11,611		16,175	
Christian and Missionary Alliance	4,214	.04	6,396	.05	18,006	.10	23,630	.10
Christian Reformed	(2)		(2)		62,257	.30	83,390	.40
Churches of Christ, Disciples	21,260	.18	14,920	.10	19,512	.10	16,405	.07
Confucian	22,282		5,791		5,089		2,165	
Congregationalist	(3)		(3)		(3)		(4)	
Doukhobor	16,878		13,175		13,234		9,170	
Free Methodist	8,805	.08	8,921	.06	14,245	.08	19,125	.09
Greek Orthodox (5)	139,845	1.20	172,271	1.20	239,766	1.30	316,605	1.50
Hutterite	(6)		(6)		(6)		13,650	
Jehovah's Witnesses	7,007	.06	34,596	.20	68,018	.40	174,810	.80
Jewish	168,585	1.50	204,836	1.50	254,368	1.40	276,025	1.30
Lutheran	401,836	3.50	444,923	3.20	662,744	3.60	715,740	3.30
Mennonite (7)	111,554	1.00	125,938	.90	152,452	.80	168,150	.80
Methodist	(3)		(3)		(3)		(8)	
Mormon	25,328		32,888		50,016		66,635	
Pentecostal	57,742	.50	95,131	.70	143,877	.80	220,390	1.00
Presbyterian	830,597	7.20	781,747	5.60	818,558	4.50	872,335	4.00
Roman Catholic	4,806,431	41.80	6,069,496	43.30	8,342,826	45.70	9,974,895	46.20
Salvation Army	33,609	.30	70,275	.50	92,054	.50	119,665	.55
Ukrainian Catholic (9)	185,948		191,051		189,653		227,730	1.00
Unitarian	5,584		3,517		15,062		20,995	
United Church	2,208,658	19.20	2,867,271	20.50	3,664,008	20.10	3,768,800	17.5
Other	158,337		196,720		277,508		293,240	
No religion	19,161		59,679		94,763		929,575	

Notes:

(1) Exclusive of Newfoundland prior to 1951.
(2) Figures not available.
(3) Included with "United Church".
(4) Included with "Other".
(5) Includes those churches which observe the Greek Orthodox rite, such as Russian Orthodox, Ukrainian Orthodox and Syrian Orthodox.
(6) Included with "Mennonite".
(7) Includes "Hutterite" prior to 1971.
(8) Assigned alternately to Free and Wesleyan Methodist.
(9) Includes "Other Greek Catholic".

indication is possible by taking figures for most of the major evangelical bodies, say Baptist, Christian and Missionary Alliance, Free Methodist, Mennonite, Pentecostal and Salvation Army. In 1941 these numbered a total of 700,389 in the census figures (6.08 per cent). In 1971 they numbered a total of 1,221,205 (5.66 per cent). The decline in percentage of population is significant. To these need to be added the Christian Reformed Church, evangelicals in the mainline churches, unaffiliated Christians and independent churches. A dramatic rise in strength of the Jehovah's Witnesses, Mormons and Unitarians is noteworthy.

Evangelicals hold that true Christianity is a certain understanding of its early biblical form. They believe that in true faith one experiences God redemptively directly through Jesus Christ and the power of the Holy Spirit. This experience is life-encompassing and life-transforming. There are many parties among evangelicals, including groups with extreme theological, social and political ideas. Most evangelicals, however, are conventional Protestants. There are now growing numbers of evangelicals, especially charismatics, among Roman Catholics.

The mainline church evangelicals comprise the traditional evangelical cause in Canada. They include the residue of evangelical commitment of nineteenth and twentieth century Christianity in Canada among Methodists, Congregationalists, Presbyterians, and Anglicans. Following Church Union in 1925 the continuation of the Presbyterian Church in Canada was urged, chiefly on confessional grounds, to perpetuate evangelical faith. Among Anglicans, evangelicals are concentrated in the Low Church tradition, more especially in Wycliffe College, Toronto. The strength of Anglican evangelicalism is in the Toronto area. Up to recent years, mainline church evangelicals were a declining force, notably in the United Church. Many of them had dispersed to Baptist and other evangelical churches. In protest to the growing power of liberal theology in the mainline denominations since the 1920s, many evangelicals within the mainline churches switched their financial giving to the burgeoning parachurch evangelical home and foreign mission agencies, dozens of which were concentrated in the Toronto area in the 1930s and 1940s. Non-evangelicals have rarely understood the power of this hidden movement. A substantial portion of the support for evangelical causes came from mainline church evangelicals. As these evangelicals passed from the scene, the evangelical organizations which they supported looked increasingly for support from the specifically evangelical churches and denominations, including those of the Believers' Church tradition. Thus, since World War II there has developed competition between evangelical church related agencies and evangelical parachurch agencies for a share of the evangelical dollar. In more recent years, renewal movements within the mainline churches especially the Anglicans, have been significant; however, adherents of the new evangelicalism often have little understanding of, or loyalty to, the traditional evangelical mission agencies. So far as perception of cultural status is concerned, evangelicals of the mainline churches, in particular preachers of that tradition, such as Anglicans and Presbyterians are accorded a deference that evangelicals attached to evangelical churches and denominations rarely enjoy. An elitist mentality touches all parts of Canadian religious life, including evangelical life.

The vast majority of Canadian evangelical Christians are attached to the specifically evangelical churches, denominations and organizations. These present a variegated picture. Some churches maintain complete independence as individual congregations. Some espouse extreme political, social and doctrinal views. At times, the extremes have to do with overemphasis on a theological or social issue. Most evangelicals in Canada are traditional in their beliefs and co-operate with other Christians locally, regionally and sometimes nationally. The vast majority of Canadian evangelicals are in the Believers' Churches. When one considers that most are in churches such as Baptist, Mennonite, Pentecostal, Christian and Missionary Alliance, Nazarene, Assemblies of God, Associated Gospel Churches, Plymouth Brethren, as well as independent congregations, it is evident that the strength of Canadian evangelicalism is in the Believers' Church tradition. The denominational groupings usually reflect active internal co-operation and strong programs of church extension, education and overseas missions.

Some Canadian evangelicals are open to ecumenical dialogue, but most resist it. The reasons for this are complex. The most obvious reason is evangelical resistance to liberal domination of ecumenical activity in Canada and the United States and concern that the theology and principles of historic Christianity are not firmly espoused. Equally important reasons include the feeling that the time spent in inter-church dialogue quickly reaches a point of diminishing returns and that one's time and money are better invested in evangelistic enterprises. Ecumenical dialogue is also usually dominated by those of the Episcopal and Reformed traditions. Those of the Believers' Church tradition feel that co-operation is difficult when irreconcilable differences on the nature of the church as a believing fellowship are simply glossed over, to say nothing about polity as an issue of the ambiguities that inhere in the concept of church unity. Questions of theology and polity also divide evangelicals, as will be discussed later. Some of the issues that persist between evangelicals generally and the Believers' Churches, as to the nature of the church, are identical to those that divide Believers' Churches from the ecumenical movement.

The major criticism of Canadian evangelicalism, especially from the standpoint of the Believers' Church tradition is the issue of kerygmatic residue. Is the evangelical cut off from the world? Does he pursue primarily inner consolation without compassionate regard to the evils of the world? Does he concentrate upon personal salvation and neglect his responsibility in the church and in the community? Is there among evangelicals a great deal of fruitless reiteration of shibboleths, which reiteration is largely self-serving but which brings few to Christ? It serves rather only to reassure the enclave that the "Word of the Lord is proclaimed here"?

The most sensitive issue within Canadian evangelicalism is the relation of Word to **kerygma**. While the vast majority of Canadian evangelicals are of the Believers' Church tradition, evangelical identification in Canada has largely consisted of adherence to the authority of scripture, not the authority of scripture as expressed in the gospel, its practice and residue. This rock is barely beneath the surface of channels that ministerial associations and steering committees attempt to navigate when they plan joint evangelistic enterprises. It is not an issue of creedal dogmatism, as some have thought. Rather, it is the issue that evangelicalism in general sees the irreducible minimum to be the individual pledge of faith in Christ which seems to result in a granular faith, whereas the Believers' Church tradition sees this as a truncation of the gospel. For them the issue of faith must be public confession in baptism as part of the **kerygma**, identification with the people of God in the believing fellowship and obedient discipleship combined with sacrificial ministry.

THE BELIEVERS' CHURCH IN CANADA

On any given Sunday in Canada the majority of people attending non-Catholic Christian worship services are most likely in the Believers' Churches. Who are the Believers' Churches in Canada? What do they stand for?

1. Ideological Characteristics

The term "Believers' Church" is attributed to the German sociologist Max Weber. It is a useful shorthand to distinguish a certain Christian tradition from the other two major ones, namely, the Episcopal tradition and the Reformed tradition. However, the use of the term is not intended to be pejorative. Its use does not disparage the faith of Christians in the other traditions. Nor does its use make the self-serving implication that all who attend or even belong to Believers' Churches are in fact genuine believers, though they ought to be. It expresses an ideal on the nature of Christian experience and on the nature and polity of the church. Nor is this ideal expressed in a single form. The tradition comprises many denominational forms clustered around several key-feature ideals.

The Canadian Believers' Churches derive from the Free Church and Pietist traditions of Britain and Europe. Puritan separation and Lollard and other English pietism are the roots from which originate Baptists, Methodists, Plymouth Brethren and Quakers. Continental Anabaptists, Baptists and Pietist life are the roots of Mennonites, Church of the Brethren, and some Baptists and Brethren in Canada who are of European origin. From these and from evangelical movements which are indigenous to Canada and the United States there have sprung up many other Believers' Church groups. These include Pentecostals, Holiness groups, Christian and Missionary Alliance, Nazarenes, Evangelical Free Church, Association of Gospel Churches, the

Apostolic Church, the Christian Church, and the Brethren in Christ Church. In addition, there are independent churches of many labels, and also many parachurch organizations and agencies which practise certain Believers' Church principles.

A common error Canadian Believers' Church Christians make is to suppose that their true home is in the Reformation cry **Sola Scriptura, Sola gratia**. Well and good. But for the Baptists and Anabaptists this was a half-way house. The Radical Reformation principle was that the church must be a body of believers. Socially the system must allow for diversity under the rule of law, rather than monolithic uniformity. Canadians continue to think of the church in organizationally monolithic terms. Believers' Church Canadians continue to affirm freedom from hierarchical control, regenerate membership, voluntarist commitment and congregational government, but they have little perception of the historical origins of these ideas, or of their theological and social rationale, or of their conceptual cohesion and dynamic as a model for the church in the modern world. The Canadian establishment-minded attitude assumes that Canadian conditions are not conducive to a Believers' Church mass movement, as in other places such as the United States. Needed is a new awareness of the reasons for the existence of Believers' Church denominations and a new vision of mission to overcome the inferiority complex which afflicts the Believers' Church in Canada.

The progress of the Believers' Church tradition in Canada calls for nothing less than the re-orientation and re-education of the public mind. It is likely that the media and the political and educational establishments will be the slowest to respond to these modes of thought. The ideal of a composite society has been won politically but not fully culturally or religiously. The view persists that believers' baptism and disciplined discipleship within the believing body divide Christendom.

Consider the ideological teaching and practices which characterize Canadian Believers' Churches. Foremost is the view that the church as a fellowship of believers is restitutionist in character. The aim is to restore the church to its dominical and apostolic character through the gospel. Certain key elements of scripture are normative. These include proclamation, conversion, faith-baptism, reception of the Spirit, membership, disciplined spiritual life under the Word of God, works commensurate with one's profession, and obedient witness in the name of Christ.

The church is properly made up of those who have personally professed faith in Jesus Christ the Lord and have been baptized. There is the principle of the believing people who alone constitute Christ's body. Their fellowship is thus inevitably and irrevocably socially discontinuous. There is a line between the church and the world. Society must function on a footing of temporal laws. Voluntarism and compositism become the social and political ideals. It is not the business of the state to approve or subsidize religion.

The Believers' Church urges upon its members obedient discipleship.

The body should be self-disciplining. The marks of discipleship include prayer, high spiritual ideals, works of kindness, and concern for the social as well as the spiritual welfare of men.

The church is a **koinonic** body. This breaks the claim of the monolithic structure of the **Corpus Christianum**, yet encourages faith in the unity of believers in the Lord Jesus. The vital unity of the church historically is the local assembly. This view enhances the responsibility of each member, compels attention to the life in the Spirit under the Lordship of Christ, encourages mission to the community in which the church is located, and discourages the tendency to pyramid religious power locally, nationally or internationally.

2. Kerygmatic Effectiveness

(a) **Identity**: Like all minority groups in a society, the Believers' Churches in Canada have developed toughness and persistence. Regrettably at times some have been reactionary and fratricidal. Establishmentarianism as a frame of mind in Canada generates an inferiority complex among the Believers' Church denominations. They need a thorough re-education and re-indoctrination as to their historical roots, on the critical role the Radical Reformation has had on the North American political structure, and on the thoroughly irenic and accepting nature of their faith. While most Believers' Church members are well taught on the nature of Christian experience and terms of membership in the believing church fellowship, few have much notion about their historical roots, social and political ideals, or even churchmanship. Affirmation of identity and interpretation of biblical and social principles are urgently-needed denominational and public media tasks.

As a parallel component of the interpretive process, there is needed affirmation of the apostolic character of Believers' Church Christianity. The legitimacy of the continuity between apostolic Christianity and the Believers' Church faith and practices requires public re-statement. Regrettably, controversy and reaction have cast the movement in the light of spoiler, not as a legitimate branch of Christianity.

It is likely that provision for ethnic ministries in Canada, as provided by Believers' Churches, is unrivalled among non-Catholic bodies. Nevertheless, a new view needs to be taken of cultural relations and practices in church life, not only as regards ethnic Canadians but also working class Canadians. During the past half-century many Believers' Church people, for example Baptists, Mennonites, and Christian and Missionary Alliance, have become predominantly middle class and in some cases elitist in outlook. A middle class status combined with an inferiority complex produces an effective deterrent to witness and growth. As long ago as 1961, three American Baptist analysts were invited by the Toronto Baptist Association to report on Baptist church strategy in Toronto. Commenting on the inferiority complex of the business-suited Toronto Baptist, they said, "Perhaps if it could be said of the Baptist Church in Toronto that she associates with publicans and sinners, it would be discovered that her message would be much more winsome for today's generation."

Three comments are appropriate here. First, Pentecostals and independent churches have displaced Baptists and the Christian and Missionary Alliance as churches of the common people. There are notable exceptions of course. Mennonites have also become largely middle class with the added ethnic barrier. Second, few churches have learned how to minister to ethnic people. My own family experience is instructive. We were never so lonely as during the years following our conversion from Eastern Orthodox tradition and thereby separated from many relatives and friends. We found evangelical faith among predominately WASP churches, but it was a lonely existence. One had to have been thoroughly converted to stay with it! Few English language and culture Christians realize that people must be won to themselves as to the Lord. The language and culture of ethnic Canadians has been too much ignored or denigrated in WASP evangelical churches. Third, while evangelicals generally have an excellent record of ministry to the socially deprived in detoxification ministries and in other social and rehabilitation ministries, frequently they have used these ministries as an excuse for not practising horizontal evangelism as against downward speaking ministry. It is easy to target social assistance to the needy and to speak down to them about religion along with gifts of meals, lodging, money, or medical assistance. But this must not continue to comprise a tradition of excuse for not practising horizontal, eye to eye, peer-level evangelism.

(b) Focus: Many legitimate ministries can include elements of personal style and emphasis, especially as regards the peculiar needs of a church and the gifts of the leaders and congregation. One need not here recite a litany of the incredibly diverse and effective ministries Believers' Churches undertake. Occasionally, churches and leaders go off on tangents. But the vast majority of churches and pastors have a clear sense of vision and vocation, which is that, beyond ministering to the spiritual needs of the congregation, they should unceasingly strive to win new converts to faith in Christ.

Subtle misinterpretation of the essential task and witness of the church does occur. For example, some evangelicals think that the focus of confessional emphasis must be almost solely and exclusively upon the inspiration of the scriptures. This has become in our time a rallying point of evangelical concern. Now, it goes without saying that belief in the integrity and authority of scripture is critical to evangelical faith. Surely scripture is the mother that nurtures all that is authentically Christian. Nevertheless, at the risk of misunderstanding, it is important to state that this plays into the hands of the Reformation theology. The witness and life of the Believers' Church espouses a different ideal— different, that is, in the sense that essential features of the Christian evangel as a coherent whole are taken to interpret the meaning of biblical authority. That was the point of the Radical Reformation in Europe and Britain. The point is not biblical authority in the abstract, but to a certain issue. We do not confess the Word alone, but the Word as expressed in the apostolic gospel, mandate and mission.

In this respect the Believers' Churches in Canada need to take the lead in attesting to and practising the form of the **kerygma** that reflects their faith, and not to be so completely dominated by the least common denominator approach of the general evangelical stance. I plead for co-operation. Let that be understood. I plead strongly nevertheless for Believers' Church vitality, visibility and leadership which call for untruncated commitment to Christ, baptism, church membership and church body life.

In a new and fresh way the Believers' Churches in Canada must take as their norm the apostolic mandate of the day of Pentecost. This is the model for mission today. Surely the Book of Acts presents to us the fulfilment of our Lord's Commission in the activities of his disciples:

> Turn away from your sins, each one of you, and be baptized in the name of Jesus Christ, so that your sins will be forgiven; and you will receive God's gift, the Holy Spirit. For God's promise was made to you and your children, and to all who are far away—all whom the Lord our God calls to himself. And Peter made his appeal to them and with many other words he urged them saying, "Save yourselves from the punishment coming to this wicked people!" Many of them believed his message and were baptized; about three thousand people were added to the group that day. They spent their time in learning from the apostles, taking part in the fellowship, and sharing in the fellowship means and the prayers (Acts 2: 38-42).

This is the Believers' Church mission: to preach the word of love and grace and redemption. To call men to repentance and faith in the Lord Jesus Christ. To baptize them without delay, upon the profession of their faith, which in the New Testament is the door into the church and into ministry. Conversion, baptism, reception of the Spirit, and membership are one event in the New Testament and in the post-apostolic church. Further, the task is to lead believers to develop the life in the Spirit which they have received, the life of obedient discipleship, and to teach them the biblical necessity of the local church of believers. This simple pattern needs to be repeated over and over again.

The Believers' Churches must resist displacement of the church in their understanding of the Christian mission, because the dominical mandate relates the mission of Christians and the life of Christians to the egalitarian believing fellowship, not to special interest groups. That is the genius of the New Testament model. Peter did not establish a Galilean Fishermen's Fellowship. Paul did not organize a Tentmakers Christian Association. Lydia did not establish a Sellers-of-Purple Christian League. Philemon did not organize a Christian Business Men's Group, nor Onesimus a Christian Slaves' Society. Nor did Apollos establish a Pan-Hellenic Christian Alliance. All were part of the body of Christ as expressed in the local believing fellowship. This focus does not deny that there are believers in other Christian bodies, but affirms that the Believers' Church reflects distinctive concepts about Christianity.

(c) **Growth**: The traditional church bodies can never quite understand the drive of evangelicals, including the Believers' Churches, to win new converts. The sense of urgency to communicate the evangel, if needing to be renewed for each generation, is itself not based on novel or whimsical grounds. Rather, it is based on the crisis of the ultimate divine judgment of human sin, warmly complemented by the truth of God's compassionate grace in Jesus Christ and his saving Cross. The fundamental issue for evangelicals is that without Christ men are lost. How can one then withhold life-encompassing commitment to preach the gospel?

Up until the present generation in certain instances, a sectarian and competitive spirit might have been justifiably alleged against some evangelical churches and bodies. Today the secularization of modern man and the resulting alienation of many Canadians from the traditional church bodies have created new conditions. Believers' Churches must see that current problems are in fact opportunities. Periods of intellectual, social, cultural and religious change are periods which tend to disorient the establishment minded. Historically they have been periods of golden opportunity for the Believers' Church tradition. The opportunities will be missed if we persist in an enclave mentality, if we superciliously talk about quality not quantity, if we advance pseudo-theological reasons to justify no-growth, and if we fail to develop strategy and to deploy human and material resources with growth in mind. This must include a more egalitarian frame of mind, more concern about French Canada, greater awareness of the changing social and cultural characteristics of the nation, and a jettisoning of our traditional inferiority complex.

Each Believers' Church denomination should carefully assess its growth pattern. Recent renewal and growth trends are heartening because some groups, such as Baptists, actually declined as a proportion of the population since 1901. We need the resurgence of life that outreach brings.

To achieve growth at an on-going rate, the single most important requisite is to create a pervasive mission-mood. Growth depends first of all on a mood, and only second on methods. The problems associated with inspiring and assimilating growth are greater than those associated with no-growth. Growth occurs best where strategy places mission at the top of the priorities' list. Unless growth is measured at a compounded rate and as a ratio of population, we deceive ourselves.

Growth calls for leadership. It also throws up leadership. A mission-mood which targets and achieves growth natively implants in the consciousness of the next generation of lay and ministerial leadership the assumption that mission and growth are the normal pattern of church life, not an extra mood to be periodically cranked up. Lay and ministerial leadership need to assume a "take charge" attitude in relation to goals. Power trips by some church leaders during the past half century have forced Canadians generally to be leery of religious leadership. This needs to be corrected. Part of the cure is the primacy of mission-mood as a norm not only for programs, but also for leadership. The Believers' Church congregational and denominational model provides the framework to call leadership to taks. Responsibility to the people should include a continuing demand for growth, not simply preservation of the status quo.

(d) **Co-operation**: Advocates of monolithic church unity have assumed that denominations perpetuate the so-called scandal of disunity. This assumption is challenged by the Believers' Church tradition in more than one way. F.A. Norwood has observed that denominations affirm the legitimacy of Christian churches beyond toleration by establishments. As well, in comparison with movements, denominations are strengthening and uniting forces.

Movements are sometimes forced to by-pass the church and denominational life because inertia plagues institutional church life. However, movements are undisciplined whereas churches and denominations are coherent and stable. Where churches overcome spiritual inertia, the prospects for their productive long-term growth are great today. Add to this the dynamic of the conventicle as the seed of the local church, and one can understand why explosive growth of the Believers' Church tradition can easily occur. The dynamic is wedded to a stable, recognizable kerygmatic tradition. Churches are coherent, stable and hard-working. Cost effectiveness is controlled. They are repositories of true doctrine and preserve continuity. They mobilize moral and spiritual energy. They efficiently dispense charity and public service. Churches act as shepherds. They keep tab on the flock. Churches are resilient. They ride through rough times and carry the people through rough times.

In short, the church is essential to the nurture of Christian experience. Like Felix Manz, the Anabaptist martyr of Zuerich, Believers' Churches today must re-emphasize that true faith results in a new life and that this makes secret, invisible Christianity impossible. The new life entails public commitment to the people of God. We must dismiss in our day the idea that one can authentically be biblical as a Christian, or as a local church, in isolation. Granular independence is unknown in the New Testament.

Co-operation is thus a theological as well as administrative issue. Co-operation is essential within the local church, between the local church and the denomination, and between the various denominations of the Believers' Church tradition. Co-operation entails more trust and less edginess; more encouragement of one another, and less criticism. Increased awareness of the historical principles of the Believers' Church will generate greater confidence that co-operation fosters a common goal of the church as a fellowship of believers. Thus co-operation can reflect a unity of the heart and mind which finds its joy in results. There can emerge an implicit federalism through co-operation without the threat of enlarging structures.

(e) **Model**: Lack of consistency as to model, programme and aesthetic values in church planting remains a problem and possibly a hindrance to dramatic Believers' Church growth in Canada. This may well be the case, despite the extensive similarities among the various denominational traditions as to hymns, songs, worship forms, preaching style and content, structure of religious education, age group ministries and activities. This may be true also even where there is indicated the need for distinctive aspects in church life due to socio-economic, cultural or ethnic differences.

Clarity and consistency as to kerygmatic structure, the confessional core, and mission as expressed through the church are critical contemporary issues facing the churches in Canada.

Before us is the question of model. What is transferrable? It is a mistake to transplant the untransplantable. Special ministries usually require special men. That is a form of growth and a form of gift which, like the results of co-operative evangelistic crusades, may be regarded as icing on the cake, but such results are not the cake. It is the cake that the Believers' Churches should be setting out to bake. To state the matter again for the sake of clarity, what is "replicable"? What is "duplicable"? What is duplicable not by the expert, but planned in such a way that effectiveness can be readily duplicated? We must fix attention upon **that which can be ordinarily duplicated by ordinary people in ordinary circumstances**. The truth of this, as expressed in methodology adapted to time and place, is a key feature of the phenomenal growth of the church during the first three centuries of the Christian era, during the Anabaptist movement of the sixteenth and seventeenth centuries, and the revivals of the eighteenth and nineteenth centuries in Britain, the United States and Eastern Canada.

Ready "duplicability" entails certain basic characteristics of the church. Christianity and the local church become an attractive alternative because the believing fellowship is essentially person-preserving and people-caring. The true Christian conventicle has a powerful sense of community and is radically egalitarian. There emotional social security is found. Ethical standards are high, religious devotion to the one true God is intense, and discipleship is demanding and life-encompassing. Converts must make a commitment, and are screened. Confession of faith is public. Separation from the world and evil is total. Dedication to the welfare of others is unceasing.

These qualities are functions not only of Christian experience but also of the church, and of Christian responsibility within the church. The church is more than an **ecclesia**; that is, more than a called out, identifiable, organized assembly. There is a plus factor which is identified by the term **soma**. The church is an **ecclesia** in the sense of **soma**. It is more than a body politic; it is the body of Christ in every place of its life and witness.

The duplicability of this model centres on the genius of its simplicity and directness. Of the many New Testament characteristics of the church in its congregational form, we may take five to epitomize it in periods of rapid growth. These are: **leiturgeia** (worship), **koinonia** (fellowship), **didache** (teaching), **kerygma** (gospel), **diakonia** (service). They are the corporate worship and praise of God, the fellowship of the Spirit expressed in the assembly, the communication of Christ's teaching and nurturing discipleship, proclamation of the gospel which issues in faith-baptism and church membership, and loving concern for people in need.

3. Confessional Integrity

The turn of the intellectual wheel furnishes to Believers' Churches in Canada an unparalleled opportunity. Contemporary modes of thought, such as oriental mysticism and naturalism which are prevalent today, reduce man to non-personal status or to a bundle of responses, just as their ancient idealist and atomist counterparts did. In holding that each man is a permanent spiritual reality, Christianity is essentially person-preserving. The Believers' churches espouse a view that conserves the human spirit, freedom and dignity. They comprise the majority of evangelicals in Canada and have the best opportunity of any non-Catholic tradition in Canada to achieve nation-wide penetration of the gospel in this generation.

Confessional integrity is encouraged by the re-affirmation of an important heritage, which includes: the belief that all doctrine and procedure must be based on biblical teaching and practice; refusal to be bound by creeds; the principle that the individual local church is self-governing; the requirement of credible evidence of regeneration as a prerequisite to church membership; the practice of baptism by immersion upon profession of faith; the principle of a free church in a free state; the duties of loyalty and good citizenship; rejection of state support for religious work. All of these are vital principles for today, but if they are held as shibboleths they will not preserve the churches, except as monuments to the past.

The proclamation and practice we need must join vision to kerygmatic integrity and loving concern. Let us take care not to adopt the ethos of the times as issues of eternity. Is there a right to enjoyment, as some evangelicals now maintain as a thesis for life, but not obligation to work? Should aspiration to self-fulfilment mute teaching on sacrifice? Are we in danger of seeking relationships, but forgetting how to love? Bypaths on these and many other current questions are not of themselves guarantees that the gospel is becoming relevant to modern man. They are not, unless spiritual renewal, altruism and self-sacrifice, as they derive their meaning from the Cross of Christ, reinfuse in us the devotion to Christ and to the service of man, which our forefathers knew and call us to imitate.

THE BELIEVERS' CHURCH IN CANADA: FUTURE

Roy D. Bell

The complications of dealing with the future are virtually impossible to resolve. The future, for one thing, rarely conforms to our expectations. Furthermore, we are living in a period of time when the rate of change is seen as exceeding man's capacity to adapt to it.

There are those who argue that the future can be understood by the process of extrapolation. This assumes that the future will be like the past. But it is clear in our day that this is not accurate. Who for example, could have forecast the massive decline of the traditional Canadian churches?

David Virtue has attempted to document the decline in Sunday school enrollment in the United and Anglican churches. He sets the national context first. "Since 1962, Anglican Sunday school rolls have declined by 68.6 per cent and those of the united Church by 62.1 per cent." He then takes a look at British Columbia. "Of the more than 80 parishes in southern B.C. only nine have a Sunday school with more than 100 pupils." The United Church in British Columbia had a Sunday school enrollment in 1964 of 66,147. It is thought that today it is "closer to 6,000."[1]

There are, of course, other suggestions for discerning the future. John Kettle summarizes them:

> There is a school of futurists that despises trend extrapolation, the contemptible "numbers game", as an abandonment of judgment. Extrapolators, these scholars say, are surrendering to whimsy. There are only a handful of acceptable ways to investigate what is going to happen in the future, they say. One is to calculate the effect of social, economic, political and technological changes on the population by sociological analysis (or perhaps by intuition). Another is to ask people and institutions what their intentions for the future are ("How many children will you have?" "How much does your company plan to spend on new buildings and machinery next year?" and so on). A third is to pre-empt the future by causing more desirable things to happen.[2]

There are other substantial difficulties as well. Will there be another world war? Will there be a major outbreak of plague? Will there be a major economic collapse? Will there be a religious revival? Will Canada itself survive? Will there be a future or will the Lord's return pre-empt it?

In the light of these difficulties, it would be tempting to abandon the task I have been assigned. Rather than do that I will confine myself to some general observations about the immediate future of the Believers'

Churches in Canada.

I am assuming that there will be no major changes in the expressed convictions of the Believers' Churches, as summarized in **The Concept of the Believers' Church** and in **The Believers' Church**.[3] In all of these there is obvious effort made to marry doctrine and ethics. The theology of the Believers' Church includes convictions about life-style. The Believers' Church may emphasize separation from the world but it is also committed to living for the world.

There are several reasons for satisfaction with the Believers' Church Movement in Canada today. The convocation of this conference and the response to it may be regarded as one of the indicators. We are beginning to sort out our identity and enjoy our true heritage.

We also appear to be prospering at the local church level. There is enough evidence to support the claim that our congregations constitute a "worshipping majority" in the larger English-speaking communities in Canada. Increasingly those Canadians who are prepared to consider the Christian faith as a viable option are coming to us. The immediate future is bright when viewed in terms of people at worship in churches of our conviction.

It is interesting to note that many of the para-church groups which receive a good deal of their support from our constituency are gaining considerably in strength and influence when compared with the serious decline of support for the large religious denominations in Canada.

There are a number of other areas where we are doing well. These include concern for overseas missions and world relief, spiritual vitality of many local churches, and leadership in evangelism. While our view of social involvement has often been narrow and limited, the scope is widening and we are becoming increasingly effective and vocal.

At the same time, there are other areas in which we are functioning far less satisfactorily. We have done poorly in producing and/or retaining leadership. We have made commitments to high quality theological education but in many of our churches the active ministry continues to be sustained by people trained outside Canada. There is little evidence to expect a substantial change in the immediate future even though there is adequte training available in Canada. A significant contribution could be made by a joint effort in theological education.

A second major failure has been our inability to cross cultural boundaries. Many of our church groups are separated only by ethnic origins. The process of time may modify some divisions but there is as yet little evidence of real progress. Cultural differences must yield to the Lordship of Christ.

A further problem is our failure to keep in touch with the so-called working class or the blue collar worker. Our churches tend to be right wing politically and anti-union in bias, and this in spite of our origins. In addition, many of our groups appear to show little identification with the dispossessed. The single parent or the family on welfare are hardly seen as desirable church members. We can sometimes persuade ourselves to patronize such persons, but to identify with them requires radical change in attitudes.

There are a number of other matters which affect our co-operation. Modes of baptism are a source of division among us and must be resolved. Better policies in co-operative church extension work should be sought. We are divided in our attitudes toward the ecumenical movement. It may be argued that this is not too significant because of the failure of the ecumenical movement itself and its own loss of impetus. Nevertheless, the two most commonly recognized barriers to co-operation between major Baptist groups are: theological education and attitudes to the ecumenical movement.

Thus far we have looked at the future in terms of extrapolation. Now, we need to raise some fundamental questions.

We seem to be far removed from the depth of spiritual concern that marked our forefathers. It was said of them (Conrad Grebel, Felix Manz and George Cajacob):

> They came to one mind in these things, and in the pure fear of God they recognized that a person must learn from the divine Word and preaching a true faith which manifests itself in love, and receive the true Christian baptism on the basis of the recognized and confessed faith, in the union with God of a good conscience, henceforth to serve God in a holy Christian life with all godliness, also to be steadfast to the end in tribulation. And it came to pass that they were together until fear began to come over them, yea, they were pressed in their hearts. Thereupon, they began to bow their knees to the Most High God in heaven and called upon him as the Knower of hearts, implored him to enable them to do his divine will and to manifest his mercy toward them. For flesh and blood and human forwardness did not drive them, since they well knew what they would have to bear and suffer on account of it. After the prayer, George Cajacob arose and asked Conrad to baptize him for the sake of God, with the true Christian baptism upon his faith and knowledge. And when he knelt down with that request and desire, Conrad baptized him, since at that time there was no ordained deacon to perform such work. After that was done the others similarly desired George to baptize them, which he also did upon their request. Thus they together gave themselves to the name of the Lord in the high fear of God. Each confirmed the other in the service of the gospel, and they began to teach and keep the faith. Therewith began the separation from the world and its evil works.[4]

We can argue that we continue to give intellectual assent to the major theological principles that belong to our heritae. But do we really hold them with the passion our fathers did? In a slightly different context, have we fallen into the errors mentioned in James 2: 4-26? Is our passion consistent with the logic of our affirmations? Could it be that God is raising up in our day those who are unaware of our historical background, but who are now and will be increasingly the real successors to the Believers' Church Movement?

Carl Lindquist's article in the January 17, 1978 issue of **Christianity Today** brings these questions into focus. He reports on a six month, 50,000 mile world tour of forty-three "centres of Christian renewal". These represent a small sample of what is now a significant new force in the Christian world. He outlines the beliefs and emphases of these groups. A dominant one is that "each group wants to share the common life in Christ with searching, often suffering people".

He identifies six principles that are common to all the groups.

1. Jesus is Lord. "Every group from the simplest to the most sophisticated found unity in a common allegiance to Christ, an allegiance that tends to obliterate other points of division." "What the ecumenical movement has been unable to accomplish organizationally in all these years, the renewal movement has effected spiritually overnight. It has made us one in Christ."

2. The Importance of Scripture. Although Dr. Lundquist encountered varying hermeneutics and interpretations he found "people genuinely relying on scripture. Usually the approach was devotional rather than systematic and at times comprehensive exegesis was lacking, but it was nonetheless valid."

3. A Rule to Live By. Most of the centres visited had a rule of life, usually printed. Some were more demanding than others. The less stringent vows included daily scripture reading and prayer, weekly attendance at worship, tithing one's income and consciously seeking to serve Christ. "Only in rare instances did I find an open community in which no spiritual discipline was demanded."

4. A Simple Life-style. This was a way of life at most renewal centres. "It stands in contrast to the over-indulgence of the western world, and aligns itself with the hungry of developing nations."

5. Involvement with Suffering People. "I did not find a self-centred preoccupation with a person's interior life that dulled sensitivity to the wounds of others. Social action—tender loving care—became a normal way to express a personal devotion to Christ."

6. Celebration Through the Arts. Lundquist perceived a desire to "joyfully relate all of life to God." The art forms ranged from hundreds of songs composed to cover various life experiences to special festivals, musical plays, biblical symbolism and biblical dance. "There is a light-hearted care-free spontaneity about all of these expressions. They grow out of a rich personal experience that says it's a joy to be a Christian."[5]

While I believe that the most urgent need is the renewal of the institutional church, and more specifically the Believers' Church, it must be acknowledged that God is using these centres of renewal to meet needs we have traditionally met. These people express and exemplify many of the concerns that lie at the heart of the Believers' Church Movement.

Could it be that our future will be largely determined by our sensitivity to the needs which these groups appear to be meeting? Have we become so middle class, so right wing in our outlook, so inhibited emotionally, that we can no longer hear what is being said so loudly by the very existence of these "centres of renewal"? Is it possible to retain the conceptual framework of the Believers' Church Movement without the spiritual concerns of the Believers' Church Movement?

There is an obvious lack of a coherent theology and an adequate doctrine of the church in most "centres of renewal," and more specifically in the Charismatic Movement. Yet if we dismiss them without considering their implications our future will be dark. There are three groups which command attention in our day: the centres of renewal, the Charismatic Movement, and a thrust expressed by **Sojourners** magazine.

The issue of life-styles must be faced. Too many of our churches mirror an uncritical acceptance of comfort and privilege inappropriate in a world like ours. We live in a world where the West is under attack for devouring the world's resources. There are, of course, complex economic factors at stake. As well, it would be wrong, in my judgment, to believe that the New Testament demands that all of us live a life of poverty. But it is noteworthy that at least within the Baptist sector of the Believers' Church Movement, this concern has never been a significant emphasis.

In his article, cited earlier, Carl Lundquist illustrates Christian commitment to a simple life-style and includes the following observation:

> ...nor did I find a spirit of criticism about fellow Christians who chose to live differently. One thoughtful leader said that this way of life was not for everyone and that it required a special call from God. There was recognition that God uses both poverty and wealth and that the ultimate issue is the way we use whatever God gives us.[6]

Generous as this comment may be, we can no longer use this kind of argument as an excuse for a lifestyle that is extravagant and, in effect, indifferent to the needs of the world in which we live. I do not believe that God will continue to bless a group which does not seek to come to terms with this issue.

Related to simple life-style is the concern for community expressed by such books as **The Joyful Community** and **Living Together in a World Falling Apart**.[7] The Mennonite churches have sought to embody a community lifestyle far more effectively than Baptists. What kind of authority do we give to the Christian community? What kind of discipline do we expect it to exercise? What kind of resources do we put at its disposal? I believe that our effectiveness and our appeal to young people will at least in part depend on our response to these questions. They do not arise from one's economic theory, but rather out of one's concern to glorify God in the release of one's time and money for the Lord's work.

The fundamental issue appears to be expressed in the following question: In what sense can we continue to be regarded as a force for radical Protestantism in the kind of world in which we live today?

I find myself uncomfortable, emotionally and politically, when I read and reflect upon attitudes mirrored by magazines such as the Sojourners.[8] In our (Baptist) tradition, the issue of peace and pacifism has not been considered as basic to Christian witness. Nevertheless, the kinds of concerns that are highlighted in the Sojourners are more than legitimate. We must be prepared to find and demonstrate other ways of dealing with the same concerns. We cannot be silent on the social issues of our day.

In what sense, then, can we be regarded as radical? Among most Baptists, neither our life-style, nor our theological beliefs, nor our service to the community can be viewed as radical. We are no longer radical in our views of church membership and in our expectations of members. Church discipline barely exists. We are not radical in our views of the significance of the laity. We are very anti-radical in our appropriation of the work of the Holy Spirit. We are no longer radical in evangelism. Most of us are not radical in social concern.

In what sense, then, can we call ourselves heirs of radical Protestantism and to what extent will the answer to that question mark our future? It is clear to me that unless we begin to go back to the roots from whence we have come our future will be bleak. We must ask ourselves whether in fact, like other traditional denominations, we may have fulfilled the function for which God has raised us up and whether now, He may use other instruments to meet the present needs. It is my belief that when we desert the convictions which gave rise to the Believers' Church Movement God will raise up others to make that witness.

Wheeler Robinson made the point in a slightly different context:

> It is often said today that the older denominational barriers are
> breaking down, and, if not wholly removed, are yet largely
> disregarded. So far as this means the removal of narrowness of
> outlook, and bitterness of judgment, it is surely a sign of Christian
> progress. But so far as it springs from an unconfessed indifference
> to the principles which gave birth to the several denominations, it
> is simply a feature in the decay of genuine religious vitality.... It is
> sometimes suggested that Baptists ought to amalgamate with
> Congregationalists and drop their own distinctive testimony. If that
> were to be brought about, it would simply mean that a new Baptist
> testimony would arise from other lips and lives to replace that
> which had condemned itself.[9]

A further serious issue is our image among Canadian people. We are seen as a group of churches prone to schism and division. Many factors have contributed to the divisiveness within the Believers' Church Movement in the past and need not be reviewed in this context.

The kind of mergers which have been sought by other church groups are not seen by us as desirable. But we have to ask ourselves whether our lack of influence on the national life is, in part, related to our divisiveness. Too often we are schismatic by nature and temperament, rather than due to divergent convictions. If that be the case, we should give far greater external recognition to our internal agreement on the basic principles that characterize the Believers' Church thrust.

In the foreseeable future, we shall face unparalleled opportunities for witness in the political arena of Canadian life. In most cases, only through co-operative efforts among the Believers' Church groups can our voice be heard. We will be listened to as we address ourselves to areas of concern where our witness has been ignored in the past. We shall have an opportunity to influence the whole fabric of Canadian society, and need to pray that He will enable us to do so.

There are theological areas in which we need to redefine our beliefs in order that we might be able to consolidate the gains that we anticipate.

We need to clarify our understanding of Christian initiation and see baptism as a significant part of that process. Too often, we tend to look at ordinances as empty and bare, as a sort of optional extras. This is surely not tolerable in a church which claims to derive its teachings solely from the Bible. It is unlikely that we will be spared some controversies arising out of the attempt to redefine the authority of scriptures. I will leave it to better minds than mine to work out that particular issue.

I continue to believe that the issue of community is one of the biggest concerns in our day. Only rarely in our church life is real community experienced. People come emotionally alone and leave, apart from whatever may be gained from the act of worship itself, without any real experience of community. This is not acceptable and cannot continue if we are to see our work grow. Ways of understanding community and ways of expressing it to the single, to the emotionally deprived, to the dispossessed, as well as to the alienated and disenchanted middle classes are essential.

In several bodies that make up the Canadian Believers' Church Movement, the issue of spiritual gifts has become an explosive issue. Do we not believe in the priesthood of all believers? Do we not agree with the statements in I Corinthians 12 regarding the nature and purpose of spiritual gifts? It is difficult for me to believe, without clearer evidence, that the Spirit of God has withdrawn certain of these gifts because we are uncomfortable at the ways in which some other groups exploit them. We surely believe that all gifts are inspired by the one and same Spirit who apportions to each as He wills. We believe also that to each is given the manifestation of the Spirit for the common good. It will never be enough to denounce the excesses of others if we do not seek a proper biblical understanding and implementation of the gifts in our church life and worship.

I can wholeheartedly endorse the reminder: "There have been times in the history of the Believers' Church when its adherents did not fear breaking with tradition. From the initial stages of the Anabaptist movement there was no hesitancy to cut away the unholy accretions of the ages...Reformation was out of the question. The Anabaptists saw their task as building anew on the original foundation."[10] May God grant to us a like spirit, and as a result, a like freedom to glorify His name.

"A basic question that confronts all churches today is, how can we effectively extend the ministries of the church in today's world? To make the effective contribution God intends for His church some radical changes will no doubt be necessary."[11]

In a society as volatile and creative as ours we must be open to the Spirit. Leadership training, extension, modes of baptism, ideas about initiation, life-style, spiritual gifts, convictions about community, our response to social and political issues, all of these and more will need to be clarified. We are being summoned, not to elevate a tired and jaded denominationalism, but to invigorate a nation that has set for its goal "that He shall have dominion from sea to sea." The wind of the Spirit is blowing. We are made for such a time as this. We must bend our wills to the will of God. The tools are available for the renewal and revival of His church.

In conclusion I want to highlight a few particular concerns where progress ought to be attempted if our future is to be in any sense a function of our deliberate choice.

1. Can we take a fresh look at theological education in Canada as it serves the Believers' Church Movement?

2. Can we do extension work, especially in urban areas, in a co-operative fashion so that it may further the growth of the Believers' Church Movement, and not merely a particular denominational advantage?

3. How can we reconcile differences in the mode of baptism which hinder ready transfer of membership within the Believers' Church Movement?

4. How can we broaden our social concerns without losing our evangelistic zeal?

5. Can we set up some continuing structures which would facilitate continuing conversations and fellowship among our respective groups?

THE BELIEVER'S WORLD

Address at the Banquet by
R. Fred Bullen

We share a concern for the improvement and effectiveness of the church and are now met at considerable effort and expense to study the Believers' Church. The history and theology of the Believers' Church is a major concern. As Kris Kristofferson has said, "There is a great future in my past." By this he meant that his ballads and music were expressions of his total experience; perhaps of his inheritance. There is no doubt that the scholarly appraisal of the road by which we have arrived is a determining factor in where we are going. The subjects also are essential to our judgments of present circumstances, challenges and opportunities. The Christian who accepts the tenets of the Believers' Church has a specific motivation for his life and witness. A Believers' Church has a different approach to its programme of education and evangelism. The projects of such a church have known ends far beyond human means and programs. The problem that faces the Believers' Church and all churches today is that we are not as effective as we ought to be. Except in rare cases, church growth is at a standstill. Statistics—especially in proportion to the population growth—display a weakening of our strength and influence. There is a plethora of books and articles describing what is wrong with the church, extensive analyses of conditions in the world and descriptions of social problems that militate against the church.

Our real problem is related closely to a story told by a foreman who hired an enthusiastic worker to paint the white line down the middle of the highway. The first day he painted carefully and with dogged determination. To the foreman's satisfaction he painted a mile of the white line. The foreman was pleased with his performance, but was less pleased the next day when the man painted only three-quarters of a mile, and less pleased when in succeeding days he painted a half mile, quarter of a mile and then down to one-eighth of a mile. In desperation, the foreman took the man aside and remonstrated with him. The man replied, "I'm working just as hard as I did the first day, but it's taking me longer to go back to the pail of paint."

I am impressed by the intellectual wealth of church historians and theologians. Their books, lectures and discussion make me wish I had studied more, if for no other reason than I would have been saved from being a general secretary-treasurer. But as an administrator and as representative of our denomination in ecumenical discussions for nearly twenty years, I have to ask whether or not we are spending a great time retracing our steps over fields where scholars have a wide divergence of opinion, and whether we fail to see the relevance of our mission to a world that is increasingly indifferent to the message of the church.

The Canadian Council of Churches personnel—in the last eighteen years of my membership on its executive—has had repeated sessions of navel-gazing, as though unified structures, authority to speak for all the churches, and institutional stature would be sufficient to persuade the world to believe. Meanwhile, a merger of the Anglican and United Churches failed. A general trend to conservatism has flickered like a candle in a gigantic cavern, and even now falters under backlash. Even the World Council of Churches revived the use of—but with semantic gymnastics—traditional words such as evangelism. We confound wisdom with words.

Federation Baptists are the only representatives of the Believers' Church Movement in the Canadian Council of Churches. Our voice has exceeded our size. We are accepted courteously much of the time ("We thank the Baptists for helping to keep perspective"). But sometimes there is an expressed impatience ("This is the typical unco-operative Baptist"). Both views are found within our own fellowship. Generally Believers' Churches have shied away from being different from other churches, and consequently we have lost the cutting edge of our sectarian origins.

Often we have claimed to be the link between the covenant theology churches and the sects. By and large our membership often requires a watch-dog attitude. For example, we resist and reject the production of a common baptismal certificate and protest the publication of brochures over the names of all CCC members in which a phrase such as "united by our baptism" occur. On the other hand, we do not want to be smug or self-righteous. Exclusiveness has shown its own cancerous erosion of Christian love. When we cannot "dialogue" with a brother and, as in the New Testament reference, we treat him as a barbarian, we must answer the question, "How does a Christian treat a barbarian?" Also, we have found dedicated and rational believers in churches that are not technically Believers' Churches.

The new wider ecumenical fellowship now in formation will lay the present Canadian Council of Churches to rest. Theoretically, the Canadian Catholic Conference of Bishops and all national churches, may become members. Politically, or expediently, there is a softening of the concept of unity and the hope of being spokesman for all churches. But for Baptists and other Believers' Churches, our priority goals and motivation, our worship and programming raise serious concern as to whether or not we have an obligation to witness to other churches as well as to the world. We cannot escape the challenges of the world. Can the Believers' Church avoid the discipline of dialogue from our minority position? Will we exercise Christian love in diversity, and do we have Pauline skill to prevent compromise?

In the light of this, we might be discouraged and ask ourselves whether it is worth the effort. In our dismay, we might be like the man who applied to his superintendent for sick leave. In his letter he wrote: "Dear Sir: You sent me to a house and I examined the chimney which was damaged by a hurricane and estimated the number of bricks that would be needed to repair it. I set up a pulley, returned to the ground and began to fill the bucket with the number of bricks needed for the job. I then hoisted the barrel and on its way I realized that it was heavier than I expected. As it got to the top, the bucket of bricks was heavier than I, and I could not control it, and holding tightly to the rope I began to be pulled up. As I went up, I met the barrel coming down at the halfway point; it bruised me badly but I continued to the top, where my fingers jammed in the pulley. The barrel continued to the bottom where it hit other bricks, and burst. The bricks spilled out of the barrel. I was now heavier than the barrel and I proceeded down. Halfway down I met the barrel coming up. It bruised me again, very badly. I then fell on the bricks that had been spilled, and broke a leg. The pain caused me to let go of the rope and the barrel which was now at the top came down with a crash on top of me, causing further damage. I therefore apply for sick leave."

There are many occasions in the life of the Christian when he would gladly apply for a sick leave. However, the work of the Christian, whether as a professional or a layman, is a calling. Our Lord did not promise an easy life; indeed, he warned his followers that the demands upon themselves in terms of energy, sacrifice and even worldly goods would be far beyond their expectation. As a matter of fact, the Christian worker cannot even expect appreciation, thanks or recognition.

Nevertheless, if there is to be a Believers' Church, it ought not to major upon any adjective preceding the noun **church**, not even the term **believers**. Jesus said, "I will build my church and the gates of hell shall not prevail against it." Our role is to accept his invitation to be part of his enterprise of saving the world, and the very best that we can do is to participate to the utmost of our capacity. As James Denny is reported to have observed, "The Kingdom of God is not for the well meaning but for the desperate." Today is intimidating. Tomorrow threatens to be overwhelming. Whatever the church's tactics, its strategy must be fixed with confidence in the living Word and a disciplined willingness to let Christ confront persons through us. Every member in any congregation anywhere is free to do that. The results are in the hands of God. He requires only that his stewards be found faithful. But Christian faith—critical, flexible, daring—exists only in the world. And as Paul said to the Ephesians, "The world is waiting for the evidence of this to be manifest through the church."

We are not insignificant persons doing insignificant work. We are sons of God called to do His work. Humbly we claim Jesus as Lord. In faith we wait upon the Holy Spirit for the dynamic.

Newspapers cover the full gamut of the daily experiences of our society, indicating the variety of human needs, social malaise, and impossible questions that face modern man and create insoluble problems. Even so called new improvements of man's progressive development carry him farther from the original paint pot, as the job took the highway painter. New developments in the field of armaments and the implications of their manufacture, sale and stockpiling create apprehensions for our children and our children's children. Mass communications, three dimensional holography, urbanization, technological impositions, predictive medicine, education, travel, biology and other sciences, etc. impose innumerable adjustments upon mankind. Never before has the citadel of man's mind required such a ministry of stability. Man needs a power outside himself to set personal goals and to see the world as something we anticipate, plan for and control in the manner which we believe is God's will. Interests, skills, projects, man-nature relationships, freedom concepts, value and moral judgments, etc. tax man's limits. Even the instant face-to-face encounter with universe-wide problems, by means of television, stagger our conceptual powers and affect our capacity to reason cogently, because we are more conditioned to deal with situations within the direct reach of natural senses. Wheels and wings extend our legs. Machines extend our arms and hands. Electronics extend our voices, ears and sight. We are a cosmological people. Wheels within wheels! But with Ezekiel we know that the Spirit must motivate the wheels. Thus the church alone can minister to the minds and hearts of a generation in motion. The world is engaged in a history. It is therefore a world of possibilities. We live in a day when there is a superabundance of demands for recognition of permissive human rights. There is little acceptance of the dignity and necessity of divine rights for the good of mankind. The challenge to the Believers' Church is that it must minister to this world. We can serve the future with a promise of truth, righteousness and peace. This is another age of **diaspora**, a sowing of hope of self-surrender, a sacrifice. It is an age which stands within the horizons of the new future. It is God's age. Therefore it is the church's age. The battle for man's mind, soul and body is joined. The church is involved. Living successfully within this kind of society requires a magnitude and scope of inner resources of faith, confidence and hope we have not yet fully demonstrated. The hope of the future lies not only on secular grounds, though they will be part of it; the hope of the future lies in man's confidence in the ultimate outcome. If the world is to know that God is involved in its total life, it must see the evidence of it in the involvement of God in the lives of believers. Believers must rethink their commitment and understanding of the mission to which Christ has called us.

The church can present the quality of man's existence, his meaning for himself, the world and God; the quality which is not moulded by his environment but which conquers his environment and himself in the all-embracing love of the Father. It is in the confidence of undertaking a holy task, divinely committed, divinely shared, that the church continues its own existence and regirds itself for each engagement. Ezekiel's commission is contemporary: "Son of Man, stand on your feet...whether they hear or forbear, yet will they know that a prophet is among them." This is the high and holy calling of the Believers' Church and indeed of any institution which dares to call itself the church.

The Believers' Church, therefore, must choose to be renewed. This is not a call to a repetition of the past, but to be contemporary in the understanding of the Word of God, as it has relevance and bearing upon today's society.

In the Art Gallery in Ottawa there is a beautiful picture by Holman Hunt. The painting is of a man whose face indicates that he has come to life-changing decision. In one hand he holds the Bible, and in the other a newspaper. The picture could have been painted in any age in the long history and theological labyrinth of the Believers' Church. I examined the painting for a long time because, with a very limited art appreciation, I expected that either the Bible or the newspaper would be the points of focus for the artist. But I failed to find the focus in either of those publications. The most important point in Holman Hunt's painting is the man's eyes. They burn with a fire and an excitement of discovery. They reveal the churning of an expectant soul, and that so often is the factor that is missing in the Christian church today. The world with all of its problems and anxieties is waiting for the sons of God to reveal themselves as the people of God.

Before the onslaught of paralyzing analyses, surveys, stockpiling of secular criticisms, the devastating statistics of declining institutions, the rejection of the traditional ministry by seminarians and some frustrated pastors, and the general indifference of the world at large, the church has two choices: to wither and die, or to put on the whole armour of God and fight the wiles of the devil, principalities and powers with the dynamic of God.

The admonition is, "Brethren make your election and calling sure." The insecure, the unready, the undisciplined, the unwilling, the fearful, the self-confident and self-satisfying have no place in this ministry. Joshua weeded them out by the brook. Jesus weeded them out of his followers. By some miracle, the critics within and without are weeding in the church today. Those who identify with Christ's call hear the promise "Fear not, little flock, it is the Father's good pleasure to give you the Kingdom." Those who view the task with justifiable misgiving hear, "Satan has desired to have you that he may sift you as wheat, but I have prayed for you that your faith fail not. When you are converted, strengthen your brethren." It has been gloriously declared that in the fulness of time, God sent forth His Son who was clothed in human flesh. The fourth Gospel says the Word was made flesh and dwelt among us. It is essential that today the Word be incarnate again in human flesh. As the Lord was involved with the world, so must His church be. The New Testament defines the church as the Body of Christ, the people of God, a new Israel, a temple to be inhabited by the Holy Spirit. Perhaps the first, the Body of Christ, is the most fruitful New Testament model for our times. The incarnation meant the redemptive involvement of the living God with this world. In this redemptive divine involvement, the church is intimately concerned and serves as a central instrument in the continuing acts of Christ in the world.

In its mission, the church must be the maker of opinions. Oliver Cromwell described the results of irrelevance when he said, "A man never goes so far when he does not know whither he is going". This can also be said of the church. The objective must be clear and often restated. No doubt new vocabulary, new methods and techniques will replace traditional ways of persuasion. Some activities of the church may not exercise pressure, but the task of communicating the reconciling love of God in Christ, within the milieu of human history, envisions the molding of opinions. Personal values are at the centre of its life. Individual man is of such value that the Son of God died for him. In a society where the impersonal is taking over, the church is the one institution which, because of its spiritual grounding, can witness to and perceive the work of human personality. In addition, the church has a responsibility for challenging the changing structures of society which inhibit full personal development. While modern man gives lip service to "a new life-style," the church **alone** is the proclaimer of new life and the dynamic of style. Here two functions are essential: (1) to encourage members to undertake careers in public, governmental and social services in which the Christian opinion will be expressed, and (2) to witness to and to act the Christian ethic through individuals and groups in all of society. We believe that Christian opinion is both desirable and necessary in such a world as ours. The task of developing it in the church and out in the world is evangelism and Christian nurture at its ultimate.

One report not long ago stated: "There are more than fifty million people in America today who are not effectively related to any religious body. They constitute a vast mission field right under the noses of American churches, and any Christian who takes his faith seriously must be concerned about proclaiming the gospel to them." If this period of history is correctly called the post-Christian era, it is the church which must bear the stigma.

There is a variety of methods by which the Christian church can both develop and create Christian opinions. Our centres of training are one of the most significant factors in the vitality of our ministries. I find it difficult to accept completely the idealistic hope that pastors and leaders can give Believers' Church congregations the optimum stimuli for participation in Christ's mission out of university and college classes that cover the religious waterfront with the naive hope that all students are astute and objective, and given intellectual freedom and honesty they will automatically sift wheat and tares and become evangelical scholars, pastors and biblical opinion makers. The professors of the Believers' Church must accept a role of opinion makers and persuaders, without fear of criticism by their peers in other colleges. To give information without persuasion will feed the mind without touching the heart and will. It will create introversion and take extraversion for granted, leaving them to intuition and to chance. Attitudes, moods, disposition, dedication and motivation are caught, not taught. Called men come from called churches; they also come from called schools and teachers.

There is a strong need for our seminaries to give leadership in the art of proclamation. For a quarter of a century, there has been very little emphasis upon a homiletics which takes into consideration the modern techniques of persuasion and communication. In a world that buys its breakfast cereal, its daily bread and all of its junk foods as a result of persuasive communication, the Believers' Church has to take its rightful place as announcers of the good news. We may criticize some religious manipulators, but the criticisms of the pulpit cannot be ignored when they describe many sermons as "long, rambling, dry, uninteresting and remote from the current realities of life." Many years ago, Pierre Berton's book was devastating in its comments on sermonizing, but one wonders how the pew cannot but be comfortable when "many sermons of today tend to be spiritless, irrelevant, dull and badly delivered." Why is it that having announced a text, as though that were the most important beginning for a sermon, many preachers find little biblical background for the development of positive, creative, and life-giving opinions for the needs of today's society? We must avoid the criticism of the farmer of his clergyman, reported 100 years ago in **The Canadian Baptist**, "He's a fine man but he rakes with the teeth up."

Our failure to be positive persuaders can be found in caricature texts. For the Ground of all being so empathized with the totality of men and things that it donated unique progeny, so that anyone (without discrimination as to race, religion, or national ancestry) who takes a leap in the dark towards Him should not endure the consequence of existential estrangement but experience vitality in perpetuity.

> Except ye repent, as it were, and be converted, after a manner of speaking, ye shall all likewise be damned, more or less.

Other churches may or can rely on liturgies. The Believers' Church—with the authority of God's Word—must revive the power of personal, positive, persuasive, opinion-creating proclamation.

Beyond proclamation, there is a growth of action groups in our churches seeking new forms or structures in the present age. Such groups often consider themselves to be radical. One should bear in mind that the term radical really means "from the root of." In other words, when Christians consider these innovating expressions of the church ministry as outlets of their urge to "do their own thing," to be creative, to break out of the stifling moulds, to emerge from traditions, they must remember the pit from which they have been dug. If God is calling them to new patterns of ministry, it is still ministry to the lost: those who have lost or never found life in this world, and certainly not in the next. If their concern for people is more than that for institutions, it is people who have personality, minds, patterns which require careful nurture to develop Christian opinion. If we are to have the mind of Christ, it is to be identified with His ministry, which was to mould opinion. The church is composed of heralds of God. We are opinion makers whatever nomenclature of evangelism, social involvement and functions may be adopted.

The church's obligations starts where it is, with the people it has. It must be patiently impatient in creating and building motivation and mission concepts. Some people will not be easily moved. The church must be able to dream of its own shape, size, destiny and style of life. Proclamation and action must have personal and social redemption as clear primary and secondary goals; neither of which can be ignored.

One church asked four questions: (1) What kind of layman are we trying to deploy in the world? (2) What kind of church deploys that kind of layman? (3) What kind of official board makes possible that kind of church? (4) What kind of clergy makes possible that kind of official board? These are serious questions which those who are associated with the Believers' Church must consider. There is significance in the fact that the task is unending, incomplete, sometimes leaving the labourer with a feeling of incompetence, and yet still striving. Paul wrote, "I count not myself to have apprehended." That is challenge with promise: "Lo, I am with you!"

To the world which demands bread, we cannot give a stone. To the world that asks for a fish, we cannot give a scorpion. To the world that asks for one mile of compassion, understanding and ministering fellowship, we must give a reconciling two miles. To the world that asks a covering shirt, we give also a cloak of comfort. To a brother who longs for neighbourliness, we must give Christian love.

To Christ who demands life, we give ours to be replaced by His. To God who demands the strange twins of righteousness and a humble walk, we give our time, talent and possessions for His consecration. To the Holy Spirit who convinces us of sin, we give confession and receive the seal of adoption and calling. To the Church of Christ, we offer body, mind and spirit, reconciled by the triune God beyond our deserving, to be regenerated, redirected and blessed in His service. And even then we have done only that which we ought to do, and are altogether unprofitable servants. We choose to be personally bound to Christ, instead of religiously tied to an organization. We choose to be used of Christ in order that the institution may be His instrument.

> Is this the time, O Church of Christ, to sound retreat?
> To arm with weapons cheap and blunt
> The men and women who have borne the brunt
> Of earth's fierce strife, and nobly held their ground?
> Is this the time to halt, when all around
> Horizons lift, new destinies confront
> Stern duties wait the nations, never wont
> To play the laggard, when God's will was found?
>
> No! Rather strengthen stakes and lengthen cords!
> Enlarge thy plans and gifts O thou elect,
> And, to thy Kingdom come for such a time!
> The earth with all its fullness is the Lord's.
> Great things attempt for him, great things expect,
> Whose LOVE imperial is, whose POWER sublime
> Fills all the earth, if we, who follow Him—
> Build in this world, HIS CHURCH, unconquerable!

The key to all this is beyond **diakonia**, service, and deeper than **koinonia**, fellowship: it is **persona**, individual! Whatever other factors we find in excavating historical facts or examining theology we come again and again to the voluntary principle and personal choice which is our recurring example in the lives of all biblical characters. This must be the thrust of our discovery of the who, what, how and why of the Believers' Church.

Therefore, share with me a personal pilgrimage. In the city of Boston I visited the great church of the persuasive and eloquent Phillips Brooks. In the garden there is a statue of Brooks, with open Bible, proclaiming the eternal invitation. The artist caught his secret. Immediately behind Brooks he sculpted the Christ with his hand on the preacher's shoulder. For me the goals of ministry were clarified. But what of the means? Inside, at the front of the church, the Communion Table is surrounded by a beautiful carved rail. Kneeling there, I read the inscription: "For their sakes I sanctify myself."

The Believers' Church—any church—to be relevant in any age and effective in the world, must share the Master's firm resolve: For their sake I consecrate myself, that they also may be consecrated in truth."

II

The Believers' Church
In The Congregational Context

Seminar Papers and Responses

BIBLICAL AUTHORITY, PAST AND PRESENT IN THE BELIEVERS' CHURCH TRADITION

Clark H. Pinnock

INTRODUCTION

Although we cannot speak of a normative dogmatic or ecclesiastical tradition for the Believers' Churches as we might in reference to the conservative Reformation, on the matter of standing beneath the authority of scripture we can confidently identify an almost universal determination to affirm and to apply the teachings of the Bible on the part of our early forebears, and to do so more radically and in reference to more topics than was the custom in the contemporary Christian traditions. In this paper I want to call attention to the high view of scripture the original Baptists and Anabaptists espoused, and deplore the state of some uncertainty about its absolute authority which is so widespread today. As many contemporary spokesmen have noted, there is a widespread confusion regarding the nature of the Bible, the older position having been dropped without a new one being found to replace it. Recovering the high doctrine of scripture I regard as a top priority item for Believers' Churches.[1]

Because we are all aware these days how social and contextual even our theological convictions are, I should begin by a short testimony arising out of my life experience. My own entre into Christian faith took place within the matrix of evangelical religion in which one's attitude to scripture was taken to be a matter of central importance. I came to feel, almost with my first spiritual milk, the crucial nature of this conviction, and the threat posed to it by what is imprecisely called the 'liberal' experiment. It seemed to me that there was an undefined group of Christians quite concerned about the humanity of the Bible (in some ways I could not identify with), but very uncertain about its infallible divine authority. This confused and alarmed me then, and I would have to confess, it still does. Because of the large importance I attached to a strong stand on biblical authority I tended to trust, say, a Presbyterian who shared my conviction above a Baptist who did not, and developed a kind of ecumenism in which the significant lines of agreement and disagreement fell, not vertically **between** Presbyterian and Baptist denominations, but horizontally **across** them both.

Since the earliest days of my Christian experience, however, I have also been developing my understanding of biblical authority, a process which is still continuing. Although my conviction has not altered as to the Bible being our divine teacher, I have learned to balance this belief with a fairer recognition of the human aspect of the Bible as well. It was sometimes a painful process because the conservative doctrine I first learned ultimately from Warfield made it difficult, though not impossible, to recognize what one might call the human 'weakness' of scripture which is also an integral aspect of the form of divine revelation. Perhaps my studying under evangelical scholar F.F. Bruce will help to indicate the struggle that went on in my mind over the bipolar nature of the Bible, and not in my mind only, but I suspect in the experience of a large number of others. In recent years I have been listening to much of the exciting fresh research into the meaning of biblical authority, from Barr, Stuhlmacher, Childs, Dunn, and Kelsey, and although I cannot yet say to what extent I have been influenced by them, I am certain that their influence has been considerable.

It is important to explain one's theological development and present stance because, as Gadamer has been telling us, no critic or interpreter of scripture is completely detached and unbiased. It is important for my hearers (readers) to know where I am coming from, because it will help them to understand why I take the stance that I do. My view is, and I am open to correction, that on the matter of biblical authority all is not well in the Believers' Church traditions, nor for that matter in the church as a whole. I maintain that we are not following our forefathers as faithfully as we should at this point, but are in fact somewhat distanced from them in it. Whereas they maintained an unwavering conviction about the final cognitive authority of biblical teachings over them it is rather rare to find modern exponents of these traditions expressing themselves so forthrightly on the character of the Bible as the Word of God written.[2] I for one grieve over the decline of an unshakable confidence in scriptural truth, and seize this opportunity to call us back to it. If things prove, through our discussion, to be healthier than I fear, I shall be the first to rejoice, and if I can be corrected in my present stance by those present, I shall be grateful and not disappointed.

1. Biblical Authority in the Early Phases of the Believers' Church Traditions

In my reading of the evidence, the resemblances between the Radical Reformation, the early Baptists, and the conservative Reformers are much more significant than the differences that can be identified. As Yoder put it, "None of the early Anabaptists intended to do anything more than apply faithfully the fundamental **sola scriptura** of the Reformation."[3] This is not to minimize the importance of applying scripture to ethics and ecclesiology as the Anabaptists uniquely did, nor their orientation to the Bible as a practical guide rather than a doctrinal textbook, nor their insistence on the competency of the congregation to interpret the text for itself — all these are real gains, and deserving of our appreciation.[4] Nevertheless, the basic confidence the early evangelical Anabaptists had in the divine authority of the Bible was a conviction they shared with Calvin and Luther. Henry Poettcker cites the words of Menno Simons which illustrate my point:

> I pray and admonish all my beloved brethren...not to allow and
> consent to glosses, innovations, nor human explanations...I confess
> that I would rather die than to believe and teach my brethren a single

word or letter concerning the Father, the Son, and the Holy Ghost (before God I lie not) contrary to the plain testimony of the Word of God which so clearly points out and teaches through the prophets, evangelists, and apostles.[5]

For the majority of Anabaptists as for our Lord Jesus, scripture is divine, tradition human, scripture obligatory, tradition optional, scripture supreme, tradition subordinate.[6]

The situation is with the Baptists, and particularly the Calvinistic Baptists, if possible, even clearer since their English Puritan roots align them more closely to the Reformed tradition in which doctrinal precision and confessional statements are more prominent than in Anabaptism. From several of these historic documents we gain a clear impression where the Baptists stood on the matter of biblical authority.

In the Second London Confession of 1677 and 1688, for example, we find an eloquent paragraph modelled on the Westminster Confession:

The Holy Scripture is the only sufficient, certain, and infallible rule of all saving knowledge, faith and obedience...The supreme judge by which all controversies of religion are to be determined, and all decrees of councils, opinions of ancient writers, doctrines of men, and private spirits, are to be examined, and in whose sentence we are to rest, can be no other but the Holy Scripture delivered by the Spirit, into which Scripture so delivered, our faith is finally resolved. (ch. 1)[7]

More familiar to Baptists in North America are the words of the New Hampshire Confession of 1833 which read:

We believe that the Holy Bible was written by men divinely inspired and is a perfect treasure of heavenly instruction; that it has God for its author, salvation for its end, and, truth without any mixture of error, for its matter; that it reveals the principles by which God will judge us; and will remain to the end of the world, the true centre of Christian union, and the supreme standard by which all human conduct, creeds, and religious opinions should be tried. (art. 1)[8]

And from the Continent of Europe we hear the confession of the Evangelical Association of French-speaking Baptist churches in 1879:

We believe that the canonical writings of the Old and the New Testaments are the Word of God and constitute the only and infallible rule of faith and Christian life and the only touchstone by which every doctrine, every tradition and every religious and ecclesiastical system as well as every method of Christian action are to be tested. We believe that the Holy Scripture is a providential document and that the Holy Spirit presided in a sovereign manner at its origin and at the formation of the biblical story. We believe that He has Himself assured therein the perfect teaching and the entire historic truth, despite the imperfection of the human instruments who, by His divine inspiration and under His control, have contributed toward communicating to us the divine oracles. We believe that the Holy Scriptures reveal to us all that we must know in the spiritual realm. We believe that they need not to be modified or completed by any other revelation in the course of the present dispensation. (art. 2)[9]

Individual Baptist thinkers of the past, too, like John Smyth, John Gill, and Andrew Fuller all agree that the Bible is God's written Word, the supreme authority for life and thought.[10]

It seems plain to me that there is a historic high view of scripture and that the early leaders in our Believers' Church traditions held to it without hesitation. They did so basically because it is the doctrine the Bible teaches about itself. In saying this, I do not wish to deny that subsequent research into the hermeneutics of the New Testament writers introduces some subtleties into our perspectives into scripture, but only to insist that in receiving the Bible as the God-breathed Word they were following the lead already clearly established in the primary documents themselves. That is not to say, however, that later concerns, most notably the anxiety about the perfect errorlessness of the original autographs of scripture, were of concern either to the biblical authors or the early Baptists and Anabaptists who sought to follow them.

2. The Crisis of the Scripture Principle in Believers' Church Traditions.

Having briefly sampled the encouraging record of faithful adherence to biblical authority on the part of our spiritual forebears, the mood changes as we begin to characterize the sad and melancholy history of a great defection. It is not that biblical and historical criticism in themselves are threatening, as if making use of scholarly tools and striving assiduously to arrive at the historically precise sense of the text were intrinsically a bad thing. The problem arises out of the fact that post-enlightenment criticism has taken to itself some novel features which are threatening indeed. The historical critical method in this modern sense, while claiming neutrality and detachment, approached the biblical text in a manner destined to destroy it. Because of an assumption about the uniformity of reality and the omnipotence of analogy, this method proposes to tell us what could and what could not have happened in the historical past, and where it has been consistently practised it has practically destroyed the text as text. I do not think it is possible to exaggerate the effect on the older conviction and upon the whole enterprise of theology itself of the new negative critical view of the Bible spawned in the nineteenth century.[11] In order to grasp what happened in its briefest essence let us hear from Father Burtchaell:

Christians early inherited from the Jews the belief that the biblical writers were somehow possessed by God, who was thus to be reckoned the Bible's proper author. Since God could not conceivably be the agent of falsehood, the Bible must be guaranteed free from any error. For centuries this doctrine lay dormant, as doctrines will; accepted by all, pondered by few. Not until the 16th century did inspiration and its corollary, inerrancy, come up for sustained review. The Reformers and Counter-Reformers were disputing whether all revealed truth was in Scripture alone, and whether it could dependably be by private or official scrutiny. Despite a radical disagreement on these issues, both groups persevered in receiving the Bible as a compendium of inerrant oracles dictated by the Spirit. Only in the 19th century did a succession of empirical disciplines newly come of age begin to put a series of inconvenient queries to exegetes. First, geology and paleontology discredited the view of the cosmos and the cosmogony of

Genesis. Next, archaeology suggested that there were serious historical discrepancies in the sacred narrative. Later, as parallel oriental literatures began to be recovered, much of Scripture lay under accusation of plagiarism from pagan sources. Literary criticism of the text itself disclosed that the writers had freely tampered with their materials, and often escalated myth and legend into historical event. After all this, considerable dexterity was required of any theologian who was willing to take account of the accumulation of challenging evidence, yet continued to defend the Bible as the classic and inerrant Word of God.[12]

Putting aside the fact that Burtchaell may be grossly exaggerating the actual force of the new criticism, he has certainly not exaggerated the importance of the shift which took place away from the historic conviction about scripture. Pannenberg is not exaggerating either when he writes: "The dissolution of the traditional doctrine of Scripture constitutes a crisis at the very foundation of modern Protestant theology."[13] In that same essay he expresses his own scepticism about the history recorded in the gospels, and casts doubt on the unity of biblical thought. In his book on the Apostles' Creed he rejects the miraculous conception of Jesus, and in his book on Christology alludes to legendary elements in the resurrection narratives. On every hand, even in theologians like Pannenberg who are not radically unorthodox, we encounter a willingness to stand in judgment over scripture which is nonexistent and inconceivable in the founders of our traditions. Without doubt a new theology, together with a new view of the Bible, has been born,[14] and there are not many signs of improvement in the situation across the churches.[15]

But the question that concerns us most in this paper is not the defection of Christians at large from the historic high view of inspiration, sad though that it is, but rather the extent to which the Believers' Church movement has been involved in and been affected by this shift in conviction. Although we do not have access to a historical study comparable to Lefferts A. Loetscher's **The Broadening Church,** which traces the change in the northern Presbyterian denomination in the USA from 1869, we are fortunate to have a substantial article by Norman H. Maring and a supplementary article by James L. Garrett. For Anabaptists we have even less, and more study needs to be done.[16] In attempting to evaluate the extent of these changes in Believers' Church traditions, and to determine the exact state of affairs that actually exists now or in the recent past, I am conscious of severe limitations, in not feeling very surefooted in this area of historical theology, and on account of the difficulty obtaining documentation to warrant bold conclusions. Therefore, I am compelled to write in a tentative vein.

The modernist impulse affected Baptists in the northern United States and Canada very considerably, and the extent of the defection from belief in inspired scripture was great.[17] Already in the 1860s Thomas F. Curtiss, who taught theology at a Baptist college in Lewisburg, Pennsylvania, felt compelled because of the negative criticism filtering in from the Continent to jettison belief in the infallibility of the Bible, and began to emphasize instead the experiential authority of the fallible Bible. This view was brought to very consistent expression by William N. Clarke who "surrendered all conceptions of a unique biblical authority."[18] Clarke wrote:

> The Bible itself releases us from all obligation to maintain its complete inerrancy, in the sense of freedom from all inaccuracy and incorrect-ness of statement, and shows us a higher quality, in which is manifest a higher purpose than that of inerrancy.

> Christ was saving sinners before the New Testament was written, and could do the same today if it had not been written.

> When Christ was departing, he trusted his gospel in the world to the keeping of the Holy Spirit, who was to abide with men. He never promised an infallible church, or an infallible book, or any infallible visible guide, but committed his kingdom to the Spirit and the divine life.

What was needed, Clarke believed, was not truth expressing itself in language, but in life: "truth rich, free, spiritual, plentiful, alive, self-imparting." The authority of Christ had clearly shifted from the text of scripture to the present activity of the Spirit in Christian hearts.[19]

Further to the south there was the case of Crawford H. Toy, professor of Old Testament at Southern Baptist Seminary in Louisville, who felt compelled to resign in 1879 because he could not honestly suppress the doubts he felt, and who subsequently became much more radical in his theology. Meantime, over at the University of Chicago a group of Baptist academics led by Shailer Matthews espoused very radical views of scripture. Although a great deal of biblical study went on there, the Bible was less and less regarded as a source of normative divine truth, being supplanted by the newer insights discovered in sociology and psychology.

Obviously all Baptists did not follow these innovations. In the north there were articulate spokesmen like A.H. Strong and Alvah Hovey who resisted them, and new seminaries like Northern Baptist (1915) and Eastern Baptist (1952) and later the California Baptist Seminary at Covina were opened, all of this indicating a strong ongoing conservative theological tradition. In Canada one would have to mention the conflict between T.T. Shields and McMaster University, and the subsequent rise of two conservative Baptist groups with their own seminaries, as well as an ongoing conservative tradition in the original Baptist groups, especially in the west and the east, but also in the Baptist Convention of Ontario and Quebec. Apart from exceptions represented in certain Southern Baptist seminaries and colleges over the years, the large majority of that denomination has followed the lead of conservative luminaries like A.Y. Mullins and A.T. Robertson and remained within the bounds of conservative Christianity, almost unaffected by the newer trends.

On the Anabaptist side of the equation, the picture at first sight looks quite different. In Baptist circles the new approach to scripture made deep inroads, as we have seen, into the theological and pastoral leadership of the northern denomination at least, provoking after a few decades a vigourous debate and eventual schism as the fundamentalist forces reacted violently against the new theology. But among Mennonites, as Kraus argues, the fundamentalist reaction to modernism gained control of the group both in the leadership and among the people so that modernism hardly gained a foothold at all.[20] A small but influential group of Mennonite leaders such as Daniel Kauffmann, in fact, allied themselves with the fundamentalist cause and guided the denomination in that direction for a generation early in the twentieth century. For the doctrine of scripture this meant assenting to the concept of verbal inspiration as it had been expounded by Warfield and the Princeton theology, and insisting on a high degree of precision in doctrinal language not previously required in the earlier Anabaptist movement. A good example might be Chester K. Lehman who took his theology at the 'Old' Princeton, served Eastern Mennonite College and Seminary in Harrisonburg from 1924-1971, and whose two-volume work **Biblical Theology** is surely a scholarly expression of Mennonite biblicism. Another example would be J.C. Wenger. A turning point was reached, according to Kraus, with Harold Bender's pamphlet **Biblical Inspiration and Revelation** (1959), in the wake of which has been emerging a conservative but non-fundamentalist approach to scripture. If this analysis is correct, it means that Mennonites were largely spared the wrenching experience the Baptists went through as liberals and fundamentalists reacted so bitterly to one another.

The question which I have in regard to Mennonites and which I find difficult to answer is, to what extent the modernism once denied access has made a belated appearance in the atmosphere of openness now existing. It would certainly help if we knew more about the attitude taken toward the Bible and its authority by the faculties at the Mennonite seminaries and colleges in the US and Canada. Such information I suspect would have to be gained through personal relationships I have not made because, to my knowledge, these scholars have not often placed their views in print. In desperation I have resorted to the work of Mennonite theologian Gordon Kaufman who may be atypical in his views but who at least shows the new critical view of scripture is represented in these circles. In his work, the authority for theology is not the text of scripture itself, but the revelatory event attested in the text, and arrived at by means of historical reconstruction. Consider two quotations:

> The historical faith characteristic of the Bible can become ours only as we revise thoroughly and rewrite the biblical account of the course of human and Hebrew history in accord with our modern understanding of its actual movement.

> Just as the historian often finds it necessary to correct both his primary and secondary sources, as well as his own prejudgments, in the light of the reconstruction he finally produces, so the theologian

frequently needs to reinterpret and amend the portrayal of Jesus
Christ which he finds in Scripture and tradition, or in his own
preconceptions, in terms of the understanding of God's act which is
forthcoming in his work.[21]

The result of working along these lines is predictable but need not be
surmised. After acknowledging that the Bible as a whole and Jesus in
particular speak often about the threat of divine wrath upon disobedient
sinners, Kaufman dispenses with it in his theology because it would not
fit into the pattern of truth he is developing (p. 154, n.11). As for the
incarnation, although admitting that the New Testament writers think
in terms of Christ's eternal deity, Kaufman takes that to be
mythological language, and settles for a merely human Jesus who
reveals God decisively for us (p. 189). Reflecting on the appearances of
the risen Lord to his disciples, he concludes we should understand them
as 'hallucinations' (p. 424). I hope that unbiblical theology of this kind is
rare in the contemporary Mennonite movement, and I look to others for
a more informed reading of the situation. Meantime it can stand as
evidence that what happened to the Baptists can happen to the
Mennonites, too.

3. Maintaining the Scripture Principle in the Believers' Church Traditions

Although I am not unsympathetic with the agonies of soul which
accompany the shift from the older to the newer view of scripture, and
not unaware of some of the objective factors which called for a re-
examination of the historic position, I think we would be foolhardy to
refuse to recognize the extreme dangers implicit in the new approach.
William N. Clarke seemed to sense this danger when he wrote:

> I tell no secret—though perhaps many a man wished he could keep
> it a secret—when I say that to the average minister today the Bible
> that lies on his pulpit is more or less an unsolved problem. He is
> loyal to it, and not for his right hand would he degrade it or do it
> wrong. He longs to speak with authority on the basis of its
> teaching, and feels that he ought to be able to do so. He knows that
> the people need its message in full power and clearness, and cannot
> bear to think that it is losing power with them. Yet he is not
> entirely free to use it. Criticism has altered the book for his use,
> but just how far he does not know.[22]

On a darker note still, A.H. Strong warned Baptists in 1918 of the severe
potential and real dangers in the new radical biblical criticism. He
wrote:

> What is the effect of this method upon our theological seminaries?
> It is to deprive the gospel message of all definiteness, and to make
> professors and students disseminators of doubts. The result of such
> teaching in our seminaries is that the student, unless he has had a
> Pauline experience before he came has all his early conceptions of
> scripture and Christian doctrine weakened, has no longer any
> positive message to deliver, loses the ardour of his love for Christ;
> and at his graduation leaves the seminary, not to become preacher
> or pastor as he had once hoped, but to sow his doubts broadcast, as

a teacher in some college, as editor of some religious journal, as secretary of some Young Men's Christian Association, or an agent of some mutual life insurance company. This method of interpretation switches off upon some sidetrack of social service many a young man who otherwise would be a heroic preacher of the everlasting gospel. The theological seminaries of almost all our denominations are becoming so infected with this grievous error, that they are not so much organs of Christ as they are organs of Antichrist. This accounts for the rise, all over the land, of Bible schools, to take the place of seminaries. We are losing our faith in the Bible, and our determination to stand for its teachings. We are introducing into our ministry men who have lost their faith in (Christ) and their love for him. The unbelief in our seminary teaching is like a blinding mist slowly settling down upon our churches, and is gradually abolishing, not only all definite views of Christian doctrine, but also all conviction of duty to "contend earnestly for the faith" of our fathers. We are ceasing to be evangelistic as well as evangelical, and if this downward progress continues, we shall in due time cease to exist. We Baptists must reform or die.[23]

These are emotional words, and perhaps the final reflections of a somewhat discouraged older man. But they are not to be swept aside lightly. At the Reformation we contended for the unique authority of the Bible, and opposed any raising up of an independent source of revelation to rival it. But now, ironically, at the very time when the Roman Catholic Church seems to be moving closer to acknowledging the supreme authority of scripture, we Protestants seem to be drifting away from it. If we cannot be sure of the revelational data of the Bible, we have lost the basis of normative theology and the possibility of clear, bold preaching. The alternative to a trustworthy Bible is human subjectivity, however we may define it, and that is not the foundation on which our traditions were established.

What doctrine, what conviction can survive the loss of confidence in the cognitive authority of the didactic thought models of scripture? At this very time there is widespread scepticism, for example, about every aspect of traditional Christology: the unique deity, the miraculous conception, the atoning death, the bodily resurrection, and the glorious **parousia** of Jesus. We are living in the midst of a revolution in the history of Christian theology. Salvation is being defined in this-worldly terms, eschatology reduced to the vague symbol of a political utopia brought about by human effort, and universal redemption is almost an axiom. There is no point in continuing this dreary list except to insist that none of it would be possible if we shared the view of scripture our forefathers held.

We are living in a time when rebellion against authority is regarded as the mark of maturity, whereas in actual fact its rejection is a mark of adolescence. As Dulles writes:

In practically all the affairs of daily living, mature persons rely upon authority in the sense that they depend upon the advice of experienced and knowledgeable persons—those whom they have reason to regard as experts in the particular field. If we do this in law, in medicine, in history, and art criticism, why not in religion?[24]

The Believers' Church traditions have always rested on the belief in a definite revelation given in the past and authoritatively attested in the scripture. Its special status occupies a central place in our religion; so much, so that it is surprising its position is being threatened. Why would those for whom the Bible, and not some creed, is the final authority succumb to a low view of it? Perhaps there are some simple explanations. A slight twist can easily convert the principle of "soul competency," which originally applied to the believer's right to search scripture for himself, into a humanistic principle of human competency **apart** from scripture. Or again, the accent on the importance of a personal encounter with Christ can be deflected into an orientation to experience apart from biblical controls. Or again, an admirable emphasis upon ethical practice can blind us to other themes of scripture. In such ways it can easily happen that traditional believers can be initiated into a subjectivist theology detached from external authority.

A Postscript for the Sake of Balance

In this paper we have reacted sharply to the historical critical method in its modern form, and deplored the influence it has had upon the time-honoured conviction about the Bible in our traditions. We object strongly to the assumption that the divine is never a causative factor in history, that all events are imprisoned in a tight homogeneity, that the integrity of the text can be sacrificed on the altar of speculative reconstruction. Thus the drift of the argument so far gives the strong impression that developments on the liberal side have been mostly harmful, while the witness of the conservatives has been generally wholesome. However, things are not that simple. There have been disturbing shifts on the conservative side too, which must not go unnoticed lest we leave a badly distorted impression. Undoubtedly the most serious weakness here is the significant shift in the list of preferred tests of orthodoxy from, what do you think of Jesus? to what do you think of the Bible? Of course conservatives are correct to sense an important relationship between the fate of the Bible and the strength of this confession of Christ historically and practically. But, nevertheless, whatever one thinks of the Bible, he is saved only by Jesus, not by a theory of inspiration. Another serious problem on the conservative side is an unwillingness to see diversity in the Bible itself, and a **consequent** unwillingness to affirm diversity in the contemporary church. How often the "biblical" position is equated with a single scriptural statement, ignoring the presence of other perspectives also in the Bible, and used with devastating effect against other believers whose attention has been caught by other nuances. These shifts from christology to bibliology, and from catholic openness to bigoted narrowness are errors of a serious kind and demand confession and repentance.

In addition there are less serious mistakes in large numbers. There is, for example a curious belief in the almost magical efficacy of creedal formulae to guarantee orthodoxy, e.g. "inerrancy." There is the inexcusable neglect of the godly use of scholarly tools in Bible study which prevents the radical nature of scriptural revelation from calling into question our cultural patterns and theological traditions. There is the transformation of the Bible from an instrument in the hands of the sovereign Spirit into a compendium of fixed absolutes to be rationally manipulated, from a Word that sets us free into a weapon of condemnation. It is important that we face the facts as they are, and not try to patch over a pretty sorry record. For what does it profit if we flee from modernism only to end up in a decadent fundamentalism?[25]

Putting our point more positively, we do not follow our spiritual ancestors faithfully by seeking to transpose ourselves into **their** century and in the process turning a blind eye to the aberrations which have crept in because we were not really striving to be faithful in **our** context. Somehow we have to learn to face twentieth-century questions in the same spirit of docility to God speaking in scripture as our fathers did earlier. They were faithful in their generation precisely because they grappled with the issues of contextualization existing in their day, and we only follow them truly when we face the questions before us with the same flexibility and integrity. The essence of heresy may well be what Dunn points out, the **refusal** to face up to new challenges and to apply the gospel creatively in the new context.

In closing, let me offer a short list in outline form of some of the actions we have to take if we hope to render credible any call for a return to the high doctrine of inspiration in our day. First, we will have to show some leadership in the development of a **reformed** historical critical method, along the lines of what Stuhlmacher called a "hermeneutic of consent." At a time when Christians who have gone through a period of negative criticism in which the text of the Bible has been virtually shredded and who now seem to be wanting to return to a greater respect for the authority of the Bible in the text as it stands, surely our historic belief in the God-breathed character of scripture is highly relevant again in undergirding this wholesome tendency. We must seize the opportunity to articulate what many are sensing instinctively in regard to the divine authority of scripture.[26]

Second, we will have to work toward a greater balance between the desire to demonstrate the unity of the biblical message, which rests on our conviction about its divine authorship, and the growing recognition in recent study of a considerable **diversity** in the canonical context taken as a whole. While this diversity may be less than Dunn argues, it is certainly more than our conservative traditions have ever acknowledged, and signifies a demand for us to be more open and receptive to styles of Christian existence different from our own. It also means not so incidentally that Believers' Church advocates too cannot write off so easily the Catholic, Calvinist, pietist, and fundamentalist styles as orientations lacking all scriptural support. At the same time, recognition of diversity also guarantees a place for our own witness in the symphony of voices of the greater Christian witness.[27]

Third, we will have to learn to be less flippant in our dismissal of such influential programmes as "demythologizing" the Bible. It is all too easy to reject Bultmann for abandoning crucial N.T. historical and onto-logical affirmations about Jesus in favour of his narrow anthropological programme, and fail to notice that the problem he identifies does not disappear with that gesture. We still have to explain how **we** propose to relate the mesage of the N.T. in all its first-century conditionedness to its modern hearers in all their twentieth-century conditionedness. We still have to work at the task of rendering meaningful a message of hope and love first expressed in a language in lots of ways remote from our own, in such a way that it really lives again. At least Bultmann can be said to have **tried** to solve this problem. Any effort must be judged to be better than no effort at all.

Fourth, there simply has to be profounder and more relevant exposition of scripture if we are to make good our doctrine of inspiration. Unless we can show that the Bible is a living word capable of effecting spiritual change in the modern context, as it did in ancient times, and not the frozen and burdensome letter of Pharisaic doctrine, our witness should and will have no effect. What a travesty to trumpet our convictions about biblical authority and fail to inform the people at a profound level what God really has to say to them from the scriptural text. Surely God is not pleased with lip-service in the matter of inspiration and authority if at the same time his word is not being heard and obeyed.

In summary, the high doctrine of scripture which is everywhere assumed in the foundation witnesses of the Believers' Church traditions has come under severe attack in recent times as a result of the inroads into Christian thinking of humanistic themes, and it needs to be defended and vindicated again in our day, but not in a manner that obscures rather than illumines its true character, relevance, and power.

BIBLICAL AUTHORITY:
A RESPONSE

William Klassen

Professor Pinnock has attempted to clarify a very complex matter. Although he has said more about the present state than he has about the past, he has attempted to cover a large area. Consistent with the Believers' Church tradition, it is our privilege to suggest areas that were neglected, and to come to different conclusions. Certainly we would all recognize that we are dealing here with a very difficult problem. I shall therefore indicate some of the issues which deserve further discussion.

Before doing so, however, I would like to affirm the conviction expressed by Professor Pinnock that the crucial test in all of this is christology. We dare never allow christology to be replaced by bibliolatry. Consistent with our tradition also, it is clear that we are never done when we have made an affirmation or subscribed to creed. The ultimate test is always how we obey what we recognize as God's word to us. One recalls here an anecdote about the famous New Testament Professor, Adolf Schlatter, who was once greeted effusively by an American graduate student with the words, "Ah, Professor Schlatter, I am so glad to meet a professor who stands on the Word of God." To which Professor Schlatter replied, "Young man, I stand not **on** the Word of God but **under** the Word."

Furthermore, I speak as one who is not a systematic theologian and has never pretended to be. My approach to the Bible may seem somewhat simple, therefore, to those who are interested in theology in a more systematic way.

1. The first question to which we must address ourselves is, what has our tradition said about the Bible? Professor Pinnock's paper assumes throughout that there is a "high view of scripture" in our tradition. It would have been helpful if he had given us some citations from the early writers and placed them alongside of more recent ones. Surely there is a big difference between what the Anabaptist leaders said about the scripture and what contemporary writers have said. In four centuries, the shape of the question can change drastically. It is, therefore, simply not fair to those writers or to any writer to take him as a spokesman for our position four centuries later. Where, for example, would support be found for his statement, "For the majority of Anabaptists as for our Lord Jesus, scripture is divine, tradition human..."? The word that is particularly poorly chosen here is "divine." To divinize scripture is surely very far from our heritage.

In Jesus' context we might say that the Pharisees, the sect of Qumran, and to some extent the Zealots and Sadducees divinized scripture. The Pharisees added tradition to it, parting ways with Sadducees precisely here. The affirmation that the Bible is holy in the sense that it points to God and originates from God is saying something quite different than saying that it is divine.

Two scholars, one Baptist (Torsten Bergsten), the other Mennonite (Paul Peachey), have urged that we see the Anabaptists as representing not an orthodox verbal inspiration theory but rather a combination of a real and personal theory of inspiration. Paul Peachey argues that, "Anabaptist Biblicism in modern times has become widely identified with the Fundamentalist view of scripture. It is the view of the present writer that few outside influences have so adversely affected modern Mennonites as this confusion."

We can then ask whether our tradition has said about the Bible what it says about itself. Unfortunately not! We have gone far beyond what the Bible claims for itself. Professor Pinnock himself has made the remarkable observation that references to infallibility of the scriptures appear among French Baptists about the year 1879. Does it not strike you as interesting that at the same time the Roman Catholic Church was beginning to talk about an infallible dimension about some of the statements of the pope? It is almost as if we are saying that we too in the Free Church tradition, must have our infallible authority — our final fallback position.

Fortunately, we do not need to repudiate our position to restore sturdy confidence in the truth of the Bible and the reliability of its message, and above all the adequacy of the salvation which it heralds. We can stress the functionality of the Bible — what it is given for and what it has achieved precisely — what the New Testament writers claimed for the Old Testament (II Timothy 3: 15-17). If we stress the use of the Bible rather than the nature of the Bible, then the confidence in the Bible as a reliable guide to point us to God will be restored.

It is pedagogically a very important point that we invite people to read the Bible and to study it, and that whatever they eventually conclude about the nature of the Bible may come out of that kind of an experience. My best Bible teachers taught that, and it is a privilege to continue that approach in teaching the Bible to university students. It is the only consistent approach; that is, consistent with the biblical message itself. The invitation is to come and see for yourself what the Bible is, read it, study it, and let the Holy Spirit lead you. Those who come to the conclusion that the Bible is God's word, on the basis of personal experience, cannot be easily shaken from that conviction.

Our Free Church ancestors said that the Bible is meant to be used, to be studied, to be preached, and that it has a message which changes life. They also said that it is a reliable dependent witness to God's care for us, as shown especially in the gift of his son. We believe that the picture of Jesus as shown in the Bible is reliable and is a guide for those who wish to follow Christ. If the Bible is viewed as a flight plan, it is our conviction that our job is not to spend time praising the adequacy of that flight plan, nor to spend time examining it to be sure that we can establish all the flaws in it; rather it is our task to use the flight plan or roadmap, and in the usage of that our confidence grows. The purpose of the Bible, as expressed particularly in I John 1: 1-4; and in II Corinthians 1: 20 is to increase joy. As joy grows, the confidence in the Word also grows.

It was this conviction that lead some of the most prominent Anabaptist leaders to speak of the Bible as a witness to God's acts in history. They speak of it as a material means which God uses to make himself known. As the physical flesh of Jesus was the material means in which God chose to dwell, so the scriptures are the material means through which he calls attention to his will.

That is a "high view of scripture" — the highest view there is. Instead of affirming this, Pinnock unfortunately "deplores the state of some uncertainty about the absolute authority of scripture, which is so widespread today". Throughout his paper one has the distinct impression that in large measure he holds scholars responsible for this state of affairs, for his illustrations all come from the realm of higher education.

That approach is fundamentally in error. It is doubtful that a high view of scripture and certainty about the "absolute authority of scripture" have come about through the work of biblical scholars. That is seriously to over-estimate our influence. It may have come about through incredibly poor adult education materials or even the children's Sunday school materials we have produced. It may have come about through the fact that there is hardly anything in the Bible which we can today treat as "absolute." In an age where literally nothing has absolute authority, it is not surprising that the Bible has also lost it (if in fact, it ever really had it), and I think that it will never be regained. Primary authority, determining authority, is one thing. Absolute authority is quite another, and I doubt that the term has any meaning for our students or our parishioners. In any case, it would be difficult to reconcile the use of this term with Pinnock's acknowledgement of "human weakness of scripture." Can anything that has human weakness, at the same time be described as absolute in authority? If so, then the term "absolute" means something quite different than what we are accustomed to.

To use one example, you may convince people that the one thing Jesus never did was to kill anyone and that even the most radical scholars are convinced that he commanded his disciples to love their enemies. Once that has happened, the sport begins. For it is not only the critical scholars who have worked their way around those clear and simple teachings of Jesus: it is many preachers as well. Foolish preaching, we may call it, especially much radio preaching has killed confidence in the Word. Vain repetition and heaping up of empty phrases are what Jesus describes the heathen as doing and urges his followers not to do. It is my judgment, after years of listening to it, that 90 per cent of all the preaching done on the radio by Baptists and Mennonites and others in the Free Church tradition should be removed from the airways. That might be a first step in helping to restore some confidence in the Bible. At least it will allow people to look at the Bible directly, rather than through some distorted version or perversion of the scriptures.

This brings us, then, to the quote from Dulles, offered by Professor Pinnock. While the context of that citation is not given, it is disturbing that Pinnock seems to be calling for a curb against questioning the authority of the tradition or rebelling against authority. We in the Believers' Church tradition, whatever we wish to learn from our brothers and sisters in the Roman Catholic tradition, can never again return to bondage. We dare not install our own popes, and while rebellion may often be a mark of adolescence, it is also a profoundly human experience essential to the children of the Radical Reformation. We should be the first to affirm the validity of such a rebellion. Those are children of the Free Church movement who continue to press the question on all of our members, does the Word really mean that? Does God speak to us thus today?

But most important, the authority and only authority to which we defer, is the Holy Spirit. The Holy Spirit as he expresses his presence within the community and as he confirms the lordship of Christ. No other authority is absolute or authoritative for us. All others are open to question. Jesus Christ is Lord, and that means the only one who receives any ultimate authority. While we can say we are hooked on the Bible, it is because the theme of the Bible is the Lordship of Christ that it has become so important to us. If Pinnock is warning us against subjectivism, that warning is well taken. But surely we also must stress that central to our tradition has always been what one believes. It must be personally appropriated. My faith may be similar to that of my father, but it is not something that I have inherited and it cannot live unless it lives within me. The English Baptist Charles Spurgeon, when he was asked, "How do you defend the Bible?" gave the best answer. "How do you defend the lion? Let it loose, it will defend itself!"

2. This brings us to the central question of "how has the Bible been used in our tradition?" Few topics have been given as much concerted study in the last number of years as the question of hermeneutics. How has the authority of the scripture been expressed? For some 350 years, it was done primarily by uneducated ministers and laymen. It was believed that since the people who crucified Jesus knew Latin, Greek, and Hebrew, one should not learn these languages. Thus, there has been a heavy strand of anti-intellectualism in the Believers' Church tradition. How much have we been influenced by this tradition? One needs to look only at the basically unbiblical way in which Billy Graham approaches the topic of angels in the Bible to realize that it is one thing to use the formula, "The Bible says," and another to really capture what the Bible says. Or one has only to look at the disproportionate emphasis given by modern believers to the theme "Jesus the Saviour," in light of how seldom it appears in the New Testament, to notice again a basic difference. Pinnock's assumption is that we have been influenced by liberalism, but I find very little evidence for that.

To be sure, some scholars in the last thirty years have actually taken the trouble to become biblically literate and to learn Greek and Hebrew. Baptists have even come out with a series of commentaries on the Bible, published by Broadman Press. On the whole the results are not too encouraging. We still have to come up with a Free Church hermeneutic.

Fundamentally, however, we have proportionately fewer biblical scholars than we have medical doctors, psychiatrists, business persons etc. The reason for this seems to me to be relatively simple. We have not been able to create a climate of study in our churches and in our institutions. Mennonite scholars are found in the sciences or humanities and yet our greatest area of need is still in the Bible. Particularly we need exegesis. Very few commentaries are written, there are a few attempts to wrestle with the text and its meaning and relevance for current life. There have been no modernists in the sense of anyone who has taught the Bible but believed it not to be the Word of God, although there have been disagreements on how to define that. So when Pinnock asks the question about the influence of liberalism, I would suggest that for all practical purposes, it has had no influence at all. The example that he uses of Professor Gordon Kaufman is not pertinent to the discussion at all. The consultation on Anabaptist Mennonite Theology held in 1969, and the papers presented there which were published do not indicate any difficulty in this area.

Yet we must come to terms honestly on this situation. There need be no sacrifice of the intellect, and we must refuse to be trapped in the rhetoric of Professor Pinnock's paper, when, for example, he warns "that the integrity of the text may be sacrificed on the altar of speculative reconstruction." What does he mean? Surely he does not suggest that we hide from our students the fact that the story of the adulterous woman (John 8:1-11) has no firm place in the textual tradition? Surely we owe it to our students to indicate that here is a story which is genuine and may indeed go back to the early church. It was not written by the author of the Fourth Gospel and in fact, for four centuries of the church's history was rejected by that part of the church which wished to take a strict and harsh attitude toward this kind of sin. What we must be able to do is to move through a pre-critical to a post-critical study of the Bible. Thus, when we study the book of Jonah, the question is not to try to find out whether there are whales in the Mediterranean big enough to swallow a man, but does the Word of God really achieve its purpose? What is the intention of the book? May it be, for example, that the intention of the book is to show that God loves even his enemies and the power of God's words is such that even the enemy can be converted? It is a point which Jonah would not accept. He would rather sulk. It is a point likewise that Billy Graham cannot accept.

I find it also strange that there is an objection to the entrance of humanistic themes into Christian thinking. Surely, humanism is not bad. A healthy dose of good Christian humanism which confirms the human as it is seen in Jesus is surely preferable to some of the zeal without knowledge and intolerance which come out of Fundamentalist circles.

Finally, I would urge us to have an absolute commitment which reflects honesty. The truth lies through the critical problem, never around it. I find it striking that Jesus lived in a century when there was a great deal of discussion about the inspiration and the authority of the scripture and that he said so little about it. Perhaps we too can follow Him in staying with the main point. That main point seems to me to be the question: How can we build a covenanted community in which there is serious searching for the will of God? Can such a community be built? We raise that main point because we believe that question can be answered. There are those who under God live by His will.

BIBLICAL AUTHORITY AND DENOMINATIONAL TRADITIONS

David Schroeder

Christians throughout the centuries have affirmed the scriptures as the Word of God and as vested with the highest authority. The central place that has been given to the scriptures in the lives of people and in the life of the church is evidence of the authority of the scriptures.[1]

From time to time Christians have attempted to say in precisely what way they are authoritative. This has happened especially where the scriptures were being called into question, and this is to be expected. But this also meant that the explications of the authority of the scriptures were usually given in a conflict situation with the result that any arguments advanced tended to be argued to the extreme. The limitations of all such explications were not respected sufficiently.

A. The Limited Nature of All Theories Designed to Affirm and Explain the Authority of the Scriptures

1. Most of the theories have advanced either a subjective or an objective base for their affirmation of biblical authority. The subjective base is not enough because anything that one **believes to be** authoritative would then **be** authoritative, and this is not the case. To base it on objective data only would mean that the Bible must be taken to be its own witness to the authority of the Bible, but this could only be the case if the authority of the Bible were already established. An authority claim cannot be self-validating and it does not suffice to say it needs no validation.

In order to give at least some evidence on the basis of which a reasonable claim to the authority of scripture can be made, the subjective-objective dichotomy must be transcended or overcome. If we cannot do this we will remain with the traditional dichotomies. If we base the affirmation of authority on purely subjective grounds, then it is based on ineffable experience, for it will be of the nature of mystic experience and therefore not communicable; if we base the affirmation on purely objective grounds then the argument should have the kind of evidence that anyone examining it should know it to be true, and such evidence is not available.

It has always struck me as strange that conservative scholarship in America, which has so strongly defended the verbal infallibility of the original autographs, has not been actively involved until recently in textual criticism. One would have expected that these scholars would have been engaged in seeking to get at the original text. Most have been content not only with the Textus Receptus (KJV) but even with paraphrases of the text (The Living Bible).

Similarly, liberal scholars, who have questioned the historicity of the biblical record of the life of Jesus and have been open to concede that there may be errors in scripture, have contradicted this belief in being extremely anxious to get at the original text and have not hesitated to omit in new translations those sections that were based on later manuscripts.

Because of this inner contradiction in both positions it has been very difficult for conservative scholars to communicate a position that does not fit into either extreme, without the subsequent polemics forcing those persons into one or the other camp.

The polemics on both sides are set up in such a way that this must happen. Each position is carefully honed to present an either-or argument on the basis of exhaustive categories. The case is not argued on the basis of let's say "black" and "white" for then one could speak about "green." The case is argued in terms of "white" and "non-white" so that no other color can be named without it being in fact "non-white." Thus if one rejects any one item on either side of the argument, one is immediately taken to be fully and totally in the other camp. For this reason such arguments are next to useless because they are designed more to be successful than to be truth-finding.

Another feature of the polemics involved is that the arguments are so often couched as deductive arguments. As such they may be perfectly valid arguments without being at the same time sound or true.[2] In order to establish the soundness of the argument empirical evidence has to be given on the basis of inductive arguments. The inductive approach again demands that all the different disciplines of critical scholarship (archaeology, linguistics, historical research, literary analysis, etc.) be used to gather the necessary evidence for such reasoning. Even when the evidence is in, it is of the nature of inductive arguments that conclusions can only be reached to a degree of probability.

My attempt will be to make an argument for the authority of scripture on an inductive approach. It will be an attempt to do greater justice to both the subjective and objective elements involved. Beyond that, I can only testify to the fact that I believe the evidence is strong enough for me to accept the scriptures as the Word of God and seek to live according to that Word.

2. Specific theories of inspiration have sometimes been advanced in such a way as to seek to guarantee the authority of scripture. This seldom succeeds. People who hold to the authority of scripture do not do so on the basis of a theory of inspiration but rather, the theory of inspiration is an attempt to spell out why in fact they believe as they do.

I am not arguing that we should not have theories of inspiration. We will in fact develop them if we believe in the authority of scripture. I am arguing that we do not accept the authority of the scriptures on the basis of our own arguments about scripture. It would in fact be possible for our theories of inspiration to be false, and still to believe in the authority of scripture. The acceptance of the authority of scripture gives rise to the theory of inspiration and not vice versa.

Rather than demanding that people accept our theories of inspiration, we should be intent to point to those actions of God in history which can serve as reasonable evidence for a belief in the authority of scripture. What we need to point out is how God himself has established his Word.

3. Whatever theories of authority and inspiration of scripture we may have, they will be totally beside the point if somehow we are able to interpret scripture in such a way as to give it a message and a content that God did not intend. This can be done very simply by interpreting passages out of context; by reading a specific system of dogmatics into the scriptures; by claiming that certain passages are meant for some future age (e.g. Sermon on the Mount); by not taking things literally (do not swear), or too literally (cut off your hand) where such is not intended; or by any form of **eisegesis** in which we define the terms and concepts in such a way that we read out of scripture our own intended and pre-determined message.

The battle for and against the scriptures is not won or lost as much on the question of authority and inspiration as it is in the interpretation of scripture. More will be said about this later.

Even though there are distinct limitations to explicating the authority of scripture, I must nevertheless state what evidence I think might be helpful to others, with respect to the question of authority. I cannot give a distinctly "Mennonite" position for there would be a variety of approaches to the subject in the Mennonite church as in other churches. It will therefore be a paper in which a Mennonite wrestles with the question of the authority of scripture.

B. The Authority of Scripture Rests in God and in the Way in which He Has Made Himself Known

The authority of God's Word, i.e. revelation of himself, was known to Abram, Isaac and Jacob long before there was a written Word. Also those who were instrumental in recording the Word of God knew it to be God's Word, and therefore authoritative, before it was committed to writing. The prophet in most cases first delivered his message orally to the people, but it was nevertheless the Word of God and he was aware of its authority. The prophets were not less sure of the authority of the Word that came to them than we are about the authority of scripture today.

The nature of God's revelation of himself, whether in Word or deed, is such that authority is an accompanying characteristic of revelation. It is not possible for there to be a true revelation of God without it also being authoritative, or God would not be God. It is important, therefore, to consider in some detail the nature of God's revelation of himself to mankind.

1. God's revelation is personal in nature. The "personal" emerges where two persons are present to each other. It is not a matter of existing together in the same time and space, but a matter of being aware of each other's presence and knowing themselves addressed by the other. The personal emerges there where there is communion, dialogue, response and interaction.

God in this way made himself known to Abraham and to Moses. He was present to them and addressed them. He revealed himself and his will to them. They knew themselves addressed of God, and they responded to his call. Revelation solicits response and dialogue. The same could be said of the prophets. They knew that it was God himself who was present to them and his word had unquestioned authority to command (Amos 7:14). The revelation of God began with God being present to people and soliciting from them unquestioned obedience.

Revelation also calls forth or creates theological language. God spoke to people in a language they could understand. Sometimes it was in a dream, sometimes in visions. It was acknowledged later that "in many and various ways God spoke of old to the fathers by the prophets" (Hebrews 1:1). The language used was at first ordinary language. As time went on, it carried more and more meaning as God's revelation came to be known more fully. Thus in Jesus people experienced the "good news" that Jesus is the Messiah. As this became fully known, "good news" took on the technical and theological meaning it has in the word "gospel." In the Greek the word remains the same, however.

Were we to stop, however, with God's personal appearance to people, it would not yet be a Word that could be known to be true by someone to whom God had not appeared in this way. Though there is both a subjective and an objective element present, it cannot yet be **known** to be more than subjective by others.

2. God's revelation is of the nature of promise and fulfilment. The revelation of God came to people most often in the form of a promise. God came to Abram with a command ("Go...into the land that I will show you") and a promise ("...and I will make you a great nation, and I will bless you..."). So the promise came also to Isaac and Jacob as well as to David (Genesis 12:1-2; 22:15ff; II Samuel 7:12-17).

The promise of God to Israel is an integral part of the covenant God established with them. God gave to his people a knowledge of his will in the law (Exodus 20:2ff); he set before them life and death, and asked them to choose life (Deuteronomy 15:24f; 30:19). God gave them his word that if they would do all that he had commanded, he would bless them and fulfill the promises already given to Israel through the patriarchs.

It is through the promise that God solicited from his people faith, trust and obedience. The promise was not yet knowledge, even though it was recognized as, or perceived to be, a promise from God. The recognition that it was a Word of God, however, called forth the response of obedience: "We will do all that the Lord has commanded" (Exodus 24:3). Had Israel not obeyed the command with promise, they would never have known the promise to have in fact been of God.

The truth of the promise became known to Abram in its fulfilment. As Abram responded in faith and obedience to the promise of God and went out in faith, the signs of fulfilment began to appear. He received a son. The son was not yet a great nation, but was to Abram a sign that the rest of the promise would also be fulfilled by God. Through these signs of fulfilment Abram knew that God was faithful to his promise.

The same could be said about the covenant. As Israel obeyed the will of God as expressed in the law, God was on their side giving them the land, and sending them judges to lead them. In the fulfilment of the promise they received tangible, empirical evidence that the Word of God, which had come to them as promise, was in truth God's Word. It had the very stamp of God on it, and it would be used by the prophets to call a people back to this covenant relationship.

Even now God comes to us as promise. The promise is given to us through the scriptures and through Christ and the Spirit. His Word indicates which way we are to walk. If we take that way in faith and find the promise fulfilling itself, or showing the signs of fulfilment, we will know it to be of God; we will know the authority of his Word.

3. God's revelation is covenantal in nature. Through his revelation, God calls people into a covenantal relationship with himself. God not only saved Israel from slavery in Egypt but bound them to **his** will in the covenant. They became his people. As they yielded obedience to God's will they became a different people, separated from the world of idolatry and immorality.

The direction of the revelation through the covenant is always toward salvation. God made known to them what would lead to life and what would lead to renewed captivity and death. If they bound themselves to his will they would experience the salvation of God just as they had experienced it in the exodus from Egypt.

In binding themselves to the Word and will of God they would be free; free from captivity, free to be servants of God. In the wilderness wanderings it became clear to them through judgments of their unfaithfulness, that it was indeed the Word of God and carried his authority.

4. God's revelation of himself is historical in nature. God has revealed himself in history: to specific persons, living at a specific time and in specific circumstances. The revelation occurs in and through events in history: physical events, language events, visions, etc. The revelation of God came to people through God's acts in history, through his mighty acts of redemption.

For Israel God's saving power could best be seen in the Exodus. They had been helpless before the might of the Pharaohs, but God came to them and in a miraculous way saved them and set them free. It was in and through this mighty act of God that Israel came to know God as a saving God.

Through such acts of power (authority), God's saving will became manifest. It was there for all the world to see. If someone would have asked, "What is God like?" they would have responded by telling them what he did. The events that could be pointed to as evidence of the saving power of God were there for all to see.

So too in language events. The prophets claimed to speak for God. But there were also false prophets who made similar claims. In such cases Israel waited for the confirming action of God. They said: we will wait and see which one God honours. Then, in the fulfilment of the words of the true prophet, Israel would know who spoke for God; whose Word they ought to hear. Both the revelation in deed and in Word came in history, as did also the confirmation of its authority.

In the events of history Israel began to understand to an ever increasing degree that God is sovereign Lord over all of creation, over all the nations and especially over his own covenant people. This was why there was no question but that God's Word was ultimate authority.

5. The revelation of God is parabolic in nature. The revelation of God came in and through historical events. But historical events are not in and of themselves revelation, for they are not unambiguous. The event is not a self-evident statement of some truth, i.e. demonstrative proof. Rather, the revelation of God is given in and through those events. The event is the medium through which God communicates himself and his will; in the event is given the possibility to apprehend the truth of God.

Even in the event of the incarnation we see the parabolic nature of revelation. God came in the flesh. There was no clearer revelation of God anywhere. Yet this was not yet a demonstrative statement of truth in such a way that people of necessity had to believe him to be God incarnate. There were those who saw his authority (power) to cast out demons but assumed He did so by the power of Satan (Mark 3: 20ff). Yet it was in and through the life of Jesus that people could apprehend the truth of God.

Apprehending the truth of God in His mighty acts, depends on how people respond to that revelation; it depends on whether people have ears to hear and eyes to see; it depends on whether people meet that revelation in faith and trust and commit their lives to it, or whether they reject it for one reason or another; it depends on whether they recognize it as in truth being of God in the first place.

Jesus taught in parables. In them you have the same phenomena. A parable is an ordinary story, and yet it brings the story in such a way that the transcendent kingdom of God could be seen through it.

6. The perception of revelation is progressive in nature.[3] Where the revelation of God is responded to in faith, trust and obedience, there is a growing knowledge of God, His purpose and His will. Every confirmation of the revelation of God in a person's own experience and history sets the stage for a greater and fuller revelation of God. This is reflected in Paul's statement: "When the time had fully come, God sent forth His son..." (Galatians 4: 4).

Conversely, where the revelation of God is rejected in unbelief, there is a hardening of the heart so that with every rejection of God's truth a person will know less and less of God in history. In this way from him that has not, even that will be taken which he has.

The law of an "eye for an eye" was given to overcome the sin of taking revenge sevenfold (Genesis 4: 24; Exodus 21: 24). This then opened the way for a new revelation that one need not take an eye for an eye but rather meet the offender with mercy just as God met David in mercy, even though he had forfeited his life. Jesus built on this further when he asked us to forgive each other and to love even the enemy.

Not all of God's will was known to the people immediately. They grew in their knowledge of the will of God so that things that were still part of their lives early in their history (polygamy, war, divorce, circumcision) were later known to be contrary to the will of God or no longer required.

Jesus appealed to the Scribes to recognize that they could not simply freeze the revelation of God to His people in Moses' day (law) and then make it apply to all future times. To do this would be to refuse to see the progressive nature of revelation. Jesus recognized that the ceremonial law, given of God, had fulfilled its purpose and was no longer needed (Mark 7: 1ff). Not to recognize this progressive movement is to give uniform authority to all aspects or items of scripture. But Jesus indicated that the law to honour father and mother carried greater weight than the law of Corban (Mark 7: 9ff).

7. The authority of God's revelation is seen most fully in the revelation of God in Jesus Christ. The Old Testament prophets, Moses, in the giving of the law, and the Scribes all asserted only a delegated authority, but Jesus spoke as one who had authority in Himself (Mark 2: 21-22). He made a clear distinction between the authority of the tradition handed down from generation to generation, and His own authority. He said, "You have heard that it was said to men of old...but I say unto you" (Matthew 5: 21-22). He could claim "all authority has been given to me in heaven and on earth" (Matthew 28: 18) and He exercised this power not only in Word but also in deed. He Himself interpreted His action and its significance: "If it is by the finger of God that I cast out demons, then the kingdom of God has come upon you" (Luke 11: 20). Those who responded to His call and followed Him were sent out to proclaim His Word, and received from Him the power to substantiate that Word in a form that was visible for all to see (Mark 6: 13).

C. The Authority of the Scriptures rests in God and in the Way in which He Confirms His Word

1. We have already indicated that God, through the fulfilment of the promise, confirmed and established the Word of promise to those who believed. The fulfilment came in concrete historical events that could be observed by all people. In that way, the Word, though it was at first subjectively received, was substantiated through empirical events. The revelation could be talked about and shared with others.

Wherever the revelation of God came to be known in truth as the Word of God, there people could not help but witness to the revelation received. It had to be shared because it was either a word of life or a warning. Paul said, "Woe to me if I do not preach the gospel" (I Corinthians 9: 16). So also the prophets (Amos 7: 15; Jeremiah 1: 9f). They had not only a subjective experience to communicate but a knowledge of what God had done to redeem His people and the assurance that God would so act in the future. Thus, out of the confirmation of the Word came a witness to the Word. They could invite others to receive that Word (Acts 2: 36ff).

This proclaimed Word, whether oral or written, then functioned again as a promise of God to those who now heard it. As the hearer responded in faith and obedience, the Word was confirmed in his own experience and he too knew the truth of that Word.

Where something was proclaimed as the Word of God, when it was not God's Word, it did not find an ongoing fulfilment or confirmation and did not establish itself as the Word of God. Rather it lost its power and authority (Acts 5:33f). It is in and through history that His Word is established.

2. The Word as proclaimed by Abram, Moses and others who had received it, revealed its power to create a new community under God. Because of its power to give life, this Word became a sacred trust to the people of God and was faithfully transmitted from generation to generation. Some was written and some was at first only transmitted orally (Jeremiah 26:1f; 30:2f), but all of it was treasured as the words of God. The fact that these words had been recognized to be God's Word, and had become words of life to the people, caused the people to recognize what was from the beginning the case, that these writings (scripture) were in fact the Word of God.

This process, in which the community comes to recognize the Word from God, we call canonization.[4] The community did not create this Word but recognized it for what it was, and what it had been, the Word of God.

We should not forget that there were many books and writers that purported to speak for God. Some of these are known to us in the Apocrypha and the Pseudepigrapha. They claim equally to be the Word of God. Here again God acted in history over a period of time, giving indication in history through the fulfilment or non-fulfilment of their message, which books were to be recognized as the Word of God. These events too belong to the mighty acts of God in establishing His Word.

There is evidence of this process of recognition (canonization) of the scriptures in the Old Testament itself. If we take the Hebrew division of the Old Testament into Law, Prophets and Writings, we notice that in each successive group of writings the authority of the previous set is attested.

The Law was already recognized as having divine authority at the time when God made His covenant with Israel (Exodus 24; Deuteronomy 4:2; 12:32; 31:9-13) and continued to be so regarded by the prophets (Joshua 1:7-8; I Kings 2:3) even though it is not always clear whether reference is made to the content of the law of Moses or the Pentateuch as such. The Writings (Ezra 7:10; Nehemiah 8:8) and the New Testament also affirm the authority of the Law (Luke 24:44).

The Former Prophets were recognized by the Later Prophets (Zechariah 7:12), by the Writings (Daniel 9:6,10) and the New Testament (Luke 24:44). In their turn the Writings were accepted as canonical in the New Testament in that they are not only quoted but referred to specifically (Luke 24:44).

We cannot consider here all the historic events by which God confirmed the authority of each individual book. If we did so, we would find in each case a process through which the community recognized it as the Word of God and preserved it as such.

3. The most significant confirmation of God's Word came in Jesus. Jesus revealed his authority and power to all people. The people were aware that a very significant claim of Messiahship was made in His words and in His deeds. If these claims were true, then He was indeed the Sent One of God and spoke in His authority and acted in His might.

But as we said, revelation in events is parabolic. Jesus could be known through His words and deeds but only by those who believed in Him and followed Him in obedience to His Word. There were in fact many, even people learned in the scriptures, who did not believe Him to be the Messiah. As a result, there were two strong and powerful prophetic words given in that day. Jesus and the disciples claimed He was the Messiah. Perhaps the disciples did not yet fully understand all that messiahship included (e.g. obedience unto death) but they held Jesus to be the one who fulfilled the prophetic word. Jesus had so fulfilled the promises of the coming reign of God that they saw the inauguration of the coming kingdom in Jesus (Mark 7: 27-30).

The Scribes, on the other hand, interpreted the words and deeds of Jesus to be blashpemy. They knew the Law of Moses and were committed to it; they knew the tradition of the fathers, i.e. the interpretation and application of the law to all of life, and they believed that Jesus did not honour this law and this tradition. They claimed He was a false teacher and a blasphemer (Matthew 9: 1ff).

Just as in Israel, when the claim and the counter-claim of the true and false prophet contradicted each other, the people waited patiently to see which word God would confirm in history. In this case each group remained true to its conviction and acted on it; the disciples followed Jesus as the Messiah, and the Sanhedrin condemned Jesus as worthy of death. Now the world had to wait to see which word was of God.

The disciples on the road to Emmaus were beginning to believe that God would not confirm the promise of Jesus being the Messiah, for they reported, "We had hoped that He was the one to redeem Israel" (Luke 24: 21). They seemed to be in the process of giving up their faith. Other reports indicate that they returned to their fishing. In the resurrection, however, God himself confirmed the message of Jesus and the faith of the disciples. Again it was there for all the world to see. Mark 1: 1-13 argues very convincingly that it was God Himself who confirmed Jesus as the Messiah in that the heavens were opened, the Spirit descended, the voice of God was heard and Psalm 2 was spoken as His entrance into His earthly ministry. All of it was God's doing.

4. We must also speak of the authority of the apostolic tradition (**paradosis**). Jesus had manifested who He was in Word and deed. But it was not sufficient after His death simply to collect His sayings or to write an account of His life. The very meaning of His earthly ministry, His death and resurrection had to be made known.

Jesus Himself, after the resurrection, helped the disciples to understand the scriptures and how His life, ministry and death fulfilled the prophetic Word (Luke 24: 44). Again it is the fulfilment of scripture that indicates that what happened was in truth the revelation of God and would serve to be the redemption of a people.

John's Gospel refers repeatedly to the work of the Spirit in recalling for them the words of Jesus and their significance. They were made aware of the significance of the death of Jesus through the Holy Spirit (John 16: 12ff; 2: 22f). It was this new understanding of the events in Christ that the apostles communicated to all the churches (I Corinthians 15: 3f). Paul assumes (Romans 6: 17; 16: 17) that a church that he has not yet visited has received the same gospel that he has communicated to other fellowships. Though Paul had not been with Jesus in His earthly ministry he nevertheless knew that the gospel he had proclaimed to the churches was of God (Galatians 1: 9-12).

Again God confirmed this Word through His mighty acts. The Word as it was preached was powerful and people were converted so that daily people were added to the church (Acts 2: 43-47). The power of God was with the proclamation of this gospel, whether in healings (Acts 5: 12-16) or in judgment (Acts 5: 1ff), in answered prayer (Acts 5: 5ff), or in martyrdom (Acts 7: 1ff). The writer of Hebrews says it best. "It [the message or Word] was declared first by the Lord, and it was attested to us by those who heard Him, while God also bore witness by signs and wonders and various miracles and by gifts of the Holy Spirit destributed according to His own will" (Hebrews 2: 3-4). But it should be noticed that the writer was speaking about the apostolic tradition, since the New Testament was not yet in existence.

Not enough attention has been placed on the fact that the apostles were the guardians of the tradition in the time between the ministry of Jesus and the writing of the New Testament documents. The apostolic tradition, whether oral or partially written (Luke 1: 1-4), was confirmed by God in the life of the church. Paul could say to the Corinthians, "You are a letter from Christ delivered by us, written not with ink but with the Spirit of the living God" (II Corinthians 3: 3) and call to the attention of the Galatians the fact that God had established His work among them through the Spirit (Galatians 3: 5). All of this indicates that the apostolic tradition was proclaimed under the power (authority) of God and as the Word of God.

5. With time, for reasons of exhortation or information, the Epistles and the Gospels of the New Testament were written. These were based on the apostolic tradition (Romans 6: 17; 16: 17; II Thessalonians 2: 15; 3: 6; I Corinthians 11: 2) and spell out further implications of that teaching. To Paul, it is quite clear that some things have been received from the Lord (I Corinthians 7: 10; 9: 14) and some are received through the Spirit (I Corinthians 7: 40). Thus an exchange of letters occurs with the congregations.

As more of the apostles were martyred or passed away, there was a need to draw together accounts out of the apostolic tradition for specific purposes. Luke indicates that he is writing for Theophilus an orderly account, after carefully surveying all of the tradition (Luke 4: 1-4), and

John says he made his selection so that people might believe that Jesus is the Christ (John 20: 31).

Peter already refers to the writings of Paul as being written by a wisdom given to him and sets them on par with the Old Testament (II Peter 3: 15-16). Each letter and gospel was written in the authority of God and Christ, i.e. in His name.

Here again we notice the process of canonization, of recognizing which writings were of God. There were many writings [5] which purported to be of God, even gospels (e.g. Gospel of Thomas, of Peter, of Bartholomew, etc.), acts (Acts of John, Acts of Paul, Acts of Peter, etc.), epistles (Epistle to the Laodicians, Epistle of the Apostles, etc.), and apocalypses (Apocalypse of Peter, Apocalypse of Paul, etc.). Not all of them could be considered authoritative.

The Spirit of God worked in and through the church to give her the insight and the criteria by which the Word of God could be recognized. Thus by 397 A.D., at the Council of Carthage, agreement was reached that the 27 books of the New Testament should be recognized as God's authoritative Word. Here again the process itself belongs to the work of God in establishing His Word.

D. Authority of Scripture and the Transmission of the Text of Scripture

1. The task of transmitting the scriptures from generation to generation in Judaism was the responsibility of the Scribes. The New Testament was transmitted in written documents, copied and recopied by hand as the need arose. Enough copies of the New Testament manuscripts exist today that we know that errors were made in copying. Some were made by accident, and others in a deliberate effort to clarify difficult passages. What are we to say about this process? Are the scriptures to lose their authority because we do not have the original autographs? If everything hinges on the original autographs, and we have none, then surely we are in trouble in claiming the authority of the scriptures.

I would hold rather that God is still at work establishing His Word. He has given to us more and more manuscripts, better techniques in comparing manuscripts, and through the inspiration of the Spirit he is even now guaranteeing the veracity of the scriptures through those who work with the texts. True, there may be theories proposed here and there that are false, but if so, they will not abide; they will not be confirmed of God.

2. So also with respect to the translation of the scriptures into languages. Is the message to be lost because it is no longer in the original language of Greek, Hebrew or Aramaic? Is the message to be lost because it is sometimes not possible to find an exact word to translate the Greek word? We have many translations and one need only notice the attempts to translate I Corinthians 7: 36-38 to know that they cannot all be right. Are the scriptures in the end to be lost because of faulty translation or paraphrases?

Again I would hold that God is still at work establishing His Word. Though one translation may have served very effectively for many years, God may cause it to die because another says it better. There may be some very problematic translations that may be very popular for a while, but I believe God will give to the church the criteria by which, through the Spirit of God, the more accurate translations will be recognized.

At times God also may choose other ways. If in translation, for example, no word for 'sin' can be found in a language, the translator may choose the word for 'missing the mark' to translate 'sin'. As this term begins to be filled with meaning through the life and ministry of Jesus and the Word of scripture, the new word takes on the connotation of 'sin' in that language.

It is by the power of God at work in the world that the scriptures are preserved for us today. As the apostles were the guardians of the oral tradition, the church is the guardian of the text of the scriptures even now.

E. Biblical Authority and Denominational Tradition

1. The problem of biblical authority and denominational tradition can best be seen in terms of Jesus' encounter with the Scribes from Jerusalem (Mark 7:1-23). They charge Jesus with not accepting the authority of the scriptures, because He does not abide by the "tradition of the fathers" which the Scribes held to be identical with and expressive of the Law of Moses. Jesus makes the counter-charge (7:8) that it is in fact they, the Scribes, who leave the commandments of God to follow the traditions of men.

A closer look will reveal that the Scribes followed very normal procedures of biblical interpretation, procedures that we ourselves cannot avoid.

(a) It is clear that they accepted the scriptures as binding on all Jews. They accepted the Law, the Prophets and the Writings, in short the entire Old Testament, as God's Word. No one could fault the Scribes in taking the scriptures lightly. They were scholars of the Word and authoritative interpreters of the Law.

(b) They found it necessary to interpret the text of scriptures. They found that the law indicated clearly that no work whatsoever was to be done on the Sabbath (Exodus 23:12). It also stated that you could do good on the Sabbath such as freeing an ox from a well (Luke 14:5). But the law did not say in any great detail what constitutes work and what type of 'good' one could do on the Sabbath. Yet such questions needed to be decided if one were going to keep the law. To settle such questions, agreement, often after long study and debate, was reached among the rabbis, as to what would in fact be the right interpretation of the text. On some questions they could not agree, and divided into camps such as that of Hillel and Shemmai on the question of divorce. But there was no possibility of avoiding the task of interpretation, not for them nor for us.

(c) Even where agreement had been reached on interpretation, it did not answer all the questions. New situations were being faced in first century Palestine that were not spoken to in the law. The law, therefore, had to be extended to apply to new situations. Thus the law regulating negligence in the case of an ox ruining a neighbour's property (Exodus 21: 28f) had to be applied to death by negligence in the building trade. If the scriptures were to cover all of life, then this task too became necessary. They knew it was not an easy task and that it was fraught with dangers. To avoid error they made these auxiliary interpretations extra stringent. Out of the interpretation of the Law and in an effort to extend it to cover all aspects of life, a whole complex or oral laws developed.

(d) The Scribes accepted the Law of Moses as authoritative and the entire complex of laws as equally binding, since they were in fact deduced from the Law of Moses. They also made an honest effort to keep the law. Not only that, as Scribes they fasted twice a week, and gave the tithe, and lived an uncompromising life — a rigour that Paul later still regarded as impressive, as he reflected on his life as a Scribe.

The four steps the Scribes took as a result of accepting the scriptures as authority we have to take as well. We cannot avoid them.

2. The affirmation of the authority and inspiration of the scriptures on our part also does not guarantee faultless interpretation of the scriptural text. It is, as we said at the beginning, possible to get away from the intention of the scriptures through interpretation. The affirmation of the scriptures as authority does not necessarily result in uniform understanding and interpretation.

Four authors all accept the verbal plenary view of scripture, but come up with totally different interpretations of Genesis 1. Rimmer[6] holds to six days of 24 hours in the creation week; Carnell[7] speaks of threshold evolution; Ramm[8] prefers to call it progressive creation; and Ridderbos[9] sees in Genesis 1 a literary form of two sets of three days, where day one and four speak about the creation of light, two and five about the firmament above and below, together with birds and fish, and three and six speak about the dry land on which animals and people dwell. As we can see, interpretation is not governed by the particular view of authority.

There are many things besides the deceitfulness of sin that influence the interpretation of scripture. Even where we seek to be utterly sincere in seeking the correct interpretation we will still be carried into different paths. Sometimes it happens simply by the emphases we give to certain sentences. We might think that the five words from Psalm 23 cannot be misconstrued: "The Lord is my Shepherd." Yet we can make five different propositional statements out of it be accenting each word in turn. Through different communions choosing to read certain network of passages with a specific emphasis, a tradition of interpretation develops.

At other times, two persons or confessions fear different enemies and will as a result select certain portions of scripture to be more important than others, or will use the same scripture references in a different way. Thus, for example, those who fear the old style liberalism with its emphasis on the human Jesus will select the virgin birth account to emphasize Jesus' divinity. Those who fear the new liberalism of a

Bultmann, who emphasizes the divine Christ of faith, will use the virgin birth to emphasize the humanity of the son of God.

Circumstances of history and culture have a lot to do with interpretation. I would imagine that Christians in a communist country and Christians in a capitalist country might "exegete" Luke's many words about poverty and riches quite differently. So also the rich interpret differently than the persecuted.

The reasons for differing interpretations are myriad and we can only illustrate the point. What happens, however, is that a tradition gets started and eventually develops its own apologetic systems. In this way, denominations or sects that separate themselves from others through such interpretations and traditions are formed. There is a danger here of being held captive by one's own line of interpretation. Jesus recognized that the Scribes were in such a bind. Their interpretation of the law had become a burden from which people had to be liberated (Matthew 23: 13ff).

3. Jesus criticized the Scribes for having left the commandments of God to follow their own tradition. He faulted them on each of the four items mentioned. (a) He indicated that it was not the scriptures that they attached authority to but rather their own interpretation of scripture. This happens every time we fail to distinguish between the scriptures and our own interpretation of scripture. (b) They did not interpret scripture correctly. They deduced new laws from the Laws of Moses, but they did not perceive the true intention of law (e.g. law of Corban). They were to take the law as indicating the **direction** of God's intention and then to be open to an even more sensitive interpretation of that law, rather than to freeze it for all time as originally given. (c) Jesus charged that through the extension of the law they had actually introduced an interpretation of lesser laws (Corban) in such a way that it would allow them to escape the weightier matters of the law (honour father and mother). (d) Jesus broke also with their practice because they were not following God but their own teachings.

This may give us an indication as to how Jesus relates to traditions of interpretation generally. We notice, first, that Jesus identifies fully and completely with the scriptures and with the tradition that arises out of the scriptures. He indicated that he had come to fulfill the law and the prophets (Matthew 5: 17f); he accepted the Jewish feasts and often attended the festivals in Jerusalem. In short, he affirmed that, in the tradition, that was of God.

Second, there were some things in the tradition of interpretation of the Scribes that He simply rejected. He did not accept their interpretations of the scriptures to be identical with, nor necessarily expressive of, the will of God. Jesus recognized the progressive nature of revelation and on that basis no longer kept the ceremonial law. In like manner, he rejected the special customs and traditions the Scribes had set for themselves (fasting, not eating with sinners, not talking to women publicly, etc.).

Third, Jesus also responded to tradition by deepening it. Thus tradition was right in speaking against killing, but why not deal already with the feeling of hatred? Adultery is wrong, but why not deal with lust in the heart? Jesus asked that we should be perfect as the father in heaven is perfect (Matthew 5:48).

It seems to me Jesus meets our tradition of interpretation in the same way, affirming aspects of it, rejecting other interpretations, and certainly deepening it.

4. We cannot avoid the task of interpreting scripture and the task of applying it to very specific situations in our world. If the Word is to be significant for us, it must again come to us as a promise of God for our own selves and our own time.

There needs to be more than individual interpretation of scripture. A hermeneutic community is needed where the scriptures are studied with an eye to finding the will of God for the total community and for calling forth the gifts of the Spirit in that community. Several things would then become clear(er) in the process.

The community would begin to work on a proper hermeneutic and would call forth a more careful exegesis of scripture. There would be attention to biblical theology before attempts at application would be made. The point is that if people would be searching for the will of God, to which they would commit their lives, much more careful interpretation of the scriptures would be demanded, and would result.

Furthermore, the fellowship would become a binding and loosing fellowship. To be convinced of the will of God through the scriptures and the Spirit would be to commit oneself to it. In this way the church would become a binding fellowship, binding each other to the will of God. It would also be a loosing fellowship, experiencing within the fellowship forgiveness and freedom from the powers of captivity.

DISCIPLINE AND DISCERNMENT

Marlin Jeschke

In his chapter on Discipleship and Authority in **The Believers' Church** Donald Durnbaugh calls for a recovery of church discipline, noting that discipleship, by definition, calls for discipline. In **Discipling the Brother** (see chapter bibliography), the present writer bases his entire conception of church discipline on the analogy between a biblically conceived and practised evangelism and a biblically conformed church discipline.

I. THE LOSS OF BELIEVERS' CHURCH LIFE

My experience since the publication of **Discipling the Brother** in 1972 has been a growing conviction that three-fourths of the problem of church discipline is the lack of clear vision in defining church membership and incorporating members into the church through evangelism, baptism, and education. Sometimes churches try to accomplish in discipline what was not accomplished at a person's entrance into the church. Sometimes churches tolerate in members what they would not condone in a baptismal candidate. Often churches seek to save people initially through preaching of the Word but try to discipline them through application of the law. In short, churches do not have consistent standards or methods in accession and preservation of their members.

Too often today we see on the religious scene the conversions of naughty celebrities who get up from their knees, run for the nearest microphone, and make twice as much money as before, with adulation thrown into the bargain. We see the routine catechizing of twelve-year-olds in our churches. No wonder the practice of church discipline is in bad shape.

In North America, religion has for some time now served as a way to wealth and power just as railroads, oil and sports have done. The financial empires of prominent television preachers stand as exhibitions phenomenon. Religion as a road to success goes back as far as Joseph Smith, but it is more in evidence today than ever before.

Billy Graham is a highly respected evangelist whose honesty and motivations are not questioned. Nevertheless it is of concern to me that Graham, a Baptist coming out of a Believers' Church tradition, has seriously undermined Believers' Church life by compromising believers' baptism with his decision card method of registering conversions (a method adopted to gain the support of all churches in a given community), and by removing evangelism from the context of the congregation, placing it in some football stadium or other public location.

When I was a boy on a Saskatchewan farm, the means of travel and communication were such as to bind most people to some kind of neighbourhood responsibility. The main form of religious life open to anyone was therefore local church membership or participation. But the radio, the auto, television, and the jet plane have radically altered the forms of religious life of people. For some time now, cars have passed each other on the way to church Sunday morning; nevertheless, in most traditional communities people are still invited to congregational accountability.

But TV has ushered in a new pattern of religious life characterized by a guru and his clientele. The auto and jet travel have introduced the Bill Gothard type of seminar or the charismatic renewal weekend rally. These modes of religious life often present a public figure with a groomed TV studio image and a far-flung devoted public supporting constituency.

Martin Marty, in his newsletter **Context** (February 1, 1978) has drawn attention to this:

> ...invisible religion, the completely personalized faith of post-modern times....Today much converting is done not through congregations but by entrepreneurs who have clienteles, not churches. The converts feel sufficiently engaged if they find their guru in the form of a television evangelist, buy the books of a celebrity, talk the code language of 'born-again,' and consort with what the Southern Baptist Convention calls 'Para-churches.'

A radio church of God or tabernacle of the air or drive-in cathedral, while it used to (and for many people still does) supplement but not displace local membership, it now increasingly displaces such membership and becomes the only form of Christian existence an increasing number of Christians want and have.

The consequences of this mode of religious existence are apparent. There is no mutual responsibility between a radio or TV "pastor" and a scattered clientele. The personal life and financial dealings of the TV celebrity are not answerable to a body of believers (e.g. Garner Ted Armstrong). He can largely control what the people of his constituency hear and know, and government stipulations being what they are in a separation of church and state, he needs to make no financial disclosure. Moreover, individual people are far from the radio "pastor," even if he may teach and uphold a serious Christian ethic. People give their donations, too often to compensate for the absence of responsibility in other respects. And all parties to the arrangement like it that way!

It is many of the Believers' Church groups that have been hardest hit by the new forms of religious life, partly because the new organizations' leaders often come from such groups, and also because they speak the language of much of Believers' Church evangelicalism — conscious conversion, the importance of missions and evangelism, and the like.

Some of this, I am convinced, is the result of misinterpretations of Believers' Church concepts. For example, "voluntarism" is taken to mean not so much personal decision in faith as personal private taste in social and moral values. "Free church" means not so much independence of Rome or of Lutheran, Reformed, and Anglican State Churches as it means entirely independent, free-wheeling organizations that are laws unto themselves — congregationalism gone to seed.

It will be as difficult as it is necessary to recover the fundamental principles of the Believers' Church. If, however, we wish to recover authentic Christian and church life, we will need to attack the problem, a process that will no doubt bring discomfort and the loss of some cherished illusions but that will also bring healing and the recovery of biblical faith.

II. THE RECOVERY OF BELIEVERS' CHURCH MEMBERSHIP

The recovery of Believers' Church faith and life must begin with a model of what is meant by the gospel, by conversion, by faith, by baptism and membership in the church. My study of the New Testament has persuaded me that entrance upon faith and life in the body of Christ includes at least five ingredients.

A. Dimensions of Believers' Church Life

1. Entrance upon faith and membership in the body of Christ is inescapably connected in some fashion with the name of Jesus. It signifies believing that **Jesus is the Christ** — to be a "Christian." But to be a Christian means not merely a consent to the formulas and the logic of Nicaea and Chalcedon, not participation in that popular piety that often resembles Krishna worship more than it does New Testament faith. Confession of Jesus as Christ is to act upon the word of Peter that Jesus has been made both Lord and Christ. It is to accept the enthronement of Jesus at the right hand of God, and to acknowledge his reign in one's heart and life.

The appropriate way to make this christological confession is to take up the form of life of Jesus. Baptism is into Christ or into His name. Jesus is the model of the life being adopted, and that new life shows the nature of Christ, or the mind of Christ. Faith involves discipleship of Christ. Church membership means to be united with Christ, to believe in Him, to die and rise with Him, and to reign with Him. It means life "in Christ." In short, Christian life is totally Christ-oriented.

2. In the New Testament, church membership implies also simultaneously life from God's **Holy Spirit**. It means to receive the Spirit of the new age promised by the prophets and by Jesus. It is to be empowered with the life of the Spirit, to be given his companionship. And to receive the Spirit means to be gifted and ordained to a correspondingly appropriate calling or task. The life of the Spirit is nothing less than divine life itself.

3. Church membership, according to the New Testament, signifies **eschatological life**. To believe in Christ and to receive the Spirit means to cross over into the messianic era as part of the recreated community and to adopt the pattern of life of the age to come, tasting its joys and blessings, but also incurring persecution from the people of this present evil age. This move generates a hope for the fulfilment of God's purposes in a "second advent," purposes put in process by the first

advent. And to be united with Christ carries the promise of future life in and with Him.

4. Christian life also implies membership in a **redeemed community**. Faith includes reconciliation, in which the alienations and estrangements of the old age are overcome. Separation from the world leads to participation (**koinonia**) in the church. Through "membership" in the church, people cease to live in isolation.

The membership established by Christian baptism is simultaneously both local and universal, not just one or the other. Baptism is into the church of Christ, not merely into the Charleswood Mennonite Church. If it were baptism into the local church, such would be valid only locally, and transfer to a Brandon church would require a new baptism. Being globally valid, baptism, according to the New Testament model, is valid for any or every local assembly.

But the membership in the universal church of Christ does not render local membership unnecessary or even optional. Instead it makes local membership mandatory, because the New Testament knows of no church except one that finds actual embodiment at Antioch, at Corinth, in Rome, or in Winnipeg.

5. Christian life and church membership according to the New Testament also mean **a new ethical life**. This is always implied in each of the foregoing, and should not need separate mention, but because the point is overlooked even more frequently today than it was in apostolic times, it calls for separate emphasis. Christian faith (and life) means death to an old way of life and resurrection with Christ into a new way. It is called regeneration, acceptance of a new master, and is symbolized as putting off old garments and putting on new ones (which very likely was practised literally in the patristic era, when baptism involved stripping naked for the baptismal "bath").

The primitive church took meticulous care to spell out the ethical dimensions of taking up the Christian walk. Such teaching, of course, consisted not merely of verbal instruction. The church itself was, first of all, a model of the life of the kingdom. In life and word it presented the whole gospel, making sure that the nature of Christian life was not short-changed. Thus converts came with clarity concerning what their step of faith involved.

B. Correcting Distortions of Believers' Church Life

At various times and places, people in the church have thought that some of the aforementioned dimensions of church membership were optional. For example, it has been widely held that one might receive forgiveness but not neccessarily a new nature, or that one might receive spiritual life but not undertake church membership, or that one might receive forgiveness of sin but not the gift of the Holy Spirit, or, again, that one might accept church membership but not regeneration. The above-mentioned dimensions of life in the church are not, however, optional. They must all be held together in a balanced total unity. Because some of these distortions are fairly common, let us examine them briefly.

1. Church life is sometimes conceived as forgiveness without ethical renewal. In too much of western church history, faith has meant almost exclusively the washing away of original sin or remission of past sin. On this view, forgiveness is considered a cancellation of charges or remission of punishment, merely a new formal status before the moral-legal authority of God. But the New Testament shows that to be "forgiven" is to be "given" — to be given a new heart and attitude, the Spirit of Christ.

2. Sometimes faith is viewed as new life in Christ, but without church membership. For some reason it has become fairly common in some Free Church circles to baptize people into Christ's universal church without their making any concrete commitment to a local fellowship. But how is it possible to become a child of God and not accept the consequent responsibilities in the family of God? Or to be indwelt by the Holy Spirit, and not share (**koinonia**) in the community?

To some extent, it must be admitted that churches have brought this upon themselves. Churches have too often misdefined membership to carry extraneous meanings not intrinsic to the life of the kingdom (rules about clothes, hair styles, etc.), and these extraneous definitions of church membership some Christians have then protested and sought to avoid. But one mistake does not correct another. Membership must first be biblically defined and then made normative.

What should church membership actually involve? Here the most common issues immediately crowd in upon us: attendance requirements, financial obligations, and the like. The temptation beckons us to define membership by multiplying the requirements about attendance, residence, financial support or acceptance of the **mores** of the congregation. But is is better, I think, to define membership in terms of the marks given in the New Testament. Such is not an evasion into generalities, but establishing the basis of membership that makes possible a more detailed discussion of requirements and duties within a commonly accepted frame of reference.

3. Too often faith is considered to be forgiveness, but not life in the Holy Spirit. One of the tragedies (the word is not too strong) of traditional Protestant Christianity in both charismatic and mainline churches is the common notion that an initial level of Christian life is possible without the Holy Spirit and that the infilling or baptism of the Spirit is a second work of grace, or at least a separate and distinct experience in the course of the Christian life. For charismatics or Pentecostals this experience is, of course, most desirable, even urgent. For staid church people it is strictly optional, perhaps even undesirable. But both concede it to be separable from initial salvation and/or water baptism.

Here, as in many other apects of religious life, experience tends to follow the way people are coached. They are taught, in the first place, to expect a short-changed first stage of the Christian life — mere "forgiveness" without power, joy, freedom and peace. And then they are coached to expect an effervescent or ecstatic experience of the Spirit that derives a good deal of its character precisely from being divorced from the initial Christian experience of forgiveness, faith in Christ, membership in the church, or ethical life. Naturally both become distorted — forgiveness and enduement with the Spirit — whenever one of them is divorced from the other and sought and accepted by itself alone. The remedy for such distorted notions about initial faith and subsequent baptism of the Spirit is for the church to keep the components in proper connection. These components will then receive a correct definition and expression.

What about the claim, though, that the baptism of the Spirit is a second and separate experience? I personally think there are several explanations possible for this claim. First, in some cases the so-called baptism of the Spirit represents the initial conversion of the individual in question, and an earlier alleged first stage of Christian experience was not a decisive and real conversion. Second, in some cases the so-called baptism of the Spirit is an emotional experience people have been tantalized to seek, which doesn't add much of significance to their Christian life. Third, in most cases Christians have been cheated out of a full and normative experience of grace precisely because these stereotyped options have been the only ones available to them: the idea of conversion as a too-narrowly defined "forgiveness of sins" and then the idea of the Spirit as a too-narrowly defined ecstacy, a high to be enjoyed. As a result, it takes a long time until many believers finally inherit that complete life of love, joy, freedom, peace, righteousness, hope and power that is intended to be every Christian's baptismal birthright.

4. Perhaps most common today (at least in some churches such as my own Mennonite Church) is the notion that baptism involves church membership, but not much more. This notion is fostered by the many organizations all around us that require their minimal dues and then offer their limited benefits. The church comes to be regarded as just one more of these organizations. In theory, church membership may be held to have some consequence for a person's ultimate destiny, but in practice meanwhile church membership serves basically as an acceptance of social conformity, a readiness to "settle down" and to recognize the middle class social and cultural values of the community. Not much of a sense of spiritual transition surrounds the rite of baptism, little sense of "crossing over."

In the New Testament, baptism does, of course, include membership in the body of Christ. But this membership presupposes a spiritual transaction — a call, a new birth, a divine act of ingrafting that goes far beyond conventional socialization.

Meanwhile, what about the inadequate or short-changed concepts we have reviewed? Are those people "saved" who claim forgiveness without Holy Spirit, or Holy Spirit without ethical renewal, or forgiveness without church membership, or church membership without the spirit of Christ? Obviously one cannot make a blanket judgment about a wide range of actual cases. Let us fall back upon an illustration. Suppose two people have been married (in church), have achieved a satisfactory sexual relationship — on those occasions when they visit each other — but apart from that do not live together to share the task of conjointly rearing their children. Are they married? I can imagine people saying, rhetorically, "That's not marriage!" And yet, if pressed, we would concede that technically such people are married. Nevertheless, we would instinctively see some misunderstanding of marriage here, whatever its origin, and we would urge removal of this misunderstanding through proper counseling so that such people could bring their lives into line with the full meaning of marriage.

So it is with faith. New Testament believers, were some to return in our day to see, for example, the church-memberless baptism of some Christians, or the Spiritless "joining the church," would likely say, "That's no baptism!" Our churches must recover the full-orbed biblical meaning of baptism and church membership, to restore to people their rightful spiritual heritage.

The various dimensions of baptism, faith and church membership just discussed are not, according to the New Testament, separable components among which one might pick and choose. They are related and mutually inclusive, mutually implicated. We are not at liberty, for example, to make baptism mean forgiveness but not Holy Spirit, or Holy Spirit but not ethical life. We must remember to keep all the elements together, else we end up with a short-changed definition, an impoverished practice, and perhaps in some cases run the risk of a church life so far removed from its New Testament norms as to be spurious.

III. THE RECOVERY OF BELIEVERS' CHURCH DISCIPLINE

Once the church's vision or norm for church membership is established and upheld, the task of church discipline is the maintenance of such church life, the church reaching out to members who fall short of that norm and restoring them to the life in Christ they should know.

In seeking the way to a recovery of a biblical Believers' Church discipline, I really can do little better than recapitulate the thoughts set out already in my **Discipling the Brother**. The essence of restoring faltering saints, expressed in rather traditional theological language, is this:

The good news of God's grace in Christ has the power to free people from bondage to evil and to remake them in the image of Christ — to launch them upon lives of love, service, peace, righteousness, hope, fellowship, creativity, fulfilment and joy. This potential of the gospel holds not only for the church's initial mission in restoring sinners but also for the task of reclaiming believers who have offended, erred, transgressed or otherwise lost (the) faith. The gospel — the message of Christianity, the Christian faith we hold and teach — is not only a means of rescuing people from the world and from judgment: it is a way of life in this world, the way of God's new humanity.

The two misconceptions I see repeatedly in traditional church discipline are legalism and lenience.

Legalism is, of course, not new. It is a pervasive influence from the Medieval practice of indulgences and the doctrine of purgatory. The Reformers, from Luther to Menno, rejected the practice of indulgences, holding that money does not compensate for sin. God wants a renewed heart and life. The Reformation also condemned the doctrine of purgatory, which also assumed that an offender could pay for his offence, not in this case with money, but by doing time. The guilt of sin was thought to be cancelled out by suffering an appropriate amount of pain.

Despite the Reformation, however, the idea of paying fines and doing time is still ingrained in the mentality of western societies, even Protestant ones, as a means of dealing with offenders. This mentality continues to govern western systems of criminal justice and all too often informs the practice of the church in its treatment of offenders.

The legalistic mentality seems to be endemic to the natural man. It does not, for that matter, originate in the church of the Middle Ages. It is found already in an apostatizing Israel in the Old Testament, an Israel that seeks to multiply sacrifices to God in order to compensate for its transgressions of God's law. As we know, prophets such as Micah disallowed Israel's offer to "trade in" acts of merit in order to offset offences against God and the poor.

The pernicious principle underlying legalism (as I am using the term here) should be evident. Legalism presents the appearance of taking offences seriously and of discouraging offenders from continuing their transgression. In fact, however, the principle underlying legalism proposes an arrangement whereby an offender pays for bad deeds with good ones or offers to make up for offences with an appropriate amount of suffering, pain, or inconvenience. Despite its appearance of taking transgression seriously, legalism ends up excusing or justifying the transgression, since the offence is paid for, as merchandise is paid for in a commercial transaction. In this sense, legalistic arrangements for settling an offence represent an evasion of the problem rather than a resolution of it. But an assault, for example, is not made right by a fine or other punitive sentence. It is made right only by the reconciliation of the assaulter with the one assaulted **and** by his becoming a **non-assaulter**, a person who respects other people instead of hurting them.

Believers' Church thought and practice in discipline must transcend a legalist mentality. Church discipline must not function according to abstract balances of justice nor according to the principle of punishment. It must seek to create the mind, spirit and pattern of life of Christ.

Lenience in church discipline, like legalism, is also not new. Lenience represents an attempt to take seriously the themes of justification by faith, grace and forgivenss. Indeed, lenience is usually the consequence of attempts to avoid the mistake of legalism, without, however, finding the genuinely Christian alternative to legalism. In terms of our illustration above, where legalism calls for punishment of an assaulter, lenience sees the futility of such punishment and therefore merely calls for remission of punishment without pressing the demand for the given individual to become a non-assaulter, without making available the power of judgement and grace to transform the assaulter.

Lenience, in other words, makes a virtue out of compassion and tolerance in the abstract. As already mentioned, it is a retreat from the futility of punishment without an adequate alternative. Such lenience, in fact, usually proves even more futile than legalism. It is therefore used only as a preliminary measure, much as probation is in criminal justice, and/or lenience is complemented by legalism. That is, only selected offences are eligible for lenience (such as fornication or sharp business practices) because the church or state is holding the line on other offences (such as larceny, assault, homicide, or traffic violations).

Lenience in church discipline, whether or not disguised as "forgiveness," is too well known and has demonstrated its failure too often for us to need to argue the point further. There is a decided difference between "letting someone off" and holding out the possibility, value and even necessity of a regenerated mind and life, bringing the resources of the Word of Christ, the power of the Spirit and the support and counsel of the **koinonia** to bear upon the task.

Properly conceived and practised, church discipline is enablement. In the restoration of errant believers the church appropriates the power of grace and of faith to remake people. Such a task is not necessarily easy, though it is easier than legalism or lenience, and it results in positive consequences. As its cognate, discipling, indicates, discipline is not just an act, a judgment or assessment and decision. It is a sustained ministry. In discipline the believing community "hangs in there" with, for example, the person with an alcohol problem, persuaded that it is possible for such a person to receive a new mind and nature. I have seen a marriage reborn, thanks to Christian counsel. Too often the church has lost hope for people caught in problems. It no longer believes in the miracle of regeneration that it still professes and preaches in evangelism and mission.

The good news can re-mould lives. We need to recapture that vision and recommit ourselves to that ministry.

DISCIPLINE AND DISCERNMENT

J. Ernest Runions

In all its ages the church has taught that discipline inheres in the idea, nature, authority and function of the church. The notion of the church of God as a disciplined community is not special to the post-Reformation Believers' Churches. The New Testament church had a prominent discipline. Through the Patristic period discipline was formally rigourous, with a prolonged catechumenate, lengthy penitential rites and dramatic public rituals of repentance and reconciliation. During the Medieval and Renaissance periods discipline moved along two lines. With the rise of the confessional, under the influence of Celtic Christianity, discipline moved along pastoral lines. But in the same period the church developed a rigourous and legalistic attitude to capital offenders, a development ending in the Holy Office and the Inquisition.

The Reformation itself was born of disciplinary zeal. The urge to cleanse the church of everything that betrayed its pristine faith and purity is evident in Oxford, Prague, Florence, Wittenberg, Zurich, Geneva and Edinburgh. In the Radical Reformation discipline became a **cause celebre** and, unfortunately, a point of schism. In later times, the Councils of Trent and Vatican, in their different ways, spoke to the need of discipline in the church.

In the Reformed churches discipline embraced the whole order of the church and society — as witness Calvin's Geneva. The chapter headings in Knox's **Book of Discipline** illustrate how widely the net was cast.[1] Little of life, society or religion lies beyond the Scot's pale!

In the light of this history, the first task facing a study in discipline is to define limits. Jeschke's paper, which precedes this one, helpfully sets discipline in the context of membership in the church of God. In this paper we shall deal only with corrective or post-baptismal discipline. Under that rubric we will explore the New Testament foundations, both textually and theologically, and try to probe pastoral problems connected with discipline.

I. BIBLICAL AND THEOLOGICAL FOUNDATIONS
1. Old Testament Background

It is a truism that the New Testament **ecclesia** is developed against the backdrop of Israel as the covenant people of God, the assembly that seeks God's presence, affirms God's laws, adores God's glory, praises God's mercy and advances God's claims. From its inception, Israel proclaimed "holiness unto the Lord" as a covenant ideal. Forman suggests that two ideas control correction in the Old Testament:

The one motif is built on the concept that life is divided into areas which are of varying degrees of holiness...The other motif arises out of the covenant between God and Israel. In this covenant Israel's obligations are laid down. The covenant is, in the customary manner, endorsed with blessings and curses. He who does not observe and obey the laws of the covenant has thereby broken the covenant and thus no longer stands under God's protection. He is given over to the curse, to misfortune, and in the last extreme, to death.[2]

Holiness in life and religion, and the integrity of the covenant community, were clearly of great importance. Forkman finds these themes in later Judaism, both classical and eccentric; he also finds them in the New Testament, where they are leavened by the idea of the Kingdom of God.

From our point of view the tension can be described as follows. The synoptic presentation of the limits of the community is orientated from the motif of the Kingdom of God, in polemics against community limits orientated from the holiness motif. But for Paul the community limits are orientated from the holiness motif. Yet we have seen how with Paul the effect of the holiness motif was modified by thoughts which are associated with the motif of the Kingdom of God.[3]

2. New Testament Evidence

Discipline and the church come together in three major New Testament passages: Matthew 16: 13-20; Matthew 18: 15-20; Revelation 2, 3. Two other passages illustrate the apostolic implementation of discipline: 1 Corinthians 5: 1-13 and 2 Thessalonians 3: 6-16. Taken together they link the themes of covenant, holiness and the reign of God in Christ.

Matthew makes the first New Testament reference to the church (Matthew 16: 13-20) in the setting of Peter's confession and our Lord's promise of the keys. The idea, nature, authority and function of holy church are thus defined by and grounded in the Lord Christ: the church is His messianic community, gathered upon confession of His name, holding His authority and acting on His instructions.

Kenneth Hein succinctly summarizes the meaning of "the keys":

In Isaiah 22: 22, the image of the transferral of the keys from the master to the servant represents "delegated" dominion which cannot be taken away except by the master himself (Isaiah 22: 19). The symbolism of the keys and the terminology of binding and loosing are technical rabbinical terms which refer primarily to the right to take disciplinary measures. To be bound or loosed means respectively to be put under the ban or to be absolved from it.[4]

The church, then, is wholly the Lord's by establishment, gathering, appointment and action. Yet so divine an institution, holy, catholic and apostolic, is simultaneously human, visible, particular and composed of erring men and women.

Our Lord speaks to the problem of the imperfect humanity of the church in Matthew 18: 15-20. The passage outlines a disciplinary sequence which is at once the action of the church and of Christ. The simultaneity of ecclesial and dominical action in church discipline is highlighted by several features: the simultaneity of earthly and heavenly action is directly asserted (verse 18); the Lord's presence in the human gathering is so certainly assured that the prayers of the assembled believers must infallibly accomplish their purpose (verse 19); the assembly of God is gathered to and with Christ (verse 20): so that as He acts, it acts; as He prays, it prays; as it rebukes, He rebukes; as it excludes, He excludes; as it forgives, He forgives. The "power of the keys" committed to the church rests upon the absolute Lordship of Christ over His church and His utter centrality within it. He tries behaviour and tests doctrine.

The Holy Spirit focuses these teachings upon individual churches in Revelation 2, 3 when the risen Christ walks among the churches on fiery feet, sees them with His blazing eye and corrects them with His two-edged sword.

If the Gospels show us Christ active in the church's action, the Apocalypse shows us His method of action. He entreats, pleads with the churches by His Spirit. He exhorts the church by the Word of His mouth. He corrects the churches by the standards of His own holiness and integrity.

In the Apocalypse the Lord chastises the churches for their failure in discipline; Himself tests their doctrine and conduct; recommends remedies; holds forth rewards; and from within Himself declares the Word of Judgment — a Word filled with mercy, calling to repentance while there is time. Discipline in the Apocalypse begins with Jesus Christ, proceeds from Jesus Christ and ends in Jesus Christ. He grants forgiveness and restoration to repentance, or metes judgment and separation to obduracy.

In the Apocalypse, purity of faith and conduct, and integrity of community stand inseparably linked to Christ's centrality and dominion. All our teaching must advance the truth that Jesus is Lord; all our conduct must exhibit the truth that Jesus is Lord. Anything less destroys the community and falls under the sword of His mouth.

Pauline discipline likewise sets the ideas of personal purity, corporate sanctity, fidelity to the truth and the limits of community under the Lordship of Christ. A close scrutiny of II Thessalonians 3: 6-16 and I Corinthians 5: 1-13 reveals the depth of christological authority committed to the Church.

Biblical discipline is profoundly searching, for it impinges not only upon the offender but upon the whole church of God. Those who wield the authority of the keys must also undergo the judgment of God. They, too, stand under the absolute test of divine purity."[5] Judgment begins at the house of God.

To the Thessalonians Paul is bluntly authoritative when he says, "We command you, brothers" (verse 6).[6] He enjoins them "in the name of our Lord Jesus Christ." That is, as Christ's **shaliach**, Paul is commanding definitively. His command is not arbitrary nor his authority self-appointed. He is himself under the Word of Christ and sets his readers under that same sacred tradition — "the tradition which you received" (verse 6)[7] — a tradition rooted in Jesus. His exhortation to the unruly brother is as the Word of Christ: "We command and exhort in the Lord Jesus Christ" (verse 12). And he implicates the assembly in that same authority: they are to pinpoint the busybody idler and to break fellowship with him.

Here then is a clear line of authority: Christ through apostle to church. Apostolic discipline is christologically determined in the church. The authority, word and action of Christ are involved. The Thessalonian passage could scarcely be more christological. It begins with a command in the name of our Lord Jesus Christ; it appeals to the tradition; it commends the church to Christ (verse 16b).

Similarly, the Corinthian passage is christological. The incestuous member is to be separated from the church by apostolic instruction and action, proceeding under the authority of Christ. When Paul bids the church to gather with his spirit in the name of Christ, the action which he bids is a delegated action, taken in his place. The gathered church will make a decision that is the apostle's decision. But the apostle acts for Christ, so the decision will be Christ's decision. Their ecclesial action will be fully dominical and apostolic.

II. THE PRACTICE OF DISCIPLINE

In the discussion so far, we have reflected that the church by its very nature practises a post-baptismal corrective discipline. A variety of moral and doctrinal aberrations fall under the ban: impenitence, sexual licence, idolatry, avarice, evil speaking, blasphemy, Judaizing, apostasy, the doctrine of the Nicolaitans, factiousness and schism.

Virtually all interpreters understand Matthew 18: 15 to mean that the first step in discipline is to be private.

> We are agreed as follows on the ban: the ban shall be employed with all
> those who have given themselves to the Lord, to walk in His
> commandments, and with all those who are baptized into the one body
> of Christ and who are called brethren or sisters, and yet who slip
> sometimes and fall into error and sin, being inadvertently overtaken.
> The same shall be admonished twice in secret....[8]

This was evidently also St. Paul's method. An erring brother or sister was to be sought out and to be exhorted (not accused) in such a manner that the exhorter was bearing the burden with him. Galatians 5: 1-5 may read as an apostolic exposition of Matthew 18: 15.

This private correction is to be done by "you who are spiritual" — "those who are in obedience of the instruction of verses 16-26, live by the Spirit, walk by the Spirit, as against those who, failing to do so, are still following the **epithumia tes sarkos** [desires of the flesh]."[9] This, coupled with Paul's comments that the exhorter is simultaneously to be examining himself, guards the assembly against gratuitous comments, coercion (always the bane of discipline) and priggishness. The exhorter, no less than the transgressor, is set under the Word of Christ; he is in peril from the same temptations. When a Christian is conscious of being under the same word of correction and in the same peril of falling, the correction he offers is truly pastoral, undertaken in the spirit of meekness and bearing up the other party.

Paul himself gives an example of this careful and gentle exhortation in Philippians 4: 2, in the Pastoral Epistle and supremely in Philemon.

James, whose writing is among the most stringent in the New Testament, suggests much the same approach in 5: 16, which enjoins confession and absolution of sin in the care of the sick — but in such manner as to be a mutual confession and absolution: "Confess your sins to one another."

In the New Testament, the emphasis in discipline falls not upon censure, not upon assessment of guilt, but upon the restoration of the offender to the enjoyment of the benefits of salvation in the church. It is only when private exhortation is ineffectual, or when the sin of the offender is flagrant, that the exhortation is to be done in a more public manner.

"As for those that persist in sin, rebuke them in the presence of all, so that the rest may stand in fear" (1 Timothy 5: 20). "If he refuses to listen to them [the witnesses], tell it to the church..." (Matthew 18: 17). Public discussion may be necessary and even mandatory, but it should be used only as a last resort when other attempts have failed. Should public exposure not effect godly sorrow in the errant member, then the church is solemnly to exclude that member from its fellowship. The member is not merely suspended but excluded as effectively as a Gentile or publican was excluded from the congregation of Israel.

There appears to have been various degrees of banning, ranging from a simple separation, through shunning from eucharistic and social engagement (Romans 16: 17; Titus 3: 10; 2 Thessalonians 3: 14), to a "delivery to Satan." A final act was pronouncing anathema, from which there seems to have been no appeal.

The New Testament does not intend to give a tariff of penalties, but rather to take account of the obduracy of the offender, his persistence in sin (either moral or doctrinal) and the seriousness of his offence. The "anathema" appears to have been reserved for those who blasphemously rejected the gospel of grace and the finality and authority of Jesus Christ (Galatians 1: 8; 1 Corinthians 16: 22). Against the New Testament use of **anathema**, the Tridentine **anathema sit** seems almost flippant and trivial as it attempts to enforce doctrinal conformity and unity of the great church under the Roman hierarchy.

Both the Reformers and the Believers' Churches recognized the authoritative nature of church discipline and recognized that it must be the action of the whole people of God in a given place and not the arbitrary action of an autocrat (neither the New Testament nor the Reformers could tolerate Diotrephes!).

Calvin comments on 1 Corinthians 5: 1-5:

> Let us take notice, then, that in excommunicating this limitation be observed — that this part of discipline be exercised by the common counsel of the elders, and with the consent of the people, and that this is a remedy in opposition to tyranny. For nothing is more at variance with the discipline of Christ than tyranny, for which you open a wide

door, if you give one man the entire power.[10]

And in **The Institutes:**

> Moreover, lest anyone should despise the judgement of the church or count it a small matter to be condemned by the suffrages of the faithful, the Lord has declared that it is nothing else than the promulgation of his own sentence, and that which they do on earth is ratified in heaven.[11]

This was, independently, the Anabaptist view:

> Here it is, indeed, allowed the individual, if aught be done against him personally, to forgive his brother if he bettereth his way; but the full power of the key of Christ, that is to exclude and to accept, hath he not given to individuals, but the whole church.[12]

In the fullness of time it is a view being recovered in the Roman Catholic Church:

> It is the whole Church, the whole community of disciples which bears the authority to forgive sins. Matthew 18: 18 itself...indicates that the whole community of the disciples is addressed here...final judgments, particularly negative ones, are the responsibility not of the individual but of the community.[13]

III. PASTORAL PROBLEM OF DISCIPLINE

The church in all its branches has recoiled from corrective discipline. This may be partly because of a new Babylonian captivity — the church has been secularized all too successfully. But there is more than accommodation to the world in our hesitancy to invoke post-baptismal discipline. We feel revolted by the glaring misuses of discipline in every church tradition. The abuse of discipline has flourished whenever it has been prostituted to power, whether of prelacy or of the group. And its misuse has flourished whenever the fundamental pastoral motivation of discipline has been lost to the interests of institutional purity or doctrinal conformity.

Perhaps it is just at this point that a distortion of emphasis has been sufficient to permit the rise of further abuses. While moral purity in the church and orthodoxy of church doctrine are not irrelevant or peripheral to New Testament concerns, they are quite clearly not at the centre of New Testament teaching on discipline. At the heart of all New Testament discipline is the missionary call to repentance. "Never should zeal for a system, or even for the holiness of the church in the abstract, destroy pastoral care for the individual child of God."[14]

While excision of the offending member may be necessary for the testimony of the church and for the welfare of the body, it is never a desirable step. Amputation is radical surgery! Most to be desired is the godly sorrow that works repentance and the full restoration of the brother or sister.

When Matthew says that we are to "tell him his fault" he uses the verb **elegchein** [to convict]. The LXX (Septuagint) uses this verb to embrace "all aspects of education from the conviction of the sinner to chastisement and punishment, from the instruction of the righteous by severe tests to his direction by teaching and admonition." The New Testament uses the verb "to show someone his sin and to summon him to repentance, to point away from sin to repentance. It implies educative discipline."[15]

The aim of the discussion is to win the brother — ekerdesas ton adelphon sou. The term kerdainein [to win] is filled with missionary zeal. Similarly, Paul recommends that hoi pneumatikoi [the spiritual ones] are to restore or edify or establish (katartizein) the person who is apprehended in sin. The Thessalonians are to shun the idler but they are not to treat him as an enemy but as a brother. The much more severe paradosis to Satana [delivery to Satan] has as its aim the salvation of the offender — if not here, then in the Day of the Lord. "The sinner is to be excluded from every evidence of love in the church in order than he may see his sin and be converted."[16] Both references to "the delivery to Satan" (1 Corinthians 5: 5; 1 Timothy 1: 20) have in mind the recovery, and not the punishment, of the sinner. With apostolic authority, Paul had delivered Hymenaeus and Alexander to Satan "that they may learn not to blaspheme." Even the severe anathema that appears to cut off the transgressor from hope is ultimately a "devotion to the Lord." When anathema is pronounced the church has, so far as it knows, severed the wicked person from the people of God with eschatologic finality — and yet it has so bound the sinner over to God that his final destiny must be left in the hands of the Judge of all the earth.

Maintaining ecclesial purity is a secondary matter in discipline, although it is clearly present in the major Pauline texts. Paul concludes his Corinthian discussion with a quotation from Deuteronomy, "Drive out the wicked person from among you" — a clause with special reference to purging Israel of false prophets (Deuteronomy 13: 5), idolatry (Deuteronomy 17: 7), sexual irregularity (Deuteronomy 22: 24) and rapacity (Deuteronomy 24: 7).

But the purity of the church, in conduct and in gospel, is more a matter of pastoral concern than it is of institutional sanctity. Only as the church is cleansed of evil can it adequately witness to and participate in the benefits of salvation. Paul develops this theme eloquently in Ephesians 4: 25-5: 27. Greenslade wisely reminds us:

> Just insofar as this discipline was "not" intended to secure forgiveness which comes through repentance and faith but rather to preserve the purity of the Church, it may run into legalism again and may be punitive in its operation.[17]

Discipline invites abuse when it displaces reconciliation-of-the-brother with purity-of-the-church.

When purity is made central, perhaps no misuses are more obvious than the demand for behavioural conformity and increasing trivialization of discipline. Whenever conformity is demanded, coercion is inevitable. The church becomes a moral court trying trivia. Sentences and punishment become the end of discipline rather than spiritual watchcare.

Trivialization of discipline and coercion of behaviour have eroded the credibility of many Believers' Churches. Epp cites the ill repute early Saskatchewan Mennonites earned in the ugly Wiens/Friesen controversy.[18] Similarly, the history of early Canadian Baptists reflects not only their moral earnestness but also their insistence upon behavioural conformity.[19] Greenslade summarizes well the intent of discipline in the New Testament:

> Truly salutary discipline is possible when the congregation supports the sinner, sharing the sorrow of the penitent, praying for and with him, pointing forward to reconciliation. This is impossible if discipline is made trivial.[20]

IV. CONCLUSION

Discipline is an action of a community under the dominion of Christ. The action may be negative, when every attempt at reconciling the brother or sister has failed. But much more commonly, and always to be desired, it is an act of reconciliation by which the church greets the penitent. Discipline must remain the action of the gathered church, acting no doubt on the advice — but not at the bidding — of its local leadership. And the only tradition which must be allowed to condition the assembly's disciplinary action (whether of exclusion or absolution) is the Gospel tradition of the New Testament under which the assembly is constituted. As the gathered church surrenders itself to the sacred Word, in and by the Spirit, it discerns truth and error both of belief and of conduct. By that Word, the church is itself being continuously corrected and renewed; and it is the proclamation of the Word that calls the sinner to repentance and offers him a full restoration to the church of God. If the sinner remains unrepentant, the Word of mercy becomes a Word of judgment. This radical submission of the whole assembly to the Spirit's scrutiny and instruction by the Word is the only safeguard against coercion, against trivialization, against favouritism, against harshness and against relativism in discipline.

EVANGELISM: CHRISTIAN INITIATION AND NURTURE

Eugene M. Thompson

I. THE NECESSITY OF CONVERSION

Virtually all Reformation churches emphasize personal faith. However, those in the Believers' Church tradition insist that we also affirm and implement the implications of personal religion. The Believers' Church movement, which took various forms in sixteenth century Europe, held in common the view that the church is to be composed only of believers who voluntarily repent and believe. They emphasized the necessity of conversion from the world to Christ, and of a transformed life. Our understanding of the nature of conversion, then, is basic to our concepts of evangelism and Christian nurture.

In Believers' Churches people are frequently invited to become converted. This invitation is extended to young people and children as well as to adults. Can such a request be justified, or can people simply grow into the Christian life without such a "decision for Christ?" In the New Testament the word sometimes translated "to convert" is **epistrepho** which means "to turn." "In the New Testament **epistrepho** occurs thirty-nine times and the noun **epistrephe** once. Half the instances are in Luke's writings. Again about half have a spatial reference and denote physical movement."[1]

> In its varied usage **epistrephe** points toward the element of choice, which is made by a competent person who wills to turn to God. Only such a willful engagement of a whole person with God in a responsible decision is truly conversion. Although one may turn at various times in his Christian experience, there is a definitive turning that sets the total direction of one's life and it is the first step of the continuing process of personal transformation.[2]

In conversion there is the willing act of turning to God in Christ. A.H. Strong defines conversion as

> ...that voluntary change in the mind of the sinner, in which he turns, on the one hand, from sin, and on the other hand, to Christ. The former or negative element in conversion, namely the turning from sin, we denominate repentance. The latter or positive element in conversion, namely, the turning to Christ, we denominate faith.[3]

Conversion occurs when a responsible, willing person commits himself to Jesus Christ as Saviour and Lord. "Allowance may be made for conversion being a gradual rather than an instant experience. But is is always regarded as an event — the point in one's experience where he alone responds as a competent person to God's gracious offer of redemption.[4]

Repentance and faith are the two conditions for conversion. Repentance is the turning from sin to God. Faith primarily means trust and commitment in a personal relationship with God. Faith (**pistis**) is not an affirmation of a set of propositions. A person is not saved by his understanding, although understanding will be involved.

> The propositions are important in that they set before us a picture of Jesus Christ and His claims upon us in all our attitudes, action, and conduct in the world. The believer does not have to be a theologian. He is not saved by understanding. But he should be capable of enough cognitive grasp of the **kerygma** to have at least a rudimentary understanding of the gospel and its claims upon his life.[5]

Because we use such language as decision, commitment and personal faith it should not be assumed that this means that man is the author of his own salvation. "Faith is the gift of God in the sense that such voluntary surrender and obedience would be impossible unless God had first acted in Christ. Yet faith is also truly our own. If it were not, it would be purely automatic and would have been destroyed.[6]

In the minds of some, of whom Horace Bushnell was the leading exponent, children are to be trained from birth always to think of themselves as being Christians. This point of view fits in well with infant baptism but runs counter to the traditional Believers' Church emphasis upon the necessity of conversion for all, including those who are children of believing parents.

In the New Testament one finds an emphasis upon conversion. However, certain studies have pointed away from conversion being necessary for all. Some New Testament scholars believe they have discovered the core of the primitive Christian message or preaching called the **kerygma**. This is the material addressed to those outside the church family who were not Christians and which informs them concerning the incarnation of God in Christ, His ministry and death, resurrection, ascension and promised return. The rest of the writings are **didache** or teachings. Concerning Acts 2, C.H. Dodd says:

> The age of fulfillment has dawned...this has taken place through the ministry, death, and resurrection of Jesus...by virtue of the resurrection, Jesus has been exalted at the right hand of God, as Messianic head of the new Israel...The Holy Spirit in the church is the sign of Christ's present power and glory...The Messianic Age will shortly reach its culimination in the return of Christ...the kerygma always closes with an appeal for repentance, the offer of forgiveness and of the Holy Spirit, and the promise of "Salvation," that is of the "Life of the age to come."[7]

The **kerygma** includes the Gospels of Mark and John, and Acts chapter two. The **didache** consists of the teachings ascribed to Jesus, largely comprising the Gospels of Matthew and Luke. Certain scholars believe that the **kerygma** was directed to those outside the church while those within the church family were taught the **didache** without the conversion or repentance emphasis. In other words, those who were already under Christian influence (including the children of Christians) were not in need of the **kerygma** (repentance and conversion). If this is true, much of the emphasis the Believers' Churches have placed on the necessity of conversion for all is wrong. This interpretation of **kerygma** and **didache** seems to lend support to those who would teach that children of believing parents are already within the household of God and that conversion for them is unnecessary. This teaching has not gone unchallenged. In referring to this teaching about **kerygma** and **didache**, Donald Gordon Stewart in his book, **Christian Education and Evangelism**, says that "...by this division of the New Testament a dichotomy is constructed wherein the gospel message of salvation is separated from man's act of faith that issues in personal trust and commitment."[8] J. Stanley Glen made the following statement:

> This widely accepted representation of the New Testament conception
> of preaching (kerygma) and teaching (didache) fails...to do justice to
> the unity that, on biblical grounds, ought to obtain between them...the
> problem [is] due to an excessive dependence on documentary defini-
> tions...teaching is merely the doctrine and ethics which interpret
> the kerygma.[9]

It is questionable whether the division between **kerygma** and **didache** can be maintained as clearly as Dodd indicates. It would appear that there was an overlapping and interaction between the two. This inter-action can be seen in the advice of Paul to Timothy: "Do the work of an evangelist" (II Timothy 4:5). But he also said, "You then, my son, be strong in the grace that is in Christ Jesus, and whatsoever you have heard from me before many witnesses entrust to faithful men who will be able to teach others also" (II Timothy 2:2). Apparently a teacher could be an evangelist, and **vice versa**. It is questionable, from a study of the New Testament, whether we can separate nurture from conversion. Evangelism, conversion and Christian nurture are to go hand-in-hand.

II. THE HISTORICAL BACKGROUND

The relationship between conversion and Christian nurture can be traced to the beginnings of the Christian church. When Christianity became the state religion it was natural for those who were citizens of that country to be considered as Christians. Infant baptism was well suited to this situation. In some cases an emphasis was placed upon children being reared in Christian homes, but the necessity of a personal faith and conversion was not stressed. Even the Protestant Reformation did not substantially change this situation. Menno Simons (1496-1561) wrote: "We are not regenerated because we have been baptized...but we are baptized because we have been regenerated by faith and the Word of God (I Peter 1:23). Regeneration is not the result of baptism, but baptism is the result of regeneration.[10] In the seventeenth century the Pietist movement developed among the Lutherans in Germany.

> While the orthodox Lutherans emphasized that the new birth took
> place in baptism, the pietists favoured a personal, immediate

experience of regeneration by the Holy Spirit. This would begin with repentance followed by faith as grace was received and appropriated. Conversion was then experienced producing an immediate sensation in the heart. This sensation was the seal of assurance that one was converted.[11]

For the Calvinist, conversion was not necessarily immediate but often took a long time as he sought the mercy of God, agonized over sin and then with repentance eventually realized that he was redeemed.

For the Calvinists the foundation of conversion was the sovereignty of God. That some are saved is an act of grace. Later this was modified through "covenant theology" where God meets man on terms of the covenant. If man would do certain things God would do His part. The Puritans operated on the covenant theology and believed that their children were part of the covenant based upon the parent's faith.[12]

It was during the First Great Awakening of the 1700s that the emphasis upon conversion gained momentum. Beginning with George Whitefield, who arrived in New England in 1740, the evangelists of the awakening taught that man might have a direct, personal relationship with God. The outstanding preacher of the era was Jonathan Edwards. Edwards believed in the importance of conversion and sought to explain the phenomenon. "No complex of propositional beliefs, creedal affirmations, or traditional formulations guaranteed religious truth. He made it clear that true religion was more than affection — but without the affections, faith did not exist."[13] Edwards wrote: "Conversion is a great and glorious work of God's power, at once changing the heart, and infusing life into the dead soul, though that grace that is then implanted does more gradually display itself in some than others."[14] Dennis M. Campbell says that, according to Edwards, "the knowledge of God involved more than rational consent, not that religion was irrational, but rather the category of 'rationality' was itself insufficient. Faith was appropriated by the whole man, not merely by man the thinker."[15]

The impact of the First Great Awakening and its emphasis upon conversion reached into Canada and had an important influence upon the Believers' Church movement there. In 1776 a farmer by the name of Henry Alline of Falmouth, Nova Scotia, preached his first sermon and became the New Light evangelist who led a revival which was to sweep the province and see old churches revived and new ones established. Although Alline was a Congregationalist, through his preaching nearly every Congregationalist church in the province became Baptist. More than to any other single person, Baptists in Canada owe their existence to him. George A. Rawlyk says there are certain things we can still learn from Alline:

First, Henry Alline was not afraid to stress, without qualification, the central importance of the "New Birth" or regeneration...to abandon this central truth or to shove it off to some ideological periphery was to prepare the way for both disaster and spiritual hypocrisy. Second, Henry Alline obviously placed considerable stress on the mystical and pietistic side of the Gospel. Contemporary Christians abandon these at their peril. The emotional and rational appeal of Christianity must blend together.[16]

The emphasis upon the importance of conversion received a great setback in the writings of Horace Bushnell, who was born in Connecticut in 1802. His influence spread across the continent and into Canada. Bushnell felt that the Great Awakening had greatly exaggerated the role of the individual and that it did not place enough emphasis on the family and the church. He was not satisfied with any theory that tied church membership to conversion. His key emphasis was that "the child is to grow up as a Christian, and never know himself as being otherwise."[17] Bushnell also made the statement: "Train up a child 'How'? for future conversion? — No, but in the way he should go and when he is old he will not depart from it."[18]

Added to this teaching of Bushnell, which still has its influence, is the current accusation that an emphasis upon personal evangelism and conversion tends to blind people to social concerns. Certainly the Believers' Church movement cannot ignore these criticisms, whether they be from Bushnell or from modern sources such as the evangelism department of the National Council of Churches of Christ in the U.S.A. and the World Council of Churches study on the mission and structure of the church. These groups say that evangelism today must be located in the secular world and especially in its power structures. Advocates of personal evangelism are accused of being devoid of social concern. John Howard Yoder, a Mennonite scholar, asserts that the stance of the Believers' Churches cuts across the debate between social concern and personal evangelism to form a new configuration:

> The error of individualism is not adequately tempered by insisting that saved individuals will get together sometimes or that saved individuals will be socially effective. But neither is it to be corrected by replacing personal change and commitment with the remodeling of the total society. The complement to personal decision is the "new humanity" of covenant community...The political novelty which God brings into the world is a community of those who serve instead of ruling, who suffer instead of inflicting suffering, whose fellowship crosses social lines instead of reinforcing them. This new Christian community in which the walls are broken down not by human idealism or democratic legalism but by the work of Christ, is not only a vehicle of the Gospel or fruit of the Gospel; it is the good news. It is not merely the agent of mission or the constituency of a mission agency. This is the mission.[19]

Donald F. Durnbaugh illustrates how the division between an individual and a social approach to evangelism has been cut across by Believers' Church groups. Referring to the above statement by Yoder he says:

> A review of the history of the Believers' Church shows that this position is close to the truth. Anabaptists did not have the cause of religious liberty in the commonwealth in mind when they demanded freedom from the state to worship, but their suffering witness helped to

establish it. The Quakers' testimony against slavery proved to be a major factor in its abolition. John Wesley's determination to have a well-ordered church was not designed to stabilize the English proletariat, but it is assessed to have done just that.[20]

In order for the church to make this kind of impression upon society, a strong sense of community must be maintained. This emphasis upon community influences our understanding of conversion, evangelism and Christian nurture. The locus of conversion is important. Within recent years, conversion has sometimes been seen as something not necessarily related to the church nor needed to be followed up by the church. Through the Jesus Movement young people were converted and in some cases baptized without relating to a local church. In order to avoid such an extreme individualism in the conversion experience, a strong emphasis upon the church as community should be made. Although we cannot limit where and how God may speak to an individual, yet the response to that speaking seems best to be carried out in the community of faith where involvement with other persons is experienced, where social responsibility is emphasized and where Christian nurture can continue.

III. CONVERSION AS EXPERIENCE

A person's understanding of conversion grows out of his theology of Christian experience, although Christian experience is wider than that of conversion. "In common usage, experience is taken to mean the interaction which takes place between a perceiving subject and the object of its perception."[21] Religious experience is not merely a subjective feeling. "To have an experience implies the existence of the object as distinct from the subject."[22] William James in his classic book **The Varieties of Religious Experience** (in which, incidentally, he refers to Alline) says: "It is as if there were in the human consciousness a sense of reality, a feeling of objective presence, a perception of what we may call 'something there'."[23] This same experience was explained by Rudolph Otto when he said that "the nouminous is felt as objective and outside the self."[24]

A number of theologians have taken experience as the departure point for theology. These include Friedrich Schleiermacher, Rudolph Bultmann and Otto Weber. Each of these has made experience the key note of his theology, giving little place to reason in experience. Bultmann expressed his understanding of religious experience when he said:

> It remains to keep oneself open at all times for the encounter with God in the world, in time. It is not the acknowledgement of an image of God, be it ever so current, that is real faith in God; rather, it is the readiness for the eternal to encounter us at any time in the present — at any time in the varying situations of life.[25]

Applied to the situation of the local church, this approach would discourage the desire for biblical knowledge as well as discourage the use of reason in the conversion experience. It would appear from this that God makes himself known at certain dramatic moments but between times He is absent or quiescent.

The importance of conversion has been seen by Emil Brunner, but he says it is difficult for conversion to occur in certain church settings.

> Conversion to Christ is not a real possibility within the Constantinian Church situation, since there everyone is a baptized Christian. This is the reason why conversion is hardly mentioned there. This at once becomes clear when a comparison is made with the situation in the Free Churches of America. Here the concept of conversion is central, because the man who turns to the church turns thereby at the same time to Christ. It is then not only a theology different from that of the Reformers, but the historical reality, which has there kept the event of conversion true to its biblical sense.[26]

A number of recent theologians have seen the importance of linking Christian experience to the scriptures and the historical Jesus. This is especially true of the "theology of hope" theologians, of which Wolfhart Pannenberg is one. For him, Christianity must move out of the world of experience into a faith based upon the historical Jesus. He does not deny the importance of experience but insists that it must be linked with history. He even goes so far as to say: "Certainly the believer knows very well that Jesus not only lived in the past but that as the risen and exalted Lord He is also alive today. However, one cannot achieve such knowledge about the living present Lord through direct, present day experience in association with the exalted Lord."[27]

Conversion involves experience which is related to the biblical revelation. Experience which does not conform to that revelation of God as seen in the scriptures, especially as seen in Jesus Christ, is to be questioned. This is not to say that God does not speak in other ways, but the scriptures are to be the norm of our experiences. Christian experience usually issues from a variety of sources but it is more than the sum of these sources.

A variety of factors enters into conversion as religious experience. Besides being a personal encounter with God in Christ, it involves information about the Deity which we obtain through a knowledge of the scriptures. It involves the rational use of our minds as we interpret our experience. It also includes societal aspects as we experience community with others who have had, or seek to have, a similar experience. The mixture as to what is involved when a person is converted to Jesus Christ will vary from person to person. What is important to notice is that Christian experience does not happen in a vacuum but through a number of forces being used by God, many of which may appear to be very human. Evangelism and nurture leading to conversion seek to provide a background through which God may work. Conversion is not an isolated event but includes cognitive aspects as well as experiential. Conversion and nurture cannot be separated, as nurture leads to the conversion experience, is involved in it and continues to build upon it. This being so, the locus of conversion is important and the teaching leading up to conversion is of great importance.

IV. NURTURE PRIOR TO CONVERSION

In evangelical churches, Christian nurture is usually a reference to what takes place following conversion. This can be understood because of the great emphasis upon conversion, the "new birth" being the beginning. However, the importance of nurture before conversion, and leading to conversion, should not be ignored. Christian nurture should be seen as covering the total age span. In some churches a service of presentation of children and dedication of parents provides the opportunity to emphasize the important part that Christian nurture plays within the church and the family. This service should include a reminder to both the church and the family that one of their goals is to assist the child in eventually making a personal decision for Jesus Christ.

The church as the locus for both conversion and nurture is extremely important to the individual. Cyprian, the third century bishop of Carthage, wrote, "Whoever and whatsoever he may be, he is not a Christian who is not in the church of Christ." Few of us would be as certain about this as Cyprian, but the church nevertheless is the chosen vehicle of God. In providing the locus for conversion the church must see its educational programme not only as preparation for conversion, but also as preparation for living the Christian life. To place the emphasis primarily on preparation for conversion, to the neglect of preparation for Christian living, would be to neglect the formative stages of a child's development when patterns are moulded which will affect him throughout his life. To be sure, the full implications of this will not be understood nor appreciated until after he has made his personal decision for Christ, but nevertheless it should be there. The same holds true of the fellowship of the Christian community. Although in the Believers' Church one does not become a member until after conversion, yet the knowledge that one is loved and supported by the Christian community is important for the spiritual development of the person and in leading a person to make a decision for Christ and His church.

V. EVANGELISM AND CONVERSION

Although the person who has not yet professed Christ as Saviour and Lord ought to be the object of the church's nurture and fellowship, the importance of conversion and hence evangelism should be kept constantly in mind.

> Conversion is the point of transition from the old life to the new. It is the line of the demarcation between death and life, darkness and light, world and Kingdom of God, evil and goodness, sin and salvation, flesh and spirit, self and Christ...Conversion represents the **real** turning from the one sphere to the other, and the **real** beginning of a new creation in Christ. And that turning is nothing other than an authentic and responsive personal encounter between the sinner and the Saviour.[28]

Because it is through conversion and not nurture (as important as that is) that one becomes a Christian, evangelism is of great importance to

Believers' Churches.

> Evangelism may be defined as the effort to lead the individual to a
> personal acceptance of Christ and his way of life. This, evangelical
> Christians regard as the activity next after instruction and the most
> important until accomplished. It may be done privately, in a class, a
> department, or a social assembly either during a revival meeting or
> apart from one. Some religious educators think this activity is out of
> harmony with the educational method...but such is not the case. If
> education includes response to truth taught, then it involves evan-
> gelism; for it is leading the pupil to respond to the truth taught about
> Christ.[29]

The importance of Christian nurture both before and after conversion
indicates that evangelism must be an integral part of church education.
Evangelism which operates apart from teaching and nurture operates
in a vacuum and tends to produce converts who have made an emotional
response, but are lacking in Christian knowledge. If these converts
receive immediate nurture and community support they can grow, but
unfortunately many who make such decisions do not mature. Pre-
evangelism nurture is important for those who have grown up in the
church as well as those who have been outside the church. The loving
support and interest of individuals, as well as the teaching of the church
through classes and activities, lays the groundwork for effective evangelism. This does not mean that efforts to reach those who have not had
the opportunity for such nurture should be reduced. Every effort should
be made to reach every person, but the important link between nurture
and evangelism must be understood.

In a similar way, the evangelistic efforts undertaken must be in
recognition of the importance of the church. The church as the locus of
conversion has already been mentioned. Suffice it to be said here that
the scriptures teach the linking of evangelism with the church.

> The New Testament knows nothing of an evangelism that leaves the
> saved to live apart from the churches. Whatever good may be done by
> methods and institutions apart from the churches of Christ, we must
> remember that Christ has put his honour upon the churches, and has
> chosen them to be channels through which to work out his purpose
> among men.[30]

While recognizing the importance of the evanglistic work being done by
para-church organizations and by television and radio evangelists, care
must be taken to see that individuals reached through these means
become associated with the church. A form of "easy Christianity"
without responsibility and community can be misleading and
destructive to individuals as well as to the church.

When believer's baptism is viewed as an initiation into the Christian
church, as well as into the Christian life, some of the difficulties relating
to para-church organizations are overcome. In recent years, some
sections of the Believers' Church have placed little emphasis upon the
relationship between baptism and church membership, so that
sometimes individuals are baptized without becoming members. In the

New Testament, apparently there was a strong relationship between baptism and being a part of the church. On the day of Pentecost "they that gladly received his (Peter's) word were baptized; and the same day there were added unto them about three thousand souls" (Acts 2: 41). Neville Clark points out that

> between the Christ who has come and the Christ who will come, lives the church, the visible embodiment of the kingdom, the community of those who have heard the Word and responded to it, and by baptism have been engrafted into the Body of the Lord.[31]

By emphasizing the relationship between baptism and the church, those who have been brought to a saving faith in Christ through television, radio and para-church organizations can be helped to see that the church is not simply something added to their faith but an integral part of what God has intended for them.

VI. CONCLUSION

Believers' Churches in Canada have a responsibility to proclaim with a clear voice the necessity of conversion, and that Jesus' words to Nicodemus, "You must be born again," apply to all. Church leaders and workers must realize that conversion affects the depths of one's being and therefore normally involves emotion, the will and the intellect. All religious experience, including conversion, must be seen against the background of the teachings about God and man as found in the scriptures. If religious experience does not conform to such teachings, then the validity of such experiences must be questioned. Conversion is to be rooted in the historical Jesus, as well as in immediate religious experience.

There is no particular age for conversion, but it should not be expected before the age of accountability when the person is able to understand the central meaning of the event. Conversion, or the outward declaration of conversion, should be related to the church as community. The church should also be the locus of nurture for the individual Christian, leading to and subsequent to conversion. Evangelism and Christian nurture should not be seen as separate from each other, but relating to and relying on each other. Conversion and nurture are to be interrelated in the life of the individual as well as in the ministry of the church.

Conversion itself is brought about by the activity of the Holy Spirit who "reproves the world of sin" (John 16: 8) and guides men into the truth (John 16: 13). However, we have the responsibility of providing the setting and background through which the Holy Spirit may work. Let us provide that setting well through Christian nurture, evangelism and a strong, loving, believing community — the church.

EVANGELISM: INITIATION AND NURTURE

Henry J. Gerbrandt

INTRODUCTION

God created man and woman, placed them into the garden of Eden, and in the cool of the evening had fellowship with them. He set man and woman over His creation and instructed them to have dominion. The Psalmist sings, "What is man that thou art mindful of him, and the son of man that thou dost care for him? Yet thou hast made him little less than God and dost crown him with glory and honour. Thou hast given him dominion over the works of thy hands; thou hast put all things under his feet" (Psalm 8: 4-6). But man sinned, became separated from God and fell short of God's intended destiny of fellowship, honour and dominion. This broken relationship has enveloped the whole human race. "All have sinned and fall short of the glory of God" (Romans 3: 23).

The total thrust of God's revelation after the Fall is directed to man's return to felowship. The garden of Eden question, "Adam, where are you?" finds its fullest response in the eschatological vision of John in the final affirmation over evil. Fellowship has been restored.

In the intervening periods of time, from the Fall to the final victory, God is at work re-establishing fellowship with His creation. To Abraham, the Lord said, "In you all the families of the earth shall be blessed" (Genesis 12: 3). Lot was called to come out of Sodom, and Jonah was sent to call to repentance the sinning Ninevites. Ezekiel's bold invitation to Israel to return to God has echoed through the centuries, "I will judge you, O house of Israel, everyone according to his ways, says the Lord God. Repent and turn from all your transgressions which you have committed against me and get yourselves a new heart and a new spirit...I have no pleasure in the death of anyone, says the Lord God; so turn and live" (Ezekiel 18: 30,32).

The love and zeal of God for mankind's return to fellowship with Him shine forth even more clearly through the New Testament. The "joy to all people" of the angelic message on Bethelehem's hills is placed into focus by Jesus' words, "I am come to seek and to save that which is lost." The love of the father for the prodigal son incarnates Jesus' concern for the erring. Jesus' mission to return people to the fellowship of His Father took on a sobering image when He said, "The Son of Man came not to be served but to serve, and to give his life as a ranson for many" (Matthew 20: 28). And finally, the apostle Paul captures beautifully the intended inclusiveness of the saving ministry of God in his brief summary of the gospel, "It is the power of God for salvation to **every one** who has faith, to the Jew first and also to the Greek" (Romans 1: 16).

Jesus spelled out for His disciples the characteristics that would make them known in the world, "You are the salt of the earth...you are the light of the world...it gives light to all in the house...Let your light so shine before men that they may see your good works and give glory to your Father who is in heaven" (Matthew 5:13-16). Jesus also shared the secret for the source of power and the all-inclusiveness of the disciples' commission, "You shall receive power when the Holy Spirit has come upon you; you shall be witnesses in Jerusalem and in all Judea and Samaria and to the end of the earth" (Acts 1:8).

The church is the **visible expression** of the redeemed people of God who have entered into a covenant relationship with God and with each other in order to glorify God and be His agents of reconciliation. In the Believers' Church we understand that the initiation into the company of believers is not a passive induction in infancy but an active commitment of faith in response to God's invitation to a reasonably mature person.

Within the Believers' Church there is a wide range of positions regarding initiation to the faith. We believe in conversion, either gradual or sudden; either gentle or violent; either as a one-time experience at a given point in history or as a continuous process that must constantly help the believer to bring all areas of life under the light of Christ's cleansing power. We believe in the Christian nurture of our children, but we also believe in the altar call, inviting the obvious sinner to repent. We believe that baptism symbolizes our union with Christ, or we believe that baptism is an integral ingredient of the conversion experience.

These various positions are not necessarily always contradictory. Rather, they speak of the magnitude of the gospel, of the influence of our respective journeys through the centuries and of the various needs of different people at different levels of maturation. Some denominations within the Believers' Church will place more emphasis on the Christian nurture of children, whereas others will stress the radical conversion experience.

This diversity of experiencing new life is not unique to the Believers' Church. Jesus' disciples did not all have the same kind of initiation experience to the faith. Two opposite illustrations of coming to newness of life are portrayed by the turbulent journey to faith experienced by Saul of Tarsus and a more placid entry into the faith by Timothy.

This paper will not seek to give definitive answers to these various positions. Suffice it to say that I believe faith in Jesus Christ must have a beginning. I believe there must be knowledgeable faith-commitment to Jesus Christ. Though not all people can point to the moment of time when they first believed, I personally find it rather important that Christians do know when they became Christians or gained the assurance. We have many weak "Christians" who do not really know when, or even if, they ever turned around to follow Christ.

Gabriel Fackre, speaking of the current hunger for the supernatural says:

Converts are those who have done an about-face, assumed a new posture, and launched a new pilgrimage. They have turned from darkness to light, from the idols of mammon and power, from the gods of arrogance or apathy, pride or lust, to the God of mercy and justice who shines in the face of Jesus Christ. And the turned ones are those who not only see the Light, but who see in the Light the wretched of the earth, and seeing, serve the neighbour in need."[1]

This theme, evangelism and ecclesiology, or initiation and Christian nurture, contains two rather salient foci. Initiation includes the whole area of conversion, including Christian nurture in Christian homes prior to conversion. Initiation into the Christian faith is being treated by Eugene M. Thompson in a companion paper. The focus in the present paper is on the nurture that follows conversion. I am discussing the care of the baby after it has been born, the nurturing of the believer in the context of the corporate body of believers. My understanding of my theme comes out of my particular segment of the Anabaptist tradition.

INITIATION INTO A NEW PERSPECTIVE

I find Jesus' evangelism ministry very intriguing. He called Andrew, Peter, John, James and Levi to follow Him. He told Nicodemus to be born again, and He told the sinful woman who washed His feet that her sins were forgiven. Generally, it appears, Jesus was more concerned with how people followed and fellowshipped with Him than how this following began. Naturally, there can be no following if there is no beginning.

Jesus yearned intensely for the followship of men. It hurt Him very much when people turned away. Peter stabbed Him deeply when he denied Him. Jesus looked upon people who were outside of faith or fellowship as missing God's purpose of creation. Lawrence O. Richards says, "The gospel message speaks particularly to the fallen state of man. The promise of eternal life speaks of a restoration of **lost capacity**. With life comes a **new ability** to perceive reality (Hebrews 11: 13). With life comes a **capacity to experience** and **express genuine love** (I Timothy 1: 5; I Peter 1: 22). With life comes the option of living life responsively with God (Hebrews 2: 12-15)."[2]

The creation of the new person is therefore an act of God to restore to man his lost capacity, to help him perceive reality and to allow him to experience and express genuine love. That capacity to love, be loved, and to fellowship, is precisely what man lost in the garden of Eden and what the prodigal son regained when he returned to his father. Myron Augsburger speaks of evangelism as an **Invitation to Discipleship**. He says, "The gospel tells of a God who acts, involving Himself in man's problems and moving to us in grace, producing spiritual wholeness....the kerygma is a call to conversion, a change of direction that brings our perversity and rebellion to a halt and introduces us into a new life of fellowship with God in Christ."[3]

John Howard Yoder moves to a much fuller dimension of the new creation of the individual. His interpretation of II Corinthians 5: 17, "If anyone is in Christ he is a new creature," places the individual into an entirely new arena. Yoder's focus of the new creation is not limited to the individual's experience but on the new context into which his relation with Christ has placed him.

> Putting together these strictly linguistic observations it becomes enormously more probable that we should lean to the kind of translation favoured by the more recent translators: literally, 'if anyone is in Christ, new is creation,' or more smoothly, 'there is a whole new world' (NEB). The accent lies not on transforming the ontology of the person (to say nothing of transforming his psychological or neurological equipment) but on transforming the perspective of one who has accepted Christ as his context.

> This is certainly the point of the rest of the passage in question. Paul is explaining why he no longer regards anyone from the human point of view; why he does not regard Jew as Jew or Greek as Greek, but rather looks at every man in the light of the new world which begins in Christ. 'The old has passed away, behold the new has come,' is a social or historical statement, not an introspective or emotional one.[4]

CHRISTIAN NURTURE AND GROWTH

The Believers' Church practises baptism on faith in Jesus Christ. Through a careful study of scripture, much prayer and intense agony, certain believers in the sixteenth century reformation movement came to the conviction that baptism is for those who are believers.

> Conrad Grebel, Felix Manz, and others came together and found that there was among themselves agreement in faith. They realized in the sincere fear of God that it was firstly necessary to obtain from the divine Word and the preaching of the same a true faith which worketh by love, and then to receive the true Christian baptism upon the confessed faith, as the answer of a good conscience toward God (I Peter 3: 21), being resolved henceforth to serve God in all godliness of a holy Christian life and to be steadfast in affliction (persecution) to the end.

> And it further came to pass as they were assembled together, that great anxiety came upon them and they were moved in their hearts. Then they unitedly bowed their knees before God Almighty in Heaven and called upon Him, the Searcher of all hearts, and implored Him to grant them grace to do His divine will, and that He would bestow upon them His mercy. For flesh and blood and human forwardness did by no means lead them to take such a step, for they knew what would fall to their lot to suffer and endure on account of it.

> After they had risen from their prayer, George Blaurock arose and earnestly asked Conrad Grebel to baptize him with the true Christian baptism upon his faith and knowledge. And entreating him thus, he knelt down and Conrad baptized him since there was at this time no ordained minister to administer this ordinance. After this was done, the others likewise asked George to baptize them. He fulfilled their desire in the sincere fear of God, and thus they gave themselves unitedly to the name of the Lord. Then some of them were chosen for the ministry of the gospel, and they began to teach and keep the faith.[5]

J.C. Wenger says, "Baptism is to be administered to those who desire it, to those who have turned to the Lord in penitence and faith, and to

those who are ready to assume the obligation of Christian discipleship."[6]
Wenger underlines: (1) The proclamation of the Word of God;
(2) Conviction of heart of one's sin; (3) Contrition and repentance;
(4) Acceptance of Jesus as Saviour and Lord; (5) Induction into the
church of Christ by water baptism. Water baptism appears to be a
symbol of cleansing from sin. "And now why do you wait? Rise and be
baptized, and wash away your sins, calling on His name" (Acts 22: 16).
Water baptism also symbolizes one's death to sin.

> What shall we say then? Are we to continue in sin that grace may
> abound? By no means! How can we who died to sin still live in it? Do
> you know that all of us who have been baptized into Christ Jesus were
> baptized into His death? We were buried therefore with Him by bap-
> tism into death, so that as Christ was raised from the dead by the glory
> of the Father, we too might walk in newness of life.
>
> For if we have been united with him in a death like His, we shall cer-
> tainly be united with Him in a resurrection like His" (Romans 6: 1-5).

Further, water baptism constitutes a covenant of discipleship with
God through Jesus Christ. "Baptism which corresponds to this, now
saves you, not as a removal of dirt from the body but as an appeal to God
for a clear conscience, through the resurrection of Jesus Christ" (I
Peter 3: 21).

Finally, water baptism symbolizes the baptism of the Holy Spirit:
"John baptized with water, but before many days you shall be baptized
with the Holy Spirit" (Acts 1: 5). In the Believers' Church different
forms of baptism are recognized. For this topic it is not basic to discuss
forms. Wenger says, "The significance of a sacramental sign does not
reside in its material form but in the faith of the recipient who is
sincerely looking to Christ for the blessings symbolized."[7]

For many years I taught a Christian faith class, mostly of young
people in my church. Every year, a goodly number of members of those
classes were baptized on confession of faith in Jesus Christ. Many of
them experienced conversion during the instruction period. Many came
to the assurance of salvation, though they had believed in Jesus Christ
since they were children. The majority of those baptized believers of
those classes have remained true to their confession of faith and are
today active members of the church.

I find it very important that baptized people understand that they
have publicly confessed faith in Jesus Christ as Lord and Saviour; that
they have identified with Jesus in His death and that they must continue
to die to sin and live in the resurrection of a new life of victory over sin;
and finally, that they as believers have been baptized by the Holy Spirit
into the body of Jesus Christ. They must now permit the Holy Spirit to
produce the fruit of the Spirit in daily living and the gifts of the Spirit for
the upbuilding of the whole body.

New believers are babes in Christ. "But I, brethren, could not address
you as spiritual men, but as men of the flesh, as babes in Christ" (I
Corinthians 3: 1). "Like newborn babes, long for the pure spiritual milk,
that by it you may grow up to salvation" (I Peter 2: 2). They must be

nurtured in the faith. Writing to the Colossians, the apostle Paul says, "As therefore you received Christ Jesus the Lord, so live in Him, rooted and built up in Him and established in the faith, just as you were taught, abounding in thanksgiving" (Colossians 2: 6-7). The believers have "received" and are now to "so live." They have been "rooted" and are now to be "built up in Him." Jesus Himself demonstrated this better than anyone has ever done.

> 1. He stood up to read as his **custom** was. For Him the reading of the scriptures was a habit. It was an integrated activity of life. 2. He went out into the mountain to pray as his custom was. The whole life of Jesus was lived in close communion with His Father. Prayer was breathing to Him. 3. He taught them again as His custom was. He was active and again this was His habit. He shared with others the Word, His love and Himself.[8]

Reading, studying and searching in the Word of God is "milk" for the newborn Christians and "bread and meat" for the older Christian. Prayer is the breathing of the soul.

SHARING THE FAITH IN A PERIOD OF CRISIS

The Christian must share himself and his faith. Jesus' parting words were the Great Commission. The disciples were to be witnesses. Earlier Jesus had told them to feed the hungry, to heal the leper, to go to the next village and tell them of His coming. The Samaritan woman was told to tell her fellow villagers. The man healed of the demons was to go back home and tell his family. E. Stanley Jones says, "If you don't sow it you will have nothing to sow. Those who do not pass on to others are themselves empty. The converted convert, or they do not stay converted. Unless you are evangelistic you don't remain evangelical."[9]

The Free Church had its early roots in the sixteenth century reformation. Very early the Anabaptist leaders identified with Jesus' words, "If any one serves me, he must follow me; and where I am, there shall my servant be also; if any one serves me, the Father will honour him" (John 12: 26). "If you love me, you will keep my commandments" (John 14: 15). "This is my commandment, that you love one another as I have loved you" (John 15: 12). Being a believer meant total commitment. They followed the Lord in total obedience even though it meant persecution and death. They admonished each other to love one another and also their enemies. Just prior to his martyrdom, Michael Sattler admonished his followers:

> Further, dear fellow members in Christ, you be admonished not to forget love, without which it is not possible that you be a Christian congregation....[10]

Hans Denck's famous statement has been a basic tenet of faith to Anabaptist believers through the centuries. "No one may truly know Christ except one who follows Him in life."[11]

> Love means that one's life is intimately open to that of another; love for God opens one's life to Him and love for one's fellows opens one's life to what God is doing in them. Human nature knows little of love, for love is a totally unselfish giving that delights in the happiness brought

to another.[12]

The church is at a critical crossroads today. Statistically there is still some growth. But any rapid growth is primarily in the third world. The church does not grow in Europe and North America. Though the vast majority of Europeans are still considered Christian because of their child baptism, the churches across England, France, Holland, Germany, Switzerland and Austria are almost empty. It is not uncommon to see Dutch or German churches with 500 members having a Sunday morning worship service with twenty-five in attendance.

During the last six years, my ministry has involved frequent travelling. I have travelled with fine Christians who radiated their faith beautifully. I have also had as seatmates, agnostics, atheists, Hindus, Moslems, Jews, as well as nominal Christians who were completely indifferent, and others who were completely turned off. Many people who have had some involvement with the church are quite hostile. It is not uncommon to find people who refer to one's Christian associates as "freaks" or "nuts."

Much publicity has been given to great revivals sweeping the United States. If there is a mass movement to God in the United States, it has not yet crossed the 49th parallel. At the same time, it is not correct to say that large numbers of Canadians have not heard of Jesus Christ or have not had contact with some form of the gospel. The evidence suggests, not that they have not, or could not have heard of Jesus Christ, but that they cannot hear. Nietzsche said years ago, "Show me that you are redeemed and then I will believe in your Redeemer." Though I want to appreciate all honest efforts to bring people to Christ I do admit that I have some misgivings when I hear of multi-million dollar programs being launched by radio or television broadcasters and half-billion and billion dollar campaigns announced that **shall** evangelize the world in a few years. Antibiotics are very important. But sometimes it is good to look at the source of the infection. I believe the same is true in evangelism.

In his recent book, **Will Our Children Have Faith?** John H. Westerhoff speaks of the destruction of the field that at one time brought forth much fruit.[13] He lists six institutions that constituted the fruitbearing soil in which fruit could come to ripeness when life was still predominantly rural. They were: (1) The community with some sense of homogeneity. People knew each other and worked together. (2) The family. Father and mother worked together and the extended family was close. (3) The school, though not necessarily parochial, was open to scripture and prayer. (4) The church was the community. (5) Popular religious periodicals. (6) And finally, the Sunday School completed the influences that worked together to help youth find God. Today our communities are heterogeneous; our families are falling apart; our public schools are secular or anti-religious. The church is no longer the centre of the community and the mass media have replaced religious publications. This is the environment of the children and of many of the adults we are trying to reach with the good news. It is understandable that some families are so frightened that they attempt to flee the two most visible forces that threaten to destroy them, namely the city and the public school.

But who is society? Who are the unchurched? J. Russel Hale[14] describes the unchurched people of America under 12 headings. Here follows a brief summary:

Type 1. **The anti-institutionalists** see the church as being preoccupied with itself. Such people reject organizational structures as necessasry for "true religion." They protest that finances, buildings and property are considered more important by the church than peoples' needs. They may confess to be Christians, but reject the church. And, because they reject the church, they find other organizations for their activities.

Type 2. **The boxed-in** have been church members in the past but have felt repressed and shackled. Hale divides these into three subtypes: (a) **The constrained** feel cramped by too much emphasis on ethical standards and behavioural demands. (b) **The thwarted** feel the church prevents them from growing into independent and self-confident persons by treating adults like children, by telling them what to do and what not to do. (c) **The independents** voice a fierce individualism and see the church as a prison or strait-jacket which limits their freedom in a multitude of ways.

Type 3. **The burned-out** are the ones who gave so much of their time and energy to the church that they felt utterly destroyed by the effort. Among them are former leaders who were overwhelmed by the load carried.

Type 4. **The cop-outs** were never committed to the church. They never put down roots in the church, or were only peripherally involved. He sees the cop-outs as **apathetic**, having few deep feelings for the church, or as drifters who move from congregation to congregation to avoid responsibility and commitment.

Type 5. **The happy hedonists** find their fulfillment in monetary pleasure and recreational activities. They may not reject God and may even speak of conversion, but they don't have time for religious activities.

Type 6. **The locked-out** are the opposite of the boxed-in. These people feel the church does not want them because they do not measure up in some way. Again we find several subtypes: (a) **The rejected** who have been denied communion for some reason. (b) **The neglected** who may be of an ethnic minority, poor, handicapped, singles or aged. (c) **The discriminated against** believe they can cite specific examples of ways the church has excluded them.

Type 7. **The nomads** are wanderers in our North American society and span all classes. Their work takes them from city to city and from province to province. They are afraid to make friends. They fear the hurts that another separation will give.

Type 8. **The pilgrims** are searchers and are found mostly among youth, though not exclusively so. They are dissatisfied with their "childhood religion" and often continue to be disillusioned with what they find in other religions. The pilgrims need other people as they continue their searching and tend to treat others tolerantly.

Type 9. **The publicans** constitute the largest group of the unchurched. They perceive most churchgoers as Pharisees who are hypocrites, phonies and fakes. They reject the churches which do not measure up (in their eyes) to the ideals and types of life-style they preach. They cite church splits, judgementalism, behavioural demands and ethical lapses of leaders.

Type 10. **The scandalized** reject their church because they cannot accept or understand how each congregation, sect, group or denomination can claim to be "the one true church" and be so rejecting of each other.

Type 11. **The true unbeliever** may be subdivided into smaller categories. The **agnostic/atheist**. The **deist/rationalist**. The **humanist/secularist**.

Type 12. **The uncertain** have no reason for their lack of church affiliation.

I will not follow through on Hale's analysis. I find that his groupings portray to a degree what I have found in the Canadian society. He has not included adherents of non-Christian religions, the seekers of ancestral animist religions, or members of the occult.

In concluding this section I draw to your attention the probability that there are thousands upon thousands of people, immediate descendants of Believers' Church families, who are part of the 12 types of Hale's study.

BEING THE CHURCH IS EVANGELISM

There appears to be an assumption in our day that the millions of non-Christians in the western world are eagerly waiting for someone to tell them that Jesus loves them. The mass media approach lends itself well to inviting these supposedly seeking, lost people one by one to the Lord. But even in this one by one, individualistic approach there is the acknowledgement that our society is almost completely disintegrated. Even the neatly categorized groupings of Hale's studies are only sociological concepts. In actual life, our urban, industrial society is made up of myriads of individuals, living side by side, alone. The millions of non-Christians are therefore not simply waiting to be invited to come to Christ. Rather, they are people who are waiting to be noticed, understood, accepted and loved in the context of their very own particular needs or hurts. They are waiting to see, feel and experience a caring church. Jesus very appropriately asked people, "What will you have me do?"

Recent church growth studies have shown that much of our church growth today is biological growth. That is good, but it still falls far short of biological growth in society. Only a minority of those born to our families become active believers in the church. What is even more disturbing is that most church growth, especially in fast-growing congregations comes from transfers. It is astounding how much growth can be reported by various congregations without showing growth in the total number of Christians in the country. Our transient society, plus the fact that often there is growth at the expense of our neighbourhood church, may give us a feeling of well-being. Our own membership may grow, but few of the unchurched are won to the Lord.

EVANGELISM AFFIRMATIONS FOR THE BELIEVERS' CHURCH

The Believers' Church has a vital role to play in evangelizing Canada. But let us pray that God may save us from the arrogance of believing we can do it alone. We do not have an edge on all truth and action. God is also using other denominations.

Donald McGavran loves to say that we disciple people so that they can go forth to disciple more people. It is my understanding of the Great Commission that Jesus wanted His disciples to repeat what He had done with them. He had used three very important years to nurture them to be His followers. Now they were to go into the enlarging world to repeat the process.

In committing ourselves to the task of evangelism it may be well to consider some of the lessons the early disciples learned in their classroom and field work with the Great Master.

1. One of the most victorious evangelism affirmations anywhere is found in Matthew 5: 16: "And [they shall] glorify your Father who is in heaven." This victory affirmation closes off the Beatitudes of the Sermon on the Mount. Though this paper does not allow me to enlarge on the Beatitudes, I want to show briefly that we have here some basic principles by which the community of Christ's followers shall live.

These divine principles of **spiritual living, conduct** and **activity** set the church aside in whatever society it finds itself. These principles of humility, concern, purity, peaceloving and peacemaking project the church onto an eminence where it cannot be hid.

All too often the church has fallen short of these divine principles. Through the centuries, since the days of Constantine, the church has repeatedly courted wealth and power and the praise of the state. The church has sanctioned wars, colonization and the subjugation of aboriginal people, and persecution. The church has sanctioned killing, racism and the accumulation of great wealth. It is in these areas where I have heard the strongest indictments hurled against the church. The elite middle and upper classes, and people of power, still get excited about glamorous crusades and expensive religious campaigns. The masses of secular people are not challenged. To the masses, religion appears to be a means to preserve the life-style of the advantaged.

The community of the Sermon on the Mount becomes the salt of the earth, the light of the world. It gives light to all in the house. It provides fullness of spiritual life and fellowship-wealth for all its adherents, and like the early church, attracts the admiration of those who are still outside. This is the church that will cause people to glorify God.

2. A second evangelism victory affirmation is found in John 17: 21b: "That the world may believe that thou hast sent me." In this great prayer, Jesus prays that the apostles might be one as He and the Father are one. He prays that their joy might be full. He prays that they might be kept from evil. He prays for those who would believe through their

word. Then comes the inclusive prayer for the apostles and those who would believe through them. "...that they may all be one; even as thou, Father, art in me, and I in them, that they also may be in us, so that the world may believe that thou hast sent me" (John 17:21).

Once more there is the promise of victory. This time it is based on the community of believers' testimony of unity. Naturally, almost two thousand years later it seems almost academic to pray for unity. We can hardly expect to force all Believers' Church groups to conform to one church polity, one baptism form, one structure, one earthly head. That would return us to the pre-reformation era. Unity and oneness must come on a different level. Let us begin with a small prayer cell or **koininia** group in each of our churches. My children have left home and today we are five families, yet we are one. Love, support, concern, unity of goal and purpose, and mutual fellowship and enrichment keep us together. This may also apply to the church. Though we do not begin by joining structures, we can join forces in love, goodwill and mutual recognition and supportiveness.

Let me illustrate. Many years ago a fine young layman from a neighbour church asked for a transfer to our church. He was a gifted, dedicated young man. The Lord gave me the grace to look deeper and I spent the evening in helping him sort out a problem. After that he went back to his congregation and continued to serve with enthusiasm.

3. A third and very basic evangelism victory affirmation is found in Acts 5:14: "And more than ever believers were added to the Lord, multitudes both of men and women." Here we come to the very core of a congregation's evangelistic thrust. Preceding this statement there is the story of Ananias and Sapphira. It portrays the humanness of the people in the church, and the spiritual dynamic of the church. The church had the spiritual resources and the leadership fortitude to deal with sin in the church. Fear came upon all the church. They perceived God was at work. Miraculous things happened. There was togetherness. Outsiders did not dare to join themselves to the Christians, but they "magnified" them. The Christians were regarded very highly. Then comes the statement, "The Lord added to the church."

The church must have spiritual power for the need of the hour. The church must testify to life and newness, to togetherness or oneness. The church must be respected for its positions on good morals, ethics and justice, and unbelievers dare not slip in just to enjoy the club. They must perceive that the church is a spiritual entity made up of people like them. People become a part of that spiritual community by a creative act of God. My faith is simple enough to believe that an Acts 5 church would still upset any of our secularized communities today. The church that exudes spiritual power still attracts converts.

4. A fourth evangelism victory affirmation is found in Acts 2:44,46: "And all who believed were together and had all things in common...attending the temple together and breaking bread in their homes." Here we have the first church in operation. Just a little while before, the Holy Spirit had come with all His glorious manifestations.

Filled with the gift of the Holy Spirit, these believers now met together to pray, study the scriptures, to enjoy fellowship and to break bread. They gave up their independence and began to have things in common. They shared their possessions, according to their individual and corporate needs. They became one people, a truly visible community of believers with a corporate testimony of the saving grace of God, a foretaste of Paradise regained.

My thrust is not toward a Hutterian kind of community. Originally that group had a strong evangelistic outreach. They have lost it. I am also not advocating closed city ghettos. I do believe, however, that the believers of any particular congregation should have more in common than a Sunday morning worship service and possibly a second meeting on Sunday or Wednesday night.

Most Christians have accepted the Western free enterprise norm for their behaviour and decisions. They work, buy, sell, acquire, move and locate to keep abreast of the trend set by a non-Christian society. Their Christian living is as isolated as their conversion. They have not entered into a covenant with God's people.

Christians should enter into some kind of covenant living, so that evening teas and children playing together are reasonably possible. Christians should be able to share campers, cabins, special household items, snowblowers and farming equipment. It is hardly in keeping with the early church model or Jesus' admonition regarding material things when Christians add house to house, farm to farm and business to business. It does not mean the Christian will not enjoy the fruit of his labour. But a raise in salary should not be the determining factor to pull the family out of a good Christian church or neighbourhood to move to a distant city. One man's faltering business is not the voice of God to another affluent businessman, telling him to buy it at a bargain price to enlarge his own holdings.

I have seen professional people give up tempting promotions for the sake of their children, and I have seen how the Lord has blessed them. I have seen businessmen and farmers rescue their failing brother from bankruptcy, and have also seen how the Lord blessed them for it. The community of believers who have covenanted with each other to care, share, forgive and meet each other's needs will become visible. The Lord will add more to it.

5. The final evangelism victory affirmation comes from Acts 1:8: "But you shall receive power when the Holy Spirit has come upon you; and you shall be my witnesses in Jerusalem and in all Judea and Samaria and to the end of the earth." This statement is crucial and basic to all that has preceded this discussion.

In the Believers' Church there are different interpretations regarding the doctrine of the Holy Spirit. Nevertheless, we all agree on Paul's Ephesian statement that we "were sealed with that Holy Spirit." The new birth is the work of the Holy Spirit. At the same time we must acknowledge that the Holy Spirit has not been able to manifest Himself similarly in all people. Even the apostles who received that first outpouring of the Holy Spirit on the day of Pentecost were later filled repeatedly. The same Ephesians who had been sealed with the Holy Spirit were later admonished to be "filled with the Holy Spirit" (Ephesians 5: 18). Continuing to the end of the letter, Paul then points to a number of realities in the believer's life that need to be brought under th control of the Spirit. He speaks of husband-wife relationships; parent-child relationships; employee-employer relationships. Paul concludes the discussion by challenging all believers to equip themselves for the Christian warfare in a hostile society.

God's Spirit, incarnating the living Christ, dwells in believers. In the measure in which we permit Him to control us individually and corporately, He will help us be witnesses in an ever-enlarging circle. We will "do and teach" as Christ came to "do and teach."

Every believer should understand that Acts 1:8 is not in the imperative. Believers should not be made to feel guilty if they cannot articulate the faith. The joy of the Lord and the fullness of the Spirit make witnessing a natural sharing of the faith within the particular gifts which God entrusts to His people.

I believe the Believers' Church has a role to fulfill in evangelizing Canada. I believe that role will be played as we progress in our discovery of what the Christian congregation truly is to be, and as we nurture our believers to become true disciples of our risen Lord and Saviour, Jesus Christ, and members together of the visible body of people who have covenanted to live in love and unity, to care and support one another and demonstrate to the world true justice and good will.

The New Testament church, as well as the church of our sixteenth century Anabaptist forefathers, won the admiration of those who were outside. It seems reasonable to expect that an active, caring, evangelizing church cannot be popular today, according to the standards of the world. Many people may continue to find it necessary to leave it. But the caring, loving, suffering, healing church will continue to be the church that will demonstrate fellowship with the Father, and the Lord will continue to add to it those who are being saved.

WORSHIP
IN BELIEVERS' CHURCHES TODAY

Harold L. Mitton

Andrew Blackwood, in his valuable book **The Fine Art of Public Worship**, delineates five facts about the worship of the early church. First, there was a lack of emphasis upon externals. Second, there was a new sense of freedom to worship God without the use of fixed forms. Third, there was much more emphasis upon the people, and much less upon the leader. Fourth, there was a corresponding change of spirit so that one thinks of worship in the apostolic church as radiant. Fifth, there was the new access of power, the power of the Holy Spirit.[1]

It would be difficult to argue that worship in free churches today always resembles the kind of worship which prevailed in the early church. There are notable exceptions, of course, but worship in many of our churches tends to be formal, fixed, clergy-centred, staid and sterile. As someone has put it, "We may not be ritualists, but we usually are 'rutualists'." While strenuously avoiding the more formal liturgy, we often drift into a rut which we follow slavishly, using a restricted number of hymns, a limited lectionary, and a sameness of themes. It is all so stultifying and predictable and controlled. G. Don Gilmour in his book **In the Midst** has this to say about modern day worship: "The choirs sing anthems, the offertory is played, the responsive readings are read, the hymns are sung, the sermon is preached, but the main thing is missing. There is no room for something unplanned entering into the sanctuary and shaking men's lives. It is all under control: our control."[2]

The question I keep asking myself is this: Should those of us who belong to the Free Church tradition return to the simple, spontaneous, Spirit-controlled worship of the early church? There are those who say that it is both impossible and undesirable. They point out that many assemblies of worship today are much larger than those depicted in the Book of the Acts, and that what is appropriate for small groups of believers is scarcely appropriate for a larger assembly. There is, no doubt, some truth in this contention, but it cannot be denied that, for some time now, there has been a growing disenchantment on the part of a great number of people with respect to the way in which worship is conducted in many of our churches.

I. The complaints which I pick up, from time to time, are these:

1. **"In most services there is so little interaction on the part of the worshippers."** Apparently people come to church lonely and go away lonely. They come thinking that the church will put them in touch with other people, and they leave just as isolated as ever. As a result,

complaints about the coldness, formality and impersonality of ordinary worship services are widespread.

2. **"There is little that is new or spontaneous."** Someone has said that a religious observance is a way through for one generation, a form for the next generation, and a prison to the third generation. In commenting on "tradition versus innovation" John Killinger says,

> We don't have to give up everything of the past; far from it. There are elements in Christian worship which seem to persist as rich and meaningful from age to age — such things as songs, scriptures, the offering, communion, signs of fellowship, and the sermon. But in every age they must be given new shape, new understanding in the context of the time. And this is the task of every generation: to play with the possibilities until something rich happens to the old elements.[3]

3. **"There is little that is intelligible or relevant."** Explain it as you will, people brought up outside the church find it difficult to identify with our kind of worship. Our terminology and forms of worship are beyond their grasp. Why should we allow anything as precious as the gospel to stagnate? Is the church not under obligation to express a timeless gospel in the categories of the age to which it is addressed?

4. **"There is so little that is life-affirming and joyous."** Perhaps we have made the mistake of thinking that reverence and solemnity constitute the only valid way of relating to God. As a result, church services are often doleful and dolorous. Once again, Killinger remarks, "Why is it that worship in most of our churches remains the least playful activity in the world? Why do we act as though we were afraid to enjoy it? Why do we remain serious and hesitant, refusing to let ourselves go as we would in almost any other kind of activity we really enjoy?"[4]

5. **"There is little that is emotionally uplifting."** This is a common complaint: that our services of worship are devoid of feeling. They do not minister to the whole man. They tend, if anything, to be cold and cerebral, and this in an age when people are trying to get in touch with their feelings! Even in so-called Free Churches we have been conditioned to believe that we should be very restrained and respectable! Perhaps it is for this very reason — that our services very often are devoid of feeling — that the charismatic movement has had a phenomenal appeal in our time.

II. It should be obvious that without resorting to extremes or gimmickry Free Churches should be able, under God, to evolve meaningful experiences of corporate worship. Sometimes, however, we have been more resistant to change than liturgical churches! Quite frankly, this has been a real conundrum for me. It seems to me that, of all people, we should be open to the winds of the Spirit when it comes to the matter of the public worship of God. This has been my understanding of the term "Free Church": that, among other things, we are not in bondage to tradition. If you think that we possess that kind of freedom, just take note of the uproar the next time your church changes its form of worship, be it ever so slightly! There is always a large body in the congregation which remains unshakably convinced that any change is unholy, and that things would be much better if they were left "as they were." This makes it very difficult for the minister who seeks to lead the people in worship. On the one hand, he has in his congregation a large number of traditionalists who do not want any change whatever in the order of worship, and on the other hand, he has a number of people in his congregation who are completely turned off by traditional forms of worship. It seems to me that, without abandoning meaningful tradition, we should have the freedom to be innovative. Not that we should be ready to leap into any and every form of experimental gimmickry that comes into fashion, but that we should, as Free Churches, seek to be free of any resticting and unnecessary barriers that may stand in the way of genuine worship, or of bringing others in touch with the living God. The Holy Spirit is always a spirit of change and is even now seeking to lead people into new and meaningful forms of worship.

James L. Christensen makes a strong case for what he calls contemporary worship. He begins his book **Contemporary Worship Services** by referring to his niece who had never really been "turned on" by traditional worship, but who was very much helped by a contemporary service at a local church while she was a student at university. She said, "It seemed to speak to me. I became involved and actually looked forward eagerly to Sunday. The worship conveyed a depth of meaning and faith on my level of experience.[5] This led Christensen to ask himself the question, "What is it about the contemporary service that is appealing?" He came up with the following answers:

1. **Contemporary worship attempts to meet people where they are, with a vocabulary that expresses faith in terms relevant to the twentieth century.** Relevancy, he says, is the crucial issue which dominates every aspect of Christianity today. Too often the worship and teaching experiences of the church are artificial, suspended in a world nobody knows. Contemporary worship strives to use contemporary thought forms and language to express ancient truths.

2. **Contemporary worship attempts to recapture the spirit of celebration, expressing joy in what the Holy Spirit has done and is doing in the world.** Themes of worship focus on the new life and victory in Christ's love and hope. This mood is created by the tempo of music used, the festal use of banners, and so on. Christensen claims that the dull, mournful, repetitious services do not speak to today's generation.

3. **Contemporary worship is oriented to the needs of persons, rather than the needs of the institution.** Some traditional worship services, he argues, seem tantamount to a rally, encouraging support and loyalty to the organization. Contemporary worship, on the other hand, is sensitive to the feelings and aspirations of the worshippers. Whereas traditional worship has been focused upon God's transcendence above and apart from creation, contemporary worship focuses upon where God intersects humanity in everyday happenings. In worldly realities or categories we find God and are found by Him. The major emphasis of most contemporary services is upon God's judgement, reconciliation and mission.

4. **Contemporary worship strives to involve the worshipper in the process of participation both bodily and mentally.** In traditional worship, Christensen says, there is a tendency to feel that the "real thing" is taking place in the front of the sanctuary. The farther back you sit, the more you are "out of it." The effectiveness of traditional worship depends upon how professional the choir is and how well the minister performs. Worship in its true sense, however, is more than watching a performance led by the minister. Ideally, each worshipper is to be in the process; this the contemporary service strives to accomplish.

5. **Contemporary worship is characterized by a focus upon life and the social applications of faith, in contrast to the other-worldly emphasis.** A basic premise is the view that the church is a servant, a leaven in society. The Christian lives in a secular world, and contemporary worship trains the Christian for witness there. To accomplish these purposes, contemporary worship sometimes uses new forms, modern ballads, varied instruments, all kinds of arts, recorded music, films, responses, scriptures and prayers with words that are in current usage, and varied sermon methods.

III. But is this worship, or is it simply an attempt on the part of the church to be trendy? James F. White, Professor of Christian Worship at the Perkins School of Theology, Southern Methodist University in Dallas, Texas, does not think so. He is of the opinion that something extraordinary has happened to people, and consequently to Christian worship, since the late 1960s. He speaks of a new freedom which has burst upon the western world, a freedom to be true to oneself rather than conforming to traditional molds, a freedom to break with tradition which is no longer meaningful. Until recently, the church could oblige its people to fit into a particular pattern of worship. This is no longer possible or feasible. We can no longer say to people, "Like it or lump it." There is another alternative: they can leave. And many have. We may resent this "consumer attitude" toward worship, but it is a reality with which we must live.[6]

White goes on to point out that a generation has grown up which has a different way of perceiving reality. Worship in the mainline churches still consists almost entirely of a diet of words spooned out by the minister. It is as though the church has slept through the communications revolution that has taken place during the last couple of decades. White comments: "We must realize that the people have changed. They are accustomed to much more immediate forms of communication than words read from a pulpit." And they are much more accustomed to be much less inhibited in the way they respond to all of life. For at least a half century, we have been encouraged, even in Free Churches, to be proper and decorous, restrained and respectable, in the way we express ourselves in worship. White says:

> All this may have been fine for the period between 1920 and 1970. Most of the people in the churches in the major denominations had two goals in life: security and comfort, and our churches certainly echoed those virtues. Nothing unexpected ever happened, nothing ever rocked the

boat; one could worship with full confidence in the stability of things as they were. But the situation today has changed throughout Christendom. Quietly mouthed responses seem hardly enough in a world that bombards us with the visual, with movements, and with all kinds of sensory inputs.[7]

In other words, White is convinced that the forms by which worship is expressed must change significantly in the years ahead. He concedes that people over thirty feel more secure and comfortable with traditional forms of worship, but he feels that it is nothing less than suicidal for the church to fail to take into consideration the changes that have occurred in the human psyche in our time. This is not to imply that worship must become the merry-go-round for constant change, a parade of multi-media shows, rock songs, balloons and placards, a case of groovy language and psychedelic effects. Many of us can identify with C.S. Lewis when he says: "I can make do with almost any kind of service whatever, if only it will stay put! But if each form is snatched away just when I am beginning to feel at home in it, then I can never make any progress in the art of worship."[8]

IV. It remains for us to discuss some of the ways in which worship can become more meaningful and vital in Believers' Churches today. It would be approximately true to say that we have tended to place a greater emphasis upon evangelism than upon worship. Perhaps we need to re-examine our priorities. Jim Wallis, editor of **Sojourners** magazine says: "We have much to learn in recovering worship as the centre and pre-supposition of the whole Christian life, the very atmosphere in which it is lived."[9] Bernard Schalm writes in the same vein: "It would undoubtedly be of benefit to us if we returned to the New Testament pattern in which worship preceded evangelism; evangelism was the fruit of worship. If we fail in worship, we will inevitably fail in evangelism also, for we cannot meet the world until we have met God."[10] Schalm concludes: "If we succeed in leading people into a vital experience of worship, we will discover anew the dynamic thrust of New Testament evangelism, for the early church worshipped daily and the Lord added daily those who were being saved" (Acts 2:47).[11]

Christensen, in his book **New Ways To Worship**, makes several suggestions for creating what he calls contemporary worship services:

1. **Use a fuller range of musical instruments and celebrate in songs.** Traditional worship, he says, has been accompanied quite largely by the organ, a versatile, beautiful instrument. But why should it be used exclusively? Why not, on occasion, organize an ensemble of stringed instruments, and what about the sound of a trumpet at an Easter service?

2. **Use movement.** Worship involves not only the audio, verbal and visual senses; it should involve the whole body. James White agrees: "Surely we are capable of using more than just our ears and mouths in the praise of God."[12] In response to this, I must say that I am so much of a traditionalist that I still feel somewhat uncomfortable with hand-clapping and the raising of hands in praise. Yet I know that the Hebrews

and the early Christians used the whole body in the worship of God; marching and dancing were not uncommon! Christensen even goes so far as to say that at some point during the worship service, worshippers should be given the opportunity to speak, to touch, and talk with those around them. Many worshippers, he points out, see other worshippers only at church. Therefore, an opportunity for showing concern is desirable.

3. **Vary the order and content.** The key factors in contemporary worship are flexibility and variety. Worship is an awareness of being in the presence of God, and the response does not always have to be the same. To escape the monotony of sameness, and to give the possibility of fresh experiences, an occasional re-ordering of the service is desirable. I repeat, this should not be difficult for us in the Free Church tradition. In times past, our people did not have church bulletins or an order of service in front of them. We, of all people, should find it relatively easy to alter the service of worship! Perhaps we should recognize the fact that the fastest growing churches, here and abroad, tend to be of the Pentecostal variety with their emphasis on spontaneity in worship. It has to be acknowledged that innovations shock many tradition-oriented members. Hence, if even modest changes are made in forms of worship, the worship leader must exercise a great deal of discretion. Of one thing I am convinced: abrupt changes should not be made in an order of worship without advance notice and proper preparation. Whatever is done must be done in good taste and order. In the matter of worship, the issue is not a question of either form or freedom, but both. Even Christensen, who is an advocate of contemporary worship, has this to say: "It would not be wise to replace entirely, or suddenly, if ever, the traditional services. Perhaps an occasional contemporary service with youth participating and for which the congregation is properly prepared is the better way to begin."[13]

4. **Personalized prayers.** Prayers are integral to corporate worship. They tend, however, to be too stilted, wordy, meticulously eloquent, and sermonic. Sometimes, Christensen says, it sounds as if the one praying were attempting to impress the listeners with beautifully turned phrases. In contemporary worship an attempt is made to make prayer a heartfelt experience, an expression to God by the entire congregation. Hence, efforts are made to involve the worshippers in spontaneous prayers. Such prayers are less beautiful, perhaps, but more meaningful to the worshippers. In many Free Churches today members of the body of Christ are encouraged to exercise the gifts of the Spirit in the corporate worship of God. As was the practice in the early church (I Corinthians 12), members minister to one another in the presence of God through praise, prayer, singing and exhortation. Why should it be thought that God is limited to clergy in addressing Himself to His people?

5. **Preach inductive sermons.** Traditionally the worshipper has been a passive listener. The preacher proclaimed the Word; the worshipper looked to him as an authority figure. Consequently, the pulpiteer

assumed a didactic, deductive, dogmatic stance in preaching. Logic, reason, debate, proof approaches, were used. But the situation has changed: passivity in the worshipper is no longer valid for today. The worshipper's level of education often surpasses the minister's. Communication and growth are often accomplished through interchange of thought and dialogical involvement. Because of this, the style of the sermon and presentation are greatly affected. In contemporary worship, Christensen says, preaching needs to be inductive, attempting to involve the listener in thinking and feeling. The presentation is conversational in tone, non-defensive and open in approach. The pastor does not preach at the worshippers but thinks with them, taking them on a journey until they see the conclusion or destination themselves. In short, the preacher pays attention to feelings, movements, psychological methods. He allows the Word to be heard in the most creative, self-authenticating way possible. He has a disarming, honest, warm, relational approach. The contemporary style of preaching is not to talk down to or preach a proposition at worshippers. It is to walk with them, to share views with them, and to be vulnerable and open to them. The day of preaching is not over! The gospel must still be proclaimed, but the way it is done needs changing.

   6. **Brighten the atmosphere with colour.** Sanctuaries have too often been barren and drab, and in many instances worship services have been dolorous and sad. All this conveys the impression that Christianity is a repressive thing. This is lamentable. Maltby, the great scholar, is supposed to have said that Jesus promised the early disciples three things: first, they would frequently be in trouble; second, they would be absolutely fearless; third, they would be absurdly happy. But is this the impression people receive when they enter our assemblies of worship: that we are a radiantly joyful people? Perhaps a further word should be said, at this point, about church music. Some of us have been brought up to believe that God can be glorified only through classical music, but is this defensible? If we accept the truth that "full, conscious and active participation" is most desirable for the reform of worship in our time, we must reconsider our whole approach to church music. This much we know: rightly used, music stimulates participation, reaching its fullest degree in congregational song. James White says:

> Most of the new church music follows the popular music idioms of our time. Part of the appeal of the newer music is that it is already familiar. Much of this music, though not all, has a strong rhythm that pulls the body into the act. Older people still remember when this was true of church music until they were taught to be ashamed of it. Much of the new music is also readily singable...In terms of musical craftsmanship, much of this music is inferior. The melodies are often banal, the rhythms crude, and the harmony repetitious. So what? Its lack of complexity and sophistication may be an asset.[14]

He then makes this prediction:

> It seems very likely that the days of the bound hymnbook will soon end. People want to sing, but they want to sing in ways natural to their

times and in words akin to their sincere belief. The new music tries to do this, succeeds frequently, fails often, but at least makes the effort. A new song, sung with enthusiasm and conviction, is a fuller expression of our worship than an old song, sung without either.[15]

7. **Dress up the bulletin.** This is usually the first thing that is placed in the hands of the worshipper. White comments:

All too often, the bulletin is a poorly mimeographed job on cheap paper featuring some sentimental art. How many times have the Grand Canyon, a New England village, candles, and Christmas trees appeared on bulletins? To say nothing of the church's name and address though we are already there. It makes a sensitive person want to turn and run. How much better it is to use the bulletin for the publication of penetrating thoughts, opportunities for service, and information for Christian enterprise at home and abroad.[16]

In offering his suggestions for the renewal of worship, Christensen provides a warning. He says,

In my opinion, it is quite easy to be too mod and foolishly innovative. One can look upon worship as programmish, as a performance for people to enjoy. **Worship is an offering to God; it is He whom we strive to please. For this reason worship should be always more God-centred than man-centred, more objective than subjective. Praise, confession, absolution, instruction, offering of self and dedication are indispensable aspects of worship whether it be traditional or contemporary...**Keeping theological integrity is basic to whatever worship forms are assumed.[17]

This vivid reminder — that worship is primarily something offered to God — is further underscored by Kenneth Hamilton in his valuable book, **To Turn From Idols**:

Forms of worship while important are always secondary. It is the total recognition of the relation of our lives to our Creator and Redeemer that keeps worship a living act. Worship cannot always be an intense psychological experience. Sometimes it will be merely routine, so far as our reactions go; sometimes even boring. But that is true of anything that belongs to real life. Only romantics expect always to live at a fever pitch of joyous rapture. Nor should worship ever be considered as a kind of charging of our spiritual batteries, so they can run at high power for the next week. Worship cannot exist without structures. These structures may be tightly organized, as they are in formal liturgical worship, or loosely organized, as they are in so-called non-liturgical worship; but if they are not there, worship will soon degenerate into something else — an exercise in self-expression by the leader, a session for indoctrination in current ideologies, a time for psychological conditioning in 'progressive' or 'reactionary' cultural attitudes, or an opportunity for indulging in mass hysteria.[18]

CONCLUSION

It should the genius of Believers' Churches to evolve an order of worship which calls for the "full, conscious and active participation" of the people of God and allows liberty for the Spirit to suggest the content of the forms. The purpose of such worship is that God may be glorified, that His people may be built up in their most holy faith and that ultimately more and more of the world's life may be brought under God's loving sovereignty.

As far as forms of worship are concerned, Bishop Stephen Neill pleads for balance.

> The problem for every congregation is to find the right balance between spontaneity and order. Uncontrolled spontaneity may lead simply to the dissipation of energy. The maintenance of too strict an order may result in the disappearance of originality and the substitution of conformity for experiment. In its long history the church has erred more often on the side of order than on the side of freedom.[19]

John R.W. Stott adds:

> We need worship services that express the reality of the living God, and joyfully celebrate Jesus Christ's victory over sin and death. Too often routine supplants reality, and the liturgy becomes lugubrious. I think public worship should always be dignified, but it is unforgivable to make it dull. 'The longer I live,' said the late Archbishop Geoffrey Fisher, 'the more convinced I am that Christianity is one long shout of joy.'[20]

WORSHIP
AND SPIRITUAL GIFTS

John Rempel

A. BACKGROUND

I. In the Old Testament. The cultic and ritualistic acts of Israel's worship gave form to her relationship with God. It is evident, especially from descriptions in Exodus and Deuteronomy, how important the proper enactment of homage to God was for Israel.

Yet Israel's cult used forms common to religion in the Near East.[1] It was not the cultic but the covenantal nature of her religion which was unique to Israel's worship. Mendenhall (**Law and Covenant in Israel and the Ancient Near East**) and others have pointed out that the covenant form had political precedents but that Israel used it for the first time in a religious sense, i.e., where the king, the covenant giver, is God Himself. The covenant form is given in Exodus 20. God had acted on Israel's behalf ("I am the Lord your God who brought you out of the land of Egypt," v.2). He pronounced his lordship over this people in the form of the law and required obedience to it ("You shall...," v.3ff). Obedience would be rewarded and disobedience punished.

The worship assembly had the purpose of praising God. It did this by reciting God's act of grace (e.g., Deuteronomy 26), proclaiming the law of the covenant and asking obedience to it. We see from the prophets, among them Jeremiah and Micah, that the proclaiming of the law was not an exercise in casuistry but, in essence, a telling forth of the will of God. Cultic life served its appointed purpose only if it led to the ethical response asked for by God.[2]

I cannot do justice in this paper to the significance of the cult in Israel's worship. H.H. Rowley disputes the once popular assumption that the prophets were opposed to the cultus. He portrays them as opponents of its abuse. The opposition was based not on a new development in Israelite religion but on the nature of the covenant at Sinai. The cult and temple, then, were not a falling away from the religion of Israelite origins. When they became appeasements or evasions of God, ends in themselves, the prophets recalled them to the covenant in which they originated. Jesus followed in their steps.[3]

The path from the prophets to Jesus ran through the synagogue. Various attemps have been made to find its source. Rowley argues that it had its origins in the Babylonian captivity when the worship of the temple became inaccessible to the exiles. It was not intended to replace the temple, as we see from Ezekiel, and from the significance of the temple during Maccabean times.[4]

The significance of the synagogue, however, is that it developed a new worship life without the rituals of the Jerusalem temple. C.F.D. Moule refers to it as "Quaker Judaism."[5] Its most striking feature was the absence of sacrifice. The synagogue based its worship entirely on the teachings of the law and on prayer. Teachers and elders replaced priests as leaders of the community. It was congregational in form and furthered the evolution in Judaism of a religion centred on learning and action rather than mystery and sacrifice.

II. **In the New Testament.** Jesus lived within Judaism. He attended synagogue worship, had contact with the Jerusalem temple, and functioned as a rabbi. His invective against the Pharisees (Matthew 23) makes it clear that even the simplicity of synagogue worship and life can become empty and keep people from doing the will of God.

Jesus not only lived but died within Judaism. The constitutive element of Christian worship, the Lord's Supper, was instituted at Passover, probably at the supper of a **chaburah** (from chaber = friend), private groups of Jews who came together for devotional and charitable activities.[6] Jesus gave the bread and wine, which were part of the table fellowship, new meaning through his death. From earliest times, so Paul assumes, this act recalled Jesus' death when believers gathered for table fellowship.[7]

There has been a dispute among New Testament students since Lietzmann's **Messe und Herrenmahl** as to whether the Last Supper was intended by Jesus to be repeated, and whether the communion service of the Corinthian church is not a different rite altogether. Gregory Dix sees continuity between the two and argues that the breaking of bread was engrained in every religious Jew and would be repeated as a matter of custom. What was new in the Lord's Supper was not the act but its meaning: from now on when bread was broken it would recall Jesus.

The information the New Testament offers us concerning the Lord's Suppper is theological and disciplinary but not liturgical, i.e., it deals with the meaning of the rite but does not tell us how it was carried out. This is so, Dix argues, because the New Testament takes that knowledge for granted. To find out how the early church worshipped, we need to go to sources outside scripture.[8]

Before we attempt a description of early Christian worship from non-New Testament sources, we should look at events recorded in the New Testament. In Acts (2:37ff) there is preaching, baptism, devotion to the apostles' teaching, fellowship, the breaking of bread and prayers. In I Corinthians 12 Paul explicates the role of the Holy Spirit for the life of the church and particularly for its worship. In sum, "there are varieties of working but it is the same God who inspires them all in everyone" (v.6). The gifts of the Spirit are like limbs of a body, the body of Christ. Worship, then, involves our response to the Spirit and our response to each other. It happens through the whole church and not through one person. It may include prophecy, teaching, miracle working or singing all for one purpose: to teach us to love, which is the glory of God.

"Singing" probably meant chanting Psalms, the hymn book of the synagogue, quoted with emotion and affection by the church's early preachers (e.g., Acts 2). But hymns of praise to Christ used in the New Testament (John 1, Philippians 2, Revelation 5) suggest that some hymns originated in the earliest worship of the church.

The book of Revelation evokes the splendour of the Old Testament in its description of worship (especially ch. 4 and 5). Perhaps this reflected the liturgical practice of some part of the early church. In sum, there is no uniform New Testament pattern of worship. We have only fragments of different liturgies within the apostolic church.

Though the covenantal language of Old Testament worship was not explicitly carried over into the New Testament, the covenant remained the assumed basis of Christian communal life. It is evident in Jesus' teaching, particularly in the Sermon on the Mount (Matthew 5-7), where He proclaims a new law and asks obedience to it, and in His use of the word "covenant" in the Last Supper (Matthew 26:28) to explain the significance of his death. We see it also in the preaching of Paul and others in the early church (Romans 1-11, Acts 2-8, 13) who began their recitation of God's redeeming acts with Abraham and Moses. That covenant was fulfilled in Jesus.

It is not accidental that Romans 12, which comes immediately after Paul's recital of God's saving deeds, begins with a call for obedience to the covenant: "I appeal to you, therefore, brethren, by the mercies of God, to present your bodies as a living sacrifice, holy and acceptable to God, which is your spiritual worship." Worship and work, cult and covenant are inseparable.

Complete descriptions of worship by the end of the first century have been preserved in non-New Testament sources.[9] Very early it took two forms: the meeting (**synaxis**) and the thanksgiving (**eucharist**). The first was a continuation of the synagogue service (scripture readings, Psalm singing, preaching, praying). This assembly was to proclaim the gospel to believers and unbelievers. Unlike the synagogue service, it included no prayers; these were reserved for the gathering of believers only. It was apparently usual to ask the unbelievers to leave when the "meeting" was to be following by a "thanksgiving." There are varying judgements as to how often each of these gatherings was held, with or without the other.[10] It seems clear, however, that the Lord's Supper retained its **chaburah** character, i.e., a private meeting of those who belonged to a covenant.

The "thanksgiving" originally had four elements: offertory (people bringing to the Table bread, wine and other goods), prayer (like the thanksgiving prayer of the **chaburah**), breaking of bread, communion. There are scriptural and traditional descriptions of detail available, such as the practice of the kiss of peace, the reconciliation of disputes before communion, the striking role of the bishop as preacher and bread breaker (while congregational life in general is led by elders and deacons). Dix argues for the very early and widespread development of these customs because of his early dating of the Pastoral Epistles. Others would place them later.

The Christian eucharist, in keeping with its origins, remained simple and soon became universal in its practice. It was devoid of elaborate ritual, either Greek or Jewish, and of the prescribed texts and action of later Roman Catholic worship. These were gradually added at different times in different places, to be finally fixed only at the Council of Trent. But as to the essential form of the liturgy, there is a general opinion that partaking in fellowship, giving thanks, making memory in early Christian worship centred in the Lord's Supper. The act (communion) carries the same meaning and power of the gospel as does the word (preaching).

III. In the Believers' Church. The "Believers' Church" has at least five sources: Anabaptism, Puritanism, Pietism, Evangelicalism, Pentecostalism. As in the eary church, there is no uniformity of practice among Believers' Churches. Generally their worship is characterized by: (1) simplicity; (2) "word centredness" (as opposed to act, symbol or sense centredness); (3) freedom to develop according to local need and not to be bound to prescribed forms or words or to state control; (4) everyone is a minister, differing in function according to his gift, but an equal participant in worship.

The Believers' Churches are Protestant in their understanding of worship. They share the "protest" of the sixteenth century reformers against a decaying medieval church.[11] This means that our worship arose as a **corrective** to that of the Middle Ages. It emphasized preaching because church practice had used ceremonies to obscure the proclamation of the gospel. Its intended purpose was to restore worship to the model of the New Testament. At the heart of the New Testament model Protestants saw the direct, priestly relationship of each believer with God. The priestly office and sacraments of the Roman Church had made access to God dependent entirely on such mediation.

Catholics argue that Protestants went too far and ended up with a spiritualism which has no room for the material world as a means to God. Cyril Vagaggini assesses the significance of this conflict for theology and worship. "The question of the incarnation is that which separates Protestantism most profoundly from Catholicism...Protestantism implies a radical lack of appreciation of the law of incarnation because it refuses to find a place between the soul and God for a human intermediary."[12]

As it was popularly carried out, the Reformation became preoccupied with supplying those things which were missing in its time, and did not restore all that was a part of early Christian worship. Part of the reason for this is that only the explicit statements of scripture and not the practice of the early church in general were examined.[13]

Almost all Believers' Churches began as protest movements within other Protestant churches.[14] They originated as conventicles, i.e., small groups meeting privately to give solidarity and intensify spirituality, somewhat like Jewish **chaburoth**. These groups started out knowing more what worship was **not** than what it was: it was not endlessly repeated ceremonies created to carry along people who knew little of personal faith in Jesus Christ.

Their worship took form not so much through theology and tradition as through experience. The experience of knowing Christ as Saviour, and people as brothers, created relationships like those of the early church. It brought with it a closeness to the stories, to the very words of the New Testament which made more elaborate statements of faith unnecessary. The Lord's Supper was really eating together at Jesus' table. Singing and praying were natural expressions of the intensity of this new-found life. Brothers and sisters gave and received counsel, as in Corinth, because they could not follow the new way without it.[15]

The Believers' Churches developed their understanding of biblical worship through two sources: their own religious experience and reformed Protestantism. When the intensity of the first generation was lost, the simple forms, essentially spontaneous and innately communal, were inadequate to hold the community together.

The religious emotions accompanying the inception (or revival) of a movement were institutionalized and made the basis of its worship. (Such emotion does not last — indeed it should not if we believe that God's purpose in deepening or renewing our understanding of His ways is for us to live them out in the ambiguous life of the world. The intensity, warmth and spontaneity of revival are gifts God offers His people from time to time, but we should neither feel guilty about not always being at that point nor should we falsely prolong its emotions and base worship on a single point in history.)

In some cases the forms were kept but without the personal intensity which had brought them to life. In other cases, churches in the Reformed tradition were used as models. This often led to balance and made worship less dependent on experience but also led to uncritical borrowing from sources at variance with the ecclesiology and worship principles of Free Churches.

After the formative period, Free Church worship was passed on by oral tradition. It is not characteristic of Believers' Churches to fix their practices in written form, as in the Anglican Book of Common Prayer. But traditions which have developed are, nonetheless, passed on, often unconsciously.

Oral tradition is easily moulded by experience. Pastorally speaking this means: if it seems to attract people to Christ and the church, a practice finds an ongoing place in worship. We need to be aware that this is a pragmatic form of measurement and that it has led to bizarre practices and vulnerability to fads.[16]

Any sense of tradition in Free Churches is precarious. In some circles it means merely the practices of one generation becoming a barrier between a succeeding generation and the primitive church. Such a position is ahistorical since it presumes God to be absent from the church in history. A larger sense of tradition, as the accumulated practice of the church, retained because it is true to scripture, is lacking. With our limited sense of tradition we have little theological warrant to understand, reform and preserve it. On the other hand, this very limited sense of tradition as the practices of the preceeding generation becomes a tyrant in some circles. Simply because something was once done it must always be done.[17]

The task I see for Believers' Churches is to weigh their practice of worship against scripture, using it to judge tradition, within the early church and up to the present, keeping what is expressive of biblical faith, and through that process arriving at theological and practical norms for worship. Then they can consciously guide change in conformity with those norms.

B. TOWARD A THEOLOGY OF WORSHIP IN BELIEVERS' CHURCH

I. The Nature of Worship. Worship does not begin with our feelings or experience; its centre is God Himself. We come to worship God because He has already drawn us to Himself. We approach Him not because of our righteousness but because of His mercy; this conviction is the heart of the Psalter. We can be at home in the presence of the Lord because His love is larger than our hatreds, and His wisdom deeper than our discoveries. The first response to worship is awe at God's goodness, and gratitude for it. God's act (Christ's body and blood) and our response (our self-offering) constitute the basic pattern of Christian worship. Both these acts reach their fullness in the word of preaching and the act of the Lord's Supper.

What God has shown us of Himself is comprehended only by speaking of Father, Son and Spirit: God the Father made us, God the Son saved us, God the Spirit comforts and teaches us. The church life described in the New Testament assumes this threefold work of God. The pattern of Christian worship is that we come to the Father "in Jesus' name" (Gospels) or "through Him" (Paul's soteriology) in the power of the Spirit.

In worship the redemptive work of the past becomes present. This is so in the sermon as much as it is in the ordinance. Both of them "come alive" because of the ongoing work of the ascended Christ in His Spirit. Remembrance (**anamnesis**), is, therefore, much more than thinking about an historical event. It is an event and a person, who come from the past into the present.

That worship is not first of all our act but God's is recalled for us by the soaring, eternally comforting words of Paul. "Likewise the Spirit helps us in our weakness; for we do not know how to pray as we ought, but the Spirit himself intercedes for us with sighs too deep for words. And he who searches the hearts of men knows what is the mind of the Spirit, because the Spirit intercedes for the saints according to the will of God" (Romans 8: 26-27).

William Nichols says worship focuses on Christ, the incarnation of God's action, who is the true "Jacob's ladder," "upon which God's love comes down to earth, and man's response travels back to God."[18]

When we realize ourselves to be in the presence of God we see Him as He is and ourselves as we are. Isaiah is in awe, "Holy, holy, holy is the Lord God of hosts!...I am a man of unclean lips" (Isaiah 6: 3,5); the

Anglican Book of Common Prayer confesses, "We have left undone those things which we ought to have done and we have done those things which we ought not to have done."

The goal of this realization is not to feel bad and let God make us feel good without changing our way of life. God's nearness has the intent of moving us to repentance. Then we are free to hear God's "law," His instruction for how to live. His word in scripture, preaching, admonishing — all the things Paul mentions to the Corinthians — has the single intent of nourishing in us the desire and strength to will the will of God. Eberhard Arnold's distinction between prophetic and pietistic worship makes this point well.

> The tremendous chasm between the two consists in the fact that the Pietist feels satisfied when he experiences the personal sense of salvation and the presence of the personal God, whereas the prophetic spirit thereby only comes to the sense of committing himself to the decisive work of God and therewith desires, without any consideration for his personal feeling of happiness, to see the will of God realized for the whole world.[19]

God's redemptive acts, which bring us to Him, make people one. They have not been done to justify an infinite number of individuals but to break down "the dividing wall of hostility" (Ephesians 2: 14) to begin a new humanity. Worship, in its very nature, has to do with people who have been given relationships with one another and stand before God only as such, not as individuals. "Where is your brother Abel?" is always the first question God asks.

Worship can be an individual act but it is so in a derivative sense, i.e., a fisherman overwhelmed by the magnificence of a northern Ontario lake, or a person who is dying and knows himself at that moment to be safe in God's care, can obviously worship God. But they do so because of the Bible and the church, who have mediated their knowledge of God to them.

II. Believers' Church Assumptions about Worship. The first supposition concerns salvation. Those who gather for worship have come to a personal relationship of faith in obedience to Jesus Christ. The church makes it clear in its proclamation that this is the call of the gospel. It confirms each confession of faith with baptism and thereby makes the individual a member of the body of Christ.

This means that worship is not evangelism, though by being what it is, it draws people to Christ. Worship is not ceremony, given to masses of people who do not have personal faith, to please — or appease — God. To state the matter positively, worship is the activity of a community of faith representing itself before God. Liturgical order, or ritual, is significant only as it becomes the vehicle of corporate and individual response to God. No form of worship is valid aside from that.

The second supposition, in order of importance, is that the essence of worship is ethical. The Old Testament prophetic tradition, indeed, the very giving of the law, makes this point. It is everywhere assumed in the New Testament and specifically affirmed by Jesus and Paul. This is not to oppose action to piety, the scattering of the church to its gathering. From my description of the rhythm of worship, it is evident, I hope, that the living of the Christian life is grounded in the repeated recalling of the acts of salvation history, especially the death and resurrection of Jesus. The point at issue is that ritual is never an end in itself, an experience without moral content, an alternative to presenting our bodies as a living sacrifice.[20]

A third assumption is that the church is free. It is the people of God "come of age," no longer under custodianship (Galatians 3), not bound to means by which men seek to win God's favour (festivals, new moons, not touching or tasting — Colossians 2). The church is free, both in its inner and outer life, from the absolute claims of the state because it has found the only true Lord.

Its worship is, therefore, shaped from within itself and not modelled after "religious" patterns of the sort Karl Barth decries, because they try to please God and justify themselves by fulfilling "ritual" requirements but not by obeying.

A fourth assumption can be deduced from the third: there are no times or things which are holy in and of themselves. The "silver chalice" Jesus used at the Last Supper was probably not silver and the veneration given it is misplaced. The only "sanctuaries"[21] are groups of people, God's holy ones. The "things" of life, as of worship, take on meaning because of their role in our history, but in and of themselves they have only a functional role in worship, significant to the extent that they tell salvation's story.

All of the above suppositions lead to and give content to the fifth one: simplicity.

A sixth assumption is that worship is worldly. While worship unites all Christians before God through time and eternity, its purpose is to fit us for this world — as my whole presentation argues. This is not to say that worship focuses itself on man; its origin and focus are the God who, as Father, Son and Spirit, has entered our world and continues to be revealed in it and through it.

Therefore, while worship is a turning from man, as his own measure, to God, it never loses its worldliness. Mystery is opened to us in ordinary experience when it is offered to God. (Why is it so often sought in the funeral parlour-like organ music of many worship assemblies, which at once makes us preoccupied with our own feelings and sentimentally isolates us from a normal sense of things and people, as if God is not be found there?)

The final supposition of Believers' Church worship is that scripture is its only binding norm. How to make judgements, from this vantage point, on the theology and practice of Christian worship lost in the Reformation, is an urgent challenge. Believers' Churches have generally not acknowledged that the practices recorded in the New Testament are part of the over-all development within the early church. There is not a sharp demarkation between the general tradition of the primitive church and those aspects of its life recorded in the New

Testament nor does a definite line exist between the practice of the New Testament and that of the post-New Testament period.

III. Conclusion. Another section might have been inserted at this point: "The Believers' Church Practice of Worship." It, however, is the subject of the other paper on this topic.

Our practices of worship arose historically as a corrective to the abuses of the Middle Ages. The corrective the ecclesiology and worship life of Believers' Churches has supplied (see "Assumptions") is valid, I think, because it grew out of a recovery of the spirit of original Christianity. Not everything in primitive Christianity, however, was regained. Our assemblies consist of speaking but have no sense of acting in worship. We have not recovered acts like baptism and communion as integral, indispensable means of coming to God and to each other. Such they were in the early church. [22]

I sense an awareness in our churches that our "corrective" forms of worship lack the fullness of Christ. Many attempts to compensate for this try to heighten the subjective and experiential, on the "low" church end — with a dramatic style of preaching and music making borrowed from popular culture, or, on the "high" church end, with the kind of organ music I mentioned, vestments and processionals. We lack objective criteria derived from scripture, theology and tradition.

The Believers' Church principles of worship will stand us in good stead — worship based on personal faith, worship as morality, worship as freedom, worship as "holy" people and not things, as simple, worldly and scriptural. Our part in the church universal is to share them. We, in our turn, need to open ourselves to worship as action (through 'sacraments" — Latin for "signs") and to the catholic (universal, in continuity with what the church has held to from the beginning) tradition of worship. This will be done not by imitating the Roman or other liturgies but in searching with them for the fullness of Christ. Walter Klaassen points in that direction in his essay on worship. He urges us to acknowledge that the church's tradition of worship reaches back to the New Testament, through the twelve centuries (325-1525) we, as Free Church people, have forgotten. He concludes with a question, "How can we honestly and legitimately appropriate that heritage while maintaining our basic stance as Believers' Churches?"[23]

In that quest we shall discover that the "mystery" we seek is not found or preserved in elaborate ceremony or heightened experience. It is found listening to and obeying the God who is here, in Jesus and the Spirit, as we know of them in scripture, and in offering our lives, our wills to Him. The mystery which worship opens to us is that God takes what we offer Him and does with it more than we can think or ask.

WORSHIP AND SPIRITUAL GIFTS: A RESPONSE

Arthur G. Patzia

The procedure that I wish to adopt in responding to or "critiquing" these two papers on worship will be to make some brief summary comments of a positive nature and then to offer some thoughts that may cause us to evaluate critically and perhaps move beyond the scope of the papers as presented.

Harold Mitton's paper basically serves two important functions. The first is his perceptive analysis of "complaints" or "criticisms" that are commonly directed toward many worship services. It is obvious that most of these complaints echo a concern that worship isn't what it could be, or at least what many worshippers think it should be. If Mitton's observations are correct, then it is imperative for us to take a serious look at what's happening or rather what **is not** happening in church during the worship services.

The challenge for the church, I understand Mitton to be saying, is to create a worship service that is meaningful to **all** the people. The author resorts to James Christensen's book, **Contemporary Worship Services**, and lists those qualities of worship that Christensen considers "contemporary" as opposed to "traditional." Then, from another book by Christensen, Mitton tabulates specific suggestions on **how** to create these contemporary worship services.

A second value of the paper is embedded in Mitton's analysis of the material he uses. Although a major portion of this paper includes a presentation of Christensen's ideas, it is significant to note that Mitton does not buy uncritically everything that Christensen says. Along with other writers (James White, Kenneth Hamilton and John Stott), Mitton rightly cautions us to **think scripturally, move spiritually** and **relate meaningfully**. Worship, no matter what form or style it takes, must always remain "**worthship**."

Mitton is also aware of many of the tensions between the "new" and the "old"; between "traditional" and "contemporary"; between "fixed ritual" and "charismatic freedom." At a few places in the paper he offers some personal suggestions as to how these tensions may be alleviated.

John Rempel's paper also makes good contributions to our study on worship. After an all too brief history of worship in the Old and New Testament, the author delineates what he considers to be characteristics of the Believers' Church and suggests why these became important. From this, he then moves to his "theology of worship," which probably represents the Free Churches quite fairly. The main contribution of Rempel's paper is this attempt to characterize the **theology** and **form** of worship in the Believers' Church today.

Particularly significant is the author's contention that the church's worship, both in theology and practice, must be based on scripture. Thus he states his main concern: "The task I see for Believers' Churches is to weigh their practice of worship against scripture...keeping what is expressive of biblical faith." Supplementing this is his healthy caution regarding "experience and worship." Experience or emotion cannot be made the basis of worship. Nor should one substitute ritual for morality. I also appreciate the author's emphasis upon the horizontal dimension of worship. While worship is a movement of God to man and man to God, it also deals with people in their relationships, and with individuals who have been brought together in the Body of Christ.

Both of these papers are important for our understanding of worship: Rempel's as a theological perspective of worship within the Free Church tradition; Mitton's for its practicality. Any criticisms which follow are not intended to reflect upon their quality of work nor their contribution to the subject matter.

My general, yet main criticism of both papers, is that they failed to deal with the assigned topic of "Worship and Spiritual Gifts." Mitton does not even allude to this in the title, and, while Rempel's paper bears that title, little, if any, consideration is given to the relationship between worship and spiritual gifts. This was the direction that I had expected the authors to take.

Mitton does have several references to the Holy Spirit in worship. For example, he talks about "being open to the winds of the Spirit"; and again he states: "The Holy Spirit is always a spirit of change and is even now seeking to lead people into new and meaningful forms of worship." Too, Believers' Churches should allow liberty for the Spirit to "suggest forms for the order of worship." Unfortunately, Mitton doesn't define or expand upon these statements. What does "being open to the Spirit" etc. really mean for us within the context of worship? Further clarification of this would have been helpful.

At one point the author comes close to the topic when he refers to worship in the Corinthian church. However, he fails to expand upon the scripture passages which deal with this historical situation and which, I believe, are significant for us today. Is Paul encouraging the exercise of spiritual gifts in the corporate worship of God? What place should the Free Churches be giving to spontaneous praise, prayer, singing, exhortation, etc.?

I have a similar observation about Rempel's paper, although he comes closer to the topic when he states: "Worship, then, involves our response to the Spirit and our response to each other. It happens through the whole church and not through one person. It may include prophecy, teaching, miracle working or singing all for one purpose: to teach us to love, which is the glory of God."

Nevertheless, one is still forced to ask the question: "What does this mean?" What does Paul, or other writers of the scripture, have to say about worship and spiritual gifts? The Believers' Church needs to think through this relationship, particularly in this age of "charismatics," of increasing attention to experience in worship, and where "sharing" is replacing solid biblical exposition and preaching.

The Holy Spirit **was, is** and **must remain** the essential ingredient in worship. His centrality is seen throughout the New Testament writings and does, as R.P. Martin describes, have a pervasive influence in prayer, praise, instruction etc.[1] In fact, Martin, quoting Professor van Unnik, goes so far as to say that "New Testament worship **stands within 'the magnetic field of the Holy Spirit'.**"[2]

Any discussion on worship and spiritual gifts must take I Corinthians 11-14 into consideration. Some significant things that emerge in Paul's exposition when "people come together to worship" (11:33; 14:26) include: (1) God has given spiritual gifts to the church; (2) It is the work of the Holy Spirit to bear witness to the Lordship of Jesus Christ; (3) Spiritual gifts are given for the edification of the entire body. As Ferdinand Hahn has said: "...the dominant idea is that the gifts of the Spirit obligate their recipients to serve. This is why **diakonia** (ministering) is stressed";[3] (4) There must be **order** in the assembly. Charismatic activities should not disturb good order in the services; (5) True spirituality leads to a true morality; (6) The underlying principle of all spiritual gifts is subordination, self-limitation and dependence; (7) The right motive in the exercise of a spiritual gift during worship is essential; that motive is love.

We, in the Believers' or Free Church, are well aware of the excesses of ecstatic phenomena in Corinth as well as in contemporary society. But again, I ask: "What does this mean for us today?" Do we in the Free Church have a theology which prohibits or permits the exercise of all spiritual gifts within the context of corporate worship? Is there room for charismatic contributions by the congregation? Do we sanction any spontaneity in the exercise of gifts? And here I don't mean just having an "exciting" worship service with the usual "clapping," "amens," "praise the Lord," "hallelujahs," etc. Christensen, in spite of all of his good suggestions for contemporizing worship by making it "joyous," "relevant," "emotionally uplifting," etc., doesn't face the issue. When it comes to the exercise of the spiritual gifts within the context of Christian worship we have been content to relegate this to the Pentecostal and Full Gospel Assemblies. Is there a place for a charismatic ministry within **all** churches of the Free Church tradition?

While I am pleading that we take I Corinthians 11-14 seriously in our theology and practice of worship, I feel that another caution needs to be given. Our tendency is to simplify the worship traditions of the early church and to believe that all the answers to our problems lie within the pages of the New Testament. The five "facts about the worship of the early church" stated by Andrew Blackwood and quoted by Mitton are too simple and should not be regarded as normative for the entire church, or a pattern to which we need to return.[4]

The cry, "Let's get back to the way the New Testament church worshipped," needs to be countered by the question, "Which church in the New Testament" — the one in Jerusalem, Antioch, Corinth, Ephesus or Rome?[5]

Or, as F. Hahn has put it, do we talk about the worship of the "Early Aramaic-Speaking Community," "Hellenistic Jewish Christianity," "Early Gentile Christianity," or worship of the "Subapostolic Period?"[6] Let's examine all of the New Testament and not try to build a theology and/or practice of worship on any single document. If this were done, for example, one could conclude that scripture reading has no place in worship because it isn't mentioned in the chapters of I Corinthians that deal with worship.

We need to think clearly about such differences and developments, as well as consider seriously the implications of early Christian worship as it moved from a predominantly charismatic style of worship to a more conscious adherence to liturgical forms and official leadership. Even a closer examination of the Church Fathers, such as Justin Martyr, wouldn't hurt us.[7]

The task before us is not simple, nor should it be taken lightly. We shall always face the tensions that arise between "traditionalists" and those who plead for a more "contemporary" style of worship. Some persons believe that the only way to God is through a fixed ritual or liturgy, while others will opt for so-called freedom from structures — toward spontaneity.[8]

The congregations in which we worship are heterogenous in nature. Differing age groups, ethnic backgrounds, educational levels and even church architecture often determine what may or may not be done in worship. What is worshipful to one is disgusting to another; some like personal interaction during worship, others do not; what may be emotionally uplifting for one can be emotionally disturbing to another. Someone's worship is sacrilegious to another; someone's theology is someone else's psychology. The exercise of one's spiritual gifts in worship may be countered by another's insistence upon silence or order.

All of this presents a tremendous challenge to the Believers' Church. There is a place for worship and spiritual gifts. To quote F. Hahn:

> Worship can be properly ordered only when the freedom necessary for the operation of the Spirit remains. All legalism is contrary to the nature of the worship performed by the community assembled in the name of Jesus. But this means at the same time that worship must as much as possible be kept free of rigid institutional order. It is true that Spirit and law, charisma and order, are not mutually exclusive; but when office and community organization are fixed by formal law, we have probably reached that fateful limit of institutionalization that usually leaves no room for the manifold gifts of the Spirit.[9]

III

The Believers' Church
In The Canadian Context

Seminar Papers and Responses

CHURCH GROWTH:
ESSENTIAL TO THE BELIEVERS' CHURCH?

Philip Collins

Church growth, a term coined by Donald McGavran while he was a missionary in India, is basically a philosophy of evangelism. It involves all the processes which go into winning men and women to Jesus Christ, and leading them to the kind of discipleship which makes them responsible and reproducing members of the local church. Church growth is not, however, an evangelistic programme, but a conceptual framework which evaluates any and all evangelistic programmes on the basis of the results of these programmes.[1] It is "fiercely pragmatic."

This concept of evangelism has great validity for the Believers' Church movement. It reflects the great desire of God, which we see in the Bible, for winning men and women to Christ, and for bringing them into local churches. It seems to create a dynamic through which the Holy Spirit is free to work as He seeks the growth of the Kingdom of God.

Although many local congregations within those groups which comprise the Believers' Church movement seem to be "ghettoized," there seems to be evidence that in the past decade many Believers' Church denominations are growing.[2] As they grow, and as others watch them grow, many theological and biblical questions have been raised about the wisdom or the propriety of emphasizing church growth principles. Robert C. Berry, of the Canadian Baptist Overseas Mission Board, often says in public meetings, "After prayer and the work of the Holy Spirit in the lives of evangelical believers, we must take seriously the insights of church growth particularly in the area of sociology."[3]

In this paper, we will consider five major questions to which the Believers' Churches should address themselves.

I. RESISTANCE TO THE HOMOGENEOUS UNIT PRINCIPLE, OR TO CULTURAL CHRISTIANITY

Among evangelicals in the Believers' Church tradition there is considerable resistance to what is known as the "homogeneous unit principle," which has been defined colloquially by Win Arn of the American Church Growth Institute in Pasadena as "going to your own kind of people." On this view, the growth of the church is best experienced by going to those people who will most likely respond. That is, going to the "areas of response." McGavran has said, "Men like to become Christians without crossing racial, linguistic, or class barriers."[4] This particular principle of church growth has often been identified as racist.

Canadian believers respond negatively to this principle for mainly two reasons. One, it has the taint of "Americanism," and two, it seems to fly in the face of the biblical statement of oneness in Christ. This resistance to the homogeneous unit principle comes about in part by a failure to understand what McGavran and others have meant by this term. The intention is to take seriously the sociological reality of the many cultures in our country,[5] and to enhance in the minds of evangelicals the dignity of the various peoples who have come to our land. And it teaches us to allow authentic cultural expressions of Christianity whenever ethnic people respond to the gospel of Jesus Christ. It is meant to be the very opposite of racism. In fact, it is meant to put down forever paternalistic attitudes toward peoples of other ethnic groups who come among us, and to reduce a subconscious arrogance for people of various stations and classes in life.

The homogeneous unit principle has been called "cultural Christianity" by some evangelicals. Special attention was given to the phrase "cultural Christianity" at the Lausanne Congress, by Rene Padilla, a Latin American graduate of Wheaton College.[6] He criticizes Americans for confusing the essence of Christianity with the "American way of life," and objects to the compulsion felt by some missionaries to export an American Christian life-style to other cultures.

Church growth advocates applaud Padilla at this point. And as Peter Wagner, of Fuller Theological Seminary, notes,[7] they would also applaud if Padilla had gone on to mention similar tendencies among Korean missionaries to Thailand, or Vietnamese among the Montagnards, or French missionaries among the Gypsies, or Ecuadorian Mestizo missionaries among the Quichua Indians, or scores of other cases of the exportation of a specific "culture Christianity" by cross-cultural evangelists. This situation has existed in missionary procedures ever since the church was planted in Antioch and when bands of Judaizers began carrying around their own type of cultural Christianity.

Church growth advocates have no ultimate or final answers to these concerns, but they have developed some guidelines to deal with them. For one thing, they recognize that there **never** has been any such thing as "acultural Christianity." The very fact that Christianity has always been expressed in a human language at once gives it a cultural form. Even within the general western cultural tradition, Christianity has consistently been contextualized in a variety of ways, some good and some not so good, as a work like Ernst Troeltsch's **The Social Teaching of the Christian Churches** shows.[8] What the church growth people have discovered, not only in the United States but in Canada, is that concentrating on the "responsive people" as an area for ministry has often resulted in rapid growth of the Church of Jesus Christ. Church growth people are not stating that the homogeneous unit principle is a perfect word from the Lord for evangelism, but they are saying that a sociological understanding of our Canadian peoples (note the plural) would be to our advantage in reaching Canada for Jesus Christ. Perhaps Canadians can modify the homogeneous unit principle in a practical way by taking ten per cent of their missionary budget and using that money for "seeding" new areas where there is at present little response, so that in the years to come there will be a large "area of response."[9]

II. FEAR OF THE NUMBERS GAME

Because Believers' Churches historically have been reluctant to sacrifice "quality" for "quantity" and have tended to insist upon reproducing the New Testament church as they understood it, many have resisted what seems to them to be an excessive emphasis upon "triumphalism" in the church growth movement, especially in terms of numbers.[10] To them it implies that the end justifies the means. It does not matter, apparently, if the people in the churches are worldly, or poor stewards, or unconcerned about social issues. They suspect that church growth people preach a message of cheap grace, and they point out that apparently quantity is more important than quality. The great error in the church growth movement for them is "triumphalism."[11]

Most of us who have been brought up in the Believers' Church movement can appreciate these sentiments. It needs also to be said, however, that people who espouse church growth principles do not accept these criticisms as valid. The kind of triumphalism which the critics seem to be describing is not a characteristic of true church growth thinking. What then creates the impression of triumphalism?

This writer is in no sense a church historian, but it is his understanding that Canada has never experienced a **national** awakening or revival or renewal. There have been periods of revival in various areas of the country. Probably the best known is the one which occurred in Hamilton, Ontario as part of a great spiritual awakening in the New England States. But as as general rule, Canadian Christians seem to have been more reserved than their American counterparts. but a more likely reason for resistance is a misunderstanding of the general spirit of optimism that admittedly characterizes the church growth advocates.

There are two basic reasons for this optimism, one empirical, the other theological. Empirically, church growth people attempt to focus on the widest possible dimension of God's activity in the world. From that point of view, they see a contemporary spirit of Christianity unprecedented in the two thousand years of the Christian movement. While dark spots certainly can be detected here and there, world-wide, the victories far outnumber the defeats. This encourages God's people and tends to inject a spirit of joy and optimism.

Theologically, this is what people who are on God's side should expect. By nature God is a loving person, desiring that all men, alienated by sin, be reconciled to Himself. Those who are drawn to Christ by the Holy Spirit should then be incorporated into the church. When Jesus Himself gave the first news of the church to His followers, He said, "I will build my church and the gates of hell shall not prevail against it" (Matthew 16:18). Surely it is not stretching the biblical evidence to conclude that from the beginning Jesus assures His followers of "triumph" in the growth of the church. If this should produce a spirit of optimism in Christian believers, it is likely an optimism that God Himself shares.

Triumphalism, understood in this light, may really be a kind of holy or sanctified action.

This characteristic of optimism in the church growth movement has engendered "fierce pragmatism."[13] In the Lausanne Congress this emerged as the "practical" emphasis over against a somewhat "mystical" emphasis. According to E.P. news service,[14] "the mystical won out." Small wonder! The chief advocate of the mystical was John R. Stott who is well known and was a prominent member of the planning committee. A good way of sharpening the issue is to examine Stott's position in the words of the editor of the Presbyterian Journal (1974: 12): "John R.W. Stott put it as clearly as we have ever heard: 'Evangelism must not be defined in terms of its **results**...To evangelize in biblical usage does not mean to win converts (as it usually does when we use the word) but simply to announce the Good News, irrespective of results.'"[15]

Stott's assignment at the Lausanne Congress was to define evangelism for the plenary session.[16] In doing so he allied himself with J.I. Packer against the famous archbishops' definition of 1918.[17] What the editor did not mention was that the Stott/Packer definition also ran counter to Billy Graham's definition of evangelism given at the Berlin Congress of 1966. Graham said:

> It seems to me that we cannot improve on the definition of
> evangelism that was given to us by the Archbishops' committee on
> evangelism in 1918: to evangelize is to present Christ Jesus in the
> power of the Holy Spirit, so that men shall come to put their trust
> in God through Him, to accept Him as their Saviour, and serve
> Him as their King **in the fellowship of His church.**[18]

The point of this discussion is whether the definition of evangelism should include the goal of bringing unbelievers to Christ and into responsible, reproducing membership in the church, or whether it is simply the proclamation of the message. The problem to church growth people is that John Stott's definition could inhibit the growth of the church.[19]

Peter Wagner has stated his fear that some may be tempted to use the Stott/Packer statement as a "cop-out." With it, an evangelistic programme can fail with honour, so to speak. It is comforting to reduce one's objectives to a fail-safe level. Wagner goes on to say that a baseball player may well prefer to be evaluated on how many runs he makes. A business manager could be judged on the amount of cash flow rather than on the profit and loss statement. But these examples are absurd because we know that neither a baseball team nor a business can long survive unless the goals reflect production as well as effort.

The challenge or the response to the question of triumphalism and fierce pragmatism, perhaps, is to raise other questions in their place. Why do some evangelistic efforts consistently fail to bring men and women to Christ and into responsible membership in a local church? Are the evangelists in the wrong place at the wrong time? Are they using the wrong methods? Is something wrong with their relationship to God? These are difficult and not very comfortable questions.

III. QUESTIONING THE DEFINITION OF DISCIPLESHIP

It almost seems strange in the light of the tradition of the Believers' Church and its heritage that the question of what discipleship means in terms of membership in the local church should be raised.[20] Nevertheless, it seems to be the experience of many local churches in the Believers' Church tradition in Canada that the importance of church membership is minimized. One often hears people, including pastors, stating that it is important to be "a Christian," but one gets the distinct feeling that becoming a responsible and reproducing member of a local church is somehow not important.

The criticism that church growth people are more interested in quantity than quality indicates that church growth principles are not being understood by evangelicals. The hypothesis that the **quality** of Christians is inversely proportionate to their **quantity** ought to sound odd to people in the Believers' Church movement. Paul rejoiced that the Corinthians had been "called to be saints" and "were in everything enriched by him" (I Corinthians 1: 2-9), even though their divisive spirit, immorality, selfishness and false doctrine needed correcting. Church growth advocates are interested in seeing all Christians everywhere engaged in radical obedience to the Lord. They are concerned with numbers because those numbers reflect **real people** who have been born again by the Spirit of God. But they go on to say that in the Corinthian church these real people not only should have been born again by God's Spirit, **but also baptized into the local church**, and they should have continued steadfastly in the apostles' doctrine and fellowship, and in breaking of bread and in prayers (Acts 2: 42). Newborn Christians, who still need to be fed with milk, like the Corinthians, the Galatians and the Colossians, are infinitely better off, from the biblical point of view, than those who are still "dead in their trespasses and sins...walking according to the course of this world" (Ephesians 2: 1-2). Ralph Winter has put the false quantity-quality dichotomy to rest permanently in his chapter on the subject in **Crucial Issues in Missions Tomorrow** (1972).[21]

Church growth advocates stress reaching for goals, with objectives to reach those goals, usually in the forms of specific programmes and goal setting. The purpose is to win as many people to Christ as possible. But, the stress is on **biblical means** to reach those goals and the need to be obedient to Christ and to the Great Commission in Matthew 28: 19-20. A concern of church growth people is the persistent use of biblical but irrelevant, or unproductive, means in an attempt to bring about evangelistic ends. When believers insist on investing large sums of money or large amounts of Christian energy in certain programmes in the name of evangelism, but in fact disciples are not made and churches do not multiply, church growth people counsel a different approach. They propose productive biblical means for unproductive biblical means. The overall motivation is to glorify God in the church by Jesus

Christ (Ephesians 3:21). This, admittedly, does not always come through clearly, and sparks the accusation that church growth justifies all kinds of dubious means to reach set goals.

IV. A PROBLEM OF ORDER FOR THE BELIEVERS' CHURCH MOVEMENT: BAPTISM

Donald McGavran, in his book **Understanding Church Growth**[22] raises the question of baptism and how it relates to entrance into the church. He writes that there are only three ways into the church: baptism, transfer and restoration. (If the church is defined as a company of baptized believers, then for paedobaptist denominations a fourth way — confirmation — would have to be added.) McGavran states that nothing produces **real** church growth except baptisms **from the world**. No baptisms: no growth! He says this dictum can be refined to read: "Nothing produces growth except baptisms **from the world** provided those being baptized are properly shepherded and become vital Christians." Pastoral care is, of course, crucially important; but McGavran's refinement does not vitiate the statement, "no baptisms: no growth." The church, through baptisms, must obtain new Christians before it can care for them properly. It is also true to say: "no baptisms: no aftercare."

The point in raising this particular issue in regard to the church growth movement is that McGavran particularly feels that baptism means entrance into the Christian church. This would then mean that the development of discipleship of the Christian would take place **after** the person has become a baptized member of the local church. This particular view is not held by all in the Believers' Church movement. There are several variations in the doctrine and practice of baptism. If in future Believers' Churches move closer together, they will need to work through to a better understanding of the nature of baptism and how it relates to the mission of the church.[23]

Perhaps churches can follow through on the concept of baptism they now have. A unifying feature could be that all Believers' Churches would practise an annual renewal of "a membership covenant." How that covenant should read will also be a challenge, but it could perhaps be formulated gradually through discussion, and it could reflect the specific needs and opportunities of the church at a given time. It would seem that an artificial imposition of a traditional "standard church covenant" upon an unprepared denomination or local congregation would hardly lead to the practice of vital discipleship and discipline.

It will likely be the reconsideration of the meaning of baptism which will in time lead us to the development of a new form of the church and a new approach to church discipline.[24] It is quite clear that charity will be needed among those who are involved in this discussion, and even now prayer needs to be offered that at the appropriate time or times, God will give us the illumination and guidance. If the church growth concept gains significant influence in the Believers' Church movement, it will intensify the discussion because of its assumption that baptism is entrance into the Christian church at the local level.

V. PURITY: WHAT ABOUT THE WORK OF THE HOLY SPIRIT?

Believers' Church people in Canada have always regarded themselves as a people led by the Spirit.[25] Because of this vital heritage, the church growth movement is often challenged by the question of the work of the Holy Spirit. How does the free ministry of the Spirit fit into such things as goal setting, evaluation, measuring objectives and conducting a community analysis to determine the areas of response? This is a basic question for the Believers' Church movement and for the church growth people. For the Believers' Church movement comprises at least three types of traditions which flowed together.

The first tradition could be called "illuminism" or "spiritualism." The left wing of the Reformation, both on the continent and in England, was particularly susceptible to illuminism. Many Anabaptists and English dissenters valued direct new revelation of the Spirit above the "dead letter" of the scriptures. Luther's fear and repeated condemnations of the "enthusiasts" (Schwaermer) was well-founded, except when he failed to distinguish between the spiritualists and the evangelical Anabaptists.

A second stream of tradition is that of the holiness groups which stress sanctification and perfection. Few Baptists fit into this stream since they fail to pay sufficient attention to the continued work of the Holy Spirit **beyond regeneration**.

Today we have as a third element the charismatic movement. The discussion of the work of the Holy Spirit will take us in what may appear to some as an unusual direction. The ministry of the Spirit needs to be discussed in the framework of our church structures, particularly in relation to the decision-making process practised in most Believers' Churches. Decisions are usually made by a vote of the majority at a church business meeting. It could be asked in what way evangelicals in such churches find this compatible with an alleged dependence upon the guidance of the Holy Spirit (particularly through illumination). Since most, if not all, denominations in the Believers' Church tradition have historically adhered to congregational polity, probably a closer relationship in future will mean a gradual shift to elements of presbyterial and synodical church order.

The church growth movement could very well be a significant vehicle to help the Believers' Church denominations — and their local churches — to keep evangelism and church planting as the central thrust of their life in this twentieth century. Although witness has been an important element in the history of the Believers' Church movement, not all Believers' Church denominations have kept evangelism at the centre of their ministry. This is not meant to be a harsh judgement. If, however, the Believers' Churches could capture the optimism of the church growth movement, they would at the same time recapture the original concept of a witnessing people in mission, which is part of their heritage. Evangelical Anabaptists were the only people within the continental Reformation who recaptured the early Christian missionary vision and zeal.[26] To become a Christian meant to be a **witness** and mission-minded, often at the risk of life itself. Many sealed their witness with martyrdom. Without evangelism and church growth, a true Believers' Church will be extinct in one generation. Thus we need to identify the causes and factors, theological and non-theological, which have weakened the evangelistic outreach of some of the Believers' Churches. One factor is that several Believers' Church denominations have slid into a false dichotomy between personal evangelism and social service; that is, verbal witness as opposed to witness through deeds and lifestyle. The model of the historical Anabaptist witness, along with a better understanding of, and obedience to, the scriptures, with a new emphasis on prayer, and some insight into church growth principles and sociology will help us to recapture the early church's missionary vision and zeal.

VI. CONCLUSION

Ours is a period in which the Believers' Church has recovered a vision for the unity, renewal, mission and growth of the church.[27] It is also a period of time in which the theology of the church and its nature has been re-examined extensively. It is the purpose of the church growth movement to assist the church in its growth as it goes forward in preaching the gospel, baptizing the converts in the name of the Father, and Son and Holy Ghost, and making disciples who, by definition, are responsible, reproducing Christians in a local church. The church growth movement is still in the embryo stage and is open to guidance and direction. It does not believe that it is the only way to promote Christian faith.

Perhaps those of us who are part of the Believers' Church movement can help clarify the concept of church growth by stressing the sovereignty of God, that He is the Lord of the harvest, and that He prepares peoples and situations for response to the gospel. At the same time we can obey the injunction of our Lord in Matthew 28: 19-20, namely, that we should sow abundantly and, in doing so, reap abundantly. Surely this is biblical.[28] We could go on to state that we do believe in pre-evangelism. For example, if a mission board feels it is called to minister to the Muslims who seem to be an unresponsive people, it should send workers to do so. Church growth is not talking about individual mission boards. It is talking about the total evangelistic force in our country. We do believe in sowing the seed so that some areas will become responsive to the gospel of the Lord Jesus Christ.

However, we should at the same time continue to articulate church growth principles. After prayer and research, we move forward to conversion growth, leading those who are converted into the apostles' doctrine, fellowship, breaking of bread, prayer and outreach. The church growth movement counts as Christians those who have been born again, **having been incorporated into the Body of Christ**. And although there may be some debate about the methodology and pragmatism of the movement, it does not necessarily have to be in conflict with the development and growth of the Believers' Church movement.

CHURCH GROWTH
IN A BELIEVERS' CHURCH PERSPECTIVE

Dennis M. Oliver

I. THE BELIEVERS' CHURCH HERITAGE

The Believers' Church traditions — most notably the Mennonite, Baptist and Pentecostal streams — provide many lessons about the kind of evangelism that results in growing local congregations. In many cases, church growth was, rightly, not the **ultimate goal** of these movements, which were motivated by the desire to glorify God through faithfulness to His Word and Spirit. The Believers' Church heritage reflects many healthy emphases which we might well recapture or reaffirm today in Canada. These include: (1) A conscious and passionate commitment to evangelism and church growth, i.e., to "great commission missions"; (2) A rich illustration of the power of lay involvement in outreach; [1] (3) A reluctance to sacrifice "quality" for "quantity," and an insistence on reproducing the New Testament church (as believers understood it), demanding of the membership faith, faithfulness and experience; (4) An evangelism which made no clear distinction between the discipling of heathen nations and the proselytization of those with "lesser" (nominal) Christian commitments; (5) An evangelism which enfolded converts into local church fellowship. [2]

A common danger of Believers' Church movements has been excessive independence, leading to sectarian intolerance, heterodox faith and subjective spirituality.

II. BELIEVERS' CHURCH GROWTH IN CANADA TODAY

By and large, Canadian Believers' Churches evidence more growth than their "mainline" counterparts. United Church, Anglican and Presbyterian church memberships have all been declining through the past decade (from -1.65 to -2.9 per cent annually), while many Believers' Church denominations are growing. However, several additional realities must be recognized: (1) Some encouraging growth is occurring among congregations outside the Believers' Church movement; (2) Many heterodox "cults" are also showing impressive growth; (3) Not all Believers' Church denominations or congregations are growing.

The table on the next page shows some of the various church growth trends in our land. [3]

Contemporary Canadian church growth research, most notably by Canadian sociologists Bibby and Brinkerhoff, indicates that Believers' Church congregations (as those from other traditions) may often lack the will or the ability to evanglize those without a prior

Church	Membership Reported in 1977[1]	Membership Reported in 1976[2]	Annual Growth %	Membership Reported 1965[7]	Decadal Growth Annual %
Anglican Church	1,015,216[3]	1,057,012[4]	-3.95	1,359,601	-2.92
Baptist Federation	128,146	119,329	7.39	137,299	-.69
Brethren Canadian Conference	1,691	1,593	6.15		
Canadian Baptist Conference	2,304	1,631	41.26		
Christian and Missionary Alliance	26,587	25,447	4.48	16,049	5.05
Christian Church (Disciples of Christ)	4,700	4,718	-.38		
Christian Churches and Churches of Christ	5,100	5,100	0.00	7,258	-3.53
Christian Congregation	2,599	1,678	54.89		
Church of God (Cleveland)	2,085	1,680	24.11		
Church of God of Prophecy	1,810[5]	1,387[6]	30.5		
Church of Jesus Christ of Latter Day Saints	66,808	65,004	2.78		
Church of the Nazarene	7,972	7,849	1.57		
Evangelical Church	3,724	3,712	.32	3,595	.35
Evangelical Lutheran Church	82,045	82,110	.08	76,120	7.49
Free Methodist Church	5,043	4,864	3.68		
Italian Pentecostal Church	2,755[5]	2,640	2.13[8]		
Jehovah's Witnesses	60,759	58,542	3.95	41,887	3.72
Lutheran Church — Canada	96,187	96,887	-.72	93,717	2.61
Lutheran Church in America	121,815	120,592	1.01	122,029	-.17
Mennonite Brethren Churches of North America	18,459	18,009[6]	NA	15,462	1.77
Mennonite Church	9,448	9,357	.97		
North American Baptist Conference	14,138	13,511	4.64		
Polish National Catholic Church	6,000	6,000	0.00		
Presbyterian Church	171,791	174,555	-1.58	202,498	-1.65
Reformed Church in America — Ontario Classis	5,356	5,570	-3.84		
Reorganised Church of Jesus Christ of Latter Day Saints	11,304	11,312	-.07		
Roman Orthodox Episcopate of America (Jackson)	8,000	8,000	0.00		
Russian Orthodox Church — Patriarchal Parishes	10,000	10,000	0.00		
Seventh Day Adventist Church	25,143	23,890	5.24		
Unitarian Universalist Association	4,869	6,207	-21.56		
United Church of Canada	2,101,452	2,140,102	-1.81	2,635,217	-2.26
Canada	22,765,000[9]	22,436,000	1.47	19,644,000	1.47

1. "Yearbook of American and Canadian Churches, 1977", Inclusive Membership, pp. 241-243.
2. "Yearbook of American and Canadian Churches, 1976", Inclusive Membership, pp. 230-232.
3. 1975 figures reported except as noted.
4. 1974 figures reported except as noted.
5. 1976 figure reported.
6. 1975 figure reported.
7. Figures obtained from church records. The ten year analysis is assuming a constant growth rate over the period which levels off any dramatic changes which may have occured in any one year. Insufficient information results in an incomplete analysis.
8. Two-year periodicity.
9. Statistics Canada figures reported.

orientation to their style of Christianity (that is, to their particular sub-culture).[4] Our analysis would be tragically misleading if it agreed with the implication of Dean M. Kelly that evangelical churches are reaching out to the uncommitted within the ranks of the "liberal" denominations and winning them to their faith.[5] In fact, most church growth in Canada (of whatever tradition) in this era has resulted from immigration and other forms of transfer growth (committed Christians moving from one congregation to another) and from the retention of the children of the church. Much aggressive evangelism functions more to reassure the congregation that they are evangelistic than to evangelize effectively. Fortunately, we do have some models of effective conversion growth in our land. But we dare not assume that this kind of growth is dominant in Canadian Believers' Church congregations.

We hasten to recognize the encouraging exceptions. Ethnic churches often reach first-generation Canadians who are open to new beginnings in a new land. Recently planted churches seem to have a greater ability to reach out beyond the particularities of the socio-religious sub-cultures with which their parent denominations or mothering churches might be identified (thus contacting, converting, and enfolding the unchurched more than established congregations).

How and why are Believers' Churches growing? We must recognize sociological and psychological factors, as well as spiritual ones.

Most North American religious growth can be largely explained by the following factors: 'whole body involvement,' in which both the ordained and non-ordained laity are active in ministry, a balanced programme stressing growth and fellowship within the church as well as evangelism and an ability to discern those who would be responsive to the message and the ambiance of the church.[6]

Among Believers' Churches many forms of evangelism are proving effective, including visitation of "cold contacts" and prospects, friend-ship evangelism, home Bible studies, pulpit evangelism and special events (films, campaigns and crusades, etc.). Local churches which fail to develop effective on-going congregational evangelistic programmes will experience little growth from inter-church and community-wide outreach efforts. **The local church is the key to reaching unchurched Canadians.** These factors are important to recognize and apply, for they relate to the psychological and social nature of man.

Yet we cannot overstress the importance of the spiritual dimension for every aspect of biblically faithful, eternally fruitful ministry. For Believers' Churches to be true to their heritage they must be more than pragmatic — although their heritage includes a healthy biblical pragmatism. For the Anabaptist evangelists (many who became martyrs), church growth was secondary to faithfulness to God. So it should be in Canada today. Yet we can expect in our context of liberty and receptivity that faithfulness to God will result in church growth.

The expansion of denominations in Canada depends on church planting — not just local church evangelism. Those congregations and traditions which conceive evangelization only in terms of local church outreach — or who believe that Canada is already sufficiently "churched" — will limit their potential for growth. Denominations which are committed to vigourous church planting are moving forward in a marvellous way.

For many Believers' Churches, the most positive growth is occurring among "new Canadians" in demographic areas where the Believers' Church tradition has in the past been minimized. In one Canadian denomination, the most healthy growth is among its Chinese churches. The denomination is not only effective in conversion oriented evangelism, but is rapidly multiplying local churches in our land and is committed to a vigourous missionary expansion to the United States and to South America. Other denominations can report similar signs of life among their Chinese, Spanish-speaking, Filipino, Greek, Haitian, Italian and other "ethnic" congregations. Denominations seeking enhanced church growth should consider planting such "ethnic" churches. Such is a proven way to widen evangelistic effectiveness.

The present movement of God in Quebec is unprecedented. Quebec is perhaps Canada's most promising harvest field. Leaders working there unanimously testify that today's very encouraging signs of growth point to more fruitful days ahead. Denominations committed to growth (and committed to Canada) should invest heavily in ministry in Quebec.

It is encouraging to note the informal movement, in both reflection and action, of church growth in our land. A review of Canadian denominational periodicals shows an increasing concern for growth, and a focus on positive principles and patterns by which congregations and denominations can evangelize this country. Some denominations are circulating special evangelism and extension bulletins.[7] There is a renewed commitment to church planting in most traditions. Church growth seminars have been multiplying through Canada, in some instances with revolutionary positive effects on local congregations. As well, we find a renewed commitment to growth-oriented research, and to plotting strategies for growth. Some of our theological institutions are training students in church growth procedures relevant to Canadian realities. All these things lead me to be very hopeful regarding the continued forward movement of the Church in our land.

Much of the evangelism that is at present occuring in Canada is following models and methodologies "imported" from the United States. We can be thankful for all that God is supplying us through His worldwide church. But we must realize that Canada is dissimilar to our southern neighbour in several important respects.

(1) We are more Roman Catholic than Protestant (in terms of **nominal** church identification),[8] whereas the United States is much more Protestant than Catholic. If the Believers' Church movement is to significantly extend itself into Canadian society it must develop effective ways to enfold nominal, unchurched Roman Catholics.

(2) The Believers' Church tradition is very strong in the United States, whereas it is relatively minor in Canada. This is symbolized by the fact that the largest Protestant church in the United States is the twelve

million member Southern Baptist denomination, whereas the largest Canadian Protestant denomination is the United Church of Canada. Canada does not have any regional equivalent to the American "Bible belt."[9]

(3) Unlike our southern neighbour, Canada's religious traditions are notably liturgical, whether of the Roman, Orthodox, Lutheran, Anglican or Reformed variety.

(4) Believers' Church denominations in Canada are less "together" in thought and action than those in the United States (explained partly by our ethno-geographical diversity and partly by historical factors).

(5) There is an additional factor of our 'Canadian character.' Perhaps we are more introverted and cautious than Americans.

All this has important outreach implications regarding the style of worship, patterns of fellowship and methods of evangelism which are geared towards finding and enfolding those who are not oriented to Believers' Church traditions. Perhaps unfortunately (to our church growth concerns), the life and influence of these traditions are rather 'ghettoized' in one or more forms of "the evangelical subculture."

III. CONCLUDING PERSPECTIVES:
THE CHALLENGES OF FUTURE GROWTH

The needs of our Canadian nation are great — not merely for evangelism and church planting but for the leaven and life of Believers' Church righteousness. Perhaps as never before in our land the general population is willing to listen to those who have a clear gospel to proclaim. Those who are still restrained by the hesitation of the 1960s need to gain sight of the opportunities ahead, the God-given resources to meet them, and the timeless commission to "go." The time is urgent, for the open hearts of this generation might harden in the 1980s or 1990s.

In this writer's opinion, the greatest need for Believers' Churches is that of spiritual renewal. The heritage and biblical rootedness of Believers' Church traditions are rich. But today most churches reflect too much "uneasiness in Zion." In too many cases, the message and the movements of the past have fossilized and lost their dynamic. In this context a concern for growth can be quite self-centred. All this, however, is said with the grateful realization that God is renewing many Canadian churches, giving them a new interest and new church growth effectiveness. As we expose ourselves to our loving God, He will both purify us and multiply our effective service — not as a legalistic obligation ("ought") but as a natural overflow of spiritual concern.

For individual congregations to reach out into the unchurched community of conscious non-Christians and uncommitted nominal Christians we must find ways of breaking out of our "subcultural ghettos." Ethnic churches (e.g., German Mennonites) are realizing that their longterm effectiveness rests in appealing to the wider culture.[10] The challenge to reach out from one ethnic identity to the wider social mosaic is great indeed. Perhaps as great or greater is the need for many congregations to reach beyond the evangelical subculture in their attempt to evangelize and enfold those whose religious background is vastly different. We must remember that such are the majority in Canada. One positive way to transform or broaden the appeal of a denomination is to consciously plant different kinds of churches. The debate recorded in Acts 15 should inform us regarding both the cultural and the theological challenges of reaching out from an ecclesiastical ghetto.

As congregations and denominations face possible new harvest fields they must consider what Canadians they can most easily and most naturally reach for Christ. Yet they must not overlook the needs and opportunities found among Canada's "neglected peoples." I am concerned that few Canadian churches are committed to finding how to evangelize the two-million-plus Canadians at the bottom of our socio-economic ladder. While most denominations scramble to enfold middle class suburbanites, our urban poor are ignored. Much too little is planned for missionary outreach to our million-plus Italian community, the myriads of native Canadians in our cities, or other identifiable neglected target groups. God would not have His church rest content with tokenism. The resources of many denominations must be harnessed to accomplish this task.

A different kind of challenge facing Believers' Church congregations across Canada is the burgeoning lay movement. Some of the unordained laity who are turned on to the possibilities of using their skills and gifts in Christian service, or who are experiencing unprecedented spiritual growth in their lives, are frustrated by the inflexibility and fearful caution of traditional church leaders. Increasing numbers of Christians are seeking fellowship, growth and service opportunities in parachurch organizations which (whether consciously or by accident) are alienated from the local church. Parachurch ministry will continue to burgeon, and congregations must either be more attractive than these groups or learn to co-operate with them to mutual, Christ-honouring advantage. Otherwise, efforts to advance the local church will be hindered by these parachurch organizations.

The needs and challenges of our day do not permit contentment or self-satisfaction. Yet the growth of so many Believers' Church congregations and denominations indicates a measure of faithfulness and effectiveness for which we praise God. The present writer is hopeful about the potential of Believers' Church congregations to be used of God for Canadian evangelization. May we all be responsive to His movement among us, and worthy of our heritage.

CHURCH AND STATE IN CANADA; CO-OPERATION AND CONFRONTATION

John H. Redekop

A. INTRODUCTION

The problem of church-state relations is as old as Christianity itself; Jesus' statements about Caesar are imprecise and their application to specific situations fraught with difficulty. Moreover, as the role of government changes, new questions require new answers. The answers have ranged far and wide from theocracy to Erastianism, to legal separation and to assorted varieties of dualism. This paper focuses on the peculiar dualist response of Mennonites, and to some extent other pacifist groups, in Canada.

Several general considerations are basic. First, in many respects the Canadian responses were intertwined with and largely influenced by realities in the United States; second, in contrast with the British situation on the one hand, and the American on the other, the dominant theme since 1867 in Canada (though not necessarily for all groups) has been informal co-operation of church and state rather than formal establishment or separation; and third, Canadian Christians have, by and large, been very individualistic. Once the pre-confederation quarrels about clergy reserves, formal establishment, and public education had subsided or been settled, there was very little corporate Christian activism. There seems to have been considerable support for public morality and the welfare society but also a corollary emphasis on personal, individual, moral issues, often to the virtual exclusion of any broad concern with social or national questions. While American Believers' Churches have emphasized a "wall of separation" but in fact given much support to a "lowest common denominator" civil religion, their Canadian counterparts have, in the main, avoided both notions and indulged in a parochial political quietism. Additionally, I must underscore the usual caveats that official pronouncements often distorted actual situations and that the following account deals only with the major issues, and only in a general way.

In surveying the historical record it quickly becomes evident that for adherents to the peace churches in Canada, church-state relations has been a major problem right from the outset. Many dilemmas and much frustrating activity accompanied the determined effort to be separate people of God. At first there was little theorizing and much activity, but gradually the dimensions of the theological stance were made more explicit. Similarly, at first the response was largely corporate but in later years, especially after World War I, individuals acted and reacted increasingly on their own. Both of these developments reflected a very gradual but clear reversion to a more denominational orientation by an ethnic sect which had come into existence in the sixteenth century, not as a peculiar society but as the radical wing of the Christian church. As we review the evidence we shall also see how Mennonites in Canada, especially since World War II, have slowly shifted from passivity to active involvement and have come to view state-related issues not only as problems but also as opportunities.

The paper is organized as follows: Part B describes the theoretical/theological basis underlying the Anabaptist/pacifist response in Canada, emphasizing its development from Reformation roots and recent denominational stances; Part C, the major section, analyzes specific areas of co-operation and conflict, giving special attention to immigration and settlement, military matters and political participation; Part D provides a brief reinterpretation of Canadian church-state relations, in the light of changing circumstance and changing practices; and Part E sets forth some concluding observations.

Before turning to the theological base, let me suggest some definitions. By "Believers' Church" I mean,

> a fellowship of believers under the Lordship of Christ; a voluntary band of disciples...reconciling men to [Christ] and to one another through the preaching of the Word...through Christian nurture and discipline, through prophetic proclamation, and through humble, loving service.[1]

The term "state" has many meanings. In a technical sense it is synonymous with country. However, in this essay, unless the context connotes something else, I use it to refer specifically to the inclusive political structures whose office-holders, the government, control a specific population in a defined territory. In an ultimate sense, all state structures rest on coercion but to a large degree, especially in "Western democracies," state activities extend much beyond coercion and security to justice and welfare.

B. CHURCH AND STATE:
PACIFIST STATEMENTS AND COMMENTARY

An understanding of subsequent Mennonite church-state relations, in Canada or elsewhere, necessitates a review of the theological basis. During the Great Reformation the major reformers — Luther, Zwingli, and Calvin — never broke completely with the secular powers. The radical wing, led by the Anabaptists later known as Mennonites, "protested against 'incomplete Protestantism'"[2] and against all formal institutionalized religion. Commenting on their emphasis and activism, R.J. Smithson suggests that their assertions "were in reality the principles of the Reformation carried to its logical conclusion."[3] Noting that "Christians of the Anabaptist-Mennonite tradition belong to one of history's most misunderstood groups,"[4] Thomas Sanders adds that this "despised group...became the first Protestant advocates of a separation of church and state, not on rational, pragmatic, or political grounds, but as a consequence of a theology of discipleship and the church as a community of disciples."[5]

It is instructive to look at some of the early statements. The seminal Schleitheim Confession of Faith (1527), in its fourth article, establishes the framework: "...for truly all creatures are in but two classes, good and bad, believing and unbelieving, darkness and light, the world and those who [have come] out of the world, ...and none can have part with the other."[6] The dialectic dualism of Luther continues but, according to these early Anabaptists, the battle between good and evil takes place primarily not within both church and state but between them. Article six asserts that "the sword is ordained of God outside the perfection of Christ"; the magistracy is ordained of God but Christians must not hold political office. The article suggests that if Christians are "chosen" to be magistrates they should "flee" as Jesus Himself did when He was invited to become king. The themes of dualism and inevitable conflict persist.

> The government magistracy is according to the flesh, but the Christian's is according to the Spirit...their citizenship is in this world, but the Christian's citizenship is in heaven; the weapons of their conflict and war are carnal and against the flesh only, but the Christians' weapons are spiritual, against the fortification of the devil.

An early Anabaptist preacher, Hans Marquardt, emphasized the "new" insight in a 1528 sermon: "Under the Old Covenant God has permitted His people the use of the sword...[but] the old law has been replaced by the new commandment of Christ that we should love our enemies...The believer is not to be an earthly ruler or use violence..."[7] Menno Simons himself taught that, "We teach and acknowledge no other sword...in the Kingdom or church of Christ than the sharp sword of the Spirit, God's word.... But the civil sword we leave to those to whom it is committed."[8] But Menno seems not to be entirely consistent; for example, he also states that "he who is a Christian must follow the Spirit, Word, and example of Christ, no matter whether he be emperor, king, or whatever he be."[9] In another essay Menno defines at some length for rulers "what the Word of the Lord commands them, how they should be minded, and how they should rightfully execute their office to the praise and glory of the Lord."[10]

Sanders argues that the apparent dichotomy "can be explained as an appeal to the consciences of supposedly Christian rulers who were persecuting Anabaptists."[11] But in the light of Menno's general emphasis on toleration and individual freedom within the community of the believers, it is also possible to argue that Menno is allowing for at least some kind of political involvement under certain conditions. (We shall return to that question in Part D.) Be that as it may, the early Anabaptists generally had a strongly negative view of the state and firmly believed that Christian righteousness should be exercised directly in society rather than through any state structures. The Anabaptists were not concerned first and foremost in any reconstruction of human society but with biblical faithfulness as they understood it.

In assessing the fundamental significance of the Anabaptist wing of the Reformation, Harold S. Bender writes as follows:

> It was in the doctrine of the church that the divergence from the rest of Christendom, both Catholic and Protestant, was most complete. The Anabaptists broke completely with the medieval concept of the Christian social order (church-state) as expressed in the term 'corpus christianum' [Christian body], substituting the 'corpus Christianorum' [body of Christians]. They were the first to insist upon a free church, separate from the state, separated from the world, composed of committed disciples, who had through personal conversion and dedication accepted Christ as Saviour and Lord. This believers' church they conceived of as a brotherhood, with leaders but without a hierarchy, with responsibility of all the members for the total life and ministry of the church, a disciplined body, a church of order. By their doctrine of the two kingdoms (not the two kingdom doctrine of Luther), the one the kingdom of Christ, the other the kingdom of this world ruled by Satan, they drew a clear line between the church and the general social order. Since the state was in this general social order 'outside the perfection of Christ,' although instituted by God and responsible to God, the church could have no part in it nor be subject to it in matters of faith, etc. Finally, the church was understood as a suffering church, bound to suffer in its conflict with the kingdom of this world, as it sought to create the holy community of love within its brotherhood circle, but through victorious steadfastness in suffering demonstrating that it was the body of Christ and would ultimately conquer.[12]

Contemporary Mennonite church-state orientations, as set forth in confessions of faith, have not changed much though the greater positive role of the modern state is increasingly noted. The joint statement of the Evangelical Mennonite Mission Church and the Evangelical Mennonite Conference describes the state as

> an institution appointed by God to exercise His wrath. The order maintained by governments is in some measure an expression in His fallen world of God's own order. The state obtains its power from God, thus it has derived power...Just as the first century Christians refused to obey the commands of a government over-reaching its authority, so the modern Christian must be alert and also draw lines...Basically the state still belongs to the old order. Punishment for wrong and not forgiveness still is the necessary practice. It is no accident that after charging His Roman readers to pay dues recognized in the old order, He goes on to speak of the love due to every man in that new order, where Christ and not Caesar, is king (Romans 13:7,9).[13]

In August, 1961, the Mennonite General Conference adopted the following statement about "The Twofold Character of the State":

> ...On the one hand it is a minister of God for good, whose function is the maintenance of order in this present world. Its ultimate source of power is the God of history Himself. As such, the Christian owes the state respect, obedience and co-operation, with prayers for its rulers to the end that the people of God may 'lead a quiet and peaceable life in all godliness and honesty.' The primary function of the state is the

maintenance of a stable society enabling the church to pursue her divine ministry...[But] on the other hand...the state is also an institution of this present evil world, and...is at times an agent of the forces arrayed against the Lord of history. For this reason the Christian cannot always submit to the demands of the state. On the contrary, he must needs on occasion be in opposition to the state....[14]

Some statements emphasize non-involvement. Thus, for example, Article 19 of the Confession of Faith adopted by the Mennonite General Conference on August 22, 1963 concludes that,

In law enforcement the state does not and cannot operate on the non-resistant principles of Christ's kingdom. Therefore, nonresistant Christians cannot undertake any service in the state or in society which would violate the principles of love and holiness as taught by Christ and His inspired apostles.[15]

In explaining this article one spokesman says:

There are some state functions in which Christians may participate, such as teaching and administration in public schools and administering health and welfare. Because the state may rely on force in administering justice, the nonresistant Christian will quickly find limits to what he can do as a part of government. Some feel that they are responsible to get people into office who are willing to consider God's laws.[16]

The most recent major statement, that found in Article XIV of the 1976 North American Mennonite Brethren Confession of Faith, states,

We believe that God instituted the state to maintain law and order in civil life and to promote public welfare. The functions and responsibilities of the state are distinct from those of the church. The chief concern and primary allegiance of all Christians should be to Christ's kingdom. It is our Christian duty to pray for those in government and to proclaim truth, love, righteousness and redemption. We should respect those in authority, exercise social responsibility, witness against corruption, discrimination and injustice, pay taxes and obey all laws that do not conflict with the Word of God.[17]

While we find a common Anabaptist orientation in all of these typical statements, there is clearly some diversity in emphasis and a growing sense of church-state interaction if not co-operation. The following section illustrates the extent to which actual developments in Canada reflected the general Anabaptist stance.

C. CO-OPERATION AND CONFLICT IN CANADA: THE PAST

1. **Immigration and Settlement.** Not surprisingly, the search for freedom (and sometimes good land) and the fact of persecution, generated continuous, sometimes large-scale, migration. The first Mennonites came to what is now Ontario from Pennsylvania in 1786, settling mainly in Waterloo County.[18] (The first Quakers, having been promised "free liberty of conscience" by an Act of 1758, had come as early as 1758.)[19] Soon hundreds immigrated, especially after Upper Canada became a province in 1791. While many had opposed the American Revolution and sympathized with the United Empire

Loyalist perspective, very few officially claimed that status with the special land and other benefits it brought. However, in later years a descendant of one of the early Mennonite families became president of the Dominion Council of the United Empire Loyalist Association.[20] Church-state conflicts had an early start with the failure of the 1819 Lincoln County (Niagara) Mennonite request to have a parcel of land set aside for Mennonites only. The petition failed because of the view "that in future no lands be granted to persons who will not enroll themselves in the militia and bear arms in defence of the Prince."[21] However, immigration continued; the religious census of Upper Canada in 1841 produced the following figures: Tunkers 1,327; Mennonites 5,379; and Quakers 5,429.[22]

The next major influx of Mennonite immigrants occurred soon after Canadian Confederation in 1867. A major "privilege" was accorded the would-be immigrants by way of an 1873 amendment to the Dominion Land Act. This amendment, a concession to much pressure for block settlement, allowed improvement of homestead land to be calculated not for each quarter section (160 acres) but for an entire block held corporately, provided that there were 20 or more families involved. At least partial perpetuation of "communal" farming and "closed village" life-styles was thus made possible.[23]

Almost simultaneously, on July 25, 1873, a major agreement was reached between the Canadian government and a delegation representing "German" Mennonites in Russia. The various accounts of that event uniformly document the heavy political pressure which the Mennonites brought to bear during the extensive and difficult bargaining. The full two-page text is reproduced by Francis.[24] In brief, the accord stated that "An entire exemption from military service is by law and Order-in-Council granted to the Denomination of Christians called Mennonites." Under the amended Dominion Land Act, eight townships in Manitoba were reserved as free homestead lands for Mennonites and, if required, additional townships would "be in the same way reserved." (The large West Reserve was created by an Ottawa Order-in-Council in 1876. The reserve structure was ended in 1898 after which open settlement became common.) Of the various financial and other additional favours promised, two should be highlighted. The Government of Canada promised the Mennonites "the fullest privilege of exercising their religious principles...without any kind of molestation or restriction whatever, and the same privilege extends to the education of their children in schools." Article eleven added that "the privilege of affirming instead of making affidavits is afforded by law." In later years Mennonites referred to this 1873 agreement as the Canadian "**Privilegium**" (privileges); Francis terms it the "Magna Carta" for Canadian Mennonites.[25] On balance, Prime Minister Alexander Mackenzie's "Liberal" government was very magnanimous towards the Mennonites and they were very grateful.

Within three years, more than six thousand Mennonites migrated to Canada. As we shall see later, the education clause soon caused problems because education was a provincial matter and neither Manitoba nor Ontario was party to the 1873 Agreement. Perhaps the Mennonite negotiators can be faulted for not having researched more carefully sections 91 and 92 of the British North America Act, but surely the Canadian government must have known that it was making a promise beyond its jurisdiction. The extent of government culpability can perhaps be deduced from the fact that three days after the issuance of the "Magna Carta" it secretly revoked the education clause, a fact not discovered until much later.[26]

A crisis developed when the Manitoba Public Schools Act of 1890 brought an end to all denominational school systems, and public funds were used to make public schools available to all school-age children. At about the same time various forms of military teaching and training were introduced in the schools. The Ontario groups objected vehemently and sent urgent messages to governments but with only limited success.[27] In Manitoba, in 1907, Premier R.P. Roblin ordered that the Union Jack be raised in all public schools daily. The Mennonite reaction was swift. "Eleven schools which had gone public reverted to private status."[28] In some solidly Mennonite communities, Mennonite trustees closed down public schools, but government officials soon opened them again. Given all of this controversy, it was somewhat ironic that a Mennonite, Alfred Ewert, was selected Manitoba's Rhodes Scholar in 1912.[29]

In Saskatchewan, the situation was no better. In 1908 the education disputes produced a Saskatchewan Commission of Enquiry to investigate Old Colony education practices. In Ontario, educational disputes subsided somewhat after the compromise of 1900 which made German an optional subject in the schools.

The biggest crises in education came in 1916, when Manitoba, despite much pressuring by an inter-Mennonite School Commission, passed the School Attendance Act; Saskatchewan followed suit in 1919. Both statutes made English the official language of instruction and both made school attendance compulsory for children aged seven to fourteen years. Private schools were still tolerated but had to meet provincial standards. Many Mennonites, remembering the promise of 1873 and not familiar with the complexities of federalism, believed that Ottawa had reneged on written promises. Since the formation of public school districts in Manitoba in 1890, Manitoba Mennonites had reluctantly endured double taxation but the new requirements met much resistance. Between 1922 and 1927 about seven thousand of the more conservative Mennonites from the prairies emigrated to Mexico and other Latin American countries.[30]

The education problems were exacerbated by the public attitudes generated by World War I, 1914-1918. On May 1 and June 9, 1919, the Canadian government passed Orders-in-Council barring all Mennonites from entering Canada. Many Mennonites, remembering the Magna Charta of 1873, particularly resented descriptions of themselves, as well as Doukhobors and Hutterites, as being "undesirable owing to their peculiar customs, habits, modes of living, and methods of holding property, and...their probable inability to become readily assimilated to assume the duties and responsibilities of Canadian citizenship within a reasonable time after entry."[31]

As the result of extensive lobbying on the part of many Mennonites, Prime Minister Mackenzie King's Liberal government, by an Order-in-Council on June 2, 1922, lifted the ban against the entry of Mennonites. The government spelled out several noteworthy conditions: the new immigrants would be placed on land as farmers, the Mennonites in Canada would look after the newcomers so that they would not become a public charge, and the complete military exemption granted in 1873 would not apply to the newcomers.[32] Lest public opinion be aroused, the lifting of the ban was not published in the **Canada Gazette**. During the following eight years about eight thousand Mennonites from Russia came to Canada; this large influx created some problems, both social and economic. In any event, in November 1929, largely because of pressure from the governments of the three prairie provinces, led by Saskatchewan, the general Mennonite immigration to Canada was again halted, although a further one thousand or so managed to enter because of existing agreements which the Canadian government had signed with the C.P.R and the C.N.R.[33]

During the early decades of the twentieth century many Canadian Mennonites had vigourously resisted any political and social assimilation and refused to learn English. But times changed, at least for the more progressive segments. In 1930 J.J. Thiessen and Dietrich Epp could write:

> That we esteem Canada highly is shown by this fact that practically all those who have been here for five years have become Canadian citizens. The Mennonite immigrants will ever take an active part in the building of the Canadian nation.[34]

In similar vein a Mennonite educator wrote in **Der Bote** in 1933, "Let us make Canada our real homeland. If you have come to this country as an immigrant and have solemnly declared your citizenship vows before God and man, then become a citizen of this land also in your heart."[35]

The last major wave of Mennonite immigration followed World War II. As early as May, 1946, a Canadian Order-in-Council once again allowed Mennonite relatives to enter, but transportation was generally not available. On July 5, 1946, J.J. Thiessen and J. Gerbrandt, presented a petition to Prime Minister Mackenzie King to broaden the categories. The govenment agreed and the appropriate Order-in-Council was passed on January 30, 1947. More distant relatives, as well as farm, mine and forestry workers with guaranteed jobs were acceptable.[36] But medical and other Canadian restrictions forced thousands of others to remain in Europe or migrate to Latin America. During the 1950s another two thousand five hundred or so managed to enter Canada, largely because of a continuing series of petitions, delegations and case-pleadings to Ottawa. A trickle of individuals, and some families, continued during the 1960s and 1970s right to the present. If Mennonite immigration from Latin Amerida is included, the numbers during the last two decades again reach the thousands.

2. The Military Question. Clearly much of Mennonite, and for that matter Quaker, church-state interaction in Canada has involved the military question. A degree of military exemption was achieved even in the early years. The Militia Act of 1793 exempted Quakers, Mennonites and Tunkers from militia duties. However, substitute taxation was enforced. Most Mennonites paid; if they objected it was mostly for financial reasons.[37] But many Quakers objected strenuously. Indeed, those "who paid the taxes or hired substitutes were disciplined by their brothers as severely as those who actively joined the militia." Both groups tried hard to change the law. "Indeed, one of the most active lobbies in the half-century of Upper Canada [1791-1840] appears to have been that of the Quakers, Tunkers and Mennonites, acting individually or collectively."[38] For both Mennonites and Quakers, then as now, separation of church and state did not require silence but it did require a greatly qualified subjection to civil authorities. (We should note in passing that in 1809 the Mennonites and Tunkers were exempted from taking the oath — the Quakers had been exempted earlier — but this same Act disqualified these peace groups from giving evidence in criminal cases, serving on juries, or "holding any office or place in government."[39])

During the War of 1812-14 some Mennonites were pressed into military service, a crisis action which was permitted by the statute of 1809. The imposition of substitute taxation continued till 1849 when decades of constant Mennonite and Quaker lobbying finally achieved the desired end. For those eighteenth and nineteenth century pacifist immigrants, exemption from military service continued into the twentieth century.

When World War I broke out, the military situation for Mennonites in Canada was difficult but tolerable. Their generally German culture triggered public resentment but earlier governmental promises were in place — or so they thought. As the war progressed, federal legislation and administrative regulations gradually changed things greatly. The difficulties were made worse because the Mennonites persisted in factionalism both internally and in their many representations to Ottawa. Public, and even government confusion grew. Frank Epp quotes the following Regina dispatch which appeared in the **Ottawa Citizen**:

> Who are the Mennonites exempted under the original agreement?...
> We have nothing but the word of the several Mennonites, and there are
> exactly 16 branches. So who will undertake to solve the puzzle the
> problem presents?[40]

In part the "problem arose because the Militia Act was changed in 1907 so that it no longer made mention of specific groups but exempted persons who "from doctrines of their religion, are averse to bearing arms or rendering personal military service, under such conditions as are prescribed."[41] The shift of focus from group to invididuals and the vagueness of the last clause should have alarmed the Mennonites but, perhaps because of ignorance, they remained quite unconcerned, especially since the government assured them continued exemption, even after the war began. A few Mennonites volunteered for military service but that was not considered to be very serious. Many Mennonites, anxious to retain goodwill and partially because of humanitarian concerns, raised substantial sums of money; during the war years over half a million dollars were collected for the Red Cross and Victory Loan campaigns.[42]

The skies darkened when on August 29, 1917, The Military Services Act was passed and conscription became law. As the need for additional troops became critical, numerous tribunals twisted and misapplied the statements dealing with continuing guarantees of exemption as incorporated in the 1917 Military Service Act. The Act itself, in its conscience clause, changed matters drastically. The clause in question exempted any member of a recognized peace church "who conscientiously objects to the undertaking of combatant service." Church membership suddenly became important and exemption from non-combatant service could no longer be assumed. The upshot of the confusion was that because of the 1873 Order-in-Council the descendants of the Russian Mennonites were generally exempted from all service while most of the "Ontario" Mennonites and members of other peace churches were subject to the provisions of the 1917 Act. Also, debates about who was a Mennonite became frequent and heated. Then, as at other critical times, the dilemma was complicated further by the fact that the majority of the Mennonites could not finally decide whether to try to claim status as an ethnic sect, as a Christian denomination, or as both. The frustration, the confrontations, the numerous petitions, and the odd imprisonment continued until the end of the war. It should also be noted that under the umbrella of the 1914 War Measures Act scores of German-language periodicals were barred from entering Canada. These included the weekly **Christlicher Bundesbote** (Messenger of Christian Union), the official United States-based organ of the General Conference Mennonites, and the **Mennonitische Rundschau** (Mennonite Review), then published in Pennsylvania. In 1918 the **Steinbach Post** and numerous other German-language periodicals in Canada were forced to suspend publication.[43]

Anti-Mennonite sentiment flourished in Ottawa and throughout the land. One M.P., John Wesley Edwards, a Methodist, repeatedly referred to conscientious objector Mennonites as "cattle." Others were even more unkind.[44] The scope and depth of this animosity are reflected, in part, by the passage of the Wartime Elections Act during September, 1917. This statute disfranchised all aliens and conscientious objectors. Also, it stated that anyone who voted, automatically lost military exemption status.

After wartime emotions had subsided, F.C. Blair, then Secretary of Immigration and Colonization for the national government, wrote to I.P. Friesen in 1923 to assert that "exemption from military service is no longer extended by the government to any particular class."[45] However, in 1935, the same year that the Mennonites, Quakers and Church of the Brethren formed a North American Historic Peace Church Association, David Toews obtained from Blair the statement that "Mennonites are just as much exempt from military service as ever they were and that so long as their faith remains as now, they will continue to be exempt."[46] The question of groups versus individual exemption remained a problem.

In May, 1939, as war clouds darkened, representatives of nine Mennonite groups met in Manitoba to discuss the military question. A resolution affirming loyalty within a framework of Christian discipleship was adopted and S.F. Coffman, David Toews and B.B. Janz were elected as a continuing committee to prepare a statement. Later that year David Toews presented it to King George when the latter visited Canada. The statement read: "To His Most Gracious Majesty George VI, King of Canada": we want to assure "your Most Gracious Majesty and your government of our deepest devotion and unwavering loyalty...."[47] The Schleitheim Confession seemed to have taken on a new emphasis.

On September 10, 1939, Canada declared war against Germany. In the spring of 1940 wartime events began moving rapidly. On June 21 royal assent was given to the National Resources Mobilization Act which prepared the way for conscription but allowed for non-combatant service under civil authority. On September 3, 1940, the Conference of Historic Peace Churches was organized in Canada, with the Quakers joining officially shortly thereafter. At Saskatoon, on October 22, a national conference of Mennonites endorsed the idea of non-military service. The continuous bickering and factionalism which had plagued Mennonite groups during World War I dealings with government were not to be repeated — though there were some basic disagreements. On November 12, 1940, E.J. Swalm, David Toews, B.B. Janz and C.F. Klassen met with the Deputy Minister of National War Services. Another delegation followed and met with the Minister himself, the Hon. J.G. Gardiner. Eventually he and Walter Tucker, the M.P. for Rosthern, persuaded Parliament to establish an alternative service programme; it was launched simultaneously with the first military call-up on May 29, 1941.[48] The more conservative Mennonites, while retaining their own organizational identity, accepted the same general arrangements as the larger groups had negotiated.

At first, the alternative service involved work camp duties in parks and at forest experimental stations. In 1943 service in agriculture and industry were added. Also in 1943 non-combatant service in the Royal Canadian Army Medical Corps or the Canadian Dental Corps was made available. Since this service did not allow for separate non-combatant units, few church leaders endorsed it and few men took this option. Regular wages were paid with $25 to $60 a month deducted for the Red Cross. In total more than $300,000 was collected in this manner and used for the care of Canadian prisoners of war and dependents of men in the military. The total number of COs in Canada during World War II was

10,851 of whom 7,543 or about sixty-three per cent were Mennonites. About one hundred and forty others joined the medical or dental corps. Significantly, about 7,500 Mennonites entered combatant service, mainly by volunteering although some, because of their own weak testimony or because of bureaucratic manipulation, were forced to join after having sought CO status.[49]

Commenting on one of the Mennonite volunteers **The Toronto Star** observed:

> The paradoxical Peter Engbrecht is, all at once, a member of a religious sect which forbids participation in wars, of pure Germanic descent, and a member of the R.C.A.F. The 21-year-old bomber gunner can claim an unparalleled record in the Air Force. He has personally destroyed five enemy aircraft, and a probable sixth, and has won the Conspicuous Gallantry Medal.[50]

Assured that their money would be used for relief purposes, Mennonites also bought war bonds: $750,000 in non-interest-bearing certificates and about $3,000,000 in interest-bearing bonds.[51]

Since World War II there has been no military crisis in Canada, although during the Korean conflict some Mennonites volunteered for active service and various peace conferences and peace assemblies were held in major Mennonite centres.

Surveying the entire topic, D.J. Wilson concludes that "in the matter of military training, however, the federal government has always honoured its pledge of exemption for the Mennonites."[52] Perhaps so, but the basic pledge was radically changed in 1907; the 1917 Military Service Act changed the rules by granting exemption from combatant service only, and the 1873 pledge was unilaterally terminated in 1922 by the government for Mennonites who entered after that date. Bureaucratic bungling produced considerable injustice, and restrictions of press and franchise, among other things, had to be endured. From the government's perspective, of course, the situation took on a different hue. How could Ottawa be expected to grant blanket exemption to an entire group when about half of its draft age young men, on their own, volunteered for active, combatant service?

3. **Political Participation.** Despite all of the statements in the various early confessions of faith, political participation by Mennonites in Canada has a long tradition. David Reesor of Markham was elected to the Council of York County in 1850 and was re-elected five times. He also served as Reeve of Markham, and Member of the Provincial Legislative Council (Senate). One or more of the Reesor family served on the County Council for thirty-seven of its first fifty years. Others also entered politics.[53]

In the early years in Manitoba, that is after 1874, there were far-reaching controversies about involvement in politics, especially at the municipal level. Some who participated were excommunicated, but by 1881 several Mennonites held elective office.[54] Given the settlement patterns on the reserves, it developed naturally, as in Russia in earlier times, that Mennonites soon held political offices in their own communities.

Some branches continued to emphasize non-involvement. Thus, for example, the Mennonite Brethren in 1890 resolved "that members of the church refrain from participation and involvement in the contentions of political parties, but are permitted to vote quietly at elections, and may also vote for prohibition."[55] In recent years that same group elected two members, Jake Epp and Dean Whiteway, to the House of Commons, a major party leader, Werner Schmidt in Alberta, a cabinet member, Ray Ratzlaff, in Alberta, and numerous other officials in various party offices.

Other groups also gradually became involved politically. A Mennonite, Cornelius Hiebert, was elected to the first Alberta legislature in 1905. Another, J.E. Stauffer, elected in 1909, eventually became deputy speaker in the Legislative Assembly of Alberta.[56] Space limitations do not allow us to review the very great extent to which Mennonites have penetrated civic politics, party structures, public partisan offices, government bureaucracies and even the Royal Canadian Mounted Police in Canada today.

D. CO-OPERATION AND CONFLICT: A REINTERPRETATION

If the voluntary enlistment figures for World War II draw attention to the widespread compromise on military service, the Kaufman-Harder data point out the major changes concerning general church-state relations and political involvement. In response to the statement, "The State (national, provincial and state government) is basically an evil force in the world, an opponent or enemy of the church and its programme," only four per cent of North American Mennonites surveyed agreed, nineteen per cent were uncertain and seventy-seven per cent disagreed.[57] Similarly, responding to the statement that "members of our own denomination should not hold any local, state, provincial or national government office," thirteen per cent agreed, twenty-two per cent were uncertain, while sixty-four per cent disagreed.[58] Related questions elicited similar responses. Political involvement in Canada, albeit on a selective basis, has become widespread and also has widespread Mennonite support. The two researchers note that,

> the greater the [measured] assent to Anabaptist doctrines, the less the participation in the political process. In one sense this can be interpreted as loyalty to the sixteenth century position of thoroughgoing separation of church and state processes, but it does not indicate much shift to a selective participation as a fulfillment of the Anabaptists' sense of obligation to bear witness to the state in matters of love and justice.[59]

It is also noteworthy that "the higher one's socioeconomic status and education, the lower one's commitment to the separation of church and state."[60]

Obviously many Mennonites in Canada today believe that, given the vastly increased and broad nature of government activity, together with our freedoms in a democratic society, selective political activism can be seen as an opportunity and a ministry.[61]

E. CONCLUSION

Having surveyed the development of church-state relations, Thomas Sanders concludes: "The Mennonites are the chief Protestant representatives of a view which demands separation of church and state on the basis of a doctrine of the church," rather than on pragmatic or individualistic grounds.[62] He adds, "The Mennonites have been the most effective symbols of the Christian conscience that does not yield on points of religious significance, in contrast with the tendency of most Protestants to follow uncritically the national line especially in time of war." Somewhat over-graciously he concludes, "at their best they illustrate more successfully than any other Protestant groups the unassuming suffering of Christians in the name of religious loyalties more ultimate than the state."[63]

How does the Canadian experience compare with Sanders' assessment? Several observations come to mind. By and large, Mennonites in Canada are no longer pilgrims and strangers in the state; we have become part of the state. Also, especially in recent decades, there have been major modifications in both pronouncements and practices. In part these changes, some would call them compromises, came about in the name of greater relevance; in part they came about because traditional principles had to be applied to new political situations; and in part they came about because traditional principles were taken less seriously. In any event, in Canada the Mennonite penchant to withdraw from involvement and responsibility has been largely transformed to parallel the Quaker emphasis on pacifism as a broad goal and a method for political action.

In several respects, Mennonites in Canada are founding wanting in terms of church-state relations. To a considerable degree we have never taken the Canadian locale seriously. It is not a matter of emphasizing Canada's importance but involves an over-riding awareness of the socio-political setting. Equally important, Canadian Mennonites, as we have seen, tended to shun church-state interaction, especially in the earlier periods, yet they never seemed to hesitate to ask for themselves not only the usual rights but also special privileges. Where is the account telling how Mennonites sought protection for the rights of others? Further, during the first two decades of this century, the mainline churches got caught up in the "social gospel" and during the 1920s and 30s pacifism was popular. In both periods the Mennonites failed to exploit the situation; society needed to know that the full gospel includes both of these and more!

One of the problems, as Frank Epp implies, is that Mennonites in Canada could never quite decide whether nonresistance applied also to govenments.[64] The problem is still very much with us.

Perhaps, in the final analysis,

> ...the real problem of Church and State arises from one fact.
> Christianity is...not easily fitted into the categories of natural human
> life...May it not be that the many minds which have sought in vain a

tidy formula for the ideal relations of Church and State in a sinful world have failed because their task was like that of mixing oil and water...? Certainly no attempt seems to be perfectly self-consistent or stands up fully to the logic of facts. Is it possible that men have sought a synthesis where they could expect to find only a modus vivendi?[65]

CHURCH AND STATE IN CANADA:
CO-OPERATION AND CONFRONTATION

Harry A. Renfree

It is of no little significance that the church of Jesus Christ was born in the midst of a society which compelled immediate consideration of the relationships between church and state both by way of co-operation and confrontation.

The Master Himself set the tone when, in response to a question from some scheming Pharisees and Herodians as to one's national accountability, He replied: "Render unto Caesar the things that are Caesar's, and to God the things that are God's."[1] The apostle Paul added further strictures: "Let every person be subject to the governing authorities."[2] In short, the Christian is to be a good, loyal citizen — the better because he is a Christian — yet in the final analysis, if confronted with a choice between his responsibility to his Creator and the public administration, bound by the landmark affirmation of Peter and others of the apostles: "We must obey God rather than men."[3]

It was not long, of course, before members of the expanding church were in confrontation with the Roman authorities, many of them paying for their faith with their lives. Their "good citizenship" could not and did not extend to the act of denying their Master at the demand of a pagan ruler.

It was in the early fourth century, however, that a church-state relationship developed which, although apparently initially beneficent, proved far more menacing to the church than any of the earlier pressures or accommodations. According to historian Philip Schaff, Roman Emperor Constantine "opened the door to the elevation of Christianity, and specifically of Catholic hierarchical Christianity, with its exclusiveness towards heretical and schismatic sects to be the religion of the state."[4] That close relationship continued virtually unbroken throughout the Middle Ages, sometimes the state in the more dominant position, at other times the church.

It was ultimately the worst consequences of this sorry partnership that the Reformers resisted. It remained for the Believers' Church, however, with the initiation of the Anabaptists, to carry the protestation to its ultimate conclusion in espousing the principles of the separation of church and state, and religious liberty.

FOR SUCH A TIME AS THIS

That part of the Believers' Church historically called Baptist found its beginnings in the midst of an English church-state affiliation which, under the Tudors and Stuarts, was little better than that experienced prior to the Reformation. The first Baptist church of the name was·

composed of British expatriates who had fled to Holland because of persecution. There, in Amsterdam, in 1608, under John Smyth, they established themselves and their church. Three years later, under Smyth's associate, Thomas Helwys, a portion of them, determined to face the tyranny, returned to England to found a Baptist church, the first in Britain.

As Torbet points out, Helwys was the first to publish a claim for freedom of worship in England, where there was a state church which demanded religious conformity.[5] In his book, **A Short Declaration of the Mistery of Iniquity**, he wrote:

> Let the king judge, is it not most equal that men should choose their religion themselves, seeing they only must stand themselves before the judgment seat of God to answer for themselves.[6]

For his views Helwys was incarcerated in prison by James I, where he died. A similar jailing was the experience of John Bunyan a few decades later.

Baptists were among those Separatists who in the early seventeenth century emigrated to the New World in search of freedom, only to be spurned by other Separatists who became the religious establishment. Banished from Massachusetts Colony, Roger Williams fled to a territory which he purchased from the Indians and named Rhode Island. For the Colony of Rhode Island he secured from the British Crown a charter containing full civil and religious liberty, the first such charter anywhere. In the capital, which he called Providence, he founded the first Baptist church in North America in 1639.

A NEW NATION

Meanwhile, north and west of the New England Colonies, a vast new territory was being explored: Canada. From the very first, church-state connotations loomed large, the land having fallen heir to the most baneful of such relationships, both from continental Europe and the British Isles. Indeed, when Jacques Cartier made his first voyage into the Gulf of St. Lawrence in 1534, he claimed New France in the name both of his country and church, so linking them that the very marker he erected over Gaspe was a conspicuous merging of the symbols of the two. In Cartier's own words:

> On the twenty-fourth of the said month [July] we had a cross made thirty feet high, which was put together in the presence of a number of the Indians on the point at the entrance to the harbour, under the crossbar of which we fixed a shield with three fleurs-de-lys in relief, and above it a wooden board, engraced in large Gothic characters, where was written, 'Long Live the King of France.'[7]

However, the first charter authorizing colonization, rather than simply trading, was granted by Henry IV of France to a Huguenot, Sieur de Monts, in 1603, and one Huguenot minister as well as two Roman Catholic priests accompanied the first settlers to Acadia in 1604.[8]

Religious tensions quickly developed between French Protestants and Roman Catholics in New France as they did in the motherland, and Champlain urged that all Huguenots be banned, a recommendation quickly approved by Cardinal-Duke de Richelieu, who had just become first minister in France.

> Richelieu saw in New France an opportunity to combine advantages to the Roman Catholic Church with the imperial interests of France... Richelieu brought Church and the French state into a direct relationship by ensuring the exclusion of all Protestants from the colony and by provision for the presence there of the Roman Catholic Church under royal auspices.[9]

Such a relationship has continued — more recently on a **de facto** basis — between the authorities and the Roman Catholic Church in French Canada until very lately, so that the terms French Canadian and Roman Catholic have become almost synonymous. With the capture of New France, in fact, Britain chose the pragmatic approach, permitting in her conquered areas what would not be countenanced at home. By the Articles of Capitulation, Montreal, 1760, it was decreed that:

> The free exercise of the Catholic, Apostolic, and Roman religion shall subsist entire...These people shall be obliged, by the English Government, to pay their priests the tithes....[10]

Such rights were further guaranteed by the Treaty of Paris in 1763 and the Quebec Act of 1774. As Moir puts it, "As the only institution of New France to survive the Conquest intact the Roman Catholic Church became, with the British Government's support, the living embodiment of French-Canadian culture, and the Quebec Act formed the Magna Charta of the people and of the church."[11]

In regard to those parts of what is now Canada settled by the British, the picture differed little, although the ecclesiastical body involved was, of course, the Church of England. Thus, as Watson Kirkconnell, Canadian educator, maintains,

> Among the French settlers who had developed the region in 1605-1755, the Roman Catholic Church had become an instrument of imperial expansion. George III and his policy-makers after the Conquest looked in like fashion to the Church of England to strengthen the bonds of empire by regular parishes, missionaries and state supported colleges.[12]

It was into this kind of milieu that the Baptists came, bringing with them their Believers' Church concepts of religious liberty and the separation of church and state, the latter perhaps better termed a free church in a free state. Circumstances were such at the time that, like Roger Williams and his co-workers, they were immediately able to make their influence strongly felt, although that situation was not long to obtain.

As part of the struggle for the control of Canada which characterized the first half of the eighteenth century, France had ceded Nova Scotia, which then included New Brunswick, to the British. Britain, however, had difficulty in persuading the Acadian settlers to take the oath of allegiance to the British Crown. Fearing the existence of a fifth column in his territory, British Governor Lawrence resolved to remove them, and there followed the unfortunate "expulsion of the Acadians," about five thousand of them being forcibly ejected in 1755.

To take up the abandoned land, settlers were essential, the British Govenment deeming it a good opportunity to place demobilized soldiers. Governor Lawrence, however, insisted upon settlers from the older colonies because of their farming and fishing experience. Lawrence won his point and New Englanders were invited. As George E. Levy, Maritime historian, asserts, however,

> the prospective colonists were only willing to endure the rigours of a pioneer life if they were given a guarantee of civil and religious rights, that is, representative government and freedom of worship.[13]

Lawrence was instructed from London to call an assembly, this being convened on October 2, 1758, and in the following January a proclamation was issued guaranteeing civil and religious rights for all Protestants. In part it read:

> Protestants dissenting from the Church of England...shall have free Liberty of Conscience, and may erect and build Meeting Houses for Public Worship, and may choose and elect Ministers for carrying on Divine Service and Administration of the sacraments, according to their several Opinions...and all such Dissenters shall be excused from any Rates or Taxes to be made or levied for the Support of the Established Church of England.[14]

The farmer immigrants, then termed Planters, and the fishermen came in large numbers, many of them Baptists or New Light Congregationalists, holding many similar points of view, especially as to both state and church democracy. These were, as their descendants chose to call them, the Pre-Loyalists, and the churches they established beginning in 1765, soon spread throughout the region.

> Undue importance can scarcely be given this pre-Loyalist migration from New England to Nova Scotia and New Brunswick. The colonists from Massachusetts, Rhode Island, Connecticut, and one or two other states represented, were the descendants of freedom-loving Englishmen who had settled the New England colonies. Their fathers had left an indelible imprint on the religious and political institutions of New England, and they in turn were to have a major part in shaping the institutions of the new colony.[15]

The strength of their witness and influence was yet to be tested, however, as with the breaking out of the American Revolution the church-state picture in Canada was drastically altered. After the Declaration of Independence and the Treaty of 1783, literally tens of thousands of New Englanders, anxious to retain their links to the British Crown, poured northward, doubling the population of Nova Scotia in less than two years and greatly modifying the religious balance, most of the newcomers being members of the Church of England. These Anglican Loyalists, through their social standing and sheer weight of numbers, soon took over the positions of power, the Baptists and other Independents being pushed into the background, their promised liberties threatened.

The American Revolution shocked the conscience of Great Britain. What caused this catastrophe? The answer offered by contemporaries may not satisfy today's historians, but those answers were nevertheless the foundation for imperial policies after the Revolution when politicians tried to ensure that the remaining colonies would never revolt. One of these answers blamed the Revolution on the lack of a proper state church establishment in the Thirteen Colonies — if only there had been colonial bishops, republicanism would never have got hold in America.[16]

To ensure that such a foothold would not be secured in Canada, the established Anglican Church and the Government thus combined to control "non-conformist" activity. As Torbet indicates,

> The hitherto friendly relations between Protestant denominations began to deteriorate. Politically, there was a restiveness which led to the separation of New Brunswick from Nova Scotia, creating out of New Brunswick a new province under Tory control. Needless to say, the Baptists opposed the "Tory clique" and the strongly entrenched Anglican Church. They saw clearly that the advantages they had gained during the previous years were to be offset by unfriendly forces.[17]

Hence in New Brunswick, too, divided from Nova Scotia, the Church of England was established. All of the judges of the Supreme Court were of that denomination until 1851 and it was not until 1817 that a member of another denomination was appointed to the Legislative Council. For fifty years only clergymen of the Church of England, the Church of Scotland and the Church of Rome were authorized to perform marriages.[18] Indeed, Dissenters at one time had to secure a licence even to preach.[19]

A Loyalist, Charles Inglis, appointed Bishop of Nova Scotia in 1787, the first such colonial bishop in the Empire, immediately attempted to secure land endowment and later financial benefits for the Established Church. Such was the Free Church opposition, however, that Inglis wrote to the Archbishop of Canterbury under date of May 12, 1812:

> From these your Grace will perceive that the influence of the Dissenters, which was much increased by the prospect of a new election, was too powerful to allow any direct appropriation of the public money for the benefit of the Establishment.[20]

Obviously, the power of the ballot was heavily involved.

The Church of England did, however, find "an unusual source of funds for religious purposes in Nova Scotia"[21] in an Arms Fund, a special tax on liquor to buy arms for the militia. From a surplus of £20,000, three-quarters was given to the Church of England for church-building and education, and £850 went to the Church of Scotland and Pictou Academy.[22]

It was thus also in the sphere of education that Baptists found themselves confronting the state, the Established Church and the Church of Scotland in seeking to provide a liberal education for the youth of the land.

Early, the Anglicans established King's College at Windsor, Nova

Scotia and according to I.E. Bill, nineteenth century Baptist historian,

> ...shut up its advantages to those who would subscribe to the Thirty-Nine Articles...[and] bolted the door against all the young men thirsting for collegiate culture and honours outside the pale of the dominant Church.[23]

Lord Dalhousie, then governor, followed by announcing that he, a Presbyterian, would found a college upon a non-sectarian basis, but using £20,000 from a special fund which the British Government had placed at his disposal. The House of Assembly at the request of the governor, voted a supplemental £10,000 and Dalhousie College was begun in 1820, a Presbyterian being named president. When Edmund A. Crawley, as a representative Baptist, sought the vacant classics chair, his application was summarily rejected as "those in charge felt themselves bound, as they said, to connect the college exclusively to the Kirk of Scotland."[24]

With the two provincial colleges closed to them, the Baptists chose the obvious but difficult road open, establishing "Queen's College" in 1838 at Wolfville, Nova Scotia. Ahead still lay the securing of a charter, obtainable only from the Legislature. Initially it was refused, by a majority of one.

Quickly the Baptist Association moved to reverse the decision, letters, papers and petitions being poured upon the legislators, and in 1841 the charter was granted. One further hurdle — Queen Victoria refused the use of her name — was overcome by calling the college "Acadia," having from its inception "no denominational restrictions on professors or students."[25]

One of the early alumni of Acadia College, the Hon. Charles Tupper, son of Baptist minister, Charles Tupper, introduced the Free School System in 1864. "The plain fact is," wrote Bill, with a touch of pride,

> that the agitation of this educational question by the Baptists in these Maritime Provinces and their all but superhuman efforts to diffuse the blessings of an enlightened education throughout the land, laid the foundations broad and deep, for our present admirable system of free schools.[26]

While these church-state struggles were in progress on Canada's eastern seaboard, a very similar situation obtained in the central region, then termed Upper Canada, now the Province of Ontario. There, according to G.G. Harrop, "Baptist influence on public affairs was most felt during the first half of the nineteenth century," adding that "the two questions in controversy at this period were on matters of church-state relationships about which Canadian Baptists of American origin had strong traditional convictions."[27] Those struggles had their focus on the Clergy Reserves and education.

> In 1791, the British Parliament, far from seizing old church lands or recognizing a North American tendency favouring the separation of church and state, called for the setting aside of fresh lands in Canada, 'to the Maintenance and Support of a Protestant Clergy...and to no

other Use or Purpose whatever,' and of special Rectory lands 'according to the Establishment of the Church of England.' These provisions in Clauses XXXV to XLII of the Constitutional Act of 1791 would have a discordant history.[28]

Indeed, John Graves Simcoe, the first governor of Upper Canada, saw the establishment of the Church of England in terms foreign to any lover of religious and civil freedom. He wrote:

Every establishment of Church and State that upholds the distinction of ranks, and lessens the undue weight of the democratic influence, must be indispensably introduced.[29]

After Lord Dalhousie, the Presbyterian governor, took office, the Assembly of Upper Canada in 1823 passed a resolution favouring co-establishment of the Church of Scotland, petitioning the British Crown "to direct such measures as will secure to the Clergy of the Church of Scotland residing or who may hereafter reside in this Province, such support and maintenance, as His Majesty shall think proper."[30] Due to Anglican opposition, this specific petition was not granted, but the British Government did sell a large tract of land for development, providing funds for distribution to other denominations. These monies found their way to the Presbyterians and Roman Catholics.[31]

The Methodists, holding to voluntarism in religious matters, entered the fray, with Egerton Ryerson, then a youthful circuit rider, as their chief spokesman. However, as E.M. Checkland, drawing on Aileen Dunham's **Political Unrest in Upper Canada**, points out,

Many of the dissenters were not altogether consistent in principle. Among the Methodists, for example, Egerton Ryerson changed course to meet a changing situation in his own denomination...As long as state aid was limited to the Anglicans, Presbyterians and Roman Catholics, to the exclusion of the Methodist Episcopal body, he denounced such aid in the name of civil and religious liberty. When, however, the British government enticed the Wesleyan Methodists into Canada with promises of state aid, he was quite prepared to accept such aid in order to effect a union of the two Methodist groups. His support of the secularization of the clergy reserves was but half-hearted since his church was in receipt of state aid.[32]

The Clergy Reserves Act of 1840 passed by the British Parliament, ended the monopoly of the Church of England, with shares being allotted to the Church of Scotland, the Church of Rome and the Methodists, with provision being left open for other denominations. Yet the battle had not been won for, although "the division of the Reserves recognized the principle of religious liberty...it did not separate church from state."[33] Indeed an Act of the same year re-uniting Upper and Lower Canada guaranteed to safeguard these "accustomed dues and rights of the Church of Rome...[and] the Protestant clergy within the Province of Canada."[34]

Again, in a situation similar to that in the Maritimes,

in matters of education there was the same attempt at monopoly on the part of the Church of England. Archdeacon Strachan, leader of the

Church of England in Upper Canada, insisted on the dominance of the
Church of England. As president of the provincial Board of Education
he tried to keep the school system completely Anglican....[35]

That church was also first to obtain a university charter — for a
similarly named King's College — completely church-dominated and
assisted by government funding.

Upper and Lower Canada Baptists, whose earliest roots were also
from New England, had been strengthened by the immigration of
sturdy Highland Scots, who also cherished freedom, and they all spoke
out against this favouritism and religious bigotry. They supported the
creation of non-sectarian, public institutions — one each in Toronto and
Montreal. "At least in part to provide a voice for the Baptist voluntarist
position,"[36] the Canada Baptist Union was organized in 1843, the next
year at its Montreal meeting declaring:

> The great principles of Religious Liberty which they thus held have
> been grievously violated in the manner in which the Episopalian sect
> of Christians had been allowed to divert a large portion of the funds set
> apart for the education of the youth of the Province, from their original
> purposes, and to obtain undue influence in their distribution of the
> benefits and management of the affairs of the University of King's
> College at Toronto.[37]

With opposition mounting, the Ontario Legislature in 1849 passed a
new university bill transferring the endowment of King's College to the
new University of Toronto, founded on a non-sectarian basis. The
Baptist position had been vindicated.

As to the Clergy Reserves, meanwhile, the question continued to
simmer. In 1848 the Reform party, whose platform included religious
equality, on taking power invited all denominations to apply for a £1,800
surplus in the Clergy Reserves fund. The Roman Catholics, Lutherans,
Moravians and five Free Church of Scotland congregations did
(although the Free Church synod later repudiated the action of its
churches.)[38]

Once more the Baptists stood almost alone in absolutely refusing state
grants, although general dissatisfaction was growing. The Canada
Baptist Union of the same year, 1848, sent the following resolutions to
the Legislature:

> That the manner in which the funds arising from the sale of the Public
> Domain, called Clergy Reserves, as are now appropriated, is unsatis-
> factory to all — that the law upon which that arrangement is based,
> has always been looked upon in the light of compromise — that most, if
> not all parties, have only been waiting for a suitable time for
> opening the question afresh in order to [gain] a final adjustment...and
> that, in the opinion of this Union, all the said funds ought to be spent
> in the support of Education, to be enjoyed by all the people.[39]

That resolution, writes Moir, "is representative of the reaction of all the
voluntarists."[40]

In 1854, although postponed for a generation, the voluntarist position
triumphed. With the approval of the British Government, the

Legislature, while providing a life income for clerical incumbents, turned over the balance of the Clergy Reserve fund for municipal public works."[41]

As to these significant contributions which Baptists had made to Canadian public life, Harrop quotes W.G. Pitman from an article, "Baptist Triumphs in Nineteenth Century Canada," printed in **Foundations**, April 1960:

> The Baptists had won a real victory. In a sense they had led the way in creating a climate of opinion which would accept this solution, leading many who were Anglican, Methodist, and Presbyterian to a realization that the existence of such support for religious enterprises was a disadvantage even to the denomination that benefited. There is little doubt that those who maintained no formal connection with the church were also influenced by the logic of the Baptist argument. In spite of the resistance of every major denomination, the Baptists saw their principle of voluntarism and their ideal of the separation of church and state triumph.[42]

Moir would seem to agree with such an assessment when stating that "probably the staunchest supporters of voluntarism have been the Baptists..."[43] Arthur R. Lower, one of Canada's most distinguished historians, makes an arresting appraisal of the importance of the issue from a most vital perspective:

> The Canadian struggle against privilege in church and state was conducted in a backwater, but it turned out one of the major factors in securing the ancient institutions. Canada kept together the British Empire of the nineteenth century; it made the Commonwealth possible...Canada injected new elements of vitality into the ancient institutions, extended their orbit and in due course brought its contributions of experience and spirit to the welfare of the modern world.[44]

CENTURY TWENTY

From the foregoing record it might be presumed that in the eighteenth and nineteenth centuries the Baptist position in Canada vis-a-vis the state was one more of confrontation than co-operation. On the other hand, there are those who might maintain that Baptists in more modern times have tended to rest on their oars, leaving to other Believers' Church colleagues, notably the Mennonites, the responsibility of continuing the encounter.

Neither conclusion is entirely valid, although admittedly the pioneers were more than willing always to mount a sturdy defence of their principles. Too, with the vigour of their Anabaptist forebears, the Canadian Mennonites of this century have assumed burdens hardly to be expected of their numbers, as John Redekop's monograph makes evident, often with greater stamina than present day Baptists — and occasionally for ends with which Canadian Baptists would not always agree. H.U. Trinier, former editor of **The Canadian Baptist**, writing in the 1950s, reflects the changed position from the point of view of the denominational press which was then a century old:

> By entering fully into the struggles of that time [the 1850s] The Cana-

dian Baptist became a molder of opinion and a shaper of national and denominational destiny. But with the settling of major disputes, the maturing of the nation, and the growth and tolerance among the religious denominations of Canada, the function of the paper has changed. It has become less argumentative and critical...[and] has promoted fellowship and unity among the Baptists of its own increasing constituency...[45]

It is also true that regional and national Baptist groupings in Canada in our day have been more reticent to speak out publicly and especially representatively than were their forebears. Edgar J. Bailey, at that time president of the Baptist Federation of Canada, made the point in an address to a Special Joint Committee of the Senate and House of Commons in 1966, referring to the Baptist genius as being

> found in the willingness of its people to share in decision making
> without requiring that large committees and boards must first of all
> present definite findings. The doctrines of the separation of church
> and state and that of local church governments militates against
> what might be called church statements, and against the church
> being a pressure group for our favourite point of view in a local situa-
> tion. Responsible leaders are expected to make their views known
> and to accept the consequences of the views expressed.[46]

The fact remains, however, that Bailey's presence at the hearings on a question of great public importance — divorce — must have been viewed by many as being representative, and Baptists have taken action and continue to do so in this century on a variety of matters of church-state concern both on a personal and corporate basis.

One of the areas in which this is obvious is that of education, where Baptists have traditionally been strong supporters of the public school, although Canadian Baptists have never been as thoroughgoing as their American brethren in upholding such a strict view of separation that the public school must not be involved in religious "exercises." There, strong backing has come from the prestigious Baptist Joint Committee on Public Affairs, with headquarters in Washington, D.C., for the action of the Supreme Court which ruled "the practice of devotional Bible reading and the recitation of the Lord's Prayer to be unconstitutional."[47] In Canada, Baptists have shown equal concern that public schools be kept "public," while generally accepting the provincially provided opportunities for at least a modicum of religious seasoning. When the Ontario government in 1944 made religious studies a part of the curriculum in the public schools, Baptists agreed to be a participating denomination.

The British North America Act placed responsibilty for education entirely with the provinces, yet precluded them from effecting any statute which would "prejudically affect any Right or Privilege with respect to Denominational schools which any Class of Persons have by Law in the Province at the Union."[48] Hence, Roman Catholic schools have traditionally functioned alongside and often as part of the public school system, the particular relationships depending on the province involved.

In that the arrangement has long been acknowledged in law and generally accepted. Baptists have largely confined their major concern to preventing further inroads through Roman Catholic pressure. They were in the forefront of the winning battle in Ontario in the 1960s to prevent the Roman Catholic hierarchy from forcing an extension of the separate school system to secondary schools and claiming a greater proportion of public tax monies. Neil G. Price, minister and lawyer, forwarded the Baptist position ably in his little volume, **Education — Religion — Politics in Ontario.**[49]

In the Atlantic Provinces, where the objective to provide an alternative form of liberal higher education, Christian in orientation but without denominational tests, had been achieved in the first half of the nineteenth century, difficulties surfaced once more well over a century later, in the mid 1960s. Sensing a growing secularization of its Acadia University, founded in 1838, the United Baptist Convention of that region struck a committee on higher education at its 1964 assembly, to "re-examine and re-state its philosophy with regard to the Christian orientation of higher education as well as its policy in educational matters."[50] Reporting the next year as directed, the committee presented recommendations which, when adopted by the assembly, resulted in vigourous opposition from the university Board of Governors and the alumni. The report called for a reaffirmation of the philosophy of higher education, a requirement that faculty members be "Christian...[but] with no thought of religious tests," and "that academic and campus activities and publications be consistent with the Christian orientation."[51]

Powerful forces appealed to the Nova Scotia Government to remove the university from Baptist aegis. Because in Canada the Legislature is supreme, with no appeal to the courts except on a matter of constitution, the government was able to act prejudicially to the denomination, and did so under an Act of 1966[52] which repealed the previous statute and effectively removed denominational control. It must be admitted that the receiving of significant state funds for Acadia over many years seriously weakened the church position.

The defence of the cause was not in vain, however, for the premise may be maintained that specific benefits have accrued. Through long, hard negotiations over several years, the Convention body retains the right to name 14 of the 35 governors of the university — making possible continuing Christian input without the sometimes undesirable reflections upon a group which only in theory has regulatory powers. What is most important, however, is the fact that the Convention secured direct and complete control of the School of Theology, now its Divinity College, gaining funds from the university to aid in its establishment. Out of an intense church-state confrontation, with the press powerfully aligned against the church position, the church, though suffering losses, made important gains.

With regard to the raging country-wide debate on the subject of national unity — undoubtedly the most serious controversy facing the nation since confederation, accentuated following the election of a separatist government in the Province of Quebec — churches by and large have not been vocal. This has been especially true in that province, where the powerful Roman Catholic Church has been strangely incommunicative. As recently as 1978, the Roman Catholic bishops in another province, Alberta, jointly urged their members to "enter the debate" about Canadian unity, claiming that Canada's constitutional crisis "must not be left to the politicians and the media to decide."[53]

Both the Public Affairs Committee of the Baptist Federation of Canada and that of the United Baptist Convention of the Atlantic Provinces had taken an early interest in the aspect of Canadien/ Canadian relations, and made a number of submissions before the Royal Commission on Bilingualism and Biculturalism, with Maurice Boillat, who has subsequently become general secretary of the Union d'Eglises Baptistes Francaises au Canada, as chief spokesman.

The Boillat brief recognized that the situation could become explosive (more than twelve years before the election of the Parti Quebecois), and recommended among other things a gradual national effort to dissociate language and religion; the reinforcement of the separation of church and state by integration rather than apartness and in nonsectarian schools, with a federal system of education; the teaching of two languages to all children; an impartial presentation of Canadian history to both cultures, and a strong federalism.

The brief was published by the Baptist Federation of Canada under the title **Creed in the Canadian Crisis**, and distributed widely.[54]

A large well-illustrated volume, written by William Sturhahn, and published by the North American Baptist Immigration and Colonization Society in 1976, points to yet another way in which the denomination, with leadership by that conference, has very recently been involved in a church-state setting — in this instance the immigration of refugees into Canada from Europe following both World War I and World War II. States Sturhahn: "From the very beginning church organizations were the most prolific promoters of immigration and the greatest source of men and women from Europe."[55]

In addition to all of these contributions, there is yet another, more difficult to assess, perhaps as great as or greater than any — the furnishing of strong capable Christian leadership to the governments of country and its regions. In this Baptists have held a modified view from some others of the Believers' Church.

Two of the nation's prime ministers, the Hon. Alexander Mackenzie and the Hon. John G. Diefenbaker have so given their witness, as have many federal cabinet ministers and a number of provincial premiers. Among the latter are the Hon. T.C. Douglas, the Hon. E.C. Manning, the Hon. William Aberhart, the Hon. Alan Blakeney and the Hon. Richard Hatfield.

Mr. Diefenbaker was the author of the Canadian Bill of Rights, which asserts that freedom of religion has "existed and shall continue to exist without discrimination by reason of race, national origin, colour, religion or sex." James Penton, whose book **Jehovah's Witnesses in Canada** is definitive from the point of view of a strong member of a body which itself has been intimately involved in church-state matters, including persecution, characterizes Mr. Diefenbaker as "the Witnesses' old parliamentary advocate."[56]

In philosophically separating church from state and denying the right of either to dominate the other institutionally, the Baptist holds that the individual Christian may and, if so led, should share his unique endowment in positions of leadership in the world as opportunity affords, not abdicating to non- or anti-Christian sentiments.

Of tomorrow and the remaining tomorrows much might be written. For the foreseeable future the times would seem to be uncertain, the choices difficult, the decisions formidable. The nation, like most of the western world, is being rapidly secularized, and the influence of the church considerably diminished.

The prudent stance would obviously be that of withdrawal, leaving the world to its justified fate. Yet the Master did say: "Render therefore to Caesar the things that are Caesar's" as well as "to God the things that are God's." Church-state responsibilities continue, both by way of co-operation and confrontation.

Then, too, there is no place to hide.

DIVISIVE AND UNITIVE FORCES IN THE BELIEVERS' CHURCH TRADITION IN CANADA

Walter E. Ellis

THE TYPOLOGY OF THE BELIEVERS' CHURCH

The question, "Has the Believers' Church tradition been susceptible to divisiveness more than other Christian traditions, and why?" involves a recognition of the fact that our "histories are checkered with division"; that we are "pretty good scrappers" after all.[1] Indeed, the very characteristics that mark the Believers' Church are those which tend to foster disunity and division.

Historians recognize the Believers' Church as a "tradition" but sociologists regard it as a model or a type, and "typologies are not explanations in themselves, although they are sometimes mistaken for such...Only as types are usable to explain processes are they truly justified."[2]

The works of Franklin H. Littell, Donald F. Durnbaugh, Bryan R. Wilson and others are valuable in that they provide models for the synthesis of empirical data from wide religious movements and help to clarify on the basis of doctrinal, ecclesiological and ethical similarities much of the course of radical Western Christian history. However, care must be taken in development of a typology that attempts to deal with such diverse movements as Anabaptists, Baptists, Methodists, Disciples, Plymouth Brethren and Quakers, each with many distinctive attributes and histories, lest the "useful short-hand summaries of critical elements in the empirical cases they are meant to epitomize become remote from the empirical phenomena they are meant to clarify."[3]

When we discuss unitive and divisive forces we are doing so within the context of the narrower denominational families encompassed by the Believers' Church typology. Preoccupation with congruences may tend to obscure significant differences, theological, ethical, social, psychological, and ethnic, especially when dealing with religious divisions and the formation of emerging institutionalized groups. In short, it is the purpose of ideal types to give way to increasingly more complex and refined models, and this applies to the concept-type of the Believers' Church.

What likewise are we to say about "division"? Clearly we are speaking within the framework of institutional constructs and relate "division" to the emergence of new institutionalized groups from previously institutionalized movements. Religious divisions can be of different kinds. For example, S.L. Greenslade makes a useful distinction between heresy and schism. Heresy is significant departure from previously accepted doctrine (symbolic differentiation). Schism is differentiation in religious movements which takes place for personal, national, social, economic, language, or ecclesiastical reasons. Complications arise when factions are unable to agree on whether the issues are related to items of such import as to make them heresy, or merely schism. A case in point was the conflict in the 1920s between "liberals" and "fundamentalists," or more accurately conservatives and separatist fundamentalists. Ecumenical agendas inevitably function on the basis of identification of others as schismatics (separated brethren), and not heretics.[4]

What then are the characteristics of families within the Believers' Church type that make them especially susceptible to institutionalized religious differentiation? Perhaps a definition will clarify.

The Believers' Church is a voluntary fellowship of Believers (1), admitted under covenant on the basis of credible testimony (2), sealed by baptism (3), whose doctrine (symbols), life (ethics), and ecclesiology (structure) are based on Christ, the Living Word, as revealed in the Scriptures and interpreted through the confirming work of the Holy Spirit (Authority) (4). In short, "the Believers' Church...is the covenanted and disciplined community of those walking in the way of Jesus Christ."[5]

Three questions are relevant to institutions. 1. What are its shared symbols? 2. What are its conditions of membership? 3. What is its structure? In religion a fourth is: What is its authority? The manner in which Believers' Churches have answered these questions contributes immeasurably to the notorious instability of their institutions.

THE AUTHORITY OF THE WORD

Religion rests ultimately on authority. Among Christians the question is how the will of God and the mind of Christ can be known. Three alternative answers produce three characteristic types of religious institutions. Where the authority reposes in the community symbolized by the Petrine succession, the church-type appears. Where the authority is the Bible accepted as the "only sufficient, certain, and infallible rule of all saving Knowledge, Faith, and Obedience," sect-type institutions emerge. Where the authority is personal religious experience, weak forms of mystical association predominate. In reality Christian authority systems partake of all three elements and are informed by reason.[6]

After flirtations with personal religious experience, Anabaptists and denominations which had their rise in English Independency opted strongly for **sola scriptura**. They held that the only authentic and reliable revelation of God's will for churches and individuals was the Bible. Asserted Balthasar Hubmaier: "All the men who wish to speak the word of God, and are of a Christian way of thinking should assemble to search the Scriptures." He taught that every Christian "believing for himself and baptized for himself" was "competent to see and judge by the Scriptures."[7] In the **London Confession** of 1644 Baptists were even more unambiguous:

> The Rule of the Knowledge, Faith, and Obedience, concerning the worship and service of God, and all other Christian duties, is not man's inventions, opinions, devices, laws, constitutions, or traditions unwritten whatsoever, but **only** the word of God contained in the Canonical Scriptures.[8]

Because of the paramount if not sole authority of Scripture it was the commitment of Anabaptists and Baptists alike to reconstruct their personal and community life on a biblical foundation without compromise and without tarrying for any.

Radical and magisterial reformers shared a restorationist agenda. But the magisterial reformers and their descendents, confronted with political and social realities, were not "able to accept the logic of their exclusive scriptural foundations," whereas the descendants of the Anabaptists and English Separatists, persecuted minorities, had more opportunity to be "entirely logical."[9]

Further, Robert Paul convincingly argues that most if not all of the followers of the Radical Reformation and British Independency adopted a hermeneutic that was incipiently literalistic and encouraged personal interpretation, thus reinforcing individualistic tendencies. It was the plain meaning of Scripture that ordinary man could understand that was the reliable authority. Since the Bible was held to be the Book of the laws of God, a repository of His divine plan, it was accepted that men of good will could come to know as much of the truth about God as was necessary to organize society as well as save their souls. Those who refused to follow a restoration agenda, or compromised, were giving evidence of apostasy, since what was on the surface was clear and ought generally to be interpreted in its natural and intended sense.

To the charge that Scripture was not that clear, that there was danger in leaving exegesis to "the indiscriminate exercise of private judgment among the humbler classes" because it might lead to "interminable diversities of interpretation and of doctrine," the Baptist **Montreal Register** in 1844 resolutely replied:

> Such a doctrine is not merely an insult to common sense — it is a libel on the Divine Author of the Bible. Are we to believe that 'knowing perfectly what is in men,' [God] has yet so constructed the volume of Revelation that even fundamental doctrines remain an inscrutable mystery?[10]

The answer was a resounding, "NO!"

Ideally a written authority such as the Bible ought to produce an ecumenical institution universal in scope among all sincere followers, but history proved the contrary. God's will was not invariably clear even for restorationists. The Golden Age of the New Testament proved difficult to reconstruct when the Bible was held to be a blueprint for social reconstruction, since it appeared to encourage a static social and institutional order incapable of pragmatic change and evolution. Overemphasis on **sola scriptura** tended to bind believers' denominations to sectarian futures because the early church found itself in an alien world as a persecuted minority and the New Testament reflects its struggles against the prevailing political, religious and social institutions of that age. Robert Paul observes:

> [Biblical Restorationism] has been the natural response of those who have been forced to appeal to the simple meaning of the Scripture and to the simple form of New Testament Christianity — against the various kinds of legalism by which ecclesiastical establishments support their position and prestige.... In origin Baptists are of all Protestants perhaps most essentially restorationist; as a Baptist scholar commented, 'Popularly they have expressed their historical premise by a simple formula: Whatever can be learned about the beliefs and practices of the first generation of disciples must be followed conscientiously.'[11]

Throughout history, Believers' Church denominations vigourously and legitimately challenged attempts to modify their authority system based on the Bible and a populist hermeneutic. Subjectivism related to religious experience found little sympathy; witness the attacks on Harry Emerson Fosdick when he deprecated authority in religion, then asserted that the one vital thing in religion was first-hand, personal experience, and defined religion subjectively as "the most intimate, inward, incommunicable fellowship of the human soul."[12]

It is the function of the church historian to trace the precise theories of authority and inspiration held by significant theologians and church leaders. Sociologists examine their impact and interaction upon society and institutions. If Christians believe that in the Bible "the command of the Lord is clear" they must conform to the law of God and the mind of Christ and organize their personal and community life after a New Testament model, however interpreted. In popular thought this will often result in sectarian expressions of religion and in suspicion of secular and ecclesiastical authority. When a religious movement begins such a stance may foster growth, but what will be the response of believers' denominations when faced, as was fourth century Christianity, with embarrassment of Christ's own triumph and their own missionary successes?

ECCLESIOLOGY OF THE BELIEVERS' CHURCH

Believers' Churches generally forwarded, as New Testament doctrine, an ecclesiology centred in the concept of the **communio sanctorum** in contrast to the more prevalent **corpus Christianum**. Popularly understood, this has involved a view of the visible church as the gathered local congregation with voluntary membership based upon credible testimony and evidence of amendment of life. The invisible church is the sacred community of all past, present and future believers.

Unfortunately, the congregationalism which results, based on these subjective standards, is a far weaker polity than is episcopal or presbyterial order, which is grounded in a more objective view of the church and its membership. The polity of believers' denominations fosters individualism and encourages purity among the faithful, but it is very vulnerable when tensions develop and disunity occurs.

The inherent strength of congregationalism in frontier situations and under persecution soon evaporates when believers' denominations, in the interests of missions and evangelism, attempt to expand or consolidate their institutions. Adaptation often takes place in a utilitarian fashion but without modification of the requisite religious symbols or doctrines to justify these changes in polity.

For example, Baptists seldom made serious attempts to build their ecclesiology on restorationist principles. Yet they perpetuated a rhetoric that made it appear that they believed in local autonomy and congregational independence on New Testament grounds.

As late as 1926 the British Baptist Union responded to the Lambeth Conference of 1920 with a statement that scarcely recognized the Union as a valid expression of the Christian Church.

> We believe in the Catholic Church as the holy Society of believers in our Lord Jesus Christ which He founded, of which He is the only Head, and in which He dwells by His Spirit.... We believe that this holy society is truly to be found wherever companies of believers unite as Churches on the ground of confession of personal faith. Every local community thus constituted is regarded by us as both enabled and responsible for self-government through His indwelling Spirit...and we believe [His Spirit] leads these communities to associate freely in wider **organizations for fellowship and propagation of the Gospel.**

The statement identifies the invisible church, the local congregation — or visible church, but views wider associations as **organizations** with limited and utilitarian goals — "fellowship and propagation of the Gospel."[13]

The **Lambeth Reply** revealed how little Baptist rhetoric had moved from **An Orthodox Creed** of 1678 which stated that the church was "made up of the whole number of the elect, that have been, are, or shall be gathered in one body under Christ" — the invisible church; while the visible church was composed of "several distinct congregations which make up the one catholic church or mystical body of Christ."[14]

Space prevents a detailed survey of Baptist ecclesiology. Suffice it to observe that a more holistic view of the visible church emerged from time to time. Particular Baptists in their earlier **London Confession** of 1644 asserted —

> We doe therefore here subscribe [to this confession] some of each body in the name, and by the **appointment** of seven Congregations, who though wee be distinct in respect of our particular bodies, **for conveniency sake**, being as many as can well meete together in one place, yet are all one in Communion, holding Jesus Christ to be our head and Lord.[15]

Unfortunately, the decline of the General Baptists with their connexional model, persecution, and emergence of denominational and interdenominational parachurch societies in the late eighteenth century, and the individualistic tendencies of the frontier were only a few of the factors that encouraged Baptist polity to evolve towards a stricter local autonomy.

Concurrently the demands of missions and education encouraged centripedal tendencies. Andrew Fuller justified the growth of the Baptist mission societies on the grounds that the Bible provided no fixed pattern of government or worship for the church and he argued that men were free to use reason to develop their church order. However, these societies composed of individuals soon challenged and appreciably weakened the Baptist associations of churches. In North America, Francis Wayland espoused a doctrine of the church that further eroded the sense of corporate unity until even the local congregation came to be viewed as little more than a missionary organization whose sole purpose was "the conversion of souls." This view still prevails among many evangelicals in the United States and Canada.

The point is that in the minds of the average church member, there is only the invisible church and the local congregation. The denomination has evolved unjustified by biblical warrant to perform utilitarian purposes, and congregations find it easy to abandon their affiliations, and individuals their societies, when they experience a low level of strain or dissatisfaction.[16] No over-arching symbol exists to encourage unity. Hence, these "wider organizations for fellowship and propagation of the gospel," devoid of the marks of the church, are easily dispensed with, restructured or abandoned without any requirement that the schismatics prove that the existing institutions no longer bear the marks of a true church. Disunity is facilitated and schism is fostered when you merely leave an organization and not the church. The foregoing illustrates what Paul Harrison has firmly documented: the fact that "often-times the doctrine of a church remains static while the polity undergoes a radical adjustment to new situations."[17]

Not only do the believers' denominations generally lack a sound basis for their ecclesiastical innovations but they practise organizational pragmatism in a climate of prevailing distrust of centralized authority, a condition deeply rooted in their sectarian traditions. In consequence denominational leaders and bureaucrats depend upon "an expediential authority" that is unlegitimized and often highly vulnerable. Denominational agencies tend to function on the basis of informal exercise of power and lack the checks and balances to be found in a sound presbyterian or episcopal polity.

During these times of strife and instability believers' denominations appeal primarily to "ideas of efficiency, harmony, unity and togetherness," weak motivations in a contest against the relentless biblical restorationism espoused by critics. In addition the very "expediential authority" evolved leaves our bureaucrats open to the charge that they "enjoy power without performance and the right of administration without sacrifice."[18]

Not only are our denominations vulnerable because of this impoverished ecclesiology and practise, but they are vulnerable at law. Most denominations can withstand high levels of alienation because of their centralized control of property, assets and pension benefits. With congregationalism a simple vote of the local church is usually sufficient to extricate property from the denomination. Should efforts fail, self-styled 'charismatic' leaders find little inhibition in appropriating the name and history of a denomination, and selectively appeal to the broad, amorphous and often contradictory elements of its tradition.

In Canada this impoverished ecclesiology and polity has contributed to schism and, more importantly, inhibited the establishment of strong Believers' Church denominations, as is illustrated in the Canadian Baptist experience. As early as 1844 anti-establishment sentiment and the challenge of frontier expansion produced the vision of a Canadian Baptist Union. But upon what ground could Baptists unite? The editor of **The Canada Baptist Magazine and Missionary Register** answered, "We may unite upon the holy ground of missionary enterprise for our destitute townships. We may rally around the theological institution and the Magazine." This utilitarian experiment floundered on the "suspicion...that the Union [would] probably infringe upon the independence of the churches...and assume a dominant influence over their concerns."[19]

The tangled history of Canadian Baptist institutional experimentation reveals how little has changed. The one promising innovation of "presbygational" representation in the Baptist Union of Western Canada, an experiment determined by finances and geography, fell before charges of elitism in the "fundamentalist-modernist" controversy. The communion question, the settlement of Calvinist and Arminian strains from Britain and the United States, the impact of continental ethnicity, regionalism and the practical problems of geography, continued to complicate efforts to produce a national denomination.

Four regional bodies finally emerged: The United Baptist Convention of the Atlantic Provinces, The Baptist Convention of Ontario and Quebec, The Baptist Union of Western Canada, and The Union of French Baptists in Canada, each with divergent and unstable structures constantly in process of modification. With each new wave came the added complications of corporate charters, legal limitations, and the growth of regional bureaucracies to reinforce regional interests. In addition, the existence of the Canadian Baptist Overseas Mission Board reflects the vestige of the "rival polity" that emerged with the founding of the independent societies. In spite of the fact that the Baptist Federation of Canada was founded in 1944, progress towards a national church has been slow and it "has not yet assumed any major role in Canadian Baptist life."[20]

The ecclesiology, polity and practice of Believers' Churches illustrates the need for a reassessment of our restorationist rhetoric, a frank admission of our pragmatic practices and an honest commitment to the propostion of the early General Baptists who held that:

> General councils, or assemblies, consisting of Bishops, Elders, and Brethren, of the several churches of Christ, and being legally Brethren, of the several churches of Christ, and being legally

convened...make but one church, and have lawful right, and suffrage
in this general meeting, or assembly, to act in the name of Christ.[21]

Frank re-examination of our congregational practices and re-
statement of our biblical presuppositions has already begun among
British Baptists; witness the following:

> While there are undoubtedly in the New Testament evidences of the
> existence of a church order that we now characterize by the name of
> independency, there are also indications that can lend support to some
> form of connexionalism or synodal organization, and even some form
> of episcopal order, understood in the broadest sense. That only one
> valid structure was intended by our Lord, laid down by Him for His
> church and for ever binding can be maintained only by a selective use
> of such references to church order as there are....[22]

Canadian churchmen would do well to hear.

What is required is an adequate doctrine of the church and a frank re-
examination of the role of associations, societies and federations,
whatever the polity of the denomination in question. If unity is to be
fostered and schism avoided, Believers' Churches "have to decide how
far their present church organization is an essential expression of the
gospel, how far some of the things they espouse are only custom and
perhaps prejudice, how far certain traditional freedoms might well be
sacrificed for the sake of a wider fellowship and a more united Christian
witness."[23]

VOLUNTARISM AND DISCIPLESHIP

Calvin and the Radical Reformers would have agreed, prior to
Calvin's discipline and exile in 1538, that the marks of the true church
were three: (1) the Word correctly preached, (2) the sacraments
administered in gospel order, and (3) discipline. However, Calvin's
Strassburg experience encouraged him to move towards a more
objective view of the sacraments and church membership and to
abandon discipline as a mark of the church, deleting it from his later
editions of the **Institutes**. In contrast, the Anabaptists and Independents
continued to demand that members of Believers' Churches not only
embrace truth but live truth. For them the preoccupation of Magisterial
Reformers with orthodoxy was insufficient without orthopraxy.
Discipleship was the key to churchmanship, discipline the means. In
Durnbaugh's words, "Anabaptism developed around the central idea of
a righteous walk with the Lord after the experience of repentance and
rebirth."[24]

A major issue between the Radical and Magisterial Reformers, an
issue painfully contemporary, was whether a reasonably pure church
were possible, whether a righteous walk could be realized, or whether it
was an ideal set forth to demonstrate to man his frailty and inability to
attain it. Was Israel to be a righteous remnant or a contender against the
Almighty? Anabaptists and Baptists of Calvinist, as well as Arminian
persuasions, opted for the "righteous walk."

Scholars argue that conversionist tendencies toward subjective
individualism and perfectionism were tempered by the collective

concept of the **communio sanctorum**. True. But it is not pronouncements but practice that establishes the connection between
voluntarism, discipleship and schism. For example, in the **Second
London Confession** of 1677, Particular Baptists asserted that the purest
churches under heaven were subject to mixture and error. On the other
hand, they taught that members were "saints" by calling, **visibly** manifesting and evidencing (in and by their profession and walking) their
obedience unto the call of Christ. Members and congregations had the
onus to evidence "signs of grace revealed," the fruits of the Spirit, and
separation from the world by the Word and Spirit of God.[25] How much
dross or chaff a church can tolerate becomes a matter of subjective interpretation and is open to incessant pressure of cultural accommodation after the initial fires of revival and restorationism begin to die.

Until recently, when the impact of economic, social and demographic
change disrupted the gathered community, congregations confidently
distinquished between true believers and nominal Christians, between
sound and latitudinarian congregations. They demanded an apostolic
walk, with members living in the manner and the virtue of the first
followers of Jesus. But most Believers' Churches' were not perfectionist
and, as represented by E.T. Hiscox, editor of widely circulated manuals
for Baptists in the last century, they held that the church was the school
of Christ controlled by wise and kindly discipline, a family where law
and order was tempered with tenderness and discretion. Churches had
"a right and duty to exercise supervision of members, to reprove when
erring and withdraw fellowship when incorrigible." But discipline was
limited to the "laws of Christ, kindly and generously intepreted" and by
clearly defined convenant agreement. Matters not violations of New
Testament **law**, not transgressions of Christian morals nor covenant
obligations, were not subject to discipline.[26]

The tension between priestly and prophetic concerns, between
ministry and morals, is as old as Christendom, as old as the Donatist
controversy. Isidore of Seville clearly recognized that schisms often
occur "when men say 'We are righteous, we sanctify the unclean, and so
forth.' "[27] And what Believers' Church is prepared to follow with relentless logic the Puritan view that their offspring are naturally young
vipers, and provide no Half-way Covenant? The moral question is
especially pertinent when evangelicalism becomes the dominant faith
of a culture, as happened in nineteenth century America.

In Canada among Baptists the issue of open or close communion
clearly illustrates how Believers' Churches "stand between a rock and a
hard place." Strict Baptists recognized that an open Table abdicated the
minor discipline and that church discipline functioned as a tool for law
and order on the frontier prior to the arrival of the magistrate. Hence
they pointed the accusing finger at what Abraham Booth called
"inaccurate, loose, latitudinarian, or open Communion Baptists."[28]
Such over-scrupulousness, as Greenslade observes, leaves believers
and congregations unwilling to "trust the church to do justice in time to
[their] truth, meanwhile submitting to authority which voices the

consensus fidelium (the agreement of the faithful)."[29] The problem becomes acute, as in the fundamentalist-modernist controversy, when dispensational theology is espoused which presupposes the inevitability of ethical, and ecclesiological decay.

Sectarian restorationists find ready hearers when they crusade for separation from the world, against dancing deacons and secular amusements. Believers' Churches embrace a paradox. They espouse an inner-worldly asceticism that thrusts saints into the world but expect separated lives. It was Willard L. Sperry who observed that in America (and Canada) schisms relate to a spirit of perfectionism more than to individualism or liberalism; an entirely logical position for those who believe they are a city set upon a hill, a model for reform of the whole of Christendom. "It is in the bodies which inherit the Reformation passion for a church purged of worldliness and purified after the primitive pattern that we find in America these schisms and sub-schisms of the more evangelical types of Protestantism."[30]

Franklin H. Littell puts the issue in bold relief when he states, "To what degree, and in what form, are simple and plain living a part of the Christian witness becomes a matter of supreme importance within a denominastion at times of tension, and a potential contributor to schism."[31] For denominations which have abandoned discipline and allowed the concept of covenant to fall into disuse it is an even more pressing issue.

SOCIOLOGICAL GENERALIZATIONS

Our task has been to explain why the Believers' Church tradition has been so susceptible to disunity. The preceding attempted to deal directly with areas unique to the type. There are, however, some generalizations related to the processes of institutional cohesion and division which may contribute to a wider understanding of the question.

Organizations and institutions develop to meet the needs of members, and are maintained only as long as needs are met. However the saliency of individual needs differs, as does the intensity of belief in the doctrines, norms and values of the group. In religion a plethora of patterns emerge in consequence, and institutional separation can occur and attrition take place without appreciable change in the formal symbols or practices of a denomination. Moreover, as Canadian churches and sects evolve into denominations, abandoning the prerogatives of state churchmanship and sectarian defensiveness, their histories provide an increasingly divergent pattern of symbols and practices to which dissidents may appeal.

Concurrently new doctrines, values and practices emerge which result in differential recruitment of new members who respond on the basis of differing strain patterns. The New Light and the Old Light share the denominational house together, insensitive to the latent contradictions until some theological or social situation sparks the fires of controversy. Then the denomination emerges claiming the name and history of their forebears, or differential recruitment of converts, based on theology or class, contributes to a growing pluralism in the denomination, thus increasing the threat to its cohesion.

On the other hand, divisive and unitive forces operate concurrently. For example, to the root streams of General and Particular Baptists were added new denominations through schism such as the New Connexion, Regular and Fellowship Baptists. Mergers of Arminian and Calvinistic groups took place when the anthroplogical question cooled, but schisms occurred again when nineteenth century evangelicalism evolved diametrically towards "fundamentalism" and "modernism."

As with Rome, the denomination survives, evolving, changing, reacting to new social, intellectual and theological currents. But adjustment to change normally takes place in the context of a rhetoric of non-change. The faith of Believers' Churches today is not the "faith once for all delivered to the saints," and it is doubtful if the denominational founding fathers would recognize our innovations. Only Christ is unchangeable and there is no golden age to which His people can return. There is only Christ, history and change.

Today most Believers' Churches embrace a religious pluralism as wide as do the Baptists who seek to enfold within the family such contradictory beliefs as are represented by the Philadelphia Confession and Princeton on the inspiration of the Bible; eschatologies as wide as dispensationalism and the theology of hope; and worship patterns as divergent as reformed liturgy and revivalism. All are potential contributors to schism in the absence of an over-arching commitment to the unity of the body of Christ.

In addition, all Believers' Churches in North America share in and are influenced by religious movements which transcend national, denominational and confessional boundaries. The history of the Christian church in Canada may raise questions as to the appropriateness of the denominational designation, but there is a wide difference between a possible "magisterial mentality" and "state churchism," and among evangelicals continental influences far outweigh national ones. Frontier revivalism has left a profound legacy. Since the memory span of Christians is usually limited to one generation, the average member has more in common with the prevailing "Born Again" and "Neocharismatic" movements than he has with his denominational roots; the laments of church historians notwithstanding. Such currents which transcend denomination may contribute to closer ecumenism, but can foster ruinous controversy and schism.

Not only can minute changes in beliefs and values have profound consequences in attracting or alienating members, but in Canada there is a full range of ethnic, economic, regional and continental influences available, around which to catalyze differentiation.

Consider ethnicity. In spite of sincere efforts, Canadian Baptists were unsuccessful in holding Baptists of German and Scandinavian origin within a national fellowship. Their divergent histories, missionary interests and financial needs proved decisive in decisions to associate with ethnic conferences having headquarters in the United States. In 1919 the German Baptists joined the North American Baptist

Conference, while the Swedish churches joined the General Conference of America in the 1940s. Today the language barrier has all but disappeared but the separate institutional structures remain.

Consider class. Elsewhere I have argued that prior to 1920 two new theological systems evolved as a result of the reworking of evangelical symbols by two increasingly heterogeneous constituencies of Baptist leaders and supporters; that differential class recruitment followed which altered further the social characteristics of the Baptist denomination, precipitating struggles for power which eventuated in the "fundamentalist-modernist" schisms.[32]

While these sociological forces impinge on all Canadian denominations, their potential for disruption in the case of Believers' Churches is increased because they reinforce divisive influences inherent in commitment to biblical restorationism, congregationalism and ethical sectarianism.

Because this paper has concentrated on divisive forces in the Believers' Churches in Canada it should not obscure the fact that strong unitive currents are flowing which encourage closer co-operation, perhaps even unions, among denominations sharing the unifying characteristics of the type. The existence of a near-national denomination, urbanization, secularization, demographic dislocation, the challenge of world missions and the interests of Canadian nationalism encourage evangelical ecumenicity. Above all, a constructive response to the unifying forces which issued in the formation of the United Church of Canada must be made without resort to narrow sectarianism and with recognition that evangelicals exist among all Canadian denominations. The rising status, education and prestige of members of believers' denominations, the cross-fertilization of members, and the common milieu of scholars and leaders could contribute to the emergence of such a third force in Canadian Protestantism.

To date, co-operation has been limited to utilitarian concerns such as world relief and common representation before the magistrates; or to meetings for fellowship and inspiration. Intentional efforts, such as the Study Conference on the Believers' Church, expanded to mobilize and challenge the grassroots, now adds a major stream to the unitive current. What Robert Paul observed of restorationism may well provide the basic agenda for future discussions among Believers' Churches in Canada.

> To discover the essential contribution that restorationist movements have made to our common Christian history, we must look beyond the biblicism to which they have been prone, beyond their pharasaic striving for a demonstrable purity in the visible church, to their insistence that Christians must return constantly to their Source, and to their claim that the church of the gospel should reflect the nature of that gospel.[33]

A closer unity cannot be achieved by repudiation of the history or the genius of the Believers' Church movements. It will happen through renewed contact with the Source.

IDENTITY AND UNITY
IN CANADIAN BELIEVERS' CHURCHES

Rodney J. Sawatsky

The church union of June 10, 1925 may be the most significant event in Canadian Protestant history to date. On that occasion three traditions — Methodist, Congregational and Presbyterian — combined to create the United Church of Canada. Since that time some smaller groups joined the union, and active discussion with the Anglican Church of Canada aims to extend this form of unitive Protestantism in Canada.[1]

Not all of those invited to join in 1925 responded positively. The Anglicans declined, and a significant part of the Presbyterian Church maintained its traditional identity. Already in 1907 the Baptist Convention of Ontario and Quebec rejected the invitation on bases which may best be defined as Believers' Church principles.[2]

The Baptist letter of 1907 could be read as a charter for the ongoing separate identity and mission of Believers' Churches in a nation not particularly tuned to this religious style. But it hasn't! The Believers' Churches in Canada have only begun to consider their common tradition. More often these comparatively small denominations look to the United States for their identity because in that country, by contrast, this type of church approaches a dominant position.

Strengths and weaknesses follow from this situation. Believers' Church continentalism can rightly limit the ever present danger of idolizing a particular nation state. On the other hand, looking southward can readily obscure the nature and possibilities of the Believers' Churches in Canada, and thereby limit their mission to the nation. If indeed the Believers' Churches in Canada perceive themselves to have a unique and common mission in this nation, they will want to form some kind of unity to that end. Such a unity can be attained only after two conditions are met: these churches must understand their situation in the Canadian fabric and then develop an appropriate Believers' Church response.

Because these two issues have been inadequately addressed in the past, the history of unitive endeavours among Believers' Churches in Canada is fairly bleak. True, most Canadian Baptists gained some unity through the Baptist Federation of Canada founded in 1944, and most Canadian Mennonites co-operate through agencies such as the Mennonite Central Committee, but between these and similar families of denominations no steps towards significant co-operation, much less unity, have been pursued. Hence the task here is to provide a prolegomena to Believers' Church unity in Canada, rather than to rehearse past failures or achievements.

I. Application of the "Believers' Church" category to the Canadian scene may be novel but the basic idea is not new.[3] The classic "church-sect" typology developed by Ernst Troeltsch and Max Weber with particular reference to Europe has been extensively applied to the Canadian situation. Samuel D. Clark's monumental study **Church and Sect in Canada**, despite legitimate critical appraisals, continues to convince that the typology is suggestive in Canadian analyses.[4]

"Sect" and "Believers' Church" are not necessarily equivalents; however, they tend to denominate basically similar concepts. Likewise both terms are particularly usable in Canada, for this nation has never adopted a policy of the absolute separation of church and state, and, consequently, retains numerous vestiges of religious establishments. As Canada's leading authority on this subject, John Moir, concludes: "Canada has preserved churchism to preserve itself. Whenever military, economic, political or cultural absorption by the United States threatened, as in 1776, 1812, 1837, 1911 or even 1957, Canada has turned to its counter-revolutionary tradition for inspiration. And ecclesiasticism is a traditional part of that tradition."[5]

Believers' churchism gains special meaning in a society, such as Canada, where state churchism or ecclesiasticism remains. In the United States a wall separating the institutions of church and state resulted from the events surrounding the American Revolution. The sectarian, Free Church or Believers' Church style triumphed with that revolution and henceforth churches of this order can be seen as typically American. The category "denomination" emerged to identify this new religious order in a society where establishment "churches" and pro-testing "sects" lost much of their earlier meaning.[6] Denominationalism and believers' churchism thus have much in common and are alike at home in the United States.

Canada, by contrast, is counter-revolutionary. For English Canada, British loyalism meant an ever present wariness of revolution and republicanism. By extension this meant an uncertainty about de-nominationalism. According to the late H.H. Walsh, "There has been in Canada a religious mood that questions the desirability of denomina-tionalism and does hanker for greater uniformity of religious expression in the interest of cultural unity."[7] Consequently the Believers' Churches are more likely to be viewed as peripheral than as central to the Canadian definition.

This churchly bias in Canada is clearly documented by census data. The table below does violence to Believers' Church assumptions in that it does not list actual membership figures but rather calculates religious preference figures which embrace entire families, baptized and nonbaptized alike. Another limitation is that some of the groups in both listings are marginal to the particular category and could as well be included in the opposite list. Yet the point is obvious that a few religious bodies of an historically **corpus christianum** orientation dominate the Canadian scene. Even if one-half of the "Other" category is added to my "Believers' Churches" list, churches of this order embrace at best nine per cent of the Canadian population, whereas the "Establishment Churches" account for about 90 per cent.

RELIGIOUS POPULATION IN CANADA — 1971[8]

"Establishment" Churches		"Believers" Churches	
Anglican	2,543,180	Adventists	28,590
Greek Orthodox	316,605	Baptist	667,245
Lutheran	715,740	CMA	23,630
Presbyterian	872,335	Christian Reformed	83,390
Roman Catholic	9,974,895	Disciples	16,405
Ukrainian Catholic	227,730	Free Methodist	19,125
United Church	3,768,800	Hutterite	13,650
Other	1,916,515	Mennonite	168,150
		Pentecostal	220,390
		Salvation Army	119,665
Total	21,568,310		1,460,240

American statistics stand in marked contrast to those above. Approximately parallel denominations to the seven "establishment churches" embrace only about one-half of the U.S. membership figures. Accordingly the many smaller and larger Believers' Churches account for a much higher percentage of the population in the U.S. than in Canada. For example, in 1974 the Canadian Baptist churches recorded an adult membership of 196,501. In the same year, the Baptist churches in the United States listed 26,732,658 adult members. This means that whereas the population ratio between the U.S. and Canada is ten to one, the ratio of Baptists is 136 to one.[9]

These statistics do more than provide demographic support for the marginal role of the Believers' Churches in Canada. They also suggest why Canadian Believers' Churches tend to look southward for their larger identities. Not only are Believers' Church orientations more typical in the U.S., but also headquarters offices, seminaries and publishing houses serving most Canadian Believers' Churches are located south of the border. Accordingly they tend to see themselves identified more with their kin in the U.S. than with fellow Believers' Church members in Canada, and, in consequence, possibly more with American than Canadian society. This north-south axis is complemented by the weight of religious radio and television, by evangelistic personalities and by publication endeavours all moving from the south to the north. A recent compelling thesis defended by sociologist Harry Hiller, with reference to the so-called third force, might well be enlarged to include the Believers' Churches and would then read: "The proportionately greater activity in the United States leads Canadian third force [and Believers' Church] participants into strong continentalist relationships, dependencies and alliances."[10]

II. Two Canadian religious bodies are somewhat exceptional to these generalized characterizations. For one, the Baptist churches have been less marginal in the Canadian scene, by comparison with most of the other Believers' Church groups. Secondly, the United Church of Canada with its strong Methodist element cannot be characterized as establishmentarian without explanation. Clarification on these two situations follows.

Baptists became active in Canada already in the eighteenth century. As benefactors of the Great Awakening in the Maritime provinces they grew to considerable strength in that part of the country. With the passing of time this tradition became a major force in Upper Canada and in the west as well. Consequently, Baptists established colleges, seminaries, publication houses and periodicals in Canada. Besides, Baptists became extensively involved in many areas of Canadian political and social life. Only a small fraction of Canadian Baptist congregations maintained administrative links with offices in the U.S.[11]

In contrast to most other Canadian Believers' Churches, Canadian Baptists have known a strong, independent Canadian identity. The very fact that they were invited to join the union movement which culminated in 1925, as well as the more recent Anglican-United-Disciples of Christ conversations, indicates the degree to which this tradition is considered by others as central to the Canadian religious scene. Indeed, although not organically linked, Convention Baptists and the United Church of Canada shared a hymn book and Sunday school literature development, until quite recently. According to Jarold K. Zeman, the severing of those ties, the movement towards further church union in Canada and the lack of comparative growth in the Baptist Federation of Canada churches is resulting in a re-examination of Baptist identities, especially in relation to other Believers' Churches.[12] It might be argued that Canadian Baptists are shifting from a more central place in Canadian society, to at least identifying more with the periphery.

All this is not to say that Baptists in Canada have been untouched by Believers' Church continentalism. The rhetoric and style of the fundamentalist-liberal battle of the 1920s which divided the Canadian Baptist community were hardly indigenously Canadian but rather were American imports for the most part.[13] Similarly, independent Baptist congregations of more recent vintage are modelled after American prototypes. It is possibly even more significant to note that the Canadian German Baptists and Swedish Baptists are linked organizationally to their American brethren through the North American Baptist Convention and General Conference of America respectively. In summary, even Canadian Baptists, despite their institutional completeness, their history and relative strength, cannot avoid a lusting eye towards the Believers' Churches in the United States.

The United Church of Canada embraces basic contradictions. It co-opted one of the most anti-establishment forces in the nineteenth century, the Methodists; it welded together three traditions to create something radically new in a conservative, anti-revolutionary society; yet it is one of the major participants in Canada's conservative establishmentarian mood. The union of 1925 completed the classic church-sect cycle, in which a protesting sect (or sects), with time, itself becomes an establishment-type of church. In H.H. Walsh's words:

> The ideal of a national church never quite faded from the Canadian consciousness but has continued to colour the outlook of the Canadian churches down to the present time.... The long series of church unions that are so prominent in Canadian church history, culminating in the formation of the United Church of Canada in 1925, is the historical expression of an ideal that looks beyond denominationalism as the final destiny of the church in Canada.[14]

III. Is the continuing refusal of Canadian Baptists to participate in union negotiations an anti-Canadian move and an affirmation of American denominationalism? It is both insofar as Believers' Churches and denominationalism thrive in the same context. It is not, insofar as denominationalism in the United States has brought with it a certain depreciation of the church in favour of the individual and the nation, which can seriously undermine the Believers' Church concept. Canadian churchism has stayed the forces of both individualism and a national religious mythology. The Canadian Believers' Churches ought rightly to affirm this situation and proceed with their self-definition accordingly.

The 1907 Baptist letter opposing church union presumably spoke for all Ontario and Quebec Baptists, since it was formulated well before the divisions of the 1920s. If this is so, more liberal and more fundamentalist Baptists alike agreed that the true church is not creedal nor confessional, not sacramental nor hierarchical, but rather "is constituted by voluntary union of those alone who by personal repentance and faith, — not by natural birth, nor by proxy, nor by ceremony, nor by any overt act of the Church, — have come into fellowship with God in Christ."[15] This statement of Believers' Church doctrine surely continues to speak for all churches of this tradition in Canada as they define themselves over against state churchism.

Believers' Churches in the United States affirm the same propositions, but at their best these affirmations are not made in opposition to state churchism but to national religion. Offsetting the fantastic religious pluralism which followed upon the victory of Free Church principles, a faith developed which ascribed to the American nation a unique destiny under God. Indeed it was the nation itself which inherited the historical churchly functions of providing the individual with a focus for personal and group identity, becoming the community of righteousness and serving as the primary agent of God's meaningful activity in history. Denominational religion, on occasion, stood in opposition to this nationally oriented religiosity, but more frequently the two were indistinguishable, or at least mutually supportive.[16]

For present purposes, a detailing of this messianic self-understanding, which united divergent denominations and ethnic groupings under a common faith, is unnecessary. Although this chosen people "set apart by God to serve a peculiar purpose in the history of mankind," formulated and pursued its mission variously, basic themes emerge.[17] This commonality, as the recent extensive literature on the subject indicates, includes the following elements: a borrowing, reinterpreting and extending, expecially by the Puritan tradition, of Anglo-Saxon providential mythology; a melting-together of biblical and national event and exegesis under such concepts as a chosen race, a holy people, sacrifice, blood atonement, salvation, millennium concepts which place the Constitution, the Revolution and the Civil War alongside the Bible as religiously normative; a perception of America as a model in constitutional liberties and spiritual religion, with a destiny and mission interpreted in millennial terms to share this ideal by example, persuasion, missionary enterprise, expansion and even war; a WASP-ish restriction on the vision which by the mid-twentieth century was seriously undermined, requiring redefinition to correspond with American reality; and a two-edged ethic which could both bless the American way of life and provide prophetic critiques of the same.[18]

Canadian mythology, so far as English Canada is concerned, does not include a common sense of providential destiny. Herein is to be found the essential difference between the Canadian and American religious experience. French Canada, however, developed its own powerful providential self-appraisal. Spurred on by a minority status, by a struggle for preservation despite a conquered status, no less than by a long-standing missionary drive — different but no less religiously motivated than that of the Puritan "city set on a hill" — nineteenth century French Canadians established a nationalistic mythology which welded language, race and religion into an inseparable whole. "I cannot doubt that this religious and civilizing mission is the true vocation and the special vocation of the French race in America," said Msgr. L.A. Paquet in but one sermonic example.[19] Besides clergymen, historians led in defining this mythology which although secularized, especially in recent formulations, provided a nationalistic ideology throughout French-Canadian history.[20]

Obviously English Canadians (i.e. non-French) could not share this French-Canadian Catholic nationalism. Although the English followed the same Christian calendar, as Everett Hughes has shown so well, they were far removed from the religious and patriotic ceremonies characteristic of French Canada and which provided much of the ritual and symbol structure for its culture religion.[21]

Neither did English Canadians develop their own common sense of destiny. Unlike American pluralism, even Canadian Protestant sectarianism was not offset by a unifying mythology. S.F. Wise found, especially in the ideas expressed by Bishop John Strachan, a concept of British North America as God's "Elect Nation" inherited without modification from Britain. "But in the hands of Strachan and his fellows," Wise added, "the providential sense of mission was too narrowly conceived, too deeply rooted in the defence of a dying order to catch the imagination of the people, and to provide the basis for an emergent Canadian nationalism."[22] Similarly, Goldwin French, in his examination of the non-Anglican Canadian evangelical denominations in the nineteenth century, noted a common emphasis on providential theology among these groups, but also noted that these conceptions "lacked one vital ingredient, whose absence helps to explain one crucial distinction between Canada and the United States" — namely, the belief in the special destiny of the nation. He therefore concludes: "The failure of the churches to agree on a single providential interpretation of our destiny, and the inability of the Church of England to secure a dominant position in the colonies, deprived us of a myth sufficiently powerful to serve as the focus of a new nationalism."[23]

While the United States has a religion of the American nation, Canada has its "state" churches. Historian William Kilbourn summarizes this situation in this fashion:

> There is a lingering aura of the European established Church in Canada which is very different from the American separation of church and state and its consequences, the political religion of America that has prevailed so long in the United States. The Canadian churches' influence and status can be a strain on some people's liberties, but they are also a bastion against the more absolute dogma of an all-embracing spiritual patriotism.[24]

This lack of a religion-of-the-nation in Canada leaves to the churches their rightful task as the primary agent of God's work in the world. While in the United States the Believers' Churches particularly must constantly assert their rightful place versus the nation, not so in Canada. Yet, according to some interpreters, there are Canadian evangelicals who, in keeping with their continentalism, are also borrowing elements of the American national religion.[25] That Leslie Tarr's title **This Dominion, His Dominion** proposes to affirm a version of American national mythology in Canada could be debated. If it does, it would be in keeping with certain kinds of individualistic evangelicalism, but it would certainly run counter to Believers' Church evangelicalism.

IV. Even as the large Canadian identity is typically characterized by way of contrast with the United States, so too the Believers' Church situation in Canada is illuminated by contrast with its counterparts in the United States.

Evidence abounds to indicate that the Canadian Believers' Churches are situated quite differently from their American counterparts. The Believers' Churches have unique problems and possibilities in this nation. This fact must be recognized before the Believers' Churches can define a common mission in this nation and before they can proceed to any kind of unity for mission. Models of mission and unity cannot simply be borrowed; they must be relevant to the situation.

What precisely the role of the Believers' Churches in Canada ought to be cannot be examined in detail here. It can be said, however, that these churches will want to affirm the important role of the church in Canadian society. It is the church as an organism which is God's primary agent of redemption, not the state, or the individual. But they will also go one step further: they will emphasize, as only they can, that the disciplined church of believers is the most powerful witness of God's work in the world.

It is this high doctrine of the Believers' Church which can also unify more liberal and more fundamentalistic Christians. Although differences remain, the larger Mennonite bodies in North America, after some very difficult times between conservatives and liberals in the 1920s and 1930s, were able to regain a dynamic unity when they rediscovered the Anabaptist doctrine of the church.[26] The biblical roots of that vision were spelled out earlier by Harold S. Bender in **These Are My People**[27] and most recently by C. Norman Kraus in **The Community of the Spirit.**[28] The Anabaptist nuances are articulated in Franklin H. Littell's **The Origin of Sectarian Protestantism**[29] and Walter Klaassen in **Anabaptism: Neither Catholic Nor Protestant.**[30] As younger evangelicals, particularly, seek to move beyond the limitations of earlier dichotomies between liberals and fundamentalists, they too are finding the same view of the church to be a most creative and biblical option.[31] As they plumb the depths of that perspective, earlier divisions will fade in importance.

What is the essence of this view of the church? The church is premised not on inerrant words, nor on lofty ideals, nor on personal experiences, but on the following of Jesus Christ who is the ongoing judge, example and renewer of this his body in the world. Doctrinal squabbles pale under the searching question of faithfulness to the way of the firstborn son of God. Divisions between personal and social redemption become folly as the life of Jesus becomes the norm for the life of the church. The church is the new creation of God drawing to itself throughout the ages those seeking new life, and witnessing as a sign to the nations that under the lordship of Christ all will be made alive.

Believers' Churches are by definition evangelical in that they hold, above all else, the evangel, the good news of new life through Jesus the Christ. "Evangelical" in recent years has come to denote a particular party in the church with its particular leaders, schools, projects and statements of essential Christianity. It is an inheritor of earlier fundamentalism, although with some significant modifications. Not all Believers' Churches, although truly evangelical, identify with this evangelical party, for various reasons and, as that label is now used, it is not coterminous with Believers' Churches.

The evangelical "party" in Canada knows various kinds of unity. It has for decades co-operated through non-denominational missions, Bible schools and, more recently, seminaries. Inter-denominational ventures like evangelistic crusades and the Evangelical Fellowship of Canada are similarly notable. There is no doubt, as recent innovations in publications and seminaries indicate, that Canadian evangelicals are concerned to formulate an indigenously Canadian enterprise. But since not all evangelicals hold to the Believers' Church position, many of these unitive efforts cannot be seen as necessarily Believers' Church endeavours. Indeed, some evangelicals, with their more experiential and creedal emphases, tend to undermine Believers' Church theology. The Believers' Churches need to call their allies in the larger evangelical movement to a unity built not on creedal formulations nor on subjective experiences but on a disciplined church of believers following the way of Jesus.

V. These reflections on the nature of Christianity in Canada, assisted by comparisons with the American scene, indicate the location of the Believers' Churches in this nation and suggest in broad outline the basis for Believers' Church unity. While the weight of the past is powerful, particularly in a conservative country like Canada, observations of the present and prognostications of the future suggest that other dynamics must also be considered.

Canada, together with the rest of the western world, is rapidly entering a post-Christian era. The age of grand ecumenical schemes and church unions may well be past. Canada's high regard for the church as an institution which embraces most of her population in one of several mainline denominations is severely "eroding." The current evangelical renaissance seems to suggest that in the midst of a secularizing world, individuals are still groping for meaning in their lives.[32] Ours is an evangelical, not an ecumenical age.

The Believers' Churches in Canada need to share in both the ecumenical and the evangelical movements. With ecumenical proponents, the Believers' Churches affirm the importance of the church as God's reconciling agent in the world. Yet in contrast to much of ecumenism, Believers' Churches insist that the church is not all-embracing of the population but is premised on personal adult commitment. With evangelicals, Believers' Churches affirm the importance of a personal commitment of faith. Indeed, evangelical popularity tempts Believers' Churches to abandon all in favor of individual conversionism. To accede would undermine the Believers' Church concept, which maintains that nurturing personal faith commitments is only a part of building Christ's body in the world.

In an increasingly post-Christian world all churches will inevitably, once again, as in the days before Constantine, become Believers' Churches. Believers' Churches in Canada need to provide a model for the semi-establishmentarian churches in this transition. Simultaneously Believers' Churches must provide evangelicals with a more biblical view of the church.In this middle ground between the ecumenical and the evangelical Believers' Churches may well find their Canadian mission and a basis for co-operation to that end. If the 1907 Baptist statement could be seen as a rallying point for Canadian Believers' Church commonality, it should be seen in 1978 not as a rejection of ecumenism, but as a proposal for the future, to be considered by all Christian churches in Canada.

PUBLIC EDUCATION AND THE BELIEVERS' CHURCH TRADITION: AN HISTORICAL APPROACH

Kenneth R. Davis

Except for a few scattered references, largely to post-secondary education, especially ministerial, and to concerns for religious education, manuals of modern church history on the Believers' Church in Canada (and the United States) are remarkably silent on the subject of the relationship of the Believers' Churches to public education. Even the very small number of more specialized studies largely follow the same pattern.[1] It is the intention of this paper, therefore, to approach the problem from the broadest possible perspective; initially to review the basic principles within the Believers' Church tradition which might logically apply, then to trace how Believers' Churches have reacted over the sweep of church history, and finally to focus on reasons for and the challenge of the present crisis.

I. CHURCH AND SOCIETY: SOME BASIC BELIEVERS' CHURCH PRINCIPLES

Fundamental to the development of the modern Believers' Church tradition was a unique view of the relationship of the church to society which was worked out first in modern times by the Anabaptists during the Reformation of the sixteenth century. Anabaptism broke with the concept of the sacral or unitary society, the Christian state, as upheld in one way or another by both Roman Catholics and Magisterial (Lutheran, Reformed and Anglican) Reformers. Anabaptists were convinced that a biblically based reform of the church did not mean just a rearrangement of priorities and powers in the unitary society, nor just a purification of its theology (with reference to individual forgiveness of sins) and of its principles of operation. Indeed, the reform (or Christianizing) of society was not believed to be the proper objective at all. Rather, they sought for the freeing of the church (actually, churches) entirely from the temporal, civil powers so that it could be and function truly as Christ's Church.

The church was perceived as a separate, alien society functioning on entirely different principles from all other "worldly" societies. The most Christianized state was still never a Christian state but essentially "worldly" and must (according to Scripture) operate, even when functioning properly, on different principles than Kingdom ethics and could never be identified with the church. Accordingly, the church's membership and its visible communities were never coextensive with the civil society but rather made up of those who, while living as much as possible peacefully and responsibly for divine purpose within the "worldly" society, chose freely, voluntarily, sincerely and with primary loyalty to follow Christ in the context of a distinctive, separate Christian community.

Their numbers were expected to be "few"[2] and they saw themselves as essentially an alien, pilgrim remnant, a suffering, witnessing church — a view derived both from Scripture and from persecution from nominally Christian societies.

The fundamental Anabaptist principle of the separation of the church as a Christian society, its principles of operation and its lifestyle, from all other societies meant far more than an organizational separation of church and state.[3] It was based on the firm desire to reproduce fully the New Testament ideal of the holy community (Ephesians 5:27), as witness and in preparation for Christ's return, and on the conviction that the principle of separation must be applied thoroughly in order to do so. The restoration of the correct gospel order (proclaiming the gospel, personal repentance and baptism, producing disciples, followed by teaching and fellowship) required a different understanding of the mission of the church — as a "calling out" of disciples from an essentially worldly society,[4] and not a Christianization of "worldly" societies. New Testament church discipline also, without which there was no true church, in their view,[5] implied the exclusion of the sinner from the Christian community only, and into the worldly, civil society.

The Anabaptist emphasis on separation was also rooted in a strong belief in the spirituality or otherness of the church. The church was a unique physical manifestation of the spiritual Kingdom of God. This they derived in part from what has been called by R. Friedmann the theology of the two kingdoms. He notes that there was in Anabaptist writings "the acceptance of a fundamental New Testament dualism, that is, an uncompromising ontological dualism in which Christian values are held in sharp contrast to the values of the 'world' in its corrupt state," a Christ/world dualism.[6] The churches as limited expressions of the eschatological kingdom are in constant tension with the kingdom of the prince of this world whose systems are destined for destruction, not salvation. Friedmann adds: "It is obvious that the mood, piety, and other aspects of life are affected by whether one lives by kingdom theology with its dualism of 'Christ/world' or by the traditional theology of 'salvation by faith alone' with its own dualism of gospel and law."[7] Similarly, kingdom theology emphasized a new "resurrection" life in an other-worldly Christian society rather than individualized forgiveness in the context of the old society.

Kingdom theology, with its call to a new other-worldly citizenship and loyalty, found its greatest practical (this-worldly) expression in the unique idea of the **Gemeinde**, that is, the church as a brotherhood community, as a social unit (indeed, an alien social unit), not just a congregation of individuals (which is biblically too limited) nor the whole civil society (which is biblically too large). As a social unit it engulfs all aspects of everyday living and requires community responsibilities and expression in relation to the material, physical, and social well-being as well as the moral and spiritual development of its members (e.g., some Anabaptists refused to baptize new converts unless they were prepared to pledge a willingness to share their material things with a brother in need).[8] It was to be a developing foreshadowing of the future fulness of the Kingdom of God, and at the same time function as a redemptive community. With such communitarian ideals predominant, total education also becomes a church function and responsibility. The whole educational process is just another part of the mechanism for growth to mature citizenship in the new kingdom. Sanctification involves more than biblical studies and listening to preaching; it takes place through involvement in the context of the total functioning of the community. Kingdom education is totally other than "worldly" education.

Witness too was never just individualized personal evangelism nor preaching; it was also corporate. The proclamation of the gospel correlated with the kingdom community on display in all its living facets, its superior institutions and life-style (e.g., marriage, social relationships and education).

The modern Believers' Church tradition has its roots deep in a movement that perceived of the church as a separate entity from worldly society. The fulfilling of its task included the creation of a clear-cut alternative society and life-style. It "reasserted the legitimacy of the New Testament's pattern of relationships between churches and society — a relationship which...closely parallels the modern model of a counter-culture."[9] With such a vision, the responsibility for the education of their children could not easily be turned over to society at large. Indeed, as Friedmann noted, "It is almost a truism to say that most of the values of Western civilization — aesthetic, scientific and philosophical — do not fit into this dualistic vision and the implicit hope for the kingdom."[10] In this they were not innovating. The emphasis on "simplicity of faith," rooted in the New Testament itself, had been reasserted also by St. Bernard in the twelfth century and Tertullian in the third, that is, "What has Jerusalem to do with Athens, or the Church with the Academy?"[11] Not that the Anabaptists were anti-intellectual per se, but as with many second and third century Christians they were gravely suspicious of a close alliance with the knowledge patterns of this "world" and of education apart from "the perfection of Christ."[12]

II. HISTORICAL APPLICATIONS

Most Christians in the past have recognized and accepted, even insisted on their responsibility for the total educational task. The church in the Roman Empire, before Constantine, derived its basic attitude from the Hebrews who placed the responsibility primarily on the family, although assisted by organized schools established everywhere alongside the synagogues. The early Christians, however, did not initially establish separate Christian schools both because they could not and because the Roman primary (elementary) system was adaptable. In the first two centuries education was neither compulsory nor, at the elementary level, state controlled and operated, and the teacher was paid directly by and was responsible to the families concerned.[13]

There were tensions, however. They took the form of opposition to some aspects of classical culture and to educational alliances with it. The **Didascalia Apostolorum**, a Christian manual of wide influence in the third century, said bluntly: "Have nothing to do with pagan books," and asserted that a proper biblical education was able to provide for all one's cultural needs — "all these outlandish books that come from the Devil must be hurled away."[14] As more Christian young people went beyond the elementary basics to grammar schools, a process of expurgation, revising and rewriting of curriculum materials to Christianize them, increasingly took place and Christian teachers multiplied at all levels.

When in 362 A.D., under Emperor Julian, the state took more direct control of the schools and the curriculum, turned against Christian ideals and even forbade Christians to teach from a Christian perspective, it forced the setting up of the first alternative Christian school system with a completely independent Christian curriculum. It was the first major confrontation over state control in education that parallels our own situation today.

These tensions ceased when the Roman Empire became officially Christian and in Western Europe almost full control over all education passed to the church for a thousand years.

The Protestant Reformation did not change the long-standing pattern of close ties between education and the church, except that as state churches the Magisterial Protestant denominations (Lutheran, Anglican and Reformed) tended to turn over the actual education controls and system to the state; but it was assumed that the system still would be Christian and function in co-operation with the church in a unitary Christian state. In one way or another up to the nineteenth century, including colonial U.S.A. and Canada, most Christians, both Protestant and Catholic, still accepted, either directly or indirectly through a co-operative Christian state, their responsibility for the total educational task.[15]

Beginning with the Anabaptists, Believers' Churches often felt threatened by state controlled, denominationally established educational systems, though they were at least not secular or pagan. Moreover, Believers' Churches had little opportunity to set up alternatives of their own and for the most part did not do so. One exception were the Hutterites, the one group of Anabaptists in the sixteenth century with the greatest opportunity on their Bruderhofs in Moravia to apply the basic Believers' Church principles to education. Given the freedom to act, plus their extra strong communitarian ideals, from the first they assumed responsibility for the total education of their children according to the principles of Christ. Formal post-elementary education, however, was not encouraged and was replaced by applied education in the context of specific tasks in the community; but at nursery and elementary levels it was a completely integrated and unified Christian educational system undergirded by a catechism and the primary goal of inculcating the knowledge of and reverence for God. Basic practical skills, Bible knowledge, devotional practices, moral developent, healthy living, all in the context of a peaceful environment, loving discipline and the godly example of the teachers, fit together in their ideal.[16] Its success is in part demonstrated in the way it has helped them preserve their communities and ideals to this day.

Mennonite Anabaptists, after the mid-sixteenth century, were scattered among a dozen different and mostly intolerant political regimes. Consequently no single pattern of educational policy emerged. When the opportunity was provided, however, which happened only in Russia where they were granted full freedom after 1789, they developed an extensive educational system of their own at both elementary and secondary levels. Their objectives were made clear by a delegation to St. Petersburg in 1876, which asserted: "Both the village and the secondary schools and also the teachers' seminary must have absolutely the character of church schools, and only if they are confirmed as such do they fulfill their purpose...."[17]

In the New World, colonial education at the elementary levels in what later became Canada and the U.S.A. was largely parochial and established, that is, under the auspices of one or other politically favoured denomination. Nevertheless, when given the opportunity, the major representatives of the Believers' Church tradition, the Baptists, attempted to set up their own schools. Torbet notes: "Along the frontiers Baptist settlers in Somerset and Cambria Counties (southeast and east of Pittsburgh) used their churches as schoolhouses from the first."[18] But sources are scanty and no fully developed educational policy emerges.

The major Believers' Church adjustment came in conjunction with the establishment in North America, largely in the nineteenth century, of the modern public educational system. Reaction to it was varied and cut across all denominational lines. Most Roman Catholics insisted on retaining separate Catholic parochial education, preferably state supported (as in Ontario and Quebec) but private if necessary. The majority of Protestants of state-church background, except for some Dutch Reformed and some Lutheran mostly, in the face of a complex pluralistic sectarian society, supported the development of the public system at both elementary and secondary levels, though they established numerous private colleges.

Believers' Churches in both Canada and the U.S., especially Baptists and the smaller sects, also strongly supported the public ideal, although many Mennonites as they arrived were more hesitant; the more rural and conservative groups especially set up numerous private schools. Yet even many of these Mennonites were ambivalent in their attitude to the public system and the Mennonites have never set up a complete alternative system at any level.

Among Canadian Baptists, most educational concern, with a few exceptions (such as Moulton College, a high school for girls), centred on establishing more advanced schools, largely though not exclusively for developing a trained clergy.[19] Horton Academy was established in 1828 and quickly developed into Acadia College (1839). Canadian Baptist Theological College was set up briefly in Montreal (1839-49). Woodstock Literary Institute opened in Woodstock (Ontario) in 1860 but soon moved to Toronto and evolved in McMaster University (1887). Commenting on a parallel development to Baptist Colleges in the U.S.A., Torbet notes that though clearly Christian in perspective, most of these colleges were not strongly sectarian. "Baptists had suffered too many educational restrictions at the hands of the state churches to inflict the same kind of treatment upon others."[20] This concern for post-secondary Christian education has continued as the principle focus of educational effort and in the twentieth century has added to it the Bible College movement, which also has catered strongly to Believers' Church denominations.

Overall, Protestant Christianity, including those in the Believers' Church tradition, overwhelmingly supported the development of the new public school system, and largely it still supports it, in both Canada and the U.S.A. The reasons for this broad acceptance, with some pockets of resistance, were varied and complex. Derived from Old World traditions, most Roman Catholics and some Lutherans and Reformed retained strong convictions about Christian education as an integrated, total world view, and therefore the necessity for some direct church involvement in education in order to sustain a strong Christian (especially denominational) commitment. On the other hand, most denominations, and the Believers' Church Christians too, because of a background of oppression from and distaste for established denominational schools (in the Old World and initially in the New), favoured the complete disestablishment of any one denomination. Since Canadian and American society was much too pluralistically Christian and the population much too thin and scattered, and distances too great for all denominations to operate their own educational systems, the public school was considered the best alternative by most.

But equally important, most Christian parents and denominational leaders thought the new public system could be compatible with traditional Christian values and the most essential of their Christian educational obligations. This was true even in the U.S.A. where there was (unlike Canada) a constitutional requirement of separation of church and state but which was interpreted nevertheless in approximately the same way as on the Canadian scene, namely as primarily meaning the non-establishment of any one denomination. As Timothy Smith has noted, official ecclesiastical separation was not understood even in the U.S.A. as the establishment of secular education nor as the abandonment of, or inconsistent with, a "voluntary" non-denominational Christian base for the educational system. Rather public education was expected to support and maintain an already existing and increasingly growing "Christian" society.[21] In the nineteenth century, nominal Christians and committed believers made up the bulk of Canadian and

American society. Few envisioned or wanted a public educational system that was essentially or necessarily secular, non-Christian or even neutral (except denominationally).

Furthermore, the inculcation of morality was considered by almost all citizens and educators to be a vital part of sound education and an integral part of the whole educational process. It was assumed that this morality would be the community accepted one, that is, generally and broadly orthodox or biblically Christian — after all in the U.S. their coins said "In God We Trust." As L. Cremins has reported, in the nineteenth century U.S. Methodist preachers continued to serve in many areas as superintendents of public schools, baccalaureates were openly religious (Christian) services, and prayers and Christian social festivals were fostered in the schools.[22]

Public schools were really semi-private in that they were largely locally financed and controlled and were expected to be a reflection of parents and the local community, which were dominantly nominally Christian and strongly Protestant. As Protestant Christians especially saw it, the U.S.A. was to become increasingly a Christian society with common Christian presuppositions supported by a broadly non-denominationally Christian social, educational and legal framework. Even government continued to adopt and support measures that "belied its professed neutrality in religious affairs."[23] It interpreted separation of church and state largely in non-secular terms, i.e., statutes required Sabbath observances, proclamations called the nation to prayer, laws were enforced against blasphemy, chaplains officially served in legislative halls, and so on. De Tocqueville, a French observer, wrote in 1833 that "citizens of all classes and shades of political opinion held Christianity to be indispensable," and he notes it held sway indirectly **through the community** and thus controlled social manners and morals, including the public educational system.[24]

In Canada, a parallel development for parallel reasons took place. Three active Baptist laymen in Nova Scotia, E.A. Crawley, Charles Tupper (the premier) and Theodore H. Rand were much involved in the introduction by 1814 of a free school (public) system in that province. But Rand subsequently became superintendent of education for Nova Scotia and later for New Brunswick.[25]

"The Ontario (public) schools system, so well developed by Egerton Ryerson, became a model for the new provinces [of the West]...."[26] Writing in 1917, W.T. Gunn could by then comment proudly, "The settlers of the days to come will find everywhere a splendid public schools system, free of sectarian control, and fitted to educate and bring together our future citizens."[27] But again, non-sectarian did not mean non-Christian. Similar in intent to U.S. attitudes, the Education Act of 1850 of Upper Canada (Ontario), which completed the setting up of the public system there under a Council of Public Instruction as totally non-sectarian (except for a provision for separate Christian schools, mostly Roman Catholic), never intended the new system to be secular. "Ryerson was as opposed to a purely secularized school system as were the Roman Catholics."[28] That it was a non-secular system is also clear from the instruction material; e.g., in the nineteenth century log school house at Doon Pioneer Village in Kitchener, Ontario, two large lesson posters for teaching reading are on the wall, both authorized by the Council of Public Instruction. At the end of one, Lesson 19, in big print is the injunction, "Let us not walk in the paths of sin," and at the end of the other, Lesson 8, these quite non-secular words, "It was God that made us." This was the typical way of ending every lesson, and these posters were a part of the decor of every school house.

Moreover, the fight for the disestablishment of Anglican control over education that preceded the founding of the public system in Canada was closely linked in the minds of many Believers' Church leaders with the fight for religious liberty.[29] From that vantage point, in spite of basic theological principles that seem to indicate a different course, most strongly supported the public school idea.

In addition, many nineteenth century Christians in both Canada and the U.S.A. adopted a post-millennial eschatology which coincided with the belief that the common public educational system should and would promote and nurture the ideals of the new society, namely progress, democracy and faith, and the last was generally understood as Christian, at least in morality and values. Even for the immigrants, a Christian public education was to be a major vehicle for cultural assimilation, that is, "We shall Canadianize the foreigner by Christianizing him."[30] The creation of a Christian America coalesced with the notion of the American "destiny"[31] and similarly the new nation of Canada (1867) was called the Dominion of Canada, derived from Psalm 72: 8 which refers to God's dominion from sea to sea. A Christian Canada and U.S.A. were to be the springboards for the Christianizing of the world.

Finally, public education offered the attractive provision that basic education would henceforth be free and thus available to all citizens, not just the privileged and wealthy. In the frontier environment, private wealth for the most part was simply inadequate to maintain either a sufficient number of private schools or sufficiently inexpensive ones.

In summary, it is abundantly evident that the public school system as originally set up was intended either by actual legislation, as in Ontario, or voluntarily in response to community wishes, as in the U.S. and some provinces, to teach, promote and inculcate the basic Christian values for the building of a homogeneous Christian society, while home and church would be exclusively responsible for indoctrination in denominational distinctives. Private separate schools, especially (and mostly) Roman Catholic, often were looked on with disapproval as divisive and unnecessary. Most Believers' Church Christians found the public system to be the best available option, efficient, available, non-secular, non-threatening and superior to either established denominational systems or to private systems largely for the wealthy, and gave it full support.

III. CHANGE AND CRISIS

Underlying the acceptance of public education was the assumption that Canadian and American society would remain Christian, and public education would help it happen. But as R. Handy has noted, "Instead of the church having Christianized civilization, they [Protestant leaders] found that civilization had captured the church."[32] Moreover, Western civilivation has become radically secularized. Canadian and American society is no longer nominally Christian (at least not in the orthodox, biblical sense of the mid-nineteenth century) and similarly the public educational system for the most part (in spite of the involvement in it of many Christian teachers) is no longer Christian either; since public education by definition must reflect, adapt and align itself with the **mores** of the society it serves.

Jacques Ellul, C.F.H. Henry and a host of other Christian thinkers refer to the second half of the twentieth century as a post-Christian era in Europe and North America. The futurologists, H. Kahn and A.J. Weiner of the Hudson Institute, refer to a "multifold" trend "towards an increasingly sensate, secular, pragmatic culture...."[33] A recent intellectual history describes the secularization of life as "a condition which has dominated Europe for the past couple of centuries [North America only more recently] and which is something unique in human history. Secularization means turning the attention to things of this world and arranging society according to non-religious principles."[34] It is common knowledge that for several decades now, changes in community social **mores** and in the laws have been informed essentially by popular, secular criteria rather than by biblical standards.[35] As a result, modern public education is increasingly "dedicated to the postulates that man is self-sufficient, that human society is the arbiter of its own morality, and that knowledge is exclusively the product of scientific inquiry."[36]

Not only is the public educational system being forced to adapt to the new secularism of society, but also to a new pluralism. The Christian value-consensus which undergirded the "Christian" public system is gone. While according to the partial response of a poll of over 70,000 homes taken in Halton County (Ontario) slightly better than fifty per cent of the population still support an educational system based on the traditional values, and many expressed alarm that it was no longer so, obviously the erosion of public support for the old consensus has been extensive.[37] The public system has failed to Christianize the immigrants and sustain a homogeneous society. Indeed, as the secularism attests, it failed to sustain even the children of the faithful. Canadian society now reflects a much broader pluralism than just a pluralism of Christian sects, rather a pluralism of religions and of value systems, which at times are in serious conflict with traditionally Christian ones.

But not only is public education adapting to the new secularism and the new pluralism, it is also adjusting to a new pattern of social and state control, to centralization through massive bureaucracies, and to the dominance of efficiency and the specialist. In Canada, we have witnessed in recent years a steady transition from family and local community influence on education's patterns of operation, to the government and its professional educational bureaucracy. These new control patterns also influence educational philosophy towards non-Christian values. For example, Jacques Ellul has asserted that though the professed god of contemporary secular and progressive education is the "happiness" of the child (which is also in part expressed as the avoidance of complexes, respect for the person of the child, and negative attitudes to traditional authority coupled with advocacy of the discovery method) its real goal is the new personality, one optimally prepared for the new tasks of the new society in which happiness requires adaptability. The new technique is psychopedagogy. This "new education is a governing principle of every modern political system and of technique as a whole." It is usually implemented and guided increasingly by the state, since it alone has the necessary financial resources and if (to quote Mme. Marla Montessori, as he does) the children are to be freed "from the slavery of [traditional? Christian?] school and family," the new system must encompass all of society. But, writes, Ellul, this emphasis on adaptability is such that "what looks like the apex of humanism is in fact the pinnacle of human submission" and the parallel emphasis on usefulness creates technicians and fits its subjects into the new social "machine." This new freedom becomes instead a tool for social control and for the complete reshaping of society in terms of the good of humanity which ultimately is defined the same way whether in **Life** magazine or the **Soviet News**.[38]

The recent Keiller Mackay Commission (Ontario) admits that the original "public" educational system has undergone (and is undergoing) a massive secularizing transmutation.[39] There is mounting evidence of growing awareness, concern and alarm in Canada (and the U.S.) by many Christians, but it is becoming a major crisis of conscience for many upholding Believers' Church principles.

Many contemporary Believers' Church Christians are finding it increasingly intolerable to support an educational system that is openly (1) not compatible with or tolerant towards biblical standards of morality and values (public and private, social and personal); (2) not sympathetic towards a biblically Christian view of reality — God, man and nature; (3) not supportive of the traditional roles of home and church, including parental rights and authority; (4) not giving priority to the academic functions, but rather is challenging (through assuming ever increasing social functions) the traditional roles and responsibilies of home and church, thereby weakening both. For example, the Ecumenical Study Commission on Education has expressed concern that while "children are not allowed to be introduced at school to the basic principles of the Christian faith, they are being constantly indoctrinated in the fathers of secular humanism and allied religions." It also acknowledges that "it is undoubtedly this awareness that is arousing much disquietude among increasing numbers of socially alert Christian parents in this province [Ontario] — and elsewhere in Canada."[40]

That concern and awareness are gradually being translated into a recognition of the need for a total reassessment of the relationship of the Believers' Churches to the educational task, is increasingly evident. For example, the Evangelical Fellowship of Canada, representing about two million Canadian Christians and sympathizers, and whose constituent denominations (though not all of its members) are almost all part of the Believers' Church tradition, through its Education Commission has addressed itself repeatedly in the past five years to the problem (for Christians and churches) of changes in the presuppositions and philosophy of public education, insisting that if the system secularizes, Christians should be provided with acceptable alternatives. Some years ago after a similar evaluation, Menno Harder wrote: "An increasing awareness is growing in the minds of [Mennonite] leaders that an educational system at all levels will have to be operated if Mennonitism is to be preserved and perpetuated." He adds that where this hasn't happened, there has been a decided abandonment of "major original principles" and not just culture.[41] The Ontario District Conference of the Pentecostal Assemblies of Canada, in "A Brief Submitted to the Honourable T.L. Wells, Minister of Education, Government of Ontario, June 1973," expressly refers to "the rapid growth of secularistic humanism" and says that as a result the constituency is "deeply disturbed about our tax-supported public system in Ontario." It adds that these Christians are firmly convinced that the primary responsibility for the education of children "lies, under God, with the parent." Furthermore, "the tax-supported school has no right to undo the work of church and home...We believe that this secularistic brainwashing is taking place on an ever increasing degree." It acknowledges that "to the present time the Pentecostal constituency has supported the Public School System" because that system is supposed to be supportive of their religious, spiritual and moral rights and privileges. The warning is implicit that if changes to the contrary continue, Ontario Pentecostals will take whatever political action is necessary to redress the situation.[42] These issues were debated for the first time at the 1971 convention of the Fellowship of Evangelical Baptists in Canada, and resulted in a special committee of inquiry being set up which in turn produced the booklet, **Essays in Education**, which was made available to all pastors and churches.[43] It expressed great concern, even alarm, for the trends and directions of the modern public educational system. In the past three years, an organization begun by Kenneth Campbell in Halton County, Ontario, to protest the anti-Christian prejudices and the ignoring of parental concerns and desires by public public education has grown into Renaissance Canada, under the leadership of Robert Thompson. It now has strong provincial organizations in several provinces. Originally its primary goal was the re-establishment of respect for Judeo/Christian values and parental rights in the public system but it soon added advocacy of the removal of the severe financial discrimination which prevails in some provinces against private alternatives.[44] Recently in Ontario a new organization, the Ontario Association for Independent and Alternate Schools, has been estab-

lished with a full time director (Lyle McBurney) to represent and co-
ordinate the rapidly growing number of such schools in the province.[45]
Similarly, in Canada between 1971-76 private school enrollments have
risen by 54,000 students[46] and in the U.S.A. the rise is even more
dramatic, going from 652 schools in 1971 to over four thousand by 1977.
The **National Observer** comments that this is "the most significant
trend in American education."[47] As of 1977, in response to growing
pressure, British Columbia has opted to grant financial aid to private
(mostly Christian) schools for the first time in its 104-year history. One
advocate of this measure, Harvey Schroeder, MLA for Chilliwack,
asserted in the legislature that the bill was a necessary response to the
growing "humanistic" approach developing in Canada in public
education.[48] These examples are only representative; space does not
permit an exhaustive treatment, but they indicate clearly that many
responsible Believers' Church Christians are recognizing the need to
rethink their relationship to the public system in response to its changing patterns and in accord with their Christian principles.

IV. CURRENT DIRECTIONS AND POSSIBILITIES

To be consistent with our principles, in the existing pluralistic society
in Canada, Believers' Churches cannot logically press for the return by
legislative fiat of a public system dominated and informed solely by
biblical Christianity. Such would now be support for another brand of
educational establishment not responsible to the community. It would
be as intolerant, unChristian (from the Believers' Churches' perspective) and unjustifiable in our present pluralistic society as previous
state-church establishments or the monolithic and intolerably secular
one developing today and which is disturbing many.[49] We might wish for
an exclusively Christian system and be convinced of social superiority
of such a Christian base, but our principles also dictate that such could
only come by persuasion, by society turning itself around and somehow
recapturing it for Christian ideals — not likely an immediate solution,
given that their loss was at least a two-century process.

Rather, Believers' Churches represent a large body of concerned
citizens. As such we can in a democratic society (as stated in the
Renaissance brief to the Ontario Department of Education) properly
request our government to recognize our, and others' needs and rights,
educationally, and to respond positively and helpfully to all of them.
This means providing maximum understanding, awareness, sensitivity
and toleration by our educational systems towards all segments of our
society, certainly, at least to all major groupings, including Christians
of various types.

In seeking solutions to the problems of public education in a changed,
more complex society, the Keiller Mackay Report recommended
greater secularization of the public schools by the outright abandonment of all religious education courses, modification (really securitiza-
tion) of religious exercises, the elimination of all direct involvement by
the clergy, and an insistence that "religion belongs in the home and
church, not in the school." Subsequently, a national conference on

religious education in the schools was held at York University in 1973, and responses from departments of education across Canada indicate that Ontario is not along in considering major changes of a similar exclusively secularizing nature.[50] The response of the Ecumenical Study Commission on Public Education has been to recommend another kind of consensus or universalism, much broader than the nineteenth century Christian consensus upon which the public system was originally built. This new consensus for a renewed monolithic "establishment" (as with the Mackay Report) also calls for an abandonment of the traditional Christian basis for values to be replaced by character building through the study of "religion" (defined from a liberal Christian or/and scientific perspective) and through information about all religions, that is, almost a Baha'ism or at least the advocacy of some kind of common or "natural" religion (somewhat akin to that espoused by the eighteenth century humanists). While the Ecumenical Study Commission does not advocate a purely rationalistic moral or values education which is "divested from any rootage in religion," yet religion is to be non-sectarian, and non-indoctrinating with reference to any one religion; that is, clearly not exclusively Christian even regarding values. This new study of "religion" should be included in the curriculum as a respected discipline and put in the hands of teaching specialists who have been trained in secular departments of religion and culture at our universities. "This," it suggests, "constitutes a pluralistic approach to our pluralistic society."[51]

Without doubt, this solution is neither adequate nor even less threatening for most Believers' Church Christians (many of whom are evangelical and strongly committed to biblical Christianity) than Lawrence Kohlberg's or Clive Beck's proposals[52] for openly secular values education based on methodology (non-content) courses on how to reason morally (which the Ecumenical Study Commission criticizes, but very mildly).

In contrast to the E.S.C., the most historically viable solution for Believers' Church Christians, when the nature and seriousness of the problems are understood, seems to be the abandonment of all attempts at some new consensus and instead the provision of alternatives both within and without the present public systems, as presented to the Ontario Ministry in the Evangelical Fellowship and Renaissance brief of 1976;[53] that is, the acceptance of an educational pluralism consisting of one or more of the following:

(1) A full set of alternatives **within** the system, including specified schools with an educational philosophy, curriculum, staff and practices in accord with traditional Christian perspectives and moral sensitivities is one possibility (e.g., British Columbia's value schools).

(2) Carefully developed options in terms of curricula, reading material and social practices, including manifesting a much higher level of toleration and respect than at present exists for traditional Christian values and world view from all personnel, and avoidance of psychological-social pressures, is another alternative[54] — one which to

some degree should prevail in all schools whether other alternatives also exist or not; but, as other minorities have discovered, it is doubtful that this would be adequate in itself, or easily monitored.

Both (1) and (2) would be most difficult to make adequately effective because there are now numerous minorities calling for such consideration, and deep divisions even in Christianity, and difficult also from administrative and curricular standpoints.

(3) A third, and for many Believers' Church Christians the most preferable alternative, along with the maximum extension possible of sensitivity and alternatives to all minorities in the present system, would be the granting to all parents the right to choose either public or private alternatives **without excessive economic penalty** as a citizen right in a democratic society. Parents could, for example, as a **minimum** compensation, along with some additional personal sacrifice, be allowed to apply their direct school taxes to the school of their choice, i.e., if their children were in attendance there. The province would still legitimately set standards of reasonable minimal academic quality for all eligible schools.

This way, the educational system reflects properly the pluralistic society it represents, becomes less unjust by avoiding both a new secular and/or religious "establishment" counter to the convictions of many. It recovers the social and democratic values inherent in an educational pluralism and promotes religious liberty. The greater "efficiency" of a monolithic system is simply no sufficient argument when deep convictions and basic human rights are being violated. Moreover, the successes of competitive, lower-cost private alternatives may well lead to greater overall educational efficiency, rather than to the opposite.

But should none of these alternatives develop adequately, given that all provinces grant the opportunity and right to operate totally private alternatives, Believers' Church Christians are facing and will increasingly face a severe crisis of principles and conscience in continuing to support the new public education systems as these increasingly conform to a secularized, pluralistic Canadian society.

THE BELIEVERS' CHURCH
AND PUBLIC SCHOOLS IN CANADA

Peter H. Peters

Even though Baptists and Mennonites will generally both agree with statements that define a Believers' Church, there are distinct differences in practice and understanding when these definitions are applied to education. Different experiences and histories of people within the Believers' Church tradition have resulted in different practices and applications. The purpose of this paper is to try to interpret some of these differences. A brief history and analysis of public education in Canada will be given in order to give the framework in which the alternate schools developed. This paper will limit itself to stories of the Mennonite and the Federation Baptist schools in Canada.

The church has historically promoted literacy and Christian knowledge. In order to get teachers and clergy in the colony churches, colleges were often established on the frontier. The English influence was strong in early Protestant education in that both personal and financial support were given through the great missionary societies: The Society for the Propagation of the Gospel (S.P.G.), the Society for the Promotion of Christian Knowledge (S.P.C.K.), and the Church Missionary Society (C.M.S.). Some colleges received grants directly from the British government. The certification of Protestant teachers for private schools in the latter half of the eighteenth century and early nineteenth century also came under the jurisdiction of the parish church or one of the missionary societies.

In order to bring about more order and consistency in elementary and secondary education, central authorities were established. Anglicans, Methodists, Presbyterians and Baptists were generally persuaded, by the middle of the nineteenth century, of the merits of the public school. Egerton Ryerson, who had been the first principal of Victoria College (Methodist), became the first superintendent of education (1844-1876) for the Province of Ontario. Ryerson believed that it was possible to teach general Christian truth and morality without sectarian dogma.

In Ryerson's Special Report of 1847, the idea of non-sectarian religious instruction was further developed.

> While the several religious denominations possess equal facilities for the special instruction of their own youth, there is a wide common ground of principles and morals, held equally sacred, and equally taught by all, and the spirit which ought to pervade the whole system of public instruction, and which comprehend the essential requisites of social happiness and good citizenship.[1]

Ryerson elaborated the spirit of his system in the Journal of Education, January 1849:

> In the columns of this Journal we have nothing to do with parties, sects or personal controversy, but with what equally concerns persons of all persuasions and parties upon the basis of our common Christianity and in harmony with our civil institutions.[2]

By the middle of the nineteenth century, public education was supported by the various Protestant churches, not only because they helped to equalize educational opportunities but also because it was genuinely felt that there was a general Christian morality that could be commonly taught. The state was seen as an agent of Christianity.

In the development of its educational system, Ontario was often enabled by its size to do first and more thoroughly what newer or smaller provinces could attempt only partially, sometimes belatedly. Up to the end of World War I, the western provinces merely copied Ontario practice. The east was less pleased to be found doing later what Ontario had already done.

The central authority, through the Council of Public Instruction, drew up schedules of what must be taught, of qualifications teachers must have and of the textbooks they must use. The people locally, and the school trustees they elected, were given opportunity, from 1850, to raise money by taxation and to improve their schools. Moreover, they were given constant encouragement to take advantage of the opportunity.

The result was that by 1871 nearly all elementary schools were tax-supported and free; school enrollment had increased twice as fast as the population; three and one-half months had been added to the school year; most teachers had academic qualifications possessed by few twenty years before; and all teachers had certificates based on definite accomplishments.

The act of 1871 provided for free high school education as well. One function of the high schools was to educate teachers; thus uniform, province-wide examinations were set up for teachers' certificates. The course of study was now outlined with precision to show exactly what should be covered and the time to be taken. Two years later, a written high school entrance examination was introduced, and two years from then an intermediate high school examination was established to determine the efficiency of the school and the grant it should receive. Many other written examinations were conducted for various purposes. School inspectors, after 1871, were men who had been certified teachers, well qualified to appraise the faults and merits of their former colleagues.

C.E. Phillips[3] says that "by 1890 Ontario had a truly solid system of education." He makes the following observation:

> Ontario people of position were very proud of their school system in the last quarter of the nineteenth century. It was a model of formal efficiency, the envy of other provinces at the time. Even in 1950 there were some older citizens who looked back with nostalgia to the solid

programme of the Victorian schools. But a few people even in 1890 regarded the whole system as a pretentious machine incapable of true education.[4]

I. MENNONITES IN CANADA

Between 1786 and 1825, about two thousand Mennonites from Pennsylvania settled in the Waterloo, Niagara and Markham districts of what was then known as Canada West. These were Mennonites of Swiss-South German ancestry who had come to Pennsylvania to find a refuge where they could practice their faith in freedom and liberty. Pennsylvania had a charter from the English Crown that not only tolerated but welcomed religious dissenters. After the fall of the Thirteen Colonies from British rule, some of the Mennonites, Quakers and Tunkers sought to find new opportunities in British-controlled Canada West.

They took strong initiative in organizing community schools. In Waterloo County four schools were established before 1830. In that year Abraham Erb deeded $2,000 of his estate, or interest thereof, for educational purposes, especially for the poor and the orphaned. The Mennonites were not particularly worried about the lack of government support for education. To many of them, government intervention in education was an intrusion into their value system and was not particularly welcome.[5] These schools were neighbourhood schools with German as the language of instruction. They often included German Lutheran and Roman Catholic children as well. In 1885 the provincial authorities introduced bilingual legislation which had the long range objective of phasing out the second language until all instruction would be given solely in English. The last German bilingual public school ceased functioning in 1891. The Old Order and Amish decided that their children would be protected from worldly influences by establishing and maintaining their own church-operated schools.

The pressures of compulsory education also burdened the Old Order Mennonites and the Amish of the Waterloo area. They have pleaded in vain to obtain an exemption for 14 to 16-year-old children whose services are required for the farm household. Most of the Ontario Mennonites, have, however, become assimilated to the extent that they have sent their children to public schools.

In the west, the Russian Mennonites experienced similar measures belatedly from provincial authorities. Between 1874 and 1883 Manitoba Mennonites enjoyed complete school autonomy, as promised in the agreement reached by their delegates, with the dominion authorities, as a condition of their immigration. These first Russian Mennonites that came to Canada had been of the landless families from the Russian communities. Their leaders were less educated and tended to be more legalistic in the practice of their faith. They came from the settlement, first established in Russia when the movement from Prussia to Russia took place, often called the Old Colony. Economic and religious leadership among this Manitoba group was limited; they were not well-to-do economically, and the educational and cultural milieu from which they came was not as high as that of many Mennonites who stayed in Russia. This difference became quite significant later. Leo Driedger describes the first fifty pioneer years in Manitoba as the Period of Conflict (1874-1922):

> For some time following immigration into Manitoba, outside pressure was neither sufficiently direct and organized, nor sufficiently sustained to result in permanent hostilities with the larger society. Conflict developed, however, as the issue over control of schools arose. The Canadian government had promised no interference in their school system, but as time passed, wanted to: 1) integrate ethnic groups more closely into national society, and 2) wished to raise the educational standards of Mennonite schools since they were taught on a very low level with unqualified teachers, and with little knowledge of English and the larger society.[6]

The Mennonite community was divided over the school issue, some preferring to retain church schools and others opting for public schools under the Protestant section. When the dual confessional system was abolished in Manitoba in 1890, the position of the conservatives who had insisted on private church schools seemed justified. To many Mennonites, the non-sectarian public schools were "godless" schools to be shunned. Nevertheless, economic pressure in the form of school taxation was a factor in assisting these to re-evaluate the public school in 1897 when the Laurier-Greenway Compromise was implemented allowing German-English bilingual public schools. The Mennonites, having settled in "reserves" or blocs, found that their communities were quite homogeneous; therefore, if the conservative and liberal elements within their own denomination could agree on a public school, such an institution rapidly took on ethnic qualities.

The struggle for better education among Mennonites lasted for many decades. However, by the end of the 1880s, the number of public schools in the Mennonite colonies was actually declining because private schools were established, although the quality of the private schools was less than desirable. In order to remedy the situation, a group of Manitoba elders of the Bergthal church, in 1889, formed an association and opened a Mennonite teacher-training school in Gretna. The provincial authorities were very interested in the Gretna school project and gave it a charter to become a normal school. They saw it as the means of doing something about Mennonite education.

The Mennonite school association together with the provincial authority, George Bryce, combined efforts to secure the services of Heinrich H. Ewert from Newton, Kansas. He had come with his parents from West Prussia, had attended an English grade school, state Normal School, and Des Moines Institute and Theological Seminary at Marthasville, Missouri. His background differed greatly from that of the Russian Mennonites, among whom he was to work as a school teacher and a pastor. He worked hard as a leader of his people for over forty-three years and as a bridge-builder between two cultures. Although the school in Gretna was a private organization, the provincial authorities appointed the newly-appointed principal H.H. Ewert as the official school inspector for all the district (that is public) schools in the Mennonite colonies as well. E.K. Francis says,

> Ewert was deeply convinced that Mennonite children should be educated both in the Mennonite religious and the German national heritage. He realized, however, that Mennonite children had to be prepared for life in the Canadian environment and, to some extent for participation in the large society and its cultural values. Those who were to become teachers using Canadian textbooks, had to have some command of English and some knowledge of Anglo-Saxon institutions.[7]

Ewert considered the training of more and better Mennonite teachers as his primary task, more urgent even than rapid conversion of Mennonite private schools into public schools.

Educational matters among Mennonite communities would probably have evolved into a satisfactory public school system, as far as the provincial authorities were concerned, had the Roblin Government not decreed in 1907 that the Union Jack, the symbol of the British Empire, be flown over every public school building. The measure was intended to inculcate feelings of patriotism and materially assist in blending together the various nationalities in the province into one common citizenship, irrespective of race and creed. Francis reports that,

> This kind of patriotism was ill-received by the Mennonites. Their religious doctrine forbade direct participation in affairs of state. The secular ritual of showing and saluting the flag was remindful of rendering an act of worship to Caesar's image; if they refused to do so, the Mennonites followed the example of the first Christian martyrs. Moreover, they regarded the flag as a military emblem and believed that this was the thin edge of the wedge which, if consented to, would finally mean loss of their military exemption.[8]

The provincial authorities not only lost credibility themselves but they did much to undermine Ewert's authority.

In Saskatchewan and the Northwest Territories in general, the religious and second-language instruction was similarly limited to the last half hour of the day, and English had become the compulsory language of instruction. The assimilationist educational policy featured the public school as the place where children of several races could intermingle in class and play with English as the common medium of communication. When groups in question could not recommend teachers of their own kind for the school district, they had to accept outside teachers recommended by the department. Thus, "for those ethnic and religious groups seeking self-perpetuation it became imperative therefore, to get some of their own young people into the teaching profession to prevent the complete **Verenglischung** (anglicization), as the Mennonites referred to the acculturation process of the young."[9]

After a very uncertain start, the Rosthern Junior Academy was launched with David Toews as the first principal. David Toews, like

Ewert in Gretna, came from Kansas. After receiving his normal school training in Winnipeg, Toews gave strong educational leadership.

In 1908 the Saskatchewan government appointed a commission to investigate the private schools in the Mennonite communities in the neighbourhood of Hague, Osler and Warman. Instruction was permitted in German, although the provincial premier, Walter Scott, stated in a public address in 1913 that there were no bilingual schools in Saskatchewan.

The times were such that there were curtailments of privileges given earlier to ethnic communities in western Canada. War hysteria, an anti-alien feeling and a demand that schools more effectively assimilate the children of "foreigners" resulted in several closely related moves in education: the introduction of compulsory attendance legislation, the suppression of bilingual instruction, and the closing of private schools which did not meet provincial standards. Manitoba, followed by Saskatchewan and Alberta, abandoned the official policy of bilingualism and introduced compulsory attendance in 1916. By 1918 Manitoba closed the remaining Mennonite private schools on grounds of inferior standards; many parents were jailed for refusing to comply with the laws requiring attendance at public schools. The federal government supported the provincial action by blocking any further Mennonite immigration from 1919 to 1922.

After a test case, Mennonites learned that compulsory attendance laws and the certification of private schools were under the absolute and arbitrary control of provincial legislatures. The conservative Mennonites felt the solemn contract of 1873 with the federal authority had been violated. In 1918, the federal government had taken the precaution of enacting that none of the exemptions and privileges granted in 1873 should apply to new immigrants. Most Mennonites accommodated themselves to the assimilationist pressures, but between 1922 and 1924 about five thousand left for Mexico, and in 1926-27 another seventeen hundred left for Paraguay. They saw the exodus as but another flight from persecution not unlike their numerous migrations since the sixteenth century. Canadians were somewhat dismayed at the thought of having produced political refugees seeking asylum in other lands.

The places of the 6,700 who left for Mexico and Paraguay were soon filled by more than twenty thousand Russian Mennonites who came to Canada during 1923-30. These new Mennonites were of a higher socio-economic group, with more capital and more education. These new immigrants had been nurtured for over a century in Mennonite-controlled education. While the **Kanadier** had given most of the years from 1874 to pioneering, in precisely that same half century the **Ruszlaender**[10] had enjoyed the peak of their prosperity. When the revolution came in Russia, they were operating more than four hundred elementary schools. In addition, they had thirteen high schools, two teachers' colleges, three business schools, one Bible school, as well as other specialized institutions, all financed exclusively by the Mennonite communities.

When the Russian revolutionary upheavals struck the Mennonite communities, the emigrant group included a sizeable group of teachers, students and education-minded leaders and parents. F.H. Epp states that it is not surprising, therefore, that upon arrival in the new country in 1923 their thoughts turned as much to education as to agriculture. The Mennonite Educational Institute (M.E.I.) and Rosthern Junior College (R.J.C.) received new support and more than ten Bible schools were founded by 1945. Many Mennonite teachers were trained, who then found their way into teaching positions in many public schools.

After the Second World War, the advancement of technology, and farm technology in particular, resulted in hundreds of Mennonites flocking to the cities for a livelihood. The new post-World War II immigrants preferred to stay in the cities not only because it was difficult to get started on a farm but also because they actually preferred the urban environment. They soon found that in order to compete for jobs in the city, education was a necessity and they rushed into higher education in universities, agricultural and technical schools in order to compete in the larger society. They would have done so earlier had the Great Depression and World War II not stymied and restricted them.

While it may be said that public schools absorbed most of the Mennonite high school students in the various provinces, it is significant that a total of ten private secondary schools originated since 1945 in Ontario, Manitoba, Alberta and British Columbia. "These together with the older schools had a combined enrollment of 2,248 for grades seven to thirteen in 1977."[11] All of them experienced growing pains, financial crises and a critical constituency that in varying degrees questioned the validity of such schools. The value of these schools, however, has been examined and restated over the last few decades. During the times of conflict over particular religious emphases and practices, it was fortunate that most of these schools found part of their reason for existence in other distinguishing programmes and features. These additional features might include some or all of the following: high academic performance, high ratings in athletic and music programmes, the social warmth of the student body and the community life of the residences. These helped to popularize these schools with students and to legitimize them with supporters. Support arose mainly from the fact that Mennonites felt that they had a stake in the education of their children. Their experiences in Russia and their lack of preparation for the pressures of World War II prompted heavy investment in education.

In 1957 H.T. Klaassen, chairman of the Rosthern Junior College board, could say, for example,

> The school has always had leadership willing to face difficult
> situations and take action. In the new decade we are approaching, we
> will be faced with new responsibilities. We believe that a church school
> like this can add 'the plus' which helps us to realize spiritual values,
> which will help young people prepare for life in this time when our
> young people are exposed to so many influences from society. The
> spiritual values in this school are the only thing that justifies its

existence.[12]

In 1970 the "goals study" restated the reasons for the existence of Rosthern Junior College when it said in part:

> It is our belief that among the reasons for the apparent lack of purpose in our present society is that our public institutions have left the teaching of values largely to chance. Our own schools can and must teach enduring values of the Christian faith with conviction and without apology.[13]

The other Mennonite secondary school boards would echo these sentiments.

As far as higher education is concerned, Mennonites have been late-comers, and when the urbanization process hit Mennonite communities after World War II, the liberal arts college as a buffer educational institution hardly seemed applicable and adequate.

In order to upgrade the level of theological training on a post-high school level, two Bible colleges were established in Winnipeg in 1944 and 1947. The Canadian Mennonite Bible College (C.M.B.C.) has related its arts programme to the University of Manitoba while the Mennonite Brethren Bible College (M.B.B.C.) related first to Waterloo Lutheran University and now to the University of Winnipeg. Both schools are considered under-graduate theological training schools. "They together with the six Bible schools had an enrollment of 921 full-time students and 240 part-time students in 1977."[14] Canadian Mennonites have always considered the training of church workers as most important, and until recently have resisted the liberal arts model. With the increasing acceptance of trained and paid clergy there has also been a changing attitude towards liberal arts.

A number of Canadian universities have established the practice of allowing colleges to cluster with the university. Most of the older universities in Canada originated as Anglican, Baptist, Catholic, Lutheran or Methodist institutions. As these institutions became public, efforts were made to retain the church tradition in the form of affiliated colleges.

In the late 1950s and early 1960s there was interest in alternative models to the liberal arts church college, in view of the fact that many Mennonite young people, especially in Canada, were attending public universities. In 1961 Conrad Grebel College received a charter and in 1964 the residence hall functioned for the first year. The college, with J. Winfield Fretz as the first president, had affiliated with the University of Waterloo.

The purpose of Conrad Grebel College arises from its commitment to the Christian faith, its Anabaptist-Mennonite heritage, its affiliation with the University of Waterloo, and from the needs of the latter half of the twentieth century. From within this context the college seeks to be a residential, teaching, research and community college. The school emphasizes community among students, faculty and staff, and among intellectual, spiritual and social experiences. In 1977, the C.G.C. residential programme had a total of 128 students enrolled. The college is making a deliberate attempt to integrate all learning with the Anabaptist Christian faith and perspective.

II. BAPTISTS IN CANADA

The story of Baptists is different. Despite the fact that Baptists have often been a minority religiously, they still have been part of a linguistic and cultural majority. Historically, they have been one of several sects known collectively as the Dissenters in England, whose origin included contact with the dissenting minorities in the Netherlands. In the late sixteenth and early seventeenth centuries Anabaptists had participated enthusiastically in the national and commercial activities of the Dutch. Anabaptists by the hundreds had found their way into England. One Dutch statesman, William of Orange, on becoming King of England in 1689, also became the first of the English monarchs to side with the dissenters. Henry VIII had tolerated them earlier, but when he discovered that their protest hurt him as much as Rome, he and his successors (until William III) ordered them exiled, or imprisoned and executed. Thus, in Anglican England the Anabaptists disappeared from the scene, though,

> not without planting the seeds of separation and non-conformity. Their presence led directly to the founding of the Baptist church in England which, like the Anabaptists, insisted on a voluntary, democratic church, composed of newborn men and women, entirely free from the state, granting to all freedom of conscience in matters of religion. The two groups maintained some fellowship in Amsterdam, but union was out of the question since the Baptists held different doctrinal views on the oath, government, war and baptism.[15]

Some of the Baptists, Puritans and other non-conformists early found their way into one of the Thirteen Colonies of North America. One of the early leaders was John Clarke (1609-1676) who had come from England as a well-educated physician and linguist. In the 1640s a group under his leadership was formed, and it was Clarke who played a leading role in one of the early tests of religious liberty in America. He together with Roger Williams was able to obtain a royal charter for Rhode Island colony.

It is also important to know one other development in the New England states for an understanding of the Canadian background. There is the case of Henry Dunster, respected president of Harvard College. He had been forced to resign because he had refused to allow his infant child to be baptized. Donald Durnbaugh says,

> The conversion to Baptist principles of this intellectual and pillar of society made it more difficult to pass off the Baptists as merely a collection of lower class enthusiasts. Although many Baptists in fact were unlearned, they early turned to higher education. They founded the College of Rhode Island (later Brown University) in 1764.[16]

The growth of the Baptists was slow until the time of the Great Awakening that followed the New Light evangelists of the 1740s. The last decades of the eighteenth century saw a phenomenal increase in the number of Baptists along the new frontiers. It was on the frontier that

Baptists most often exhibited sectarian characteristics. S.D. Clark describes it in this way:

> The church has grown out of the conditions of a mature society; the sect has been a product of what might be called frontier conditions of social life...The church seeks the accommodation of religious organizations to be community; the welfare of society is something for which it feels responsible. The sect emphasizes the exclusiveness of religious organization; the worldly society is something evil of no concern to the spiritually minded. While no sharp line can be drawn between the two forms of religious organizations...It is the difference in outlook, in attitude of mind, which is so important in setting the one off from the other...Within the broad pattern of the social development of Canada, the persistent conflict between these two forms of religious organizations takes on meaning.[17]

The earliest Baptists came into Canada from New England to the Maritime Provinces and established churches in Sackville, New Brunswick in 1763 and at Horton (Wolfville), Nova Scotia in 1765. Henry Alline, a New Light revivalist stirred many, and these converts, together with the Baptist immigrants from England and the United States, formed the early churches in the Maritimes.

Though Baptists inherited from congregationalism a tradition favourable to education, the condition of the New Light revival resulted in discrediting a reliance upon an educated ministry, and the effect of this was to weaken an interest in education in general. Clark says that "by 1829, the lack of an educated ministry and of a literate membership had come to constitute a distinct handicap," and he goes on to quote E.A. Crawley,

> The Baptists enjoyed but a small amount of public favour, especially in Halifax, and were regarded as occupying the lowest rank in religious estimation — were in fact despised as an ignorant and deluded sect.[18]

The establishment of Acadia College in 1839 was the result of allegedly unfair treatment of a leading Baptist, E.A. Crawley, by the non-sectarian Dalhousie College. Crawley, together with John Pryor, worked through the Baptist Education Society to establish this college, which imposed no restrictions of a denominational character on the professors or students. They were determined to have higher education free of Anglican control. Religion was not to be a separate course but an integral part of courses in arts subjects. An early statement of purpose made the following comments:

> This College is open to all denominations, no religious tests being imposed either on students or professors; nevertheless, we must claim the right of aiming to imbue literature with the spirit of religion, and of inculcating, from time to time, those principles of our common Christianity, and those moral lessons which are admitted by all who wish to shun the reproach of infidelity.[19]

The programme at Acadia was broadened in 1851 to include mathematics, science, navigation, surveying and natural philosophy. In 1844 it had become a theological seminary as well as a liberal arts college. A number of the professors had been trained in New England colleges, particularly Harvard College. Acadia followed the opposite principle to that of the Baptist colleges in Ontario, the Canadian Literary Institute and McMaster University, in that it accepted government aid as early as 1843. As a school of higher learning, it has been a leader in the Maritimes for the training of people right up to the present time. The centennial celebrations of 1938 paid tribute to the courage, dedication and accomplishments of the founders, teachers, graduates and supporters of the college over the decades. At the various exercises,

> those present were reminded that Acadia graduates are still making, expounding and administering the law, advocating and defending the rights of people and guiding the thought and conscience of the country.[20]

How radical has the influence of Acadia been? It must be agreed that its existence was necessary to challenge the exclusive claims of the Church of England in the early nineteenth century. Through their college, the Baptists in the Maritimes received a symbol of identity. However, even though Baptists have consistently talked about separation of church and state, this has not meant that the leaders have challenged the state in some of its activities. Nowhere is this more evident than in the institution's unquestioning support of the war effort. The number of graduates, undergraduates and former students that served in World War I was over six hundred. In 1916 the Highland Brigade was organized and President G.B. Cutten preached the baccalaureate sermon dressed in khaki. Longley lists the people who won "coveted" medals of distinction and honour.[21] In the main, Baptists are non-pacifists and the concept of citizenship in heaven and not in a country has tended to be regarded as more of a spiritual concept than a prophetic stance of the believer.

Between 1825-1850, the Baptists of Upper and Lower Canada made no attempt to establish an arts college, but they did establish a theological college at Montreal which had a brief history (1838-1849). During this time they were vigourously opposing state-aided church colleges which the Anglicans were favouring. In 1855 R.A. Fyfe, a prominent Baptist leader who was of Scottish extraction and trained in both Canadian and American colleges, persuaded Baptists to enter the field of secular education also. He proposed an academy that should provide theological training and a good residential secondary school under Christian supervision. "He asserted that education under religious influence was the best training for other spheres of Christian activity as well as for the pulpit."[22] In 1857 the Canadian Literary Institute at Woodstock was started. Shortly thereafter the Baptists were invited to federate with the University of Toronto. In 1881 the Theological Department moved to Toronto and became Toronto Baptist College.

Both questions — federation versus independence, and Toronto versus Woodstock — were settled in 1888 when the Regular Baptist Convention decided that a permanent independent school of learning be developed. Woodstock College was to remain as a secondary school. In

1887 McMaster had received a charter from the Ontario legislasture to become a university. McMaster grew as did the other universities and in 1930 its campus was moved to Hamilton. In 1957, McMaster became a non-denominational private institution. At the same time a separate incorporation and affiliation of a theological college, McMaster Divinity College took place.

The first Baptists to arrive in Winnipeg (1869), Thomas Davidson and Thomas Baldwin, made some interesting observations about conditions in the west. They found the state of political or national feeling remarkable. They missed the official celebrations of the queen's birthday or of Dominion Day but found that when Governor McTavish arrived, the Hudson Bay Company offered a twenty-one gun salute of welcome. They were a bit miffed that Americans in Canada could celebrate the fourth of July and were outraged when they saw a Fenian flag flying on the Canadian flagstaff. "The sight of that dirty rag made my blood boil," said one of the gentlemen.[23]

They found the parochial schools inadequate.

> The creed of each church is taught to the children who are in the school its members sustain. Even the clergymen frankly admit the imperfections of the present system (if 'system' it can be called) and declare their preference for the common school system of Canada.[24]

Baptists made some bold attempts in the west, establishing colleges, but were often fraught with problems relating to financial support that would be necessary to underwrite and maintain these ventures. On the one hand, they consistently refused state aid, but they also had to contend with churches that valued their local autonomy and could not easily be talked into ventures that required co-operation. The Baptist Union was finally achieved in 1909 for the express purpose of carrying out a co-ordinated mission in the new territories that were being organized into municipal and provincial civil jurisdictions. "We have a dream," they said, "of a day when Baptists will no longer be the last of all religious forces to enter a community...coming in to find the field pre-empted and welcome forfeited."[25] In order to become a viable force in the community, they saw the need for trained and educated ministry — hence the desire to have local colleges to train ministers.

The following Baptist institutions were established in the west:

Prairie College, Manitoba (1880-1883)
Okanagan College, British Columbia (1908-1915)
Brandon College, Manitoba (1889-1938)
Baptist Leadership Training School, Calgary (1949)
Carey Hall, University of British Columbia (1959)

The colleges were to be liberal arts institutions to train both lay and clergy. The Calgary school is a Bible school while Carey Hall is a residence for fostering dialogue and community among students.

III. CONCLUSION

The brief foregoing study of Mennonite and Baptist education points out some basic differences in attitude towards education. Mennonites have generally held a more conscious view of the responsibility of parents for the education of their own children. The people of the Baptist tradition have felt a greater responsibility for the education of all children. Both have not taken enough time to work out a vision or understanding of the meaning and purpose of education. We must have a dedication to child education. As people of the Anabaptist and Baptist traditions, what are some of the practical implications of training our children in the spirit of voluntarism? There is a need to articulate a world view that is Christian and not conformed to this world. We need to know what it means for our church to be prophetic today. What kind of life-style should we be modelling for our students? If we say that we are a reconciled and a reconciling community, what skills do we need to become agents of reconciliation? Crucial issues ought to permeate all of education from the elementary grades to university.

We need to understand that the Christian school has a tremendous potential for building community in this day when the forces of fragmentism and depersonalization are rampant. Donald Kraybill offers the following conclusion:

> And so the school is crucial in articulating the vision which forms our new brotherhood glue. As the old meanings of Mennonite identity, forged in our rural experience, fade away the schools are best equipped to identify and transmit the more symbolic glue which will bind us together in the future. Although students come from diverse racial, regional, theological and occupational backgrounds and enter even more heterogeneous situations, the common understandings of Christian faith and Mennonite practice experienced in the schools transcends this diversity and provides a unifying adhesive in an otherwise fragmenting situation.
>
> This does not mean that church schools are always what they should be. Nor do I intend to suggest that they will perform some magic cure-all function. But for a denomination whose traditional social props are being torn away by urbanization, the church school plays a significant role in undergirding and enhancing the life of the church.[26]

IV

The Believers' Church
In The Global Context

Seminar Papers and Responses

GLOBAL MISSION: WORD AND DEED

Newton L. Gingrich

"Let your light so shine before men that they may see your good works and glorify your Father which is in heaven" (Matthew 5: 16).

"The Word was made flesh and dwelt among us" (John 1: 14). This is the heart of the gospel. Christ was God incarnate in humanity. That, also, is the nature of Christ's church. It is a heavenly and an earthly reality, performing in God's drama on the stage of this world. With Christ as head, God's people are a vital presence in the midst of society.

Jesus came, "not to be ministered unto but to minister" (Matthew 20: 33). His service was comprehensive. He preached, taught, forgave, healed, fed, cast out demons and performed many other miracles. Human need was his opportunity. He did not dissect persons, but came to make people "whole" (Matthew 9: 32).

The church is likewise called to minister in word and deed. Someone has aptly said: "A generation ago the church was asking if it should minister to every man.... Now we are asking if we should minister to the whole man." To be whole is for persons to realize their fullest potential as God's children on earth in the context of the faith community. Both word and deed are necessary to achieve this wholeness. There is an authentic verbal expression, the word (**kerygma**), and an essential action manifestation, the deed (**diakonia**). What is the relationship between these two?

I. THE CURRENT TENSION

Christians have varying viewpoints on the relationship of deed and word. These determine planning, policy, programme and performance. Terminology used includes faith and works, witness and service, gospel proclamation and social action, evangelism and revolution, being and doing, spiritual and human, verbalization and demonstration, speaking and acting. Nine distinct views on this relationship can be identified.

1. Only "save souls." This viewpoint claims that the task is to preach the gospel. Saving the "soul" is seen as a single event, valid for time and eternity. Spirituality is contained in fixed and correct terminology. The answer to the world's need is simple. Get people saved and the world will right itself. Deeds are considered inferior to words. Social action remains the responsibility of the unbeliever via agencies, governments and professions. This approach was expressed by a young husband frustrated with marital problems. When asked whether his Christian experience helped him, he replied, "The pastor who baptized me said

I'm ready to die, but never showed me how to live."

2. Deeds necessary to salvation. This stance recognizes that salvation is by faith. However, it is kept alive by action. The biblical injunction, "Work out your own salvation with fear and trembling" (Philippians 2: 12) is taken literally. Salvation is seen as a co-operative process; "God has done his part and we need to do ours." God gives salvation, but we must work to retain it instead of relying simply on an intellectual faith. A conference announced this position clearly in its motto: "Saved by faith: kept saved by works."

3. Social action as evangelistic technique. Some Christians see deeds as a technique to capture or entice unbelievers. Deeds are therefore a means to an end. Social action has no integrity in its own right. It camouflages one's real intentions. Deeds are justified if they can be used to bribe people into the Kingdom. Lewis B. Smeeds is very critical of this approach when he says: "It isn't Christianly decent to use...social concern as mere bait to get a hearing for the real gospel."[1] Visser't Hooft comments:

> The offer of service must, therefore, never be made dependent on the fulfilment of conditions by the receiver. He is worthy of service because he is one of those for whom Christ identifies Himself, for whom He suffered and died.... There is a tenacious and widespread suspicion that the Christian church is unable to serve without using its service as an occasion for preaching.... There are many occasions...to do nothing else than to meet the direct physical need of men in distress. ...It is a service which never forgets that God loves persons, not numbers or cards in an IBM machine.[2]

4. The holistic view. In this view people are considered as potentially whole persons with physical, mental, social and spiritual dimensions. None may be separated from the others. The doctor cannot isolate the physical and minister only to it, nor the educator the mental, the sociologist the social and the pastor the spiritual. These may represent areas of expertise but none dare claim sovereignty over the whole. The word may be mutually shared in many ways if the servant has commanded the respect and aroused the interest of those served.

The various dimensions of life cannot be separated from one another. What affects one area touches the other. Paul, using the body illustration, says, "And whether one member suffer, all the members suffer; or one member be honoured, all the members rejoice with it" (I Corinthians 12: 16). Ronald J. Sider notes: "Evangelism and social action are equally important, but quite distinct aspects of the total mission of the church. But the fact that evangelism and social action are inseparable does not mean they are identical. They are distinct, equally important dimensions of the total task of the church."[3] Visser't Hooft underscores the same point: "If we are concerned with men in the totality of their life, our service will include helping men everywhere to order their societies in such a way that men can live responsibly and meaningfully."[4] John Stoner also emphasizes the unity of life: "There is a temptation, understandable but nevertheless invidious of pious souls to shortcut God's pattern and attempt to get on immediately with the spiritual and eternal matters of life. But in God's pattern life is all mediate in human existences in body and time."[5]

5. Sacred and secular. This argument insists that evangelism is most significant and acts of kindness are important. Nevertheless, they are separated. The human and material are more obvious and immediate, but there is a conviction of the importance of the spiritual. People with this approach often find it difficult to render a spiritual ministry. They assume that special gifts, training and calling are required, and thus the spiritual ministry is considered the duty of the clergy, but not of the laity. Deed and word find little integration. The clerical role becomes a professional one. "Word" is reserved for the sanctuary and deed takes place elsewhere. People will readily respond to the call to clean up after a tornado, but do not regard the witness of the word as their obligation.

6. The "do only" stance. This posture says, "My life will bear evidence of the truth. Words are unnecessary." To communicate the gospel verbally is considered an imposition. Let people inquire. Certainly, quality of life and relationship are important. Deeds do speak loudly. However, is anyone's life performance adequate to communicate the good news? Words carry information and announcements, which deeds cannot. Deeds alone deteriorate into mere activism and humanism. Life's heavenly dimensions are ignored. Any altruistic, philanthropic and caring person can perform the doing, and should not be discouraged. However, when the spiritual is neglected part of the whole is missing. Berkhof emphasizes that, "What God has said to us in the life, acts, death and resurrection of Jesus Christ has to be spoken."[6] Visser't Hooft declares, "It is not merely that we have our mission imperialists and our service imperialists, the first saying that service is a lower form of Christian action than mission, the second saying that the day of mission is coming to an end and that service is to take over...in the light of the New Testament they are so obviously wrong."[7]

7. New meaning in old terms. Good news, evangelism, mission, salvation, redemption are valid theological terms. However, when they are applied to social ministries and environmental activities they no longer carry a uniquely Christian meaning. Sider says, "This viewpoint...[that] salvation is personal and social, individual and corporate...[and that] Jesus came to save the entire created order from the power of sin..., refers not only to the forgiveness of sin and the regenerating power of the Holy Spirit, but also to the growth of social justice."[8]

8. An isolationist approach. In this approach, Christianity is narrowly defined as the relation between God and the self. The motive for this isolation is to insure separation from evil. That includes refusal to participate in religious activities with anyone not part of the group. New Testament claims to the union of word and deed, it is said, have meaning only for first century believers. Persons holding another viewpoint are considered apostate.

9. The people of God approach. Ron Sider states this view very succinctly: "The primary mission of the church is the corporate body of believers. People can by faith in Jesus, who justifies and regenerates, enter this new community now. The church then is part of the content of the Gospel."[9] This overview moves from a position of word only to deed only or at points to a denial of both. The scripture identifies the holistic approach, which is the central thrust of this paper. It recognizes the total person and a ministry by word and deed. Peter Dyck said:

> The Christian will serve simply because it is his nature to do so. He has no "hidden agenda"...such service does not distinguish between word and deed...it is not fragmented but total.... In such service bread and the bread of life are mingled together. Serving thus in word and deed is evidence that we are a "new creation" and the extension of the incarnation...the presence of the people of God in the midst of mankind and the presence of God in the midst of his people.[10]

II. BIBLICAL OBSERVATIONS

God's dealings with His people throughout the centuries are instructive for our discussion.

1. **The Old Testament record**. The Old Testament reflects the social and religious life of God's people. Their understanding of God's desires and acts gives keen insight into the word-deed question. To them, God was sovereign being, the creator and sustainer of the universe. Keller observes: "The Hebrew original for creation is **debar** which means 'thing' as well as 'word'...it is a creative act...'For He spoke and it was done'...in Jesus the Word became flesh...God's Word is deed-word."[11] God made a man and breathed into his nostrils the breath of life. As a human being he lived in close relationship with God.

The Old Testament also speaks of the relationship of God and his people as a covenant. God had brought into existence material reality and a covenant to which belong promises and obligations. The laws for God's people dealing with religion have no more weight than those dealing with the body and society. Jacob Enz writes that "in the Old Testament either the soul (**nephesh**) or the heart (**lib**) or the spirit (**ruach**) may be spoken of in a way that will refer to the whole person,"[12] meaning that physical and spiritual reality are one. The Hebrew understanding of God's commandments also clearly reflects this: "If there be among you a poor man of one of the brethren within any of thy gates in thy land which the Lord thy God giveth thee, thou shalt not harden thine heart, nor shut thine land from thy poor brother" (Deuteronomy 15:7). That was as important as "Thou shalt fear the Lord thy God and serve Him" (Deuteronomy 6:13). Stoner reminds us that "Isaiah spoke of God hating religious feasts and prayers while injustice, oppression and bloodshed are practised. Jeremiah decries the practice of appealing to God's promises to bless the people while ignoring injustice, discrimination and the shedding of innocent blood. The writings of the minor prophets are replete with these themes."[13] A striking example is Amos, who was concerned about Israel's lifestyle, witness and action, challenging her people in a day of prosperity and complacency. "If anything is clear from the prophets, it is that God abhors unjust economic structures as much as sexual misconduct or drunkenness. A biblical presentation of the gospel must include a clear summons to repent of all forms of sin."[14]

I conclude this item with another statement by Jacob Enz: "The first of the biblical assumptions was that word and work are one. We often feel more obligated to the word of the gospel than the work of the gospel. We feel we must specialize in the spoken word. The Bible refers to no distinction between them. Along with the word as the preaching and teaching ministry of Jesus we see the action of the Son of God."[15] We then proceed to observe the further evidence of that.

2. The exemplary Christ. This writer believes that the model for Christian performance is Jesus. John identifies the reason for writing his Gospel: "Many other signs truly did Jesus in the presence of his disciples which are not written in this book, but these are written that ye may believe that Jesus is the Christ, the Son of God and that believing ye may have life through His name" (John 20: 30-31). Paul writes passionately about "all...coming unto the measure of the stature of the fulness of Christ" (Ephesians 4: 13). Mark notes that when John the Baptist's disciples came to inquire of Jesus regarding His true identity, the Master replied: "Go and tell John what you hear and see: the blind receive their sight and the lame walk, lepers are cleansed and the deaf hear, the dead are raised up and the poor hear the gospel preached to them, and blessed is he who finds no offence in me" (Matthew 11: 4-6). In accordance with that declaration, Yamauchi observes, "Christ came to die for sinful men and to reconcile them to God. But He was also quite clearly concerned about the physical needs of the masses as he went about feeding the hungry and healing the sick. The criterion He set forth for the judgement of the nations was the manner in which they would treat those who were strangers, naked and imprisoned."[16]

Matthew graphically presents this in the parable of the last judgement:

> When the son of man shall come in his glory...and before Him shall
> be gathered all the nations.... Then shall the king say unto them on
> the right hand...I was an hungered and ye gave me meat. I was
> thirsty and ye gave me drink. I was a stranger and ye took me in,
> naked, and ye clothed me. I was sick and ye visited me; I was in
> prison and ye came unto me.... Inasmuch as ye have done it unto
> one of the least of these my brethren ye have done it unto me. Then
> shall He say also unto them on the left hand. Depart from me....
> For I was an hungered, and ye gave me no meat..." (Matthew
> 25: 31-42).

The Gospel writers indicate clearly the full-orbed nature of Jesus' ministry. He taught, healed, cast out demons (Mark 1: 21-34); He healed the palsied and forgave sins (2: 3-11); He assured a blessing on those who receive a child and who give a cup of cold water (9: 41-42); He challenged people to love God with all their heart, soul, mind and strength...and their neighbour as themselves (12: 30-31); He praised the devotion given to Himself and giving to the poor (14: 3-9). He read from the scriptures:

> The Spirit of the Lord is upon me, because he hath anointed me to preach the gospel to the poor, he hath sent me to heal the brokenhearted, to preach deliverance to the captives, and recovering of sight to the blind, to set at liberty them that are bruised, to preach the acceptable year of the Lord.... This day is the scripture fulfilled in your ears (Luke 4: 18-21).

This evidence leads Stoner to conclude: "Jesus ministered to the needs of the whole person. There is no evidence that He divided needs into spiritual, physical, soul, political, etc., but a look at His ministry reveals that at various times He met all those needs which we categorize so neatly."[17]

Jesus challenged the religious leaders who pronounced the word but neglected the deed. This became a message also to his followers, as Berkhof says: "Christ charged His apostles not only to preach the gospel, but also to underline their words by deeds of healing and charity.... The two-fold ministry of presbyter and deacon reminds us of the two ways by which Christ's church has to represent **the debar**, the Lord in our own midst, and toward those outside, in witness and service, in word and deed."[18] Stoner takes this a step further: "The church does such things corporately which Christ did individually. Thus the church should be organized corporately to see that feeding the hungry, clothing the naked are done, just as surely as to organize to see that preaching the Word of the Kingdom is done."[19] Visser't Hooft adds to this: "In other words neither witness nor service are 'extras' in the Christian life.... They are simply different ways in which God's love works among men. Both express the same **agape**. The church as the instrument in God's hands used for the mission and service operation, must therefore be a witnessing and a serving church and that in such a way that its mission is the mission of a servant church and its service the service of a missionary church."[20]

3. The apostolic era. The apostles were to function as "ones sent" into a world of need. Jesus had authorized their going. They sought to minister after the model of their teacher. They "provoked to love and to good works" (Hebrews 10: 24). Paul under Christ's authority told the Corinthians, "Ye are our epistle written in our heart, known and read of all men" (II Corinthians 3: 2). Accordingly, he told the Colossians: "Whatsoever ye do in word or deed, do all in the name of the Lord Jesus" (Colossians 3: 17). Paul compares the church to the human body. Both have a variety of functions and whether prominent or demure, none is greater in God's sight than another. Each member has a particular gift to contribute to the ministry of the body, in both the physical and spiritual realms. Paul was concerned for the preaching of the gospel; he was also anxious to contribute to the physical well-being of others (I Corinthians 16: 1-3; Galatians 6: 10).

John and James both contributed classical statements on the evangelical service to the whole man: "But whoso hath this world's good and seeth his brother have need, and shutteth up his bowels of compassion from him, how dwelleth the love of God in him? My little children, let us not love in word, neither in tongue, but in deed and truth" (I John 3: 17-18; see also 4: 19-20). "If a brother or sister be naked, and destitute of daily food, and one of you say unto them, depart in peace, be ye warmed and filled; notwithstanding ye give them not those things which are needful to the body; what doth it profit?" "Pure religion and undefiled before God and the Father is this, to visit the fatherless and widows in their affliction, and to keep himself unspotted from the world" (James 2: 15; 1: 27).

We may allow Leighton Ford to sum up the matter:

> God's revolutionary power was released through the church in reverend action. Luke opens the book of Acts by saying, "In the first book...(Luke) I have dealt with all that Jesus began to do and teach" (Acts 1: 1 RSV). He implies that Jesus continued "to do and teach" through those He left behind. This dynamic combination of deed and word characterized His apostles. Their words acted and their deeds spoke! Acts is full of action verbs: they prayed, they spoke, they healed, they gave their testimony, they sold their goods, they went about preaching. So we need to match our words with our deeds, and our deed with our words.[21]

III. THE HOLISTIC PRINCIPLE TODAY

How does the holistic principle work out in actual practice? Perhaps we should begin with the words of Jacob Enz: "Words and works are one...body and soul are one...the individual and the group are one...."[22]

At this point I simply offer a number of contemporary statements on the unity of word and action.

Harold S. Bender: "The Anabaptist could not understand... Christianity which made regeneration, holiness and love primarily a matter of intellect, of doctrinal belief, or of subjective experience rather than one of the transformation of life."[23]

Leslie Newbigin: "The preaching of the gospel and the service of man's need are equally authentic and essential parts of the church's responsibility. But neither is a substitute for the other."[24]

Hendrik Berkhof: "The work always has to be a sign of the kingdom. ...God's ultimate aim is the establishing of His Kingdom on earth...this is, the full relation between God and man, between man and man, between man and his social structure, between man and nature.... A preaching church without her life and works of love and mercy has no winning powers.... So the church needs the word, to say what her deeds mean. She will show God's love in her serving.... Varying a well-known word of Kant we can say witness without service is empty; service without witness is dumb."[25]

W.S. Visser't Hooft: "It seems to me that if mission and service are thus both penetrated by the same **agape** rooted in the same gospel that they will play into each other's hands. The service, if it is truly Christian, will make people wonder about Christians. The mission will make explicit what lies behind the service. Both will build the church.

Both will manifest that the church exists for the world."[26]

Mennonite worker overseas: "I have been so deeply aware of the need for God to work through us and in us. We go back [to the Congo] with all the educational benefits and the very best the system can provide in preparation. Yet if God does not work through us by His Spirit, reaching out to others through us, then these degrees and honours will be as tinkling cymbals."[27]

Leighton Ford: "Evangelism must be love with flesh on. William Wilberforce went on a burning passion to abolish the slave trade...a campaign to wipe out the evil, not only by preaching the gospel, but also by fierce debate and political action. Such action should not be confused with evangelism. Neither should it be separated from it."[28]

Frank Peters: "The dichotomy of faith and works breaks down. Faith is a holistic response of the discipleship and can be seen in many areas of life.... To act as a Christian is to act in a holistic manner. The testimony of the healed in Jesus' day was simply this, 'he hath made us whole'.... Our Anabaptist forefathers were very quick to reject some of the well-worn dichotomies and to introduce holistic terms.... It is not faith and works but rather a faith that works."[29]

Robert Kreider: "I find particularly refreshing the sermons and addresses of the 1890s when our people (Mennonite) were just getting started in mission. I find none of the word-deed dichotomy, feeding, preaching, healing, caring, building, teaching — all this was one natural and integrated whole. It was all so natural, childlike, spontaneous. And then came...the judgemental pressures on people to do things in just the right way, above all to be sound in the use of words, and so the Word became words and deeds became 'social gospel.'"[30]

The thrust of these statements is that "we are workers together with God." Deed and word are inseparable parts of a holistic ministry. The deed authenticates the word and the word explains the deed. Although structures may zero in on one aspect more than another, they complement each other. Twentieth century society necessitates some of this separation as government provides service and the church is left to give the witness. Even then the church must retain a holistic stance, recognizing that Christians in government have a word-witness to give, and that there are still many areas of service the church can provide that the government is not geared to meet.

IV. CONCLUSION

Word and deed validate each other. Deed is no mere activism, and word no mere verbiage. Neither is an adjunct to the other; both are central and interdependent. In London's Highgate Cemetery the granite monument for Karl Marx holds this inscription: "The philosophers have only interpreted the world and the point is to change it." That change will come only in a wholesome integration of word and deed. Hans Denk, a sixteenth century Anabaptist, said it well: "No one truly knows Christ except he who follows Him in all of life."

Leighton Ford, himself a prominent evangelist, has made the case for integration of word and deed as strongly as anyone:

Christian conversion is so revolutionary because it is so complete. When a man meets Jesus Christ, God begins to heal all his broken relationships, to put him right with God, and with himself and with his fellowmen. Today when our churches are being torn apart, believers, the so-called "soul savers" at one pole and the so-called "social reformers" at the other, it's absolutely imperative that we keep in view the completeness of the Gospel and resist the temptation of both extremes.[31]

"I beseech you therefore, brethren, by the mercies of God [motivation], that you present your bodies a living sacrifice [commitment], holy, acceptable before God which is your reasonable service [performance]. And be not conformed to this world, but be ye transformed by the renewing of your mind [faithfulness], proving what is that good and acceptable and perfect will of God" [searching stance] (Romans 12: 1-2).

GLOBAL MISSION:
PAST AND PRESENT

John F. Keith

At the outset of this paper, permit me to spell out certain assumptions upon which it is based. Many of these assumptions appear to be held in common with a long line of missionaries in the Believers' Church tradition. Many of them were at the heart of that driving compulsion which motivated William Carey and Adoniram Judson at the outset of what we commonly refer to as the modern missionary movement.

I. ASSUMPTIONS

1. That the purposes and will of God, as set forth in the holy scriptures, are binding upon the church today.

2. That Jesus of Nazareth is the central figure of history; that He is son of God, son of man, saviour, and Lord of life; that He is the way, the truth and the life; that He is the hope of the world, and that no man comes to the Father but by Him.

3. That the church universal is the totality of true believers in Jesus Christ, whatever their external religious affiliation.

4. That the institutional churches, in order to be faithful to their calling, must address themselves to the task of being God's faithful servants, in order to accomplish His will in the world.

5. That His will can be determined on broad lines through a study of the scriptures; that in using our logical faculties to fill in the remaining details we have a right to claim and expect the guidance of the Holy Spirit.

6. That His will includes proclamation of, and witness to God's love and His saving grace through Jesus Christ.

7. That His will includes ministry to all forms of human need, suffering and alienation, through acts of love, kindness, compassion and concern, undertaken in His name.

In brief, it is an assumption of this paper that the task of the church is global in its scope, and that it involves in its implementation, ministries both of word and of deed.

II. THE GLOBAL NATURE OF THE MISSION OF THE CHURCH

Among the little band which gathered around the resurrected Christ, the term **church** was not yet in vogue. It appears in the Acts of the Apostles and in the Epistles, but not yet in the Gospels. Before the little fellowship knew that they were "a church," they knew that they were "sent." Writ large among the instructions given by our risen Lord to His followers one finds the element of their being sent. By the time the church emerged as such, and that name was being used, its "sentness" was clearly established.

Mission is a word of Latin extraction, and has reference to being sent (just as the Greek word **apostle** carries the same root meaning). The terms **mission** and **church** are closely intertwined. To distinguish between mission and church may be appropriate; to separate them is not. While one may distinguish among the various functions to be performed by the church, such as proclamation, witness, teaching, fellowship and service, yet it seems fair to state that the function of the church is its mission. The church is Christ's body, created to fulfil a divine purpose and commissioned to carry out the divine will.

The mission of the church is essentially the same for the church in all geographic regions, for all peoples, throughout time. How can this be summarized in a better way than through Jesus' own words, "As the Father has sent me, I also send you" (John 20: 21). His church is an extension of Himself, His body, responsible for working out the implications of that truth, but also guided by the charter which Jesus chose to read on the day when He stood up in the synagogue in Capernaum and inaugurated His public ministry with this reading from Isaiah:

> The Spirit of the Lord is upon me, because he has anointed me to preach the gospel to the poor. He has sent me to proclaim release to the captives, and recovery of sight to the blind, to set free those who are downtrodden, to proclaim the favourable year of the Lord.
> (Luke 4: 18-19)

Examination of that charter reveals a beautiful integration of ministries involving both word and action — the same integration which one is able to see exemplified day after day in Jesus' own life and ministry. If there exists in some sectors today a polarization between mission through message (evangelism) and mission through service, it is an artificial polarization, for both form an integral part of the mission of the church and they belong together.

The title assigned to this seminar is indeed an appropriate one: "Global Mission: Word and Deed." The pattern was set by our Lord, and the mandate was given by Him. It will involve ministries of word: witness, proclamation, discipling. It will involve ministries of deed: expressions of love, actions of compassion and concern.

The scope of the church's mission is global in two different senses: global ethnically and geographically, in relation to all aspects of life.

The **covenant promises** of Abraham indicated that in him all the nations of the earth would be blessed. A strong thread of prophecy throughout the Old Testament indicated a coming day when God's blessing and His spirit would be the portion of all without distinctions of nationality, profession, sex or age. The disciples themselves were commissioned to disciple all the nations (**panta ta ethne**), transliterated "all the ethnics." One of the announced conditions to be fulfilled before the termination of the present age was to be the preaching of the gospel of the Kingdom in the whole world for a witness to all the nations (Matthew 24: 14). John's vision of the end times included the song of the elders before the lamb:

Worthy art thou to take the book, and to break its seals; for thou wast
slain, and didst purchase for God with Thy blood men from every tribe
and tongue and people and nation. (Revelation 5: 9)

The other sense in which God's mission for His church is global has to
do with bringing the totality of life under His domain. Of no aspect of our
lives can we say, "Christ need not have lordship here." God's redemptive purposes in Christ are aimed at the revolutionary transformation of
all aspects of human life and all spheres of human activity.

We who are of the Believers' Church tradition may have been stronger
and louder in our proclamation of this truth as it relates to the private
life of the believers than we have been in making application to
corporate life in the societies in which we live. To that extent, then, we
have fallen short of our duty, and Christians have failed to be faithful to
that aspect of the church's mission which admonishes us to be the salt of
the earth and the light of the world. The global implications of the
mission of the church must be permitted to reach through Christians to
the practices of the business world and to the board rooms of
corporations. They must penetrate the legislative and administrative
cadres of both local and national politics. Those whose ecclesiology
differs from our own will have different expectations of "the church."
They will call for denominational pressure-group action, and cannot be
expected to understand when we say that such is not our way. Our final
accountability will not be to them but to our Lord, but accountability
there must be...to the totality of the mission to which He has called and
sent us.

III. RESUME OF HISTORY

Although individual Canadian Baptist missionaries served earlier
under other societies, independent missionary work began in Andhra
state, India, in 1874, in response to an appeal from a Telegu Christian.
By the turn of the century, missionary work had begun in Bolivia, the
oldest continuing Protestant witness there, begun in an era when it was
a capital offence to proclaim anything except the established Roman
Catholic religion.

During their first eighty years of overseas missions, then, Canadian
Baptists focused their efforts on these two countries — India and
Bolivia. From the outset, ministries of compassion and concern were
integrated with ministries of proclamation and witness. The central
strategy in both countries focused upon the planting and nurture of a
national church. In both countries, missionaries pioneered in education.
In India, a network of health care was established, and in Bolivia, the
life-style of peasant landholders was eventually revolutionized by
innovative measures undertaken first in the context of the mission, and
later copied in a national agrarian reform.

IV. TRENDS AND PROSPECTS

A. The 1970s. Now some comments on experiences and trends within
the Canadian Baptist Overseas Mission Board in our present decade,
giving some attention both to where we have been and where we appear
to be going.

In the late 1960s and early 1970s much attention and energy focused on the transition of authority and properties to the national church bodies which grew out of Canadian Baptist missionary efforts in Bolivia and India. This was accompanied by a parallel emphasis upon the importance of self-support for what was called "the basic work of the church," as opposed to "auxiliary services" such as education, medicine and agriculture. Considerable agony accompanied the entire process. Canadian motivation was often suspect, and statements such as "You don't love us anymore" were not uncommon.

During the term of office of my general secretary predecessor, Orville Daniel, serious attention was given to studies of policy and direction, with a special focus on gearing up appropriately for ministries in the 1970s. One of the driving forces behind the policy studies was a suspicion that for Canadian missionaries to continue in key positions of leadership would be to stifle the emergence of the right kind of national leadership, stifling as well any clear articulation by the national church of its goals and aims stated in their own terms.

By the time I came to office in 1970, the transition to national structures of authority had long since taken place; the struggles leading to self-support were essentially behind and the final transfers of property titles were to take place by 1973.

The results have been somewhat mixed, and this may be due to the presence of many other factors not mentioned here. In Bolivia, the policy change appears to have fortified a new self-awareness and confidence within the church, freeing its members to move on into the future with a sense of direction of their own, yet with ongoing links of fellowship both through shared missionary personnel and shared programs. In India, it is not yet clear just what has been accomplished.

Angola was another kind of experience for Canadian Baptists. Beginnings were made in the late 1950s, during the Portuguese colonial regime. Canadians continued a work begun by an independent British missionary, following his death, and the style begun was a traditional one. Most of this work terminated abruptly in March 1961 with the outbreak of the war of independence; the last Canadian couples left Angola in 1963. Since that time, constant contact has been maintained with Angolan refugees in neighbouring Zaire, and about 20 Angolan leaders have been assisted with theological studies, particularly in Zaire, but also in other countries. Working relationships in Zaire led directly into new styles of ministry and new patterns of relationships that were to develop in Kenya and Indonesia, beginning in 1970. More of that later.

The experience of Angola leads me to observe that the transition from mission to church happens most smoothly in circumstances where external factors (such as the Angolan war) removed the missionaries forcibly from the scene. The church did not go through a time of questioning as to whether it was being deliberately abandoned. Returning to Angola for a visit in March 1978, I found that the transition from mission to church had taken place gloriously, and to a degree that I had not dared to hope.

The current decade of the 1970s has marked a shift for the Canadian Baptist Overseas Mission Board to a new set of relationships with a new set of denominations overseas. Several of these either began independently or separated from parent mission bodies, dating from the late 1940s, and had upwards of 25 years of separate existence. Each of these is in the Believers' Church tradition. Three of these denominations with which we have already established a formal working relationship do not use the name Baptist. Each is characterized by an energy and vigour in evanglism which have resulted in growth by multiplication rather than by addition. In each case, growth rates in these national churches have been such that they had difficulty in keeping up with programmes of leadership development. In each case, requests for assistance in leadership development have been at the heart of the appeal made by these denominations to Canadian Baptists.

Without a lot of detail, the three bodies referred to immediately above are:

African Christian Churches and Schools, Kenya: Kikuyu. Origins with Africa Inland Mission. First CBOMB missionaries sent in 1970.

Kerapatan Geredja Protestan Indonesia, Sulawesi, Indonesia. Doctrinal influences through Christian and Missionary Alliance Schools, Southern Baptist (Indonesia) Seminary, but with a history of independent origins. First CBOMB missionaries sent in 1973.

African Brotherhood Church, Kenya: Kamba and other. Independent origins. Describe themselves as Baptist in doctrine, Anglican in structure. First CBOMB missionaries 1978.

The technical in-house terminology which Canadian Baptists use to describe the relationship with the three denominations mentioned above, and with the Baptists of Mato Grosso in Brazil, is **task force**. The special features of the relationship include the following:

1. The CBOMB contribution is essentially one of missionary personnel. Programme funds are provided by the denomination.

2. The personnel work is in fellowship with the national church and under their direction.

3. The tasks to be undertaken are defined and agreed to in advance.

4. A terminal date for the programme is established from the outset. (It turns out that the terminal date was thought at first to be fictitious, but CBOMB is insisting upon observing it.)

The influences which led the Canadian Baptist Overseas Mission Board to move in the direction of task force policy are many. Perhaps some of the most influential were the following:

1. CBOMB's commitment to a strategy of world mission built on a cornerstone of founding/strengthening national churches. This is diametrically opposed to a strategy which says mission structures are eternal, and must be kept distinct from church structures. Mission structures are seen by CBOMB as an interim step leading to the establishment of churches.

2. The desire to assist sister churches overseas without creating new dependencies upon either Canadian personnel or Canadian funds.

3. A conviction that all Christians have an ongoing responsibility and an ongoing share in the world mission of the church, through people and through funds; accompanied at the same time by a desire to see leadership and authority rest in the hands of the emerging churches of the third world.

4. A desire to demonstrate that Christian missionaries can and will work in situations where they are not in charge; a desire to fulfill obediently the spirit of Christ as described in Philippians 2: 5ff, whereby the master was willing to take upon Himself the form of a servant.

5. Having worked through periods of transition from mission to church, there was a desire that any newly established relationships undertaken in this decade be set up on a different basis from the very outset, thus avoiding the need for transition later.

6. John Gatu, well known as a popularizer of the term **moratorium** played a direct, active and constructive role in designing the features of CBOMB's first task force, undertaken with the African Christian Churches and Schools. He labeled this relationship a "post-moratorium" style of work.

B. The Future. Glimpses of the next stage, the trend of the future, have already begun to emerge. The in-house technical term we are likely to use to describe it is **joint outreach**. In a word, it will be a pioneer type of evangelistic outreach in which CBOMB missionaries will team with and assist missionaries of those churches with which we have undertaken task force ministries. We are defining joint outreach as an attempt to evangelize unreached peoples who are of a different ethnic and linguistic background from the church with which we have undertaken the task force relationship. This definition is necessary to distinguish it from "more of the same" church growth within their own area.

Joint outreach represents a return to pioneer-type evangelism, but with a difference. It is a situation in which responsibilities for administration and authority are not expected to be carried by Canadians. Those of us involved in planning it are anxious to see if many of the features of traditional missionary work can be avoided: institutionalization, immobility, heavy capital outlay. Some of the issues to be faced have not even been fully defined.

Only time will tell if missionary volunteers can be found in this generation who will bring to the task the combination of skills and dedication which will be required for them to adjust to the much higher demands of adaptation. Joint outreach will not be as easy as the leadership training tasks which characterize our present task force assignments.

In laying plans with overseas leadership for joint outreach projects in Indonesia and in Kenya, I have had a first-hand opportunity to see the practical advantages of this type of outreach. In November 1976, Indonesian Pastor Alex Tairas found door after door open as we travelled together to an animistic region of Kalimantan. None of the doors would have been open to a Canadian missionary society. Canadians working under the direction of an independent Indonesian denomination enhanced the prestige of the national church organization in the eyes of their government — they had not see anything like this at work before. The opportunities and needs which emerged from that missionary tour are very real. Two Canadian couples will be appointed as soon as the right people can be found.

The prospects for further development of CBOMB's missionary work under the two trends I have just described are particularly bright and promising. It is probable that CBOMB will experience sharp numerical growth of missionaries on the field. The numerical gauge, by itself, is a very empty one, unless the importance and quality of what is being accomplished are taken into consideration, and here I am particularly pleased.

The returns, both in terms of personal fulfillment and of visible results, tend to run high. Those involved in leadership training tasks, whether of clergy or lay people, see a direct multiplication of their efforts. The sense of appreciation and the level of true fraternal acceptance by national leadership runs high. The task force assignments have been appealing to Canadian Baptists who have been volunteering for overseas service in numbers unknown in the history of our denomination. This has permitted a careful selection process to take place.

Certain conditions must exist within the life of a national church as prerequisites to the appointment of a task force. There must be a common basis of Christian faith, experience and practice. The denomination must have reached a certain level of organization and maturity. There are intangible requisites very difficult to define, perhaps best described as integrity and credibility. The denomination must have reached a certain level of stewardship and have at least a minimal economic base.

It was at first surprising to see the number of autonomous denominations in the third world countries which fulfill these requirements and more, and are requesting specific personnel assistance. New requests continue to arrive, and require evaluation.

The first serious obstacle to be encountered will be that of financial support. This may relate to our inability to put a clear picture before the supporting churches, finance committees and Baptist Conventions. The structures and procedures which have been established do not appear to be adequate to respond to the opportunities and needs that have emerged.

V. A PARTNERSHIP IN DEVELOPMENT MINISTRIES

World consciousness among the churches of the Baptist Federation of Canada has found a noticeable expression within the last three years through sharply increased giving to the Relief and Development Fund of the Baptist Federation. Across the same span of time a working partnership has grown up between the Federation and the Overseas Mission Board. This partnership brings together on one hand certain funds which the committee designates specifically for developmental purposes, and on the other hand the experience of the Overseas Mission Board which has been carrying on developmental-type ministries for decades.

Although there may be a certain duplication or overlapping of structures between the Mission Board and the Federation, all aspects of relief and development assistance are a part of the response by the churches to their global mission. At the point of implementation, no conflict is seen between those ministries which are of word and those which are of deed. Having seen the two emphases ideally integrated in our Lord's ministry, we believe that they belong together in our ministries as well.

CHRISTIAN LIFE-STYLE IN AN AFFLUENT SOCIETY

Bruce W. Neal

Animal Crackers is the weekly social comment of a cartoonist named Rog Bollen. Each Saturday it appears as a coloured comic strip in the newspaper which comes to our house.

In a recent item of **Animal Crackers**, the white bird with the bulbous beak and large orange feet is walking up the side of a mountain. It is evening and a slice of moon is already in the sky. By the time you reach the third frame, the bird is standing on the edge of a cliff staring at a yellow dot above the moon; and this is what he is saying:

> Star light, star bright,
> first star I see tonight...
> Wish I may, wish I might,
> have the wish I wish tonight.
> I wish for understanding in the world
> and I wish for peace and tranquility throughout...
> ...and I wish that kindness would prevail
> and that everyone would live by the 'golden rule'...
> and I wish that patience would become a virtue more practiced
> and a Mercedes 450 SEL for me
> and that everyone would try to help those less fortunate
> and I wish for trust between nations.

Then, in the last frame, as he turns away from the edge of the cliff and begins to walk home, he says to himself: "...hope it comes with 'factory air conditioning.' "

I. TENSIONS

The very title of our seminar subject implies at least some degree of tension between the ideals of Christian commitment and the blandishments of a consumer world view. This is not to suggest that a Christian could never drive a Mercedes Benz 450 SEL, but, at a current list price of $34,000 it would be difficult to choose which Christian has the bigger problem: the wealthy one who has to make the decision or some of the rest of us standing around wishing we had that kind of choice to make.

Probably it is at the point of wishing, that the questions of life-style in an affluent society arise most sharply — which is also the point at which conscience becomes most active. By conscience I mean not just the guilt-feelings of the popular view of conscience but the inner-motivated awareness of personal responsibility.

Even in a period of inflation, we live richly in an affluent society. Critics of our affluence refer to us as the self-indulgent society, but defenders are quick to point out that our abundance provides increasing benefits to the world.

Within an affluent society, production and distribution ensure that the average person, not just the wealthy, enjoys both the necessities of life and something more. High health standards, education for everyone, social security and leisure time for the pursuit of personal interests are all benefits of an economy of abundance.

There is a paradox, of course, in the fact that most people in Canada do not consider themselves rich. Partly that is because most people want a lot, and it seems to be an elementary observation that the more we have the more we want. At the same time, it is important to note that it is almost impossible to live and function in an affluent society without having a lot. For Canadians, a sound, well-heated house is a necessity in our northern climate and an automobile is not the incredible luxury it would be in the lives of most people in the world: we have constructed a setting which requires it. What this means, of course, is that it is costly to participate in an affluent society and the majority are economically strained to keep up.   ·

But the costs of living in a rich nation like ours are not only monetary. Our value systems, our view of self, our attitudes to others and our purposes for living are all profoundly affected by our society of abundance. And, regrettably, an affluent economy appears to thrive by appealing to the worst motives of people rather than to their best. Advertisements appeal to pride, envy, conformity, sexual dominance, will to power, false security and self-indulgence. And, in the process, a consumer mentality is created which is inherently self-seeking. Vast numbers of people who are no longer producers, thanks to a multiplicity of machines, are nevertheless increasingly important as consumers. If we do not do our part by consuming, we are made to feel guilty for contributing to unemployment. And because of constant change, old skills become obsolete, jobs are phased out, and as some people gain, others are hurt in the process.

I suppose that one of the most difficult problems facing us in the affluent society is the power of the system itself. The structure of our economy of abundance seems to run with a momentum and direction of its own. Automated machinery is both the tool and the metaphor of the processes which operate, almost as though nobody were directing them. Decisions are made within the process and yet there is a virtual inevitability about the system which only increases its impersonal nature. Competitors are doing it, progress calls for it, growth in the gross national product demands it, and the company has to do it or lose business and dwindle away. The system really makes the big decisions and we are hard-pressed to find effective ways to question it.   ·

II. CONCERN AND RESPONSE

But into the 1970s have come three large concerns to challenge the whole rationale of our affluent society. As Christians who might prefer to see ourselves as inner-motivated, we have to admit that all three of these concerns have not arisen from within our own moral sensitivities a much as they have been forced upon us from without. One is the strident warning from environmental scientists that we are accountable for our use and abuse of the earth, air and water around us. The second is the threatening news that the energy supplies on which our economy of abundance depends are limited and increasingly expensive. And the third, which for many of us is the largest concern of them all, is the need of the have-not peoples of our world. Because of instant global communication systems, we have been made unavoidably aware of a severe imbalance in our world. There are millions of hungry, under-nourished and even starving people out there. According to the United Nations, **two-thirds of the earth's people** grow less than one-third of the world's food, lack any kind of decent housing for one out of every two families, endure idleness and under-employment of up to forty per cent of the work force, have patient-to-doctor ratios as high as ten thousand to one, have life expectancies as low as forty to fifty-five years, and see more than fifty per cent of their children grow up illiterate.

Therefore, questions of Christian life-style at this point in time have to be asked in terms of our relationships to the earth upon which we live and the people with whom we share it...both understood in a global sense. That makes the task very large, in some respects too large for individuals to handle; and yet any smaller perspective would bring an inadequate view to bear on the judgements we now have to make as Christians. When we now remind ourselves that we are responsible stewards of the earth which God has placed in our collective hands, we have to mean far more than our father's farm or our own back garden (if we have one). And when we remind ourselves that we are our brother's (or sister's) keeper — that is, that we are called of God to care deeply about the welfare of our fellows — we now (more than ever) have to mean all of the people of the world. Our actions may have to be specific and limited: to help farmers in the Chapare lowlands of Bolivia to grow food on land never tilled before or to help Liberian Baptists to develop a school at Kwendin which is uniquely appropriate to village children in rural areas; but the fact that we are there attempting to participate meaningfully with them has to be because we see them as our neighbours...and we have something to share.

Of course, our Canadian society has responded to all three of the problems laid before it. It has responded as an affluent, technological society in predictable yet innovative ways. It has attacked the problem of pollution by scientific and legislative methods. It is encouraging the wiser use of energy, and a search for new sources. And it has expended millions of dollars in "foreign aid" to third world countries during the last two decades.

There are many, of course, who would argue that only through the mechanisms of a society can anything of significance be done, that only through governments and large technological agencies can changes be effected. It is our conviction, however, that the attitudes and actions of persons are fundamental ingredients in what a society believes and does, and that the life-style of Christians is commissioned by God to set the pace. There is a risk of arrogance in that last statement; but the size of the need, an awareness of our own limitations and God's call for us to be Christ-like servants in the world combine to insist that we can be nothing else but humble and willing to give ourselves away to do God's will.

Observations of what people affiliated with the Baptist Federation of Canada have done in response to the principal factors we have been sketching can be little more than cursory and personal. Baptists appear to have benefited from our economy of abundance as have most other Canadians. In recent years our strength has trended toward the suburbs where middle class families choose to live, while long-established churches in the old parts of our cities struggle to adapt, with varying degrees of success, to minister in communities where former assumptions of culture or affluence no longer prevail. By and large we have assumed the acceptability and desirability of at least moderate wealth, as a blessing, a gift to thank God for, and perhaps even a sign of faithfulness and piety. We have furnished our houses after the style proposed by Eatons or The Bay. We have driven cars no more nor less impressive than our neighbours'. We have spent no more nor less wisely on Christmas gifts than others around us. And many of our church buildings are quite comfortably equipped. We have tried to discipline ourselves against the excesses of pride and materialism, but, generally speaking, we have been a reflection of the economic image of the world in which we live.

When the anti-pollution movement began a few years ago, some statements or resolutions came from us, but I am not aware of any significant actions on the part of the Convention Baptists to join the cause. We can assume that individuals have been responding to the need to prevent pollution and recycle wastes, but there has been no high profile church action on the matter.

When the energy crisis reached us, again Baptists on the whole did not see the issue as one for church initiatives. In fairness, I'm not sure that any of the denominations did — except, reluctantly, in accepting the necessity of higher fuel costs. In other words, the question of energy supply and demand would appear to be viewed by us as a "physical" issue and not an essential concern of the church.

The needs of the third world for relief and development are a different matter. Historically committed to overseas missionary endeavour in Asia, Africa and South America for many years, with significant aspects of it in the fields of medicine, education and agriculture, Canadian Baptists did not find it difficult to project themselves into further dimensions of overseas service. In 1972, Federation Baptists funnelled about $75,000 through their Relief Committee — largely into emergency relief assistance, particularly through relief channels of the Baptist World Alliance. In 1977, the Relief and Sharing Committee of the Baptist Federation of Canada handled some $330,000 in contributions from the churches for relief responses, development projects and fraternal aid in twenty different countries. In 1978, new guidelines were adopted for the re-named Relief and Development Committee of the

Federation. A working partnership with the Canadian Baptist Overseas Mission Board for research, implementation and evaluation in development projects is going well, and our people continue to respond with increasing generosity to the possibilities of helping to meet specific relief and development needs overseas.

What difference this is making to the life-style of Convention Baptists I cannot document. That our people are aware of the needs in third world countries is indicated by their givings. That some considerable conscience has been aroused by the evident plight of persons who do not have even the necessities of life is suggested by the generosity of the giving of many.

At the same time, many of us have been unable to avoid the questions put to us by our affluence in an economically imbalanced world. We refuse to be content with the argument that we must be rich so that we can have an overflow of abundance to rescue the poor from starvation. We have difficulty with the contention of a recent letter to the editor of **The Enterprise** (Spring 1978), the magazine of the Canadian Baptist Overseas Mission Board, that:

> Affluence is necessary for the continued economic health of the donor countries...The world society of the future will have a disparity of living styles and income similar to our own society. But limiting the ability of individuals to achieve wealth or affluence will reduce not enlarge the availability of resources to support the poor.

It is true that Jesus said "...you always have the poor with you, and whenever you will, you can do good to them..." (Mark 14: 7 RSV); but Jesus set before us a calling which is not quiet until our neighbours are fed and free. He opened the book in the synagogue and read from Isaiah 61:

> The Spirit of the Lord is upon me, because he has anointed me to preach good news to the poor. He has sent me to proclaim release to the captives and recovering of sight to the blind, to set at liberty those who are oppressed.... (Luke 4: 18 RSV)

Then he claimed that purpose for Himself; and anyone who follows Him must, in turn, claim it for himself.

To work on the premise that two-thirds of the world will remain poor, unwell and uneducated while we increase in bounty is an unjust attitude for Christians to exhibit. To justify our disproportionate use of the earth's resources on the rationale that we are the economic saviours of the third world, displays a paternalistic attitude which it is difficult to see as synonymous with Jesus' call to humility and love for one's neighbour. To love is to seek the best for another, to do what one can to make it possible for him to stand upon his feet and be a free and fulfilled person. Genuine loving action will inevitably lead to sacrifices on the part of the ones who would love as Jesus loved. The quest for a Christian life-style must discern the necessary shapes of attitude, action and sacrifice, of self-giving love.

III. A CHRISTIAN PHILOSOPHY

In addition to any concern we have for the peoples of Bangladesh, Haiti or Zaire, we also have a responsibility to be evaluators of the affluent society itself. For those of us who live within it to be uncritical of the unhealthy aspects of the economy of abundance is to be irresponsible as disciples of our Lord. Some may be required to be prophets in crucial places within the structures and attitude-shaping institutions of our society; but all of us who are Christians have a witness to make, an influence to exert, a ministry to offer in the life-style we offer to the world.

The appeal to Christian life-style is not to suggest that the task of righting an imbalanced world is an easy one. The needs for change in the economic order, in the priorities and systems of the third world countries as well as our own, and in the will to solve human problems rather than to exploit social circumstances are momentous factors in the search for justice. And the tremendous need for the gospel to be proclaimed in all parts of the world as the fundamental answer to the sinfulness of man is more pressing than ever. Yet the inner-directed Christian, the person who chooses to be guided by the Spirit of God within his heart and mind, is obliged by his faith to look to his own life-style as a priority question on his own agenda.

The reasons for asking specific questions about our life-style are usually prompted by the issues which arise before us. That seems to be part of human nature: that very few new convictions are born within us without being stimulated or ignited by needs or crises or encounters with the concerns of others. Yet how we respond, what authority we accept, what attitudes we take, what actions we choose and how we follow through are essential to our being as Christians endeavouring to be free and responsible by God's grace.

How we respond as Christians from within a Believers' Church will be a result of the experiences and convictions which have become ours, translated into situations of the moment through the decisions we will make. There will always be debate as to which comes first: the experience or the word. For us, the Word of God is definitive; yet even the good news of God in Jesus Christ cannot have its redeeming effect on us until we have apprehended it for ourselves. We are essentially Christian empiricists in that we insist that a person must experience the faith for himself. He must wrestle with his own conscience; he must repent because of his own sins; he must commit himself meaningfully to Jesus Christ as his Saviour and Lord, offer himself to the enactment of death-to-the-old/resurrection-of-the-new in believer's baptism, and work out his own salvation with other Christians in the voluntary fellowship of a church.

It is this insistence on the **personal** which has been a hallmark of our Baptist story. It is nurtured in the experiences of fellowship and belonging in the company of committed Christians. In family or congregation or caring group, we experience the presence of others and the presence of God as personal. We learn the experience of being sustained and carried forward by the surging power of a communal group. We experience claims made upon us, ethical demands, and covenant entered into and shared with others. And it includes the experience of being members of a redemptive society, of a fellowship whose faith is that through every dying come the possibilities of resurrection, of a community of trust which is willing to be a transforming agent under God in the world. From this experience of Christian community comes a sense of responsibility to share in a purpose which has shaped a history and will define a future.

Because of this context, the personal then takes shape in experiences of self-discovery and freedom, of self-commitment and creating. They include the discovering of self as an individual who can see and feel, wonder, think, purpose and make decisions, who can imagine, intend, commit oneself and, all being well, follow through. They also include the discovering of self as morally responsible: sometimes in need of control, sometimes in need of stimulus, but still in charge of oneself. This means the experience of the freedom of giving one's own assent or of self-initiating one's own actions. And with this come the experiences of creating — both as an individual and as part of a group. For the Christian this is the experience of being a child of the God who creates out of chaos. It is helping something new come into existence because of our lives, bringing into being someting new and compelling — instead of letting oneself and circumstances be subject to repetition and fate.

These ingredients of what it means to insist on the personal are essential for us to review because we wrestle with questions of Christian response in a highly conditioned context. We live and move and have our being within economic systems and cultural expectations which, in their offerings of affluence, are seductive and difficult to challenge. The depersonalizing of our social structures needs our Christian insistence on the personal. The stresses of competition and consumerism on interpersonal relations need our witness of the loving communal spirit under Christ. But, perhaps most of all, the affluent society demands the commitment and courage of personally decisive Christian life-style.

Freedom, cherished in Baptist experience, is not simply independence from certain controls whether of state, creed or culture. Freedom is the gift to be expressively spontaneous, to choose a course of action, not because it is required of us but because we believe that, in the sight of God, it is the creative thing to do. Freedom is to be a subject in the sentence, not just an object, to be an agent, not just a patient to be cared for. Freedom from our sins, from the principalities and powers which control and manoeuvre us, is a prerequisite; but freedom for us as Christians is to have the courage to give ourselves to helping to bring forth the life possibilities of situations which confront us.

Therefore, for us, life-style is the commitment-focus and expression of our Christian convictions, personally shaped by us as disciples, responsible to the judgement and grace of God, rather than by the values of society around us. Our ability to discern what are the attitudes and actions which will lead toward the life God intends for us all, and the courage to see them through, will be gifts of God's grace and products of our faithful efforts as free persons in Christ.

IV. AUTHORITY

Crucial to the whole issue is the question of **authority**. For us as Christians, as members in a Believers' Church, our Lord is Jesus Christ, the supreme revelation of the will of God for His world, our example, our Saviour and our Master. Jesus Christ is Lord of all and to Him must be rendered obedience in all things. Whether or not we follow through adequately on that confession is a question which leads more to penitence than satisfaction; but in Him we find our definition of the meaning and purpose of life.

Along with this affirmation of faith, we as Baptists take the scriptures as our one authority in matters of faith and practice. Our stance is that neither church court nor creed, but only the scriptures shall tell us what to believe or how to behave. The guidance, image and inspiration we need as Christians are to be found first in the Bible, especially in the revelation we are given there of Jesus Christ our Lord.

The authority of Christ and scripture will come to us with the help of the Christian fellowship of which we are part. Studying the Word of God together, seeking the will of God together and helping one another to make decisions of Christian life-style will enable us to be faithful disciples. As Baptists, it is a fair observation to make that we have not been strong on the group process of enabling one another to make specific, practical decisions for living in an affluent society, although our polity makes the possibilities real and lively.

Therefore, under the Lordship of Christ, guided by the scriptures, working out the process of discernment and decision-making within the fellowship of faith, and aware of the needs both spiritual and material of the world around us, we proceed to design our life-style as Christians in an affluent society. We have to wrestle with the world as we know it. We have to live in it, even if there are ways in which we are to be not of it. But we take our instructions first from the revelations of our faith, because we believe that God is still in charge.

V. GUIDELINES

Based on all this, the parameters of a Christian life-style in an affluent society may be delineated.

1. First, **trust God** and make your choices accordingly. Jesus says to us:

> Do not store up riches for yourselves here on earth, where moths and
> rust destroy, and robbers break in and steal. Instead, store up
> riches for yourselves in heaven, where moths and rust cannot
> destroy, and robbers cannot break in and steal. For your heart will
> always be where your riches are...You cannot serve both God and
> money. This is why I tell you not to be worried about the food and drink
> you need in order to stay alive...Look at the birds flying around: they
> do not sow seeds, gather a harvest and put it in barns; yet your Father
> in heaven takes care of them...So do not start worrying: 'where will my
> food come from? or my drink? or my clothes?' (These are the things
> the pagans are always concerned about.) Your Father in heaven

knows that you need all these things. Instead, be concerned above everything else with the Kingdom of God and with what he requires of you, and he will provide you with all these other things. (Matthew 6: 19-21, 24b-25a, 26-27, 31-33 TEV)

2. Second, be responsible **stewards** of God's creation...including your own resources...enhancing, using, sharing, giving, because you are accountable to the Lord for all that you have been given, both spiritual and material. Paul has written:

> ...God is able to give you more than you need, so that you will always have all you need for yourselves and more than enough for every good cause. As the scripture says, 'He gives generously to the needy; his kindness lasts for ever.' And God, who supplies seed to sow and bread to eat, will also supply you with all the seed you need and will make it grow and produce a rich harvest from your generosity. He will always make you rich enough to be generous at all times, so that many will thank God for your gifts.... (II Corinthians 9: 8-11 TEV)

3. Third, deliberately accept the role of a **servant** committed to love, justice and neighbouring. Love is "putting on one's neighbour" — which means to stand within the situation, feelings and thoughts of those on whom you are focussed and to make your strength, understanding and resources available to them. Jesus' example and words are clear:

> If one of you wants to be great, he must be the servant of the rest; and if one of your wants to be first, he must be your slave — like the Son of Man, who did not come to be served, but to serve and to give his life to redeem many people. (Matthew 20: 26b-28 TEV)

4. Fourth, use your talents, your gifts, your resources to be a **transforming agent** in the world. Give yourself to make a creative or redeeming difference, taking your measure of possibilities not from the current economic indicators but from the leading of God. And, in the final analysis, we will be judged by what we have done to redeem the times:

> When the Son of Man comes as King...he will say to the people on his right, 'Come, you that are blessed by my Father! Come and possess the Kingdom...I was hungry and you fed me, thirsty and you gave me a drink; I was a stranger and you received me in your homes, naked and you clothed me; I was sick and you took care of me, in prison and you visited me...I tell you, whenever you did this for one of the least important of these brothers of mine, you did it for me.'
> (Matthew 25: 31a, 34a, 35-36, 40b TEV)

With these guidelines, we can then begin to shape the specific actions of our days. We will re-evaluate our talents and turn them over to the Lord's purposes in our choices of employment and voluntary service. We will re-assess our use of the monetary and material resources we have at our disposal. We will choose meaningful, transforming ways of enabling others, near and far, to have a better share of God's gifts.

But in an affluent society faced by so much poverty, sacrificial adjustments we have not had to consider before are going to be required of us. Someone has said, "A floor under poverty cannot be achieved without a ceiling over affluence." Squirm as we might to try to avoid the logic of this fact, the time has come for us as Christians to adopt it as a responsible attitude and commitment in the world. Our standard of expectations has to be tempered in order that the poor person's expectations in the third world might be more hopeful.

VI. A CHRISTIAN STANDARD OF LIVING

What is a maximum standard of living for us as morally responsible Christians in our kind of world? Accustomed as we are to thinking that the sky is the limit and that one of our freedoms is to acquire as much as we want, this is a tough question. It is a difficult question because we are constantly being urged to increase our standard of living, rust and moth notwithstanding. Both advertisers and economic pundits are calling us to do better, to spend, purchase and consume more.

The irony of it all it that we **are** being persuaded to cut back some — by the need to conserve energy, the need to fight inflation and the need to make fewer demands on natural resources — but it is because of economic necessity more than noble principle. Persons are needed who will measure their life-style according to the needs of others and the wise husbanding of what God has given to all of us. And surely that means that Christians should lead the way in sharing!

What is a maximum for us? When is enough enough? In reality, it will require personal answers of considerable variety. But perhaps questions such as these can lead us toward our answers:

Do I need it?
Do I need that many or one that large?
Am I trying to be unnecessarily conspicuous?
Am I being greedy?
Am I letting things or money be too important in my life?
Am I being lazy and could I do it in a less energy-consuming way?
Will it lead to minimum waste?
Could I share ownership, borrow or rent it instead?
Is this way kind to God's earth?
Will it have a negative or positive effect on my neighbours,
    wherever they are in the world?

In the final analysis, I suspect we have reached the maximum level for a person with a conscience under God, (1) when we have reached the point of excess and waste, and (2) when we are trusting equipment and purchasing power for the salvation of our days. Somewhere below that ceiling is enough.

There are difficult choices to be made in the near future — by governments, by people who buy and sell, by people who produce and consume, and by young people choosing futures. But, important among them, there are tremendously significant choices to be made by Christians.

The changes we make in our spending patterns, the decisions we make to live more simply and share what we have with others, may make only a small material difference in the economic scheme of things. But our cause is in the field of attitudes and values; our calling is to keep alive a sense of proportion and to propose to others a more humane perspective. There is power in the commitment of lives placed fully at the disposal of God and others. There will still be the need to work for changes in public policy, but we must never underestimate the effectiveness of the leaven of a Christian life-style.

We who live in the affluent society are very aware of the riches which surround us. What we have yet to discern adequately are the tremendous resources of the spirit which we share — and which, by God's grace and our faithfulness, could effect more redemptive changes than we have recognized. The challenge to us is to choose a life-style which is expressive of the purposes of Christ for our imbalanced world.

CHRISTIAN LIFE-STYLE
IN AN AFFLUENT SOCIETY

Erwin Wiens

I. INTRODUCTION

A. Definition. Life-style is the ongoing visible, outward expression of an inner value base or value system.

B. Assumptions. 1. In a discussion of life-style, the focus must be on the underlying value base. Life-style cannot be pursued or evaluated as an end in itself.

2. There is an ultimate, universal value base. It will be referred to in this paper as God's value base or God's value system.

3. The fullest expression of God's value system which man can relate to is in the person and teachings of Jesus Christ. **Christian**, in this paper, refers to people who have an ongoing commitment of obedience to God's value system as expressed in and by Jesus Christ.

4. Because of the Christian's commitment to God's value system, the resulting life-style will be significantly different from that which is prevalent in society, for society at large is considered to be in a state of sin or rebellion against God's value system.

5. The question of what is Christian life-style must not be limited to economic factors as is often implied in discussions of the question.

Also, since God's value system is universal, Christian life-style is not a question limited to an affluent society. Living in an affluent society, does, however, increase the number of choices and decisions for the Christian. This freedom of extensive choice is one of the greatest challenges for affluent Christians.

C. A Story about the Prodigal Father, Business Man, Professor and Community. And behold, a man had an only son, of whom he was justly proud. And he heard many voices saying, "Father, make sure you give him the share of life that he has coming to him." So the father worked hard to give the son every opportunity to make good in life. He sent him to a distant university, and there the son eventually graduated from the school of graduate studies.

But after he graduated, the son experienced a great emptiness. The fulfillment of life he had hoped for just did not come to him. He tried to obliterate his sorrow with ever increasing amounts of stimulants and depressants until he ended up living in an oblivious stupor.

A business man passed by, saw his condition and said to himself, "Fortunately, we have the Ministry of Social Services to look after people with his needs. After all, that's what I pay my taxes for."

Next, an associate professor and his wife passed by, and she said "Isn't it disgusting how lazy people are these days? They just don't care." And they hurried on to his speaking engagement, for he was a distinguished lecturer, and she basked in his status.

But when the son came to himself he said, "Surely there is more than this to give my life to. I will arise and go to my Maker and say, 'Treat me as one of your servants.' "

Now when the people of his community saw that he left his home and profession and enthusiastically volunteered to work in a service organization, some said "Isn't it wonderful! If we didn't have children in school, we would like to do something like that too." Others said, "He is a fanatic!" But the father wondered "Is this what I raised my son for?"

II. SETTING THE STAGE

A. Those who want to be rich fall into temptations and snares and many foolish harmful desires which plunge men into ruin and perdition (I Timothy 6:9).

Man cannot live in a valueless state. Ever since man's original rebellion against God's value system, he has based his actions on values that are, at least initially, more attractive and seemingly easier to live with.

The most widely accepted value base in the world today is man's material standard of living. In western capitalistic society, individual and corporate economic growth are espoused as the highest good. Increased peace and happiness will apparently come from an increased standard of living.

Marxists claim that economic factors are the ultimate causal factors of history. Good and evil are measured by the relative distribution of material wealth. Even for the people of the developing nations, economic growth and the resulting materialism have been held up before them as the magic carrot which will eliminate all their problems, to such an extent that striving after an increased material standard of living is as intense in Lusaka as in London and as blatant in Nairobi as in New York.

This prevailing world wide value base, which may be paraphrased as "seek first to improve and consolidate your material standard of living and all these other things will be added unto you," has an almost irresistible appeal, for it eliminates the long-standing ethical burdens of responsibility and accountability. Lord Keynes, one of the great prophets of this value base, predicted that the time when man shall once more value ends above means and prefer the good above the useful is still some time down the road of history. For the present "we must pretend to ourselves and to everyone that fair is foul and foul is fair; for foul is useful and fair is not. Avarice and usury and precaution must be our gods a little longer still. For only they can lead us out of the tunnel of economic necessity into daylight."[1]

·In recent years there have been ample warnings of the physical, environmental and sociological impossibility of continuing the present pursuit of an ever increasing material standard of living. One of the most pessimistic, yet powerfully persuasive documents is the Club of Rome's project on the Predicament of Mankind.[2] This scholarly study suggests that unless there are drastic changes in the basic behaviour mode of the world system we are well on the road to a world society where industrial production has ceased, where population has suffered catastrophic decline and where air, sea and land are polluted beyond human redemption. At best we can say there is no evidence that an increased material standard of living has increased personal and communal satisfaction. Even though Canadians have one of the highest standards of living, public media reports and a great deal of private conversation would have one believe that Canadians are some of the most deprived people in the world.

    B. You do not get what you want, because you do not pray for it. Or, if you do, your requests are not granted because you pray from wrong motives, to spend what you get on your pleasures (James 4:3).

The Christian, in this setting, finds himself in a constant state of tension. Having made a commitment to God's value system, he finds the prevailing world system continues to call to him for attention and commitment. Some Christian groups and individuals have tried to deal with this tension by withdrawing as much as possible from society and by setting rigid regulations to control life-styles. Most Christians, however, continue to live actively in society. Many do not see in their Christianity a value base which is significantly different from that of society's. Society at large may be viewed by them as "Christian" and therefore societal values become acceptable. This experience may result in conformity to a selected set of do's and dont's, influencing certain areas of life-style but leaving large areas of life untouched and unchanged.

    For the number of Christians who continue to live actively in society, there is a very real danger of being caught in the runaway stampede of society, spurred on by the ceaseless cries of the ad men and by the fear of failure to come in with the rest of the crowd when the economic race of life has been run.

III. GOD'S VALUE SYSTEM AND ITS EXPRESSION IN THE LIVES OF BELIEVERS

    A. Justice and Love. According to the scriptural account, two outstanding values characterize God's dealings with mankind: justice and love. These two values are in fact identified as integral parts of the nature of God. Jesus identifies them as the basis for His followers' life-style in two of the imperatives He gives to His disciples. At the climax of the Sermon on the Mount, Jesus exhorts His followers: "Set your minds on God's Kingdom and His justice before everything else and all the rest will come to you as well" (Matthew 6:33).[3] And in response to a lawyer's question, Jesus implies that our total obligations to life can be summed up with the commitment: "Love the Lord your God with all your heart, with all your soul, with all your mind" and "love your neighbour as yourself" (Matthew 22:37-39).

    It would have been much easier if Jesus had left His followers a detailed list of rules to follow, but instead of regimentation, God's creativeness comes through in these most basic values which Jesus lays down as the basis for life-style. To seek, to strive earnestly, to be concerned above everything else with bringing about God's kingship of love and justice over every situation is the disciple's ultimate objective, and this objective becomes applicable in every human society and in every time period.

By using parables to illustrate His teachings, Jesus drives home the fact that once we have made a commitment to God's Kingdom or God's value system, it permeates every area of life. There can be no separation between the secular, the sacred, the physical and the spiritual in Christian life-style. Increasingly, every decision, every action and reaction of the Christian are determined by the values of love and justice. "The Kingdom of Heaven is like yeast, which a woman took and mixed with half a hundredweight of flour till it was **all** leavened" (Matthew 13:3).

B. Non-Conformity, Joyful Abandonment and Freedom from Anxious Worry. God's value system is a new order set in juxtaposition to the values of this world. Jesus said, "My kingdom does not belong to this world" (John 18:36). The apostle John, writing to Christians, encourages them not to love the world for "any one who loves the world, is a stranger to the Father's love" (I John 2:15). Writing to the Romans, Paul emphasizes this dichotomy: "Adapt yourselves no longer to this present world, but let your minds be remade..." (Romans 12:2).

One characteristic of Christian lifestyle, then, is non-conformity to worldly values, because of the Christian's commitment to God's kingdom. The immediate question arises about how this separation finds expression in the life of the believers.

According to Jesus' stories about the buried treasure and the pearl merchant (Matthew 13:44-46), once the importance of God's values has been discovered, it is worth giving up everything else for them. In fact, Jesus insists that a disciple must be willing to sacrifice to the point of risking his life: "Whoever care for his own safety is lost; but if a man will let himself be lost for my sake, he will find his true self" (Matthew 16:25). This requirement of giving up everything in the interest of true love and justice is not to be seen as an unbearable burden, but rather a joyful abandonment of worldly securities for the sake of obedience to kingdom values. The man who found the buried treasure "for sheer joy went and sold everything he had, and bought the field" (Matthew 13:44).

Another characteristic, then, of Christian life-style is the joyful abandonment of all societal values and securities because of the confidence that one possesses a treasure of far greater value.

It is interesting to note that Jesus' value-setting statement on seeking the kingdom of God and His justice is found in the midst of His discussion of the material necessities of life. Jesus acknowledges the need for food, clothing and shelter. God is obviously interested in them for He is their creator. However, these material needs must never become the focus of the disciple's being. They are not primary: they are secondary. In fact, Jesus implies that they are a by-product of striving after God's values.

The heathen, the people of this world, strive after these things, yet, as we have already seen, by their very striving they are rapidly causing a situation where these things may no longer be available to them.

Jesus insists that His followers refrain from anxious worry about their material needs. Paul writing to Timothy says, "If we have food and covering we may rest content." Contentment then, or the absence of anxiety over the material standard of living, is another outstanding characteristic of Christian life-style.

C. The Story of the Respectable Young Church Member. A respected young member of a local church came to Jesus saying, "Teacher, I have observed all that is expected of me in this church. I teach Sunday School and even serve on the church council. What do I still lack? What goals must I do to live a truly Christian life-style in this affluent society?"

Jesus said to him, "If you would be perfect, go, sell what you possess and give to the poor, and you will have treasure in heaven; and come and follow me."

But when the young man heard this, he began to justify himself saying, "Lord, I really don't have much capital. Most of my assets have been signed over as security to the bank. And, I am following you already. Didn't I go to the Holy Land with my pastor and other leading members of our conference? Didn't I get a better appreciation for your life there? I even challenged others for you when I showed my slides in churches. But you don't really expect me to sell all I have, do you? It just wouldn't be right for me to become a welfare case when I retire! I promise, though, that I will give more to my church building fund and I will be more faithful in witnessing for you. But to sell everything and to spend my life following you just isn't a very logical thing to do. You do expect us to use our common sense, don't you?"

And the Lord went away sorrowful, for he had some great plans for this man's gifts and energies.

D. Right Relationships. Justice and love, the basis for Christian life-style, refer to relational conditions. Neither justice nor love can occur in a situation of extreme inividualism. God recognized that it was not good that man should be alone so He made him a partner and gave them the ability to bear children. In this way the stage was set for the development of just and loving relationships between persons, just as God already had a just and loving relationship with His creation.

When, however, the relationship between God and His creature was interrupted by an extreme desire for individual assertion, it also resulted in ruptured relationships between persons. Now with the redemptive work of Jesus Christ having re-established the right relationship between God and men, it is also imperative to build up right relationships between men. In fact, the development of right relationships is the behavioural objective of Christian life-style. This is not to deny a Christian's individualism, or even the need to develop that individual uniqueness. However, all individual development most eventually lead to the development of more just and loving relationships with other individuals. Any action, therefore, which does not have as its ultimate objective the building of right relationships, cannot be a part of Christian life-style.

It is incredibly easy to talk about love and even to think that it is being practised by the generation of certain feelings and emotions. God always combines love with justice and justice is more than a feeling. It demands right actions. The problem is not a modern one. The apostle John brought it to his readers' attention: "It is by this that we know what love is: that Christ laid down His life for us. And we in our turn are bound to lay down our lives for our brothers. But if a man has enough to live one, and yet when he sees his brother in need shuts up his heart against him, how can it be said that the divine love dwells in him?" (I John 3: 16, 17).

Volumes could be written on the application of these words to this generation. One of the best recent studies is Ronald Sider's **Rich Christians in an Age of Hunger.** Sider makes a particularly powerful case for God's interest in and identification with the poor. Nobody in Canada can plead ignorance of the gap that exists between our level of affluence and the needs of a large majority of the world's population. Nor are those who lack the necessities of life ignorant of our abundance. A certain level of relationship has been established between all the world's people by mass communication. It is up to us as Christians to make this a just and loving relationship.

For those of us who claim to have the love of God abiding in us, how can we better testify to it than to share ourselves totally with our brothers and sisters who are in need? "Let us not love in word or speech, but in deed and truth" (I John 3: 18).

E. The Story of Gitau. A tour group booked into the Nairobi Hilton. The members were clothed in the finest Pierre Cardin fashions and each night at dinner they dined elegantly on the superb cuisine of the Simba Room. On Tuesday morning their limousine picked them up for a tour of Mathare Valley, for they were anxious to see the poverty of Africa.

Meanwhile, each morning, a grandmother named Gitau propped her shriveled body against the rusty strips of tin on the east side of her family's dwelling and watched the mostly naked children squabble and play among the hovels of Mathare Valley. She felt content this morning as the sun gradually brought warmth to numb limbs. Mathai, her son, had again found employment and there would be enough **ugali** for the family tonight. What joy to have a caring, supportive family with numerous grandchildren in one's old age.

The clamour of the children brought her to attention. A group of foreigners was coming through the shanty town, cameras clicking as they carefully manoeuvered their ample frames through the debris and mud so as not to get their white loafers soiled. As they passed within a metre of Gitau she felt a sudden nausea which soon gave way to a violent vomitting spell. Was it another attack resulting from her chronic **billharzia,** or was it the overpowering odour of the strangers' deodorant, perfume, hairspray and after-shave lotion? Moreover, the dogs soon came to clean up the mess.

That night Gitau died and was carried by the angels into Jesus' presence. Eventually the tourists also died, knocked on heaven's door and called, "Lord, Lord, did we not give large amounts of money to your work? We visited the mission field and told many people about you." Then he will answer them, "Anything you did not do for one of these, however humble, you did not do for me. For not everyone who calls me 'Lord, Lord' will enter the kingdom of Heaven, but only those who do the will of my heavenly Father" (Matthew 25: 45 and 7: 21).

IV. MODELS FOR CHRISTIAN LIFE-STYLE

In the search for meaningful Christian life-style, it is helpful to identify and examine certain models. It is difficult to identify individuals as models of Christian life-style. This is due possibly to personal modesty and embarrassment at being singled out. Also, if our earlier assumption that Christian life-style must be relational is correct, then individuals cannot serve as models and we can only look at Christian life-style models in the context of Christians in fellowship and community.

A. Living in Closed Communities. One of the characteristics of the Radical Reformation of the sixteenth century was the development of unique life-styles based on a literal interpretation of the Sermon on the Mount. Along with the Radical Reformers' emphasis on the separation of church and state came also the concept of the separation of believers from worldly society. This separation was often forced upon the Anabaptists and other groups of the left wing of the Reformation by intense persecution by moderate Reformers or the Roman Catholic Church.

The early concept of the separation of the believer from the world resulted in the development of numerous closed communities over the succeeding centuries, including the Hutterites and Amish of the seventeenth century and more recently the emergence of Old Order and Old Colony Mennonites.

Each of these groups has developed for its members a unique, integrated life-style which has become a folk culture. Separation from the world or society is of utmost importance for each group. Oral traditions and conventions are important in maintaining unity and uniformity, and each group maintains a high degree of discipline. Mutual aid within the group is both an important obligation and a privilege, and as a result, most state aid is refused.

There is a great deal in these communities that is admirable from the standpoint of Christian life-style. The rejection of society's value system, the security that comes from mutual responsibility and caring, and generally the recognition of things other than economic as being primary in life are outstanding characteristics of this Christian life-style.

Over the years, though, there have developed serious paradoxical problems which are evident to some degree in each of the above mentioned groups. Calvin Redekop proposes that "the greater the achievement of the original Anabaptist charter on an empirical level of behaviour, the greater the negation of the intent of the charter."[5] In each of these groups, the religion of the community permeates the life of the members so completely that some of the very reasons for rejecting the state religion have become a characteristic of the communities.

It can hardly be said, for example, that voluntary adult membership actually exists in any of the above mentioned communities. Thus a Hutterite or Amish youngster who grows up within the closed community naturally becomes a member of the church community as routinely as in a society which has a **Volkskirche**. Also, with the community's total rejection of involvement in social affairs, the clergy and the establishment within the community become the authority in individual life to such an extent that their authority and power to coerce are often as great or greater than that of the state in secular society, and thus the church again becomes the state.

For members of these closed communities, life-style, then, may very easily become a conformation to the values of a little society within a larger society, rather than the result of a joyful, willing submission of obedience to the Lordship of Jesus Christ over every area of life.

The histories of traditional Anabaptist Christian communities has some important things to say about Christian life-style. Yet since the body of Christ is made up of many members and every member has a unique function, it will not be possible for all Christians to fit into the Hutterite or Amish mold. The New Testament implies that Christian lifestyle is dynamic, and just as there is a variety of gifts, there will also be a variety of expressions as the gifts are used.

The decisive question is not which model all believers must follow, but rather one of ongoing personal and corporate obedience to the will of God in every situation.

B. Some Contemporary Models. It is extremely difficult for Christians to build just and loving relationships in relatively large groups where personal accountability to and liability for brothers and sisters is almost totally lacking. Within recent years, numerous groups of Christians have sought to implement viable alternative communities in which to work out uniquely Christian life-styles. Some have tried to develop cell groups, house churches, or mission groups within the context of the more formal traditional church structures, while others have separated themselves entirely from the traditional structures and developed their own setting for communities of believers.

A helpful, popular study of the movement toward more meaningful Christian community, with a number of case studies, is Dave and Neta Jackson's book, **Living Together in a World Falling Apart**.[6] Feelings of alienation and isolation in the traditional church structures, along with an intense desire to be obedient to the total teachings of the gospel are important motivations identified by the Jacksons in this move toward new forms of community. Of the communities which the Jacksons describe, all emphasize a value system radically different from that of society, a considerable degree of accountability to and liability for members of the community, with several practising total sharing of possessions and in all but possibly one case, an intense desire to bring about healing and wholeness to broken lives.

Of the thousands of small groups springing up in churches today, many have little lasting value because people commit themselves to each other in limited areas of life only. A few such as Reba Place in Evanston, Illinois or the mission groups of the Church of the Saviour in Washington, D.C. have grown for 20 or 30 years now, but even these represent rather tenuous models and it may be too early to evaluate their significance as agents of change in developing Christian life-style in the wider context of the Christian church.

V. SOME SUGGESTIONS FOR IMPLEMENTING CHRISTIAN LIFE-STYLE

1. Resign from the security of your job and offer your services to a mission board, a voluntary service agency, or ask the Lord to identify a totally new role He may have for you. If you are unemployed, consider similar service opportunities.

2. Adopt as an integral part of your nuclear and extended family, a foreign student, an immigrant family, a native Canadian or a handicapped child.

3. Make a list of your occupational and domestic activities. Identify any activities that are not actively or at least indirectly developing a relationship between yourself and other persons, and then resolve to remove those activities from your life.

4. Name the persons with whom your activities are building just and loving relationships.

5. Attempt to identify the impression you are seeking to make upon the people you meet today. Will they be able to recognize your basic values of justice and love in your actions and reactions?

6. Group your possessions into several broad categories such as wardrobe, furniture, house or apartment and transportation. Identify those you might have obtained due to the pressure of advertising or conformity to present fads. Decide what to do with them. Don't be afraid to cut back or scale down for God's sake.

7. If in your insomnia, nervous stomach or tension headaches, you recognize anxious worry about your material necessities, resolve to be obedient to Jesus' command not to be anxious. Look at your own history and recognize God's faithful provision. Increase the giving of your time, efforts and money to the needs of others, for in doing so, the material needs will fall into their proper perspective.

8. Don't just take your surplus to second-hand and thrift stores. Make some of your purchases there as well. If you are concerned that you are denying the poor by doing so, question whether you really need all your income.

9. Think of fellow Christians as brothers and sisters and feel free to relate to them and even address them as such. Be careful not to give place to title and rank in your own action or in reaction to others; for to be a respector of persons is neither loving nor just.

THE PROBLEM OF JUSTICE IN THE BELIEVERS' CHURCH TRADITION

Conrad G. Brunk

The record of social concern and service to humanity among the churches identified with the Believers' Church movement is a laudable one. The role of Methodists and Quakers in the movement for the abolition of slavery in both England and North America, and the world-wide relief efforts of Baptists, Brethren, Mennonites and Quakers are outstanding testimonials to the centrality of social concern in Believers' Church theology.[1]

At the same time, this service has been carried out within the context of a theology, and an ethic intrinsic to that theology, which creates a peculiar dilemma for the churches practicing it. It is this theological and ethical dilemma which I wish to explore in this essay. It is basically the dilemma between a view of the relationship between the church and the world, and a view of the social responsibility of the church in the world. In traditional theological parlance, it is the dilemma between the radical demands of the New Testament standard of **agape** and the demands of justice.

I propose to examine this dilemma from the point of view of the social service concerns of the Believers' Churches, and to put forward some proposals for an ethic of Christian social responsibility which will move towards the resolution of this dilemma. Such an ethic, I will suggest, must take more seriously some fundamental requirements of justice which are implicit in the concept of Christian **agape** itself. There cannot be a Christian social concern consistent with the radical demands of New Testament love which is not also guided by certain considerations of justice. The theology which tends to predominate within the tradition known as the Believers' Church has not, in my opinion, taken these considerations seriously enough.

Because the Believers' Church movement is a multi-faceted one with a rich and varied history, any generalizations about "its" ethics or theology will inevitably fail to assess accurately certain elements of the movement which move in other directions. This will certainly be true of some of the generalizations which follow in this paper. Nevertheless, the ethical outlook underlying the traditional involvement of the Believers' Churches in social service activities is, I believe, fairly generally shared across the movement. The differences between denominations within the movement, such as exists on the issue of peace and non-resistance, for example, really do not cut to the level of the basic ethical outlook which informs the question of social responsibility.

For the most part, it can be said that the service emphasis of the mainstream in the Believers' Church movement is based, not on a sense of the church's responsibility to preside over the affairs of the society in which it is immersed, either as priest or governor, but on a sense of obedience to the New Testament injunctions to concern oneself with the suffering and the needs of one's neighbour. The command to love one's neighbour as oneself is understood in the positive sense of service to neighbour as Jesus indicated in his parable of the Good Samaritan. Service is understood as required by the discipline of the individual believer to the standards of Christ-likeness, not as a mission of the church to redeem society itself or mold it in the direction of a more "Christian" order.

Thus, the social ethic of the Believers' Church is rooted firmly in what Ernst Troeltsch has termed the "sectarian" understanding of the church, as opposed to the "churchly" understanding.[2] The sect-type of religious order, according to Troeltsch, is characterized by a sense of radical separation between the church and the world. It is called out as a separate order from the fallen secular society to follow the hard demands of discipleship which cannot be expected of the world. In the sectarian view there is no expectation that the church is called to be a universal social phenomenon. Unlike the ethical stance characteristic of what Troeltsch calls the "church-type," the sectarian church does not perceive its task to be the creation and maintenance of a just or even tolerable social order. It rejects any "theocratic" notions of the state whereby the church presides over a uniquely "Christian" society, with the full coercive power of the law behind it.

Sectarian theology makes a clear distinction between the ethic to which the church is called and that which can be expected of secular society. While the ethical standard for the church is that of the radical New Testament ideal of sacrificial love, the standard for the secular society is the less demanding one of justice, or, as Reinhold Niebuhr called it, the "tolerable balance of egoisms." This standard of justice is perceived variously as being either divinely ordained for the secular order, yet "outside the perfection of Christ,"[3] or as discernible through nature or reason. However discerned, the sectarian attitude towards the moral ordering of society is that it is not the focus of the church's mission **qua** church.

There is, of course, divergence of opinion among various elements of the Believers' Church tradition on the question of the relationships of the individual Christian to this dual standard. The Anabaptists, for example, traditionally required the rejection by each member in the fellowship of all participation in the political affairs of secular society, especially those judged incompatible with the absolute demands of Christian love. The "agapeistic" standard applied to all levels of Christian activity, both individual and corporate, within and without the church. For the Anabaptists, the church had no foundation from which to make moral judgements about the social institutions of a fallen order, nor did individuals within the church have any such foundation.

Other groups within the Believers' Church movement do not apply the sectarian dualism this broadly. While they accept, with the Anabaptists, the dual standard of love and justice and the full conformity of the church as an institution to the former, they are willing to permit, even encourage, the participation of individual church members in the business of social ordering, according to the norms of the latter standard. This interpretation of the sectarian social ethic relies on the distinction between the level of individual behaviour governed by the norm of absolute **agape** and the level of social institutional behaviour governed by the lesser norms of justice. **Qua** individual actor, the believer is bound by the New Testament norms, but **qua** citizen in the secular **polis** he is subject to the norms of justice.

This latter dualism, a form of individualist pietism, rejects with the Anabaptist tradition the idea that a uniquely Christian norm of justice should govern the social order. Hence. the Christian politician carries with him in his role as citizen or politician no ideal of justice which he draws from his commitment to Christian discipleship. The standard of political behaviour is not that which governs his life an an individual nor that which governs the church. At best the Christian as responsible citizen relies upon the virtues of individual discipleship (e.g., integrity, prayerfulness, humility, purity, temperance, kindness, etc.) to have a positive moral influence on the character of the political order. To the extent that politicians are Christians also, to this extent can the political order be expected to be more "Christian," but "Christian" only in the sense that it will promote the individual Christian virtues, like those mentioned, in the society generally.

It is not surprising, then, to find that Believers' Church members have tended to be much more politically vocal on issues of personal morality such as pornography, abortion, Sabbath observance, and "morals legislation" generally than they are on structural issues of international order, distributive justice or civil liberties.

Nor should it be surprising to find Believers' Church Christians, where they do take strong stands on issues of foreign policy and economics in the political sector, affirming the kinds of policies which would seem to be furthest from the requirements of New Testament love which they would affirm as normative for themselves as individuals. Thus, it is not unusual to find pacifist Mennonite members of parliament, for example, among the strongest supporters of the death penalty in our criminal justice system.

Recently, I was asked by a friend to work in the campaign of a local member of a prominent Believers' Church. Since I did not know the candidate personally, I asked my friend what the candidate's views were on a number of political issues. The response was a good example of the traditional pietist position. My friend confessed he did not know for sure what the candidate's views were on national unity, northern development, capital punishment, or Canada's military and defence policy, but he knew him as an active member of his church who was honest, serious and a conscientious student of the Bible, who could be counted on to give prayerful consideration to these issues. I told my friend, for reasons I shall try to clarify below, that I would withhold my support until I knew to what conclusions on these important social matters his candidate's prayers and Bible study had led him.

In a recent article entitled "President Carter as Baptist Leader," Princeton professor Richard Schaull has commented on this aspect of Carter's perception of his moral task as United States President. Carter stressed throughout his campaign the need for new leadership in the White House, and he recommended himself as follows: "I cling to the principles of the Judeo-Christian ethic. Honesty, integrity, compassion, love, hope, charity and humility are integral parts of any person's life."[4] Shaull comments that despite Carter's high hopes for ministering to the country's poor and unemployed and for building world peace, his naive reliance on his own personal qualities as a Christian leader will not bring success. Given Carter's theology of institutions, which sees "Spirit-filled individuals create and maintain religious and political institutions with faith and commitment, but with little or no concern for radical criticism of and eternal vigilance over those institutions," the explanation for the failure of these institutions will be that the "right people are not in charge...not that there is something fundamentally wrong with the structure itself." This outlook, says Shaull, "when espoused by evangelical Christians in positions of security and privilege, carries with it the belief that justice can be established without transforming the structures which can create injustice."[5]

This outlook, it seems to me, is characteristic of the approach of the Believers' Church to social service generally. The imperatives to feed the hungry, to heal the sick, to visit those in prison, to be a "neighbour" to those in need, which underlie and motivate the social concern of the church, are seen to derive from the ethic of love, not from the ethic of justice. It is guided by the ideal of sacrificial giving to those in need, not by principles of fair distributions of power, opportunity or social welfare. Charity is the attitude which prevails, rather than a sense of justice. Social action means doing something **for** people in the social structure rather than doing someting **to** the structure itself, **with** the people.

This, of course, is a consistent expression of the sectarian dualism underlying the Believers' Church ethic. The norm of New Testament love is distinguished from the norm of justice just because the latter entails the ordering and reordering of power relationships as defined by political and economic institutions, and the use of coercive power which this entails. Since **agape** is understood precisely as a renunciation of power, there is no possibility of a common unity of a service of love and a service of justice.

Thus, the social concern of the church must be expressed in apolitical modes. It seeks to move within the structures of power to do its charitable work while leaving them intact and subjecting them to no more than implied criticisms. It confronts need with aid, but it does not confront power with new power. Indeed, it has become virtually a commonplace in North American Protestantism to hold that the church ought not to be "political" in its judgements or its activity. Whenever the social service agencies of the churches appear to take sides on political matters, or engage in activities which touch off a political reaction the cry goes up across their constituencies that the church is becoming illegitimately involved in politics.

The work of the Mennonite Central Committee of the Mennonite churches in Canada as well as in the United States is a clear example of this kind of problem. MCC has long found it more comfortable to provide humanitarian relief to victims of natural disasters than to victims of social disasters, though it has been involved in both. Certainly this is due to the fact that aid rendered to the former group does not carry the implied critique of human power structures which is implied either implicitly or explicitly in aid rendered to the latter group. Consequently, Mennonite Disaster Service has enjoyed virtually unqualified support by the Mennonite constituency in North America, but the recent involvements of MCC (Canada) in aid to Vietnam, in Native People's concerns, and in offender ministries, for example, have brought sharp criticism of the "politicization" of the church from across the church.

The reason is not hard to find. The latter kind of involvements, unlike the former, have immediate political implications which are difficult if not imposible to avoid. Sending medical aid to a socialist Vietnam, recommending and supervising the parole of a criminal offender, working for the preservation of a native culture threatened by a pipeline development, are all activities which have a clearly discernible political significance. They appear to take a position in political matters in a way that rebuilding a house shattered by an earthquake does not.

However, what the church needs to recognize is that it is **appearances** which are largely at issue here, not political reality. This is due to the fact that acts of social beneficence can rarely be said to be entirely a-political. This is especially true when those actions are directed at the mitigation of suffering and need which result from human institutional arrangements. It is widely recognized that acts of charity to the poor, the downtrodden and the oppressed often have the consequence of reinforcing the social structures which produce these results. The attempt to be a "peacemaker," where this is understood solely in terms of minimizing violence or overt conflict, is in many instances to affirm the existing distributions of power which is being threatened by the conflict. In cases such as these, the church's attempts to follow the ideals of sacrificial love are "political" acts in the fullest sense of the term.

Thus, the social involvements which we perceive as politically "neutral" may well be nothing more than involvements which accord with our tacit understandings of what is politically right; and those we perceive as too "political" on the part of the church are really those which run counter to our own individual political prejudices. What we object to much of the time, I am afraid, is not that the church is acting as an agent of political justice rather than an agent of love, but that its action threatens political structures we support or in which we have vested interests, or it supports political movements we oppose. Medical aid to a non-communist South Vietnam was not questioned as being "political" by the church constituency of MCC (Canada); medical aid to a communist Vietnam is questioned on these grounds by many. This example serves to illustrate the point clearly. Many others could be given.

What this suggests is that programmes of social concern carried on by the church can rarely, if ever, be neutral vis a vis the question of the justice of the political and economic structures within which these programmes are carried out. It is no more possible to carry out acts of charity independently of considerations of justice than it is to do scientific research independent of a value judgement about what is important to society. An agent of reconciliation who tries to bring peace in a conflict situation without making assumptions about what is a just relationship between the parties is like a marriage counsellor who believes one can resolve marital disputes independently of any normative ideals about the marriage relationship. The sectarian assumption that the work of the church in the area of peace and social concern can be carried out without a norm of social justice, and hence be politically "neutral," is a version of the positivistic outlook which assumes that science, education and technology can be completely "value free." The New Testament ethic of sacrificial love cannot be divorced from the ethic of justice. This is simply because justice is nothing more than the proper distribution of love.

A recent proposal submitted to the Mennonite Central Committee for a "Mennonite Conciliation Service" focuses the dilemma of sectarian dualism sharply. The thrust of the proposal is that the biblical injunctions to be agents of reconciliation should be implemented in the form of some organization within the church which could intervene in "social disasters" with conflict resolution skills. The debate generated within the church by the proposal, and the issues which it raises are instructive. The Conciliation Service proposal marks a departure from traditional Mennonite views about the meaning of the "peace witness" of the church, which generally has taken the form of personal commitment to the principle of "non-resistance."

But the debate over the proposal illustrates the fact that movement away from this basically passive interpretation of the "peace witness" to a more active conception of conciliatory intervention in social conflicts puts increasing strain on the traditional Mennonite dualism. Some of the participants in the debate see a fairly limited role for a Mennonite conciliation activity — that of intervening in crisis situations to prevent the outbreak of violence, and to reduce the hostilities between the parties. Opponents of this view argue that the role of merely "calming troubled waters" in volatile conflict situations places the peacemaker in the position of preserving the status quo in the relationship which has produced the conflict, and merely in order to "keep the peace." True peace can be achieved, they maintain, when this relationship is altered in a manner which solves the conflict in a fair and just way. Peacemaking is not simply a matter of squelching overt violence and hostility. It also may involve active advocacy roles with one party in the conflict, active confrontation of oppressive social forces, hard bargaining backed by coercive sanctions, and the development of reordered political and economic relationships.[6]

It seems evident that this latter view of the peacemaker role reflects the more accepted understanding of the complexities of human conflict. But it also clearly moves beyond the traditional sectarian bias against the church as an agent of social justice. It implies that to be a peacemaker in the world, one must at the same time be an agent of justice. Just as charity must be guided by a conception of what is just, so also must peacemaking. And not only must the peacemaker be guided by an ideal of what a just relationship between parties would be, he must also become involved in the sometimes coercive and forceful means which are necessary to reorder power relationships and social structures which produce the conflict. Thus, the traditional dichotomy of **agape** and justice leads to the paradox that the church cannot be an agent of reconciling love without also being willing to be an agent of justice.

The social concerns of the church cannot escape the question of justice. To the extent that we seem to have skirted around it in the past in our programmes of social concern, to that extent have we merged so completely with the prevailing justice norms of our own cultures that our actions raised no questions of justice. Political or moral "neutrality" is often little more than passive conformity with the prevailing political or moral norms, or even quiet support for them. If the practice of New Testament love is incompatible with the tacit support of oppressive and humanly destructive structures which are rationalized by unloving conceptions of justice, then the church cannot carry on its programmes of social concern without a clear critique of the social structures within which it works and a clear vision of a better order.

The lamentable fact is that as Believers' Churches we have for the most part ignored the issue of justice. Our sectarian renunciation of political responsibility in favour of secular powers has meant a willingness also to relegate to secular sources the task of conceptualizing what a just social order should be. In practice this means that the members of our churches tend to accept the prevailing secular norms of justice as the guide for their own political involvements, if they are politically involved, rather than any conception uniquely informed by biblical norms. So it is these prevailing norms of justice which in turn shape the social services of the church. Any social involvements of the church which threaten the existing power structures are likely to be condemned as "too political" because they run counter to the norms of justice which rationalize these structures.

The pressing agenda for the Believers' Church in the next decade is a church-wide effort involving laity and clergy, professional and nonprofessional, to promote intensive study and formulation of a biblically informed conception of justice. If the church is to become a credible and influential agent of New Testament love in the social arena it must develop a shared vision of a social order which is less oppressive, more fair, and maximizing of human welfare.

A simple preview of the issues which face us as a church in the coming generation cannot but underscore this need. The world now faces a situation of exploding population coupled with a rapid depletion of energy, food and other natural resources. Questions of how these dwindling resources are going to be shared among this expanding population are becoming ever more acute. While we as a Western church have been able up to this point to ignore the mal-distribution of resources on the worldwide scale, we will not be able to ignore it within our own society as the flow of the world's resources to our economies slows and the struggle for increasing shares of a smaller "pie" continues. What does New Testament **agape** tell us about the proper sharing of this pie? Is this merely a "political" question which the church should avoid? Should we merely try to alleviate the worst social consequences resulting from the massive inequalities which will result? Will the church resist the inevitable increase in the use of coercive violence by our military and police which will be necessary to curb the outrage of the expanding corps of the dispossessed, or will we rationalize it in the name of our conventional wisdom about law, order and justice? Does **agape** have any alternative to the "life-boat" ethics being put forward by a vocal cadre of population ethicists who are willing to sacrifice the weak to preserve the strong on our "life-boat earth"?

In Canada does **agape** mean support for preserving the Confederation at all costs? Is national unity the overriding concern of a radical New Testament ethic? Can a reconciling role played by the church in Canada ignore the issue of what a fair economic, political and cultural relationship between French and English Canada would be? What are the legitimate interests a people have in the preservation of a cultural identity, and how ought these interests to be balanced against the cultural and other interests of other parties? How does Christian "social concern" for native peoples balance their cultural interests against the economic interests of southern Canada?

The very asking of these questions points out how far we are as Believers' Churches from taking them seriously, to say nothing of formulating any sort of consensus which stands as a uniquely Christian critique of public policy on these issues. For the most part it is fair to say that the thinking in the church on these matters (as much as goes on "in the church"!) is quite indistinguishable from that which goes on in the larger secular society.

It is my view that the pressing agenda of the Believer's Churches in the remainder of this century should be a reordering of our theology of social concern in a direction which allows us to take the question of justice seriously. We need to develop a concept of the justice-implications of New Testament **agape** which can guide our social involvements. There are a number of areas in which our theology needs reordering. I merely summarize them below as suggested items on the future agenda of the church.

First, we need a **positive** image of what a loving involvement in a **fallen** society is. It is not enough to create images of what love would do in a fully redeemed social order. One of the most important weaknesses of sectarian ethics is, in my view, its tendency to assume that the church can live by a different standard from the world because it is a different world — it is the company of the redeemed called out from the unregenerate world, and hence is not subject to the same reality of evil. Even if such a clear distinction between the church and the world could be defended, it could not serve as an axiom of Christian social concern. This is simply because social concern is by definition the work of the church in a fallen world. Hence, a Christian social ethic must be an ethic **for this world**, an ethic which takes into account the fallenness of the world. It must provide an answer to the question, how does Christian love confront the **fact** of evil? A crucial aspect of the question of justice is the proper response to the consequences of evil. The church too must address this issue.

The image of justice must be a positive image, not just a negative one. The sectarian dichotomy between love and justice places the two in opposition to each other. Justice is seen as the compromise of the absolute demands of **agape** to the reality of a fallen society; hence, it is intrinsically unloving. Reinhold Niebuhr's definition of justice as a "tolerable balance of egoisms" in contrast to the ego-denying sacrificial concern which is definitive of **agape**, is a cogent, modern expression of this view. Niebuhr has done much to reinforce the sectarian notion prevalent among the Believers' Churches today, that justice requires a departure from the ideals of love in the direction of compromise with evil.[7]

A positive image of justice is one which would envision justice not as the negation or privation of Christian **agape** but as a minimal necessary condition of **agape**. If justice is basically the measure of what is properly due to each, as the ancients defined it, then clearly love cannot avoid meeting the demands of justice. For justice is simply the proper distribution of love. As long as there is more than one person in the world, and as long as these persons have interests which cannot be mutually satisfied, love will have to make a decision about whose interests, and which interests, should be most fully served when not all can be fully served. Not to make a fair and just assessment of these interests would be **unloving**.

Another sharp distinction between the ideas of love and justice in sectarian ethics is on the question of the uses of power. The idea of justice is usually associated with the distribution of rights, and powers within social institutions and the system of coercive sanctions required to maintain this distribution. **Agape**, on the other hand is understood as the absolute renunciation of power and the defence of one's rights in favour of redemptive suffering and sacrificial giving. Defined this way, of course, there is no commonality between the two. But these definitions seem to me to be far too severe. There is no escaping the question of power and its uses, neither within the church itself nor without it. Power, defined as the ability to accomplish desired ends, is in itself entirely compatible with the ideas of Christian **agape**. However, there are loving uses of power in human relationships and there are unloving uses of power. We need to do a great deal more thinking in the future about the distinction between these. Not all uses of force and coercive power by the secular order are violations of the high requirements of Christian love, but many of them certainly are. A concept of justice motivated and informed by the ideal of New Testament **agape** would allow the church not only to affirm and participate in those uses of political power which further the realization of justice, but also, and more importantly, to witness forthrightly and prophetically against the incessant abuses of power, especially the threat and use of dehumanizing violence. Such a concept might help us become more discerning of the proper uses of power within the church as well — something which the traditional power-denying concept of **agape** has not done well.

In conclusion, it must be stated emphatically that I am not calling for a return of the Believers' Churches to the theocratic conception of the church as the primary agent of justice and social order in the world. Nor do I suggest that the church should perceive its task as the ushering in of the Kingdom of God on earth through active social reforms, as did the theological liberalism of a century ago. One of the strengths of the "sectarian" outlook is its realistic assessment of the fallenness of the world and the intractability of evil in human beings and the institutions they create. While the temptation is ever present to take complete charge of history — to insure that it "comes out right in the end" — a temptation which faces the church as well as the secular powers in society, this temptation must be resisted. For, it is this temptation which leads easily to a "morality of ends" in which the hoped-for but rarely achieved end serves as a justification for the most insidious of means. This is the fundamental compromise into which the church invariably falls when it ordains itself as the governor of the world's affairs.

While the church cannot abandon its mission to be an agent of healing and reconciling love in the world, its social concern must be tempered by a humble recognition of the demonic tendencies which characterize all human institutions of social order — the "principalities and powers" of which Paul spoke. The faithful church will always stand over against the secular institutions and ideologies of its day. But it will do so only because, and to the extent that, it develops a biblical conception of justice as its criterion of judgement and witness against the "powers."

Nevertheless, the fact that God has not ordained the church as the guardian of history does not imply, as is too often inferred by the church, that the church ought not itself to act justly. The fact of overwhelming evil is never a justification or excuse for moral passivity and withdrawal from the responsibility to be agents of God's justice in the world. It is a call to this responsibility, to which the faithful church will be obedient. The faithful church will not bring in the Kingdom of God on earth, but it will give the world a glimpse of its meaning.

BAPTISTS AND PEACE

Paul R. Dekar

I. INTRODUCTION

Men of every era have most eagerly yearned for peace on earth. Now that man has discovered the means to destroy the human race, certainly no more urgent prayer can be offered by Christians than that which develops the biblical image of peace on earth: "Peace upon earth is the prayer we offer. Peace was the promise when Jesus was born. Peace to all men. Peace once again to this war-weary, war-worried world."[1] As with the biblical concepts of justice and righteousness, the biblical concept of peace is central to an understanding of the Kingdom of God. The Hebrew **shalom** embraces the totality of all relationships of daily life and the ideal, harmonious state of life in Israel. The Greek **eirene** is closer to our understanding of peace as the absence or cessation of war, but in the New Testament peace again is a comprehensive word suggestive of the normative life among Christians and of restored relations among men.[2]

The label "historic peace churches" has generally been applied to three churches, the Mennonites, the Society of Friends and the Church of the Brethren. The grouping suggests a greater degree of common history and co-ordinated peace witness than is historically or presently warranted, for it excludes not only many Christians who, as Dunkers, Doukhobors, Hutterites, Moravians, Schwenkfelders, Waldensians or members of some Holiness churches, should be included, but also Christians who hold peace to be central to their religious identity.[3] Thus, while Baptists in Canada and elsewhere have a long history of patriotic support of governments during times of war,[4] Baptists also have a long history of support for peace as a vision of salvation and the Kingdom of God. Moreover, individual Baptists such as Henry Holcombe, pastor of First Baptist Church, Philadelphia during the early nineteenth century and publisher of the pacifist periodical **Advocates of Peace**; John Clifford, British Baptist leader at the turn of this century and vehement opponent of the Boer War; and Martin Luther king, civil rights leader in the United States and recipient of the 1964 Nobel Peace Prize, have exercised powerful Christian witness for peace.

A recent book bears the happy title, **Peace — On Not Leaving It to the Pacifists.**[5] Baptists rightly are not classified among the historic peace churches, and in some respects their record as peacemakers is appalling. But peace is a matter of concern to all Christians. Baptists have not abdicated altogether their responsibility as peacemakers, nor has their congregational polity incapacitated them as witnesses for peace. Many Canadian Baptists might indeed be astonished were they to reflect on how radical were the English and American Baptists of the seventeenth century, as well as others called Baptist subsequently, with regard to the Christian image of peace, or how deeply rooted in the faith is the sense of responsibility to become instruments of God's peace on earth. The balance of this paper surveys briefly the classical Baptist stance towards peace and war, then focuses on Canadian Baptist positions and finally identifies implications for this conference.

II. CLASSICAL BAPTIST STANCE TOWARDS PEACE AND WAR

Baptist origins remain a matter of controversy.[6] For our purposes it is important to note that people called Baptists, in England, Europe and North America, had definite connections with two historic peace churches, the Mennonites and Society of Friends, during the formative period of Baptist history. John Smyth (d. 1612) and Thomas Helwys (d. 1616?) were among the earliest English Baptists, and ultimately differed in their attitudes towards Mennonite insistence upon nonresistance and nonparticipation in civil government. As has been observed by Dr. Hobbs, the 1612 Baptist Confession, **Propositions and Conclusions concerning True Christian Religion**, emphasized separation of civil and religious authority in any society. Article 85 developed a position regarding nonresistance very close to Dutch Mennonites:

> That if the magistrate will follow Christ, and be His disciple, he
> must deny himself, take up his cross, and follow Christ; he must
> love his enemies and not kill them, he must pray for them, and not
> punish them, he must feed them and give them drink, not imprison
> them, dismember them, and spoil their goods; he must suffer
> persecution and affliction with Christ, and be slandered, reviled,
> blasphemed, scourged, buffeted, spit upon, imprisoned and killed
> with Christ; and that by the authority of magistrates, which things
> he cannot possibly do, and retain the revenge of the sword.[7]

Articles 86 and 87 enjoined church members from going before magistrates, taking oaths or marrying "any of the profane, or wicked, godless people of the world."[8] Church members, in short, were to remove themselves from the world insofar as was possible.

Helwys also taught nonresistance, but principally "in heavenly or spiritual things" and not in temporal matters over which God had placed magistrates. Helwys and a number of followers broke with Smyth and parted with Mennonites on the matter of responsibility to civil authorities.[9] Declaring their intention to obey God and not men in matters of religion, early English Baptists generally acknowledged the legitimacy of rendering the state its due. As a later confession, of 1660, summarized:

> We believe that there ought to be civil Magistrates in all Nations,
> for the punishment of evil doers, and for the praise of them that do
> well, I Peter 2:14, and that all wicked lewdness, and fleshly
> filthiness, contrary to just and wholesome (Civil) Laws, ought to be
> punished according to the nature of the offences; and this without
> respect of any Persons, Religion, or profession whatsoever; and

that we and all men are obliged by Gospel rules, to be subject to
the higher Powers, to obey Magistrates, Titus 3: 1, and to submit to
every Ordinance of man, for the Lords sake, as saith Peter 2: 13.
But in case the Civil Powers do, or shall at any time impose things
about matters of Religion, which we through conscience to God
cannot actually obey, then we with Peter also do say, that we ought
(in such cases) to obey God rather than men, Acts 5: 29, and
accordingly do hereby declare our whole, and holy intent and
purpose, that (through the help of grace) we will not yield, nor (in
such cases) in the least actually obey them; yet humbly purposing
(in the Lord's strength) patiently to suffer whatsoever shall be
inflicted upon us, for our conscionable forbearance.[10]

While differences between Baptists and Mennonites were then highly
"nuanced," they did result in Baptist support for the Cromwellian
revolution, which entailed regicide and participation in war. Language
of holy warfare permeated the Calvinist tradition and, coupled with
fervent millenarian convictions, greatly influenced English Baptists
during the period 1640-1660. Baptists inveighed against the social order
and accepted force as an aspect of spiritual warfare. Even after the
restoration and movement towards accommodation and respectability,
Baptists held joint services with Congregationalists, Presbyterians and
Fifth Monarchists to condemn the wickedness of the time and to pray for
the speedy establishment of God's kingdom. While Baptists repudiated
the excesses of extreme Fifth Monarchists, they in turn were repudiated
by Quakers who perceived Baptist willingness to foment and to
participate in political war as a betrayal of characteristic Quaker
tenets, including refusal to take oaths or serve in the military.[11] John
Bunyan, lay preacher and writer generally associated with Baptists,
joined other Baptists in sharp, polemical controversy with George Fox
and other Quakers. Bunyan's language may be taken as typical of a
Baptist militancy antithetical to Quaker, or Mennonite spirituality. He
wrote in **The Holy War** (1682):

Remember therefore, O my Mansoul, that thou art beloved of me;
as I have therefore taught thee to watch, to fight, to pray, and to
make war against my foes, so now I command thee to believe that
my love is constant to thee...watch! Behold, I lay none other
burden upon thee, than what thou hast already. Hold fast till I come.[12]

A similar pattern of development may be observed among Baptists in
North America. Baptist beginnings are generally associated with Roger
Williams (ca. 1603-1683) and John Clarke (1609-1676). Both believed in
separation of church and state, and their strong views regarding civic
responsibility resulted in their rejection of pacifism. Williams despised
warfare and considered the history of Christian violence an
abomination. More than once he intervened to prevent his Rhode Island
colonists from going to war against the Indians, but he did not altogether
reject warfare in cases of self-defence.[13] Clarke served as pastor of the
First Baptist Church of Newport, Rhode Island. As drafter of the **Royal
Charter** of 1663 he also provided his fellow colonists a political theory of
great significance in United States history, and one which enshrined

Baptist concern for religious liberty. Inhabitants were to be "permitted
to pursue with peaceable and loyal minds their sober and religious
intentions" and to be peaceably and civilly governed. With regard to
peace, Clarke defined it as the ability to live together in community.
While he, too, despised warfare, he recognized the need of the weak new-
world community to protect itself: "For my part, I cannot expect that
the sword should be beaten into a plowshare and the spear into a pruning
hook, that a nation should not rise against nation, neither shall they
learn war any more...."[14] Such conviction enabled most Baptists to
support the American Revolution, even as Baptists in England had
supported the Cromwellian revolution. Agreeing that war was an
unsatisfactory and immoral method of settling disputes, Baptists
nonetheless assumed that religious liberty went hand in hand with civic
responsibility and support of the state during times of war. As the editor
of **The Maritime Baptist** summarized in 1942,

> While our Baptist fathers have ever stood for the absolute
> separation of church and state, both they and we have always
> regarded it as the privilege and prerogative of the Christian people
> to seek every legitimate means of promoting the highest interests
> of the nation to which we owe allegiance.[15]

III. CANADIAN BAPTISTS ON PEACE AND WAR

Canadian Baptists have generally supported peace in times of peace
and the country in times of war. They have developed no consistent
theological alternative to pacifism which would permit adherents to
know how and when they ought, if ever, to go to war. A variety of sources
reveal Canadian Baptist preoccupation with grace and with separation
of church and state. The first has resulted most frequently in an
understanding that peace derives from the spirit of Christ in the hearts
of individual men and women and ultimately awaits the realization of
the eschatological kingdom. The second has produced most frequently a
strong sense of responsibility for the defence of religious liberty and
western democracy.

There were few Canadian Baptist communities before 1800. American
Baptists tended to support the War for Independence, and former New
England Baptists who settled Nova Scotia and elsewhere did not
necessarily become pro-British partisans.[16] Subsequently,
consolidating the gains of the great revivals of Henry Alline and others,
settling the vast Canadian territory, establishing educational and other
institutions and so on preoccupied Canadian Baptists. They gave little
attention to peace or war until the present century.

When wars did break out, Canadian Baptists expressed concern for
those who suffered, as during the United States Civil War, and for
Canadian soldiers, as during the Boer War. Even when war did not
threaten, and it rarely did, Baptists dutifully acknowledged the
responsibility of organized society to protect its citizens. One **Canadian
Baptist** editorial did question prevailing attitudes by insisting that
Christians must not abdicate their responsibility to judge whether the
cause of any state be truthful and righteous. The Christian must remain,

"even if it costs life itself, the Lord's free man. Whether, on these principles, a Christian may ever become a professional soldier, is perhaps doubtful."[17] Some months later, doubt gave way to uncertain support for military adventure in South Africa, that Canadians might "share in the strength and the glories of the greatest empire that history records."[18] Unlike English Baptists, Canadian Baptists had no peace witness during the Boer War; an editorial in the May 11, 1899 **Canadian Baptist** summarized succinctly, "A nation must be in a position to defend itself; and however strong the arguments for peace...the right of a nation to defend itself should not be questioned or debated."[19]

In this century, Canadian Baptists have been unable to ignore issues of peace, war and reconstruction after war. From the turn of the century, concern for peace has permeated Canadian Baptist thinking regarding the building of a Christian social order. In an excellent book, **The Social Passion**, Richard Allen states, "From the 1890s through the 1930s the spirit of reform was abroad in the land."[20] No Protestant group escaped the impact of rapid social change — immigration, industrialization, stratification, urbanization — and Canadian Baptists proved no exception. As early as 1875, at the dedication of Jarvis Street Baptist Church in Toronto, an optimistic note was sounded, "The factory is up and the machinery is in." The work of radiating the glory of the Lord had begun.[21]

There were several avenues to awakened social conscience, and Canadian Baptists tended to be prompted by a combination of Calvinism, with its conception of a theocratic society subject to religious control, and evangelicalism, with its emphasis upon personal regeneration, rather than by the theological understanding of the kingdom of God articulated by Walter Rauschenbusch. Canadian Baptist social gospellers constituted "a small but vigourous group" including James E. Wells, editor of **The Canadian Baptist** from 1889 until his death in 1898; Henry Moyle of the United Farmers of Canada and secretary of the Social Service Committee of the Baptist Convention of Ontario and Quebec; and pastors like M.F. McCutcheon of Montreal, A.A. Shaw of Winnipeg and John MacNeil of Toronto. These were visionary but not radical men. They campaigned primarily on characteristic issues of individual morality (gambling, temperance), and their strategy consisted in such measures as establishing urban missions, for example, the Toronto Memorial Institute, calling for the transformation of men and women through God's Spirit and passing resolutions which might provide the basis of legislation permeated by Christian teaching.

They were not unaware of the threat which militarism posed to their vision of Christian society. In 1901 C.J. Holman, of McMaster University's Board of Governors, spoke against the formation of school cadet corps: "I have no measure of sympathy with this drilling of our public school children with guns even if the guns are of wood."[22] In 1904 the Maritime and Ontario-Quebec conventions passed resolutions endorsing the establishment of a permanent court of arbitration, and, subsequently, a number of resolutions of various Baptist assemblies endorsed efforts to resolve conflict peaceably. When a Canadian Defence League was formed in 1909, and military training spread to the scouting movement, Canadian Baptist opposition found loud and clear expression: "We should prefer seeing an attempt made to instruct the rising generation in the arts of peace." And again, "We have no desire to see militarism become as deeply rooted in Canada as it is in some other countries."[23] Finally, in 1913 the Social Service Committee of the Baptist Convention of Ontario and Quebec successfully added, to a programme envisioned by the Federal Council of Churches of Christ in America, a call "for the abolition of war, and for the adoption of arbitration as a means of settling international disputes."[24]

What impact did this advocacy of peace have in time of war? Virtually none. In 1914 Canadian Baptists decisively aligned themselves with the Allied cause. They regarded the war as a holy war and expected, as Christian duty and God's will, that Baptists would support the country during the crisis. The outbreak of war took many by surprise, enraged others and awakened a thousand anxieties, but support came from those who had opposed the war as a means of settling international conflict, as well as from those who, before the war, had supported imperialism. There is no evidence to suggest that any Canadian Baptist actively opposed the war or even went so far as to support pacifists like the Methodists J.S. Woodsworth and William Ivens. Canadian Baptists did express concern for the preservation of religious liberty, for temperance among the troops, for proportional representation in the matter of chaplaincy appointments and for the religious convictions of returning soldiers. Canadian Baptists did, towards the end of the war, participate in discussion regarding "the churches after the war." But for the duration of the war they resolved to "stand till the last gun is fired."[25]

The pattern of Baptist support for peace in times of peace and for the country in times of war held for the post World War I period. In the early 1920s, a time of resurgent pacifism, and in the mid-1930s, a time of growing threat of war, Canadian Baptists generally supported the League of Nations and efforts to put an end to war. In 1939, at the outbreak of World War II, Canadian Baptists again supported the cause of war as a matter of loyalty and the will of God. Canadian Baptists reacted to the renewal of warfare much as they had in World War I: with shock, anger, anxiety and even ambivalence, for pacifist sentiment was much stronger. In their pronouncements about the war they reiterated concern for religious liberty, temperance, receiving a fair share of military chaplaincies and prayerful support for soldiers and victims. They participated in national days of prayer, war services committees. reconstruction programmes and appeals for action:

> To defeat this Anti-Christ (Hitler) we have the unfailing promises of God. We need more and more intercessors and this great body of laymen (Baptist Brotherhood of Toronto) can have a vital part in that ministry. It is for us to go to our churches to-day resolved that,

as individuals and collectively, in our homes, in groups, at the weekly prayer meetings, and in other places we will, as Christ's Crusaders, meet the challenge and thereby help to shorten the period of terrible slaughter which the world is facing to-day.[26]

There are two interesting exceptions to the pattern of Canadian Baptist advocacy of peace and war described above. The first concerns Douglas Clyde Macintosh, Canadian-born Baptist pastor and McMaster University professor before moving to Yale Divinity School. The United States Supreme Court denied Macintosh United States citizenship in 1931 on the basis of his refusal to promise in advance to bear arms in defence of the United States. During World War I Macintosh served as a chaplain in the Canadian armed forces and briefly with the U.S. army. During the war he adopted a pacifist position, or at least accepted the idea of selective conscientious objection. He became a vigourous critic of "Christian realism" associated with the thought of Reinhold Niebuhr. Like the American Baptist preacher Harry Emerson Fosdick, Macintosh's interbellum pacifism ran deep and prevented him from blessing any future war.[27]

The second exception concerns T.T. Shields, fundamentalist founder of The Union of Regular Baptist Churches. During World War I Shields worked actively for conscription, and as war approached in 1939 he promoted a maximum Canadian war effort through his sermons and **Gospel Witness**. More bluntly than most Canadians, he admitted that he preferred war to peace and invited his constituency to consider themselves "British Canadians." Consistently his commitment to war surpassed that of other Protestant religious leaders.[28]

Since World War II the Baptist Federation of Canada and the social concerns departments of three regional conventions have sought to develop a theological framework on which basis Canadian Baptists might promote peace on earth. Central to such theological construction has been witness to the kingdom of God as the goal of human history. Recognizing the limitations of resolutions and the immense destructiveness of modern war, position papers have been drafted for discussion, prayer, study and creative integration into the evangelistic life-style emphasized by Baptists. This conference will have served a valuable function if it reopens dialogue concerning the organization of the church of Christ as an instrument of God's peace on earth.

IV. CONCLUDING REMARKS

This paper is necessarily brief. Much more research must be undertaken regarding Baptists and peace in the Canadian context, especially since resolutions, editorials and similar documentation do not adequately uncover individual belief and practice. Still, three conclusions may be warranted in the light of conference objectives:

1. With regard to the major contributions of the Free Church tradition in Canada, Baptists have differed significantly from Mennonites, Quakers and other historic peace groups by accepting war as necessary to guarantee the survival of fundamental Canadian liberties, including religious liberty, and world order.

2. With regard to the present state of Baptist life in Canada, Baptists generally endorse Canada's participation in peacemaking organizations the United Nations. As part of the Baptist World Alliance, Canadian Baptists are in dialogue with Christians in countries with alien economic, political and social systems. However, no distinctively Baptist position exists regarding the peacemaking role of the church in the modern world.

3. With regard to the future witness of Canadian Baptists on the subject of peace, much theological reflection will be necessary. As members of the family of man and God's kingdom in heaven and on earth, Baptist Christians need to search their heritage and to reaffirm, with the earliest Baptists, that we are ultimately subject to God, not men. As a basis for future witness, Canadian Baptists would do well to consider the force of this statement:

> The witness of the prophetic element in the biblical message supports us in our concluding emphasis to the effect that it is our prime futy as part of the church to confront our own people with the grim truth of our own spiritual and moral weakness as a nation. A gross materialism, a revolting love of ease and pleasure, and a repudiation of many basic decencies in life mark our present condition as a people. While there is much in the way of vital religious life and moral vigour in our nation, there is also much that requires to be condemned, challenged and altered. We need to develop a real climate of Christian righteousness in which personal and social Christian values will flourish. To create and maintain by Christian evangelism and Christian education such a climate is our great task...as also a consecrated sense of Christian social responsibility and creative action. In discharging that task with vigour and faithfulness we will as a church make our greatest contribution to the cause of world peace. (Baptist Federation of Canada, **Peace and War**)

THE BELIEVERS' CHURCH AND SOCIAL CONCERNS

T.R. Hobbs

This paper is written by one who is neither a theologian in the accepted sense, nor a professional church historian, but rather a student of Old Testament literature and history. However, I do have more than a passing interest in the topic since I am by conviction a member of part of the Christian church which has received the designation "Believers' Church," and for the past five years I have been a member of the Social Concerns Committee of the Baptist Convention of Ontario and Quebec — at present the vice-chairman of that committee.

The design of what follows seeks to present a brief interpretation of what I consider to be three of the chief motivations for social concern among some Baptists. Being more familiar with Baptist history and tradition, I shall restrict my illustrative remarks to items from their history.

I. From their beginnings Baptists have placed great stress on the individual and his relationship to God and his fellows. The earliest formal statement of Anabaptist principles from Europe, the "Eighteen Dissertations Concerning the Entire Christian Life," by Balthasar Hubmaier (1524), declares: since every Christian believes for himself and is baptized for himself, everyone must see and judge by the scriptures whether he is being properly nourished by his pastor. (Article 8)[1] Although no direct historical connection is necessarily intended, the same emphasis reappeared in the early confessions and statements from the beginnings of the Baptist movement in England in the seventeenth century.

The individualistic emphasis, of course, has a special origin and was developed in the light of special historical circumstances. At that time, what one can label today as "social issues" were not of any particular importance. Separation of church and state was obviously an issue of great importance and this is naturally reflected in these early statements. Good order in society is clearly the domain of the civil authority. The "office of the magistrate is a...permissive ordinance of God for the good of mankind; that one man like the brute beasts not devour another, and that justice and civility, may be preserved among men."[2] However, in some matters of charity, particularly those concerning the poorer members of the congregation, certain administrative duties are outlined, and provision is made for the relief of such distressed persons.[3]

II. Yet future directions of social concern are implicit in some of these statements, and lines can be drawn beyond these early stages into a more direct involvement of Baptists in problems of major proportions which concern the very structures of society, and the limitations of certain powers within society. The guardians of these limits often are the believers in fellowship with one another. What can be traced further is a number of incidents in the history of Baptists which demonstrate an involvement in issues of serious social consequence. I have detected three major motivations for such involvement among Baptists. By the nature of the cases concerned, each is slightly different, yet connected to the other two.

A. ENLIGHTENED SELF-INTEREST

A major and fairly consistent motive for Baptist involvement in social concerns has been "enlightened self-interest." That is, the criticism of existing structures in society and the resulting action on the part of Christian critics, have been for the protection of their own rights. Two examples will suffice; in each, echoes of the earlier emphasis on the right of an individual before God can be heard.

1. **Religious Liberty — Thomas Helwys.** Although in the Baptist Confession of 1609[4] and in the Confession of 1611[5] there is an emphasis upon the separation of the civil and religious authority in any society — although both are ordained by God — it is in the Confession of 1612 where notice is taken of the possible tension that could arise between the two. Article 84 of this Confession, entitled "Propositions and Conclusions Concerning the True Christian Religion," declares: "That the magistrate is not by virtue of his office to meddle with religion or matters of conscience, to force or compel men to this or that form of religion, or doctrine; but to leave the Christian religion free, to every man's conscience...."[6] That this is part of the Confession of the followers of John Smyth, after their break with Helwys, is interesting, since in the same year Helwys published his **Short Declaration of the Mistery of Iniquity** in London. It is here that the idea of universal religious freedom for subjects in a state finds its fullest and earliest exposition. The main ideas of the document are reinforced two years later by the publication of **Objections Answered by Way of Dialogue**...in which Helwys (?) goes into much greater detail on the topic. The limits of the civil power, albeit ordained by God, are clearly stated. With matters of religion, the form of religion and the conscience of the individual worshipper, the king should have nothing to do. He, with the poorest of his subjects, is subject to the law of Christ. The shadow of persecution in the interests of conformity to the newly established Protestantism clearly lies behind the work. Helwys continues: "O let the king judge, is it not most equal, that men should choose their religion themselves seeing they only must stand themselves before the judgement of God, and to answer for themselves?"[7] This reflects the strong emphasis upon the individual, as seen earlier. The book stands more as a monument to Helwys, who died shortly after its publication, than as a major treatise, but it does represent one of the earliest expositions of the principle of religious freedom in the English language.[8]

2. **Religious Discrimination — Canadian Baptists.** Closely related to

the defence of the principle of religious liberty and the relationship of church and state are issues concerning religious discrimination in which Canadian Baptists became involved prior to Confederation. One of these issues was the matter of the "Clergy Reserves."[9] This can be included in the section on "enlightened self-interest" since it was motivated in no small measure by a frustration over the legitimate grievances against a system which discriminated against those in Upper Canada who were not Anglicans. The system set aside large tracts of land for Protestant churches. Proportionately the Church of England benefitted most. A vigorous Baptist campaign was carried on in the 1840s and early 1850s to have the land turned over to the municipalities for the building of public education facilities. In spite of enormous pressure and the discomfort of standing alone on the issue, among all the denominations in Canada, Baptists saw the issue settled in their favour in 1854.

Although the issue was one involving a system in which Baptists received the least materially, there were larger and more important theological and pragmatic points at stake. The disruption of communications between pioneer settlements as a result of the allotments was an important factor in the protest. But by far the most important was the principle of "voluntarism," the rigid separation of church and state. Coupled with this was the danger to the principle of religious liberty which became an issue during the census taken in 1842.[10] Summarizing the contribution of the Baptists to this debate, Pitman states: "In a sense (Baptists) had led the way in creating a climate of opinion which would accept this solution, leading many who were Anglican, Methodist and Presbyterian to a realization that the existence of such public support for religious enterprises was a disadvantage even to the denominations which benefitted."[11]

Contemporary with the issue of the Clergy Reserves was the long debate over the alliance between the Church of England and the state in the field of higher education in Canada. With a fervour equal to that with which they opposed the Reserves, Baptists of Upper Canada opposed the granting of public funds to the newly established King's College, Toronto, where Anglicans maintained a decisive control. Undoubtedly self-interest is at play here. Anglican domination of major institutions of higher learning robbed Baptists of the opportunity to train their own clergy to sufficient standards of education. One response of Canadian Baptists was to open their own college in Montreal, but the venture was short-lived, and the college was closed because of financial difficulties in 1849. Based on the principle of the separation of church and state, the Baptists' plan was for a college of their own which could become affiliated with the projected non-sectarian University of Toronto. The founding of the Anglican King's College was greeted by Baptists in the following way: "...the great principles of Religious Liberty...have been grievously violated in the manner in which the Episcopalian sect of Christians have been allowed to divert a large portion of the funds set apart for the education of the youth of the Province (of Upper Canada), from their original purpose...."[12] In the same year that the Baptist College of Montreal had ceased to exist, the non-sectarian University of Toronto was founded. Much to the delight of Baptists, the endowment originally designated for King's College was transferred to University College.

B. OUTRAGED CHRISTIAN CONSCIENCE

This second category of motivation is somewhat less clearly defined than the first, but is nevertheless detectable in the history of Baptists' involvement in social issues. The primary difference from the first, as far as resulting action is concerned, is that the objects of the concern are groups other than Baptists themselves. Under this category we have moved from action motivated by a concern for one's own rights, which had a far-reaching effect in society as a whole, to campaigns for the rights of others who had no voice, or those whose voice was silenced. The clearest example of this kind of involvement is that of the British Baptist missionary, William Knibb, and his campaign for the abolition of slavery in the British West Indies in the early part of the nineteenth century. A second important difference in this kind of social concern is the emergence of courageous individuals such as Knibb, and the general reluctance of the Baptist body to become involved in the particular issue. If we look at the coalition of forces which comprised the British abolitionist movement, we note that it consisted of men of good will from within the varied branches of the Christian church, and without.[13] The Baptist "establishment" such as it was, which sent Knibb to the West Indies in the first place, did not officially countenance any involvement in what it knew to be a sad state of affairs in Jamaica. In fact, it cautioned Knibb never to interfere in the civil and political affairs of the colony.[14]

That Knibb took this advice lightly is now history, and the subsequent history of the church in Jamaica bears adequate testimony to that fact. Knibb's lack of formal theological education[15] might explain the lack of theological justification for his deep and dedicated involvement in the anti-slavery movement in Jamaica. Whatever the case, it is difficult to find any motivation in his work against slavery and the evils which followed its abolition,[16] other than a sense of outrage at the inhuman treatment meted out to the slaves on the plantations. He fought against an unjust system, which he called "the kingdom of Satan," and also despised the immorality which inevitably went with the system and which caused the slaves to "sink below the brute" in their behaviour.[17]

C. THEOLOGICAL READJUSTMENT

A third category of motivation is that of theological readjustment, or theological reorganization; that is, the development of a theological position in which involvement in issues of major social importance becomes inescapable. Within the history of Baptists one name stands out as exemplifying this position, that of Walter Rauschenbusch. To be sure, Rauschenbusch's initial dissatisfaction with traditional theology and seminary education in dealing with the problems of the parish (especially his) could well be labelled "outrage." But his deep thinking on the matter led him to seek for a theological foundation for the action needed to better the lot of his parishioners, action which he knew to be imperative.[18]

Whether Rauschenbusch can rightly be claimed as a "sectarian"[19] is a debatable question. His dislike of ceremonial religion, which he regarded as the enemy of true Christianity, and his love for the primitive, prophetic church, could certainly lend support to this view.[20] However, he might well be reflecting little more than the spirit of the liberal Protestantism of his day, which was by no means dominated by "sectarian" Christianity.[21] What is important, however, is that in developing his theological position, Rauschenbusch chose the socio-political symbol of the Kingdom of God as an important element in that theology. This is a symbol, it is to be noted, which received little or no attention in the previous history of Baptist social concern. That particular lack has not been made good since.[22] Rarely in the known Baptist confessions of faith does the biblical concept of the Kingdom of God receive prominence. Only in one confession, the Southern Baptist Convention Statement of 1925 and 1963,[23] does it receive a separate treatment as an article of faith (Article IX). However, from the overall design of the statement it is clear that the theological concept is seen as having little to do with social concern. "The Christian and the Social Order" receives separate treatment in Article XV. More typical of the spirit of the historic Baptist stance is the Confession of the **Bund Evangelisch-Freikirchlicher Gemeinden** in Germany in 1944,[24] in which the civil power is seen as having been ordained by God, and is therefore to be obeyed. Of interest in this confession is that older concept of the magistracy and civil officers, is replaced by the more metaphysical (and sinister) concept of the "state."

III. The above survey of motivations for Baptist social concern is, of course, incomplete. Left entirely out of the discussion is the Baptist involvement in the temperance movement, the perennial opposition to gambling, and new attitudes on human sexuality, none of which can be comfortably catalogued under the above categories alone. Certain conclusions can be drawn for further discussion among Baptists and others of a similar persuasion.

1. Motivation and methods of concern are not universal, nor of one type. Motivations for social concern have, do and will vary.

2. The frequently heard appeal to the distinctiveness of the importance of the individual and his salvation, over against "social issues," is at times meaningless. The early stress on the individual before God played a large part in the Baptist contribution to the cause of religious liberty.

3. The lack of a theologically and biblically based rationale for social concern among Baptists is noticeable, and needs correcting. Of crucial importance in such a theology of social concern is the concept of the "Kingdom of God." Its traceable roots in the Old Testament,[25] and its central place in the New Testament,[26] betray its importance. The meaning of the choice in scripture of this clearly political concept as a

description of the state of the believer needs to be explored. Along with this concept, others emerge of equal importance, such as "justice" (tsedakah), "righteousness" (dikaiosyne) and "peace" (shalom/eirene), all of which force us to look not only to our own relationship with God, but also to our relationship with our fellow creatures.[27]

RESPONSIBILITY FOR WORLD RESOURCES: CREATION AND DOMINION

Walter Klaassen

The words **ecology, ecological crisis,** and **pollution** are today household words. Most of us have developed views on the subject and have done one thing or another to express our convictions. We are concerned about the depletion of resources and the development of new energy sources. We virtually take for granted the role of government in solving the massive problems that have developed, and we can hardly do otherwise. At the same time, however, we desperately need to develop a new consciousness of the natural world and our place in it, if legislative decisions are to be carried out beyond the letter of the law. We will have to learn to extend to the natural world the same kind of love and concern that we have been taught to extend to our human neighbours. This essay is an attempt to make a contribution towards that end.

I have before me, on the table as I write, two fossils. They are the imprints of marine trilobites, both of them about 450 million years old. They are visible evidence of God's work from the third day of creation. They tell me part of the incredibly long story of creation of which they, the stars, I myself and the atoms are all a part. These trilobites have become an important part of my life since it was partly through their ministry that I developed concerns and convictions which I share below.

I doubt that Christians in the Believers' Church tradition will arrive at significantly different views on creation and ecology than Christians from other traditions. The question under discussion is a universal issue of urgent important. That is a sufficient reason for placing it on our agenda. But we share, especially with the rest of Protestantism, a legacy of relatively slight concern for the natural world of which we are a part. I shall try to identify some of the reasons for this.

The physical universe is the first fact of our conscious experience as human beings: mother's warmth, mother's breast, mother's voice. From the moment of conception we are tied to the universe about us by innumerable threads. We know that we are composed of the same chemical elements as the stars, the stones, the water, the air and the soil. Our physical environment is our very life, since it provides food, air, water and space. This world about us is the common human experience, regardless of whether we are the primitive inhabitants of a forgotten rain forest or the most sophisticated products of high culture.

But our solidarity with nature is not only physical; it is also spiritual. The brain is a physical organ, but it is the basis of what we call mind or soul, that dimension of human reality which links us especially with the Creator and for the most part separates us from other living creatures. Our minds are so constructed that they are able to receive signals by means of light, sound, smell, heat and pressure. Without these we could perceive nothing and so there would be nothing for the mind to work on in constructing and ordering our experience of the world. Hence there would be no intellect, no soul. Thus even at the point of human uniqueness we are dependent on and part of the natural world.[1]

Still, in our confession of faith we have always associated ourselves without hesitation with the first article of the classic Christian creeds: "I believe in God the Father Almighty, maker of heaven and earth." We sing "The spacious firmament on high" and "This is our Father's world." Many of us have had extensive periods in church camps as children and young people. A part of that experience was always nature study.

How is it then that as Christians we give so little evidence that we consider creation to be a basic, indispensable part of our life?

A quick survey of the work of Christian theologians during the last four or five decades reveals that the charge that modern Christians have neglected a basic part of their experience has some validity. As a matter of fact, the doctrine of creation, the Christian discussion of God's creative activity and of the place and importance of the physical universe and all that flows from it are given relatively minor attention by Christian thinkers. No one in the last few centuries has written more on the subject of creation than Karl Barth. He writes in the introduction to his treatment on creation that the doctrine of creation is a much neglected subject and that he will restore it to its rightful importance. But he specifically avoids what I consider to be elementary and indispensable today, namely to bring the findings of geology, anthropology, physics, chemistry, astronomy and biology directly into the circle of theological discussion. All he will do in the 2,000 pages of his discussion, he promises, is simply to retell the saga of creation according to Genesis 1 and 2.[2] Emil Brunner, too, gives a good deal of attention to creation, in the second volume of his **Dogmatics**, entitled **The Christian Doctrine of Creation and Redemption**. Apart from discussing the question of evolution in a short appendix, he, too, limits himself strictly to the biblical framework of neo-orthodox dogmatics. Both Barth and Brunner regarded the discussion of creation as important only for the doctrine of redemption. Apart from that they had no interest in it.

Other star theologians are equally uninterested. Paul Tillich gives a scant twenty pages to the question of creation in his three-volume **Systematic Theology**. Wolfhart Pannenberg, in his two-volume work on problems in contemporary theology does not even mention it.

Just a few theologians have paid attention to the question in helpful ways. Landgon Gilkey published a book on the subject in 1959 under the title **Maker of Heaven and Earth**. Since then, Gordon Kaufman gave it significant, if limited attention in his **Systematic Theology** (1968). The most significant important attempt to bring the whole physical reality of the universe in time and space into the arena of Christian thought has been made by Teilhard de Chardin, Jesuit scientist-theologian who died in 1955.[3] Finally, a very fine discussion of these issues can be found in **Earth Might Be Fair**, edited by Ian Barbour.[4]

There is a paradox here. In a century that continues to witness an immense scientific concentration on the investigation of the physical universe, the use of these fascinating and sometimes explosive findings as data for theology is still very scarce among Christians. With the few exceptions mentioned above, we appear not to be interested in the physical universe, in spite of the growing ecological awareness which marks our time. This phenomenon calls for some explanation.

The religious crisis of the fifteenth and sixteenth centuries reflected the breakup of the unitary world of the Middle Ages. It was brought on specifically by a discredited papacy, and with it a loss of credibility that spread through the whole church. Following strong pointers made by theologians in the fourteenth century, the religious movement known as the Reformation settled on the unchangeable scriptures as the ultimate authority. The age-old question, "What must I do to be saved?" was answered by pointing to one part of those scriptures, namely Paul's articulation of the doctrine of redemption, according to Romans and Galatians. The concentration was virtually totally on the question of salvation **from** the world as a place marked for destruction. Although the Protestant Reformers mention creation, one gets the feeling that they do it mainly because it is the subject of the first article of the creed. The Augsburg Confession, the fundamental doctrinal statement of Lutheranism, omits it altogether. The Reformed tradition was a little more aware of it, but it cannot be said to be of basic importance. Anabaptists also mention it, but only in passing, and more often not at all.

A number of theological assumptions common to the period following the Reformation seem to have contributed to a low view of the physical world among Christians. The accepted place of the material world in God's plan of redemption was one of these. As Loren Eiseley writes, the earth was "the platform of a divine but short-lived drama — a drama so brief that there was little reason to study the stage properties."[5] This was apparently directly connected with the idea that the world was running down, decaying, near its end, and that therefore man's first concern should be to gather treasure in heaven.

A further reason for the lack of interest in, and perhaps even an aversion to, the material world, was the Protestant doctrine of the total depravity of man. Total depravity was believed to be characteristic of natural man, and the natural world was believed to share in that depravity. Man and the world needed saving, not affirming.

The religious revival known as Pietism was equally uninterested in creation. Again, it concerned itself supremely with the soul, but not the body, with the supernatural, not the natural. Pietism has very signally influenced Protestant Christianity in Europe and especially in America, with its exclusive and consuming concern for conversion and the inner emotional experience of salvation through Christ. In its modern manifestation it has, until recently at least, been characterized by an extremely narrow concern for personal salvation out of the world and with little interest in social issues, let alone for the role of the natural world in man's salvation.

The coming of the age of science provided more reasons why western man, Christians included, should not think the world especially important. As long as the earth remained at the centre of the universe it was easy to see and accept God's presence in it, for if the earth was the centre of God's attention then everything in it, along with man, was also there. But with the discovery of Copernicus that the sun is at the centre and that the earth is eccentric, doubts about the earth's importance easily arose.

Astronomical observations soon led to the conclusion that the earth, the planets, sun and moon all functioned according to fixed and unchanging laws. God remained the Creator, but since all things unfolded according to unchanging laws which God had established, his continued action was no longer required to sustain it. Thus God was removed from the world and the universe, into inaction, and he was believed to be indifferent to it.

Even more important, man did not seem to function by the laws of nature in predictable fashion. His actions did not always conform to what one might expect. "It's not like him" we say today. Therefore, when everything else in the natural world functioned by clear laws — eclipses could be predicted, flowers opened in the morning and closed at night, cats killed birds for food — man himself did not. One never knew what he would do next. And so human beings began to feel like oddities, out of tune, and even in conflict with the natural world about them. They became strangers in their own home.

The scriptures and especially the Gospel of John, always much beloved, and therefore very influential, strengthened this feeling of alienation. This Gospel clearly states that what is really important comes from heaven, namely the heavenly Christ. He really had nothing to do with this world. He was the heavenly Saviour and it was his function to get all of us **out** of the world and into heaven. It can readily be seen that such a view of salvation, if emphasized exclusively, cannot easily make room for a positive view of the physical world.

Thus the idea that man is an alien in the universe was promoted both by the church and the scientific community. No wonder, then, that there was little interest among Christian thinkers in the doctrine of creation.

However, there was even more to this process of destroying the significance and importance of the natural world. Eventually somewhere in the eighteenth century the idea of God as creator was dropped altogether, since the universe was now believed to be self-existent. Thus the universe was disenchanted. The divine mystery was gone and the view became established that whatever is not now known will be known, and that when it can be explained the mystery dissolves.

Many Christians went along with much of this reasoning, so that even for them God was progressively shifted to smaller and smaller quarters, being located in those gaps in scientific knowledge which had not yet been explained. Thus Christians too, to a great extent, assumed the absence of God from the world to be a reality. Hence there developed problems with prayer, and even God himself was identified as a problem. The separation between God and the universe was virtually complete, in spite of the constant repetition of the words "I believe in God the Father Almighty, maker of heaven and earth." Thus a doctrine of creation that takes seriously the findings of science and assumes that God is present in his creation really becomes impossible. And since we no longer know the Maker, what he made can be used and abused in any way we see fit. And that is the basic cause of the present crisis.

The question now is: How can we recover a proper recognition of the importance of the natural world, and the respect necessary to begin treating it with the care needed to ensure its survival?

We need to bring to our remembrance, in the first place, the universe of which we are a part. We need to follow the action expressed in the words of the Psalmist: "When I look at thy heavens, the work of thy fingers, the moon and the stars which thou hast established..." (Psalm 8: 3), and the subsequent reflection about God's greatness and majesty.

We begin with the stars, where the Psalmist began. We are part of a universe that God began to call into being about thirteen billion years ago, an unimaginably long time. Our solar system is much younger, emerging from a vast cloud of gas that gradually condensed, forming the sun and the planets about four to six billion years ago. We belong also to a galaxy that contains about one hundred billion stars, in which old stars gradually burn out and disappear, and new stars are being created all the time. In its youth the earth generated immense heat internally, releasing a lot of steam which could then condense as rain, because the earth was just the right distance from the sun for this to happen. It was in the water so gathered and heated by the sun that God first created life as a single cell sometime about two billion years ago. It was a quiet event, an infinitely small and fragile one. But God patiently nurtured it as it grew and multiplied over millions of years, occupying the seas. Gradually an atmosphere necessary to the further development of life was produced by these one-celled creatures. It formed a protective mantle around the earth, to keep out the deadly ultraviolet radiation from the sun. Only then was it possible for life to develop outside the sea. Plants that had started in the water moved gradually on to the shoreline where they could find some sand for their soft roots, and so in turn, as they died, served to create soil which gradually spread over the rock. Over long ages, many-celled creatures were gradually created in the sea. These, too, moved on to the land, and soon the earth was populated by small and large reptiles. Mammals did not come along until after the flowering plants came which stored proteins in their seeds. These were necessary for the greater level of energy expended by these animals. And finally, about one million years ago, man appeared, made in the image of God, a thinking, creating creature. Life and its environment developed as an unbroken unitary network. The whole planet is a single organism, one pulsating, breathing unit, constantly changing. Species die out and new ones take their place. Environments change gradually, and man constructs some of his own environment.

At the same time all this was happening here at home, there were stars and planets elsewhere, spread throughout the vastnesses of the universe, some stars so large that if their centre were our sun they would include in their mass the orbits of Mercury, Venus, Earth, Mars and beyond (Antares is 428 million miles in diameter). These stars, like our sun, are burning furnaces of nuclear reaction millions of years long. Besides this, there are other mysteries such as quasars, the collapse of immense star systems, black holes and anti-matter.

Then we make a mental jump from these immensities to the building blocks of matter itself. These realities are so infinitesimal that they will never be seen because they are too tiny to reflect light. And so the scientists' imagination supplied models of surpassing beauty and complexity in atom and molecule, using the skills and gifts of artist, poet and musician. And around us we see every day the complex organisms and systems that inhabit the planet with us, trees, birds, water, stones, clouds, an infinite variety of forms made of matter and spirit.

How can we contemplate all this without, as the hymn says, being "lost in wonder, love and praise?" What endless and loving care has been given to it by its Creator! How carefully everything was planned and executed! How delicate the balance of living creatures and their environments! "This uniqueness and the wonder of the creative achievement that it has made possible mean that the earth is a rare gem of fantastic beauty, and that its desecration or destruction by any being is an act of awful sacrilege against which the heart of all meaning and purpose in the entire universe must cry out in anguish."[6]

In the light of all this we need to remind ourselves of four assertions made in the Bible, all of which we know, but have either not properly understood, or neglected too long.

1. God is not separated from the world. His Spirit continues to create and sustain. "When thou sendest forth the Spirit, they are created; and thou renewest the face of the ground" (Psalm 104: 30). God breathed into all living creatures his own breath (Genesis 2: 7; 6: 17, 22); therefore wherever we see life, whether in plant, insect, animals or man, we are in the presence of something from God. His life flows through the whole earth and universe, continuously creating and sustaining. The world, the universe, is sacred because God made it and because his spirit dwells in it. How dare we treat the work of God's hands which is a dwelling of his Spirit, carelessly and irresponsibly?

I believe that belief in a God who is the Creator and therefore above the creation, but also at the same time in it, is absolutely essential to recovering a sense of the sacredness and worth of the natural world, from which follows that we treat it with reverence and care. Those of us who are Christians should be in the vanguard of such a movement. It means giving the doctrine of creation equal time with the doctrine of redemption. That is a challenge, especially to the Believers' Churches, since they have traditionally been eloquent preachers of personal salvation. We should continue to do that, but we can no longer justifiably do it at the expense of the creation.

2. It is repeated over and over in Genesis 1 that the creation is good. Nowhere in the Bible is that denied. To be sure, in the creation, too, all is not well, according to Hosea 4: 3, and Romans 8: 19ff, but Genesis 8: 21 clearly records that God will never again curse the ground because of man. Even today, therefore, the creation and everything in it is good. Material things are good in and of themselves. "Nothing," wrote Paul, "is unclean in itself" (Romans 14: 14). We need to remember always the admonition to Peter even in the context of creation: "What God has made clean you may not make unclean" (Acts 10: 15).

The biblical references above reflect the Jewish view of creation. Not long after those passages were written, Christians began to regard spiritual realities as superior to material ones. The very idea that physical, material things are less important than spiritual things casts doubt upon the goodness of the material universe. But God created us material and spiritual. As I argued above, the material is the first fact of our existence and the spiritual grows and develops only on the base of the physical and material. And if we regard our own bodies as being good, we are more likely to regard other material things in nature as good as well.

3. Scripture tells us that God gave us dominion over the world. Hardly anything could be more obvious today than that we have achieved this dominion over the creation. No major place on the planet remains unexplored. All the creatures found on earth have been catalogued. Most natural phenomena have been analyzed and many explained. We have even escaped from the earth and asserted our dominion over the moon and the space between earth and moon. We know much about the history of the earth's origin and the development of life on earth. And we have used the resources of the earth to create a rewarding life for ourselves.

The image used in the Bible to make clear the nature of this dominion is that of the gardener: "The Lord God took the man and put him in the Garden of Eden to till it and keep it." Lynn White, in a famous and much-printed essay, charged that western Christianity understood God's mandate to exercise dominion as the right to exploit.[7] Whatever may be the truth of that charge, for the last 200 years at least, we have not been clear about the meaning of the gardener image of dominion. A gardener cares for his garden by definition; that is his natural function. If he does not care he is not a gardener. In fact if he takes actions that are damaging to the garden he has forfeited his right to be a gardener. We have been like that. The garden that sustains us is now so badly abused that unless we again become faithful gardeners we will not survive, nor will many other forms of life on the planet. We have been behaving like many people today who rent living quarters with the aim of getting everything they can out of the landlord, feeling free to abuse the quarters in any way they please, and then, when life in those quarters becomes impossible, they move elsewhere. Our reality is that we have nowhere else to move.

Exercising dominion means caring for, nurturing, restoring, increasing production and using the fruit in a way that preserves the world and everything in it, for the life and enjoyment of future generations.

4. Finally, I come back to a point with which I began, the relationship of creation and redemption. The neglect of the doctrine of creation in our theology reflects the view that the physical universe is not important. The view of Karl Barth and others that creation is important only in relation to redemption is in fact turning reality upside down. The fact is that creation comes first both in the scriptures as well as in our experience, and redemption comes later in terms of actual historical occurrence. We may not conclude, however, that we can choose the one or the other. Both are part of a single divine purpose which is to bring all things to unity in the end (Colossians 1:20).

It is entirely true that man has drawn the natural world into his own wrongdoing as suggested already in Genesis 3:17-19 and Romans 8:19-20. The present ecological crisis provides strong and persuasive evidence, confirming and filling out the scriptural texts. Man's inhumanity to man is reflected also in nature. There is that haunting passage in Hosea, written 750 years before Christ:

> Hear the word of the Lord, O people of Israel;
>   for the Lord has a controversy with the inhabitants of the land.
> There is no faithfulness or kindness, and no
>   knowledge of God in the land;
> there is swearing, lying, killing, stealing, and
>   committing adultery;
> they break all bounds and murder follows murder.
> Therefore the land mourns, and all who
>   dwell in it languish,
> and also the beasts of the field, and the birds
>   of the air;
> and even the fish of the sea are taken away (4:1-3).[8]

There could hardly be a more graphic description of the realities of our time.

But even as the creation has been drawn into man's sin, so it is also included in redemption. This was already the view of Isaiah when in his vision of the future he saw peace and harmony not only in human society but also in nature (11:6-9). Paul, in the passage in Romans already referred to, sees a liberated nature as part of the final liberation of man. He writes about nature's "bondage to decay" and the groaning of creation (Romans 8:19-22). Whatever Paul meant by those terms, they have in our time achieved a frightening reality. Certainly if we continue as we have done, the natural order will be destroyed. It is groaning under the massive burden of pollution and exploitation we have laid on it. But it will be liberated. It can begin today by our own liberation from our sins against it, and will, according to Paul and the writer of

Revelation, share in the final liberation at the end when God will become all in all (I Corinthians 15:28). For a rejuvenated nature is part of the vision of the city of God, coming down from God out of heaven (Revelation 21:10-11, 22:2). That fact, too, ought to alert us to our kinship with the natural world. We belong to it; it belongs to us. Without it, we cannot, indeed, would not be; without us, it cannot be fulfilled.

Like Teilhard de Chardin, we need to recover the sense of the presence of God in nature. He writes:

> Once again the Fire has penetrated the earth.
> Not with sudden crash of thunderbolt, riving the mountaintops: does the Master break down doors to enter his own home? Without earthquake, or thunderclap: the flame has lit up the whole world from within. All things individually and collectively are penetrated and flooded by it, from the inmost core of the tiniest atom to the mighty sweep of the most universal laws of being: so naturally has it flooded every element, every energy, every connecting-link in the unity of our cosmos; that one might suppose the cosmos to have burst spontaneously into flame.[9]

With that consciousness of God around us in all things we will never again be able to treat any natural thing with disrespect or merely as an object for our consumption. Then shall come to pass what the Lord spoke through the prophets:

> The wilderness and the dry land shall be glad,
> the desert shall rejoice and blossom (Isaiah 35:1).
> Behold the days are coming, says the Lord
> when the plowman shall overtake the reaper
> and the treader of grapes him who sows the seed;
> the mountains shall drip sweet wine,
> and all the hills shall flow with it (Amos 9:13).
> Then he showed me the river of the water of life,
> bright as crystal, flowing from the throne
> of God and of the Lamb through the middle
> of the street of the city; also on either side of
> the river, the tree of life with its twelve
> kinds of fruit, yielding its fruit each
> month; and the leaves of the tree were
> for the healing of the nations (Revelation 22:1-2).

RADICAL PROTESTANTISM AND THE EXPLOITATION OF NATURAL RESOURCES

David B. McLay

A widespread awareness of the ecological fragility of planet earth has only developed since 1962 when Rachel Carson's book, **Silent Spring**,[1] appeared and began to affect public attitudes. It was some time before evangelical theologians began to write seriously about the ecological crisis. Francis Schaeffer's monograph on the Christian view of ecology, **Pollution and the Death of Man**,[2] first published in 1970, is a landmark in the growing awareness of evangelical theologians at the beginning of this decade. Hugh Montefiore's book, **Can Man Survive**,[3] also appeared in 1970; it incorporates three theological lectures given at the Queen's University of Belfast in January, 1969, under the title "Man's Dominion." Montefiore, regarded as an outspoken avant-garde theologian, says in his preface that when he first raised at Belfast awkward questions concerning the facts about man's environment, his remarks were "greeted with incredulity." A short article by me which touched on some of those matters appeared in the April, 1970, issue of **The Canadian Baptist**, under the title "Christians in a Technological Society."[4] That article was solicited by the editor of **The Canadian Baptist** in October, 1969, and so there was some awareness of a growing malaise concerning the impact of technology upon society. Since then, there has been a spate of articles, books and conference reports concerning threats to ecology posed by technological development.

Concern with the ultimate limitations of natural resources, especially of food, is not new. It was nearly two hundred years ago that Thomas R. Malthus startled his generation with the gloomy essay entitled, "An Essay on the Principles of Population, as It Affects the Future Improvement of Society." Malthus was concerned with the effects of an exponential increase in the population upon the consumption of resources, and argued that the result would be eventual misery and starvation. Although frequent references to his pessimistic forecasts have been made in the past two centuries, the great successes of agriculture and technology in this century led to feelings of assurance that Malthusian ideas were just scare-mongering speculations.

Then in 1970 and 1971, detailed studies began to appear which forecast the eventual depletion of crucial natural resources such as food, fuel and minerals. The September, 1971, issue of **Scientific American** was entirely devoted to an examination of resources of energy and power, and it contained an article by King Hubbert which repeated his quantitative predictions of two decades earlier concerning the eventual depletion of fossil fuel reserves. By this time, it had become apparent that Hubbert's predictions were alarmingly accurate and that shortages would begin to appear in the 1970s. In Canada, F.K. North, very recently honoured by the Royal Society of Canada for his far-sightedness, was echoing Hubbert's predictions.

The Club of Rome, formed at Rome in April, 1968, at the instigation of Italian industrialist Aurelio Peccei, commissioned a wide-ranging and still-ongoing study of the predicaments of mankind. Jay Forrester's techniques of "system dynamics" were applied in the summer of 1970 to Phase One of the project and startling results began to appear in the publications and reports in 1971. In January, 1972, thirty-six prestigious British scientists endorsed the "Blueprint for Survival," a document published as Vol. 2, No. 1, of the British journal **The Ecologist**. In October, 1972, the sensational headline-making report on the imminent global disaster, **The Limits to Growth**,[5] appeared as the first fruits of the project of the Club of Rome on the predicament of mankind. One enthusiastic reviewer wrote, "Mark this book. It may be as important to mankind as the Council of Nicaea and Martin Luther's 95 Theses. It is a revolutionary new way of looking at man and society." The Club of Rome has recently published less sensational and more balanced analyses after a number of detailed criticisms of **The Limits to Growth** were published.

Whatever may be the shortcomings of the world model simulation used in **Limits to Growth**, it has inspired feverish activity around the world to appraise the many dire consequences of the unchecked exploitation of natural resources. In the autumn of 1973, the O.P.E.C. oil embargo brought home to citizens of Western Europe and the U.S.A. what hardship could be brought on by the shortage of oil reserves. Although that embargo was politically motivated by the Arab-Israeli conflict, it had a very salutary effect on the perceptions of the average citizen who had taken the copious flowing of oil supplies for granted. In March, 1974, a sub-committee of the Public Affairs Committee of the Baptist Convention of Ontario and Quebec produced a report entitled, "Christians and the Ecological Crisis"[6] which dealt with the impending shortage of energy reserves in the context of its impact upon ecological concerns. That report was subsequently printed in **The Canadian Baptist** in January, 1975.

There is no point in blaming "radical Protestants" for their lack of awareness of the theological dimensions of the ecological crisis and of the depletion of natural resources. They probably shared the views of the ordinary citizen in the 1960s that the "eco-maniacs" were raving over irrational and frantic misapprehensions concerning the world's future. Schaeffer, in **Pollution and the Death of Man**,[7] reluctantly conceded that the hippies had more insight than most professing Christians in unmasking and opposing "the plastic culture." A case could be made for the thesis that conservative and orthodox Protestantism not only hallowed the "Protestant work ethic" but also was largely responsible for the dynamic and irresistible capitalistic drive to exploit earth's natural resources for profit and power.

However, this is no time to be negative and fault-finding in a time of widespread re-appraisal and soul-searching. Almost every independent Christian college and Protestant seminary in the United States has introduced at least one course on Christian responsibility for the environment and for the husbanding of natural resources. Accounts of these courses appear almost monthly in the **Journal of the American Scientific Affiliation**, an association of evangelical scientists in North America. The 1978 annual meeting of the Affiliation will be held at Hope Christian College near Grand Rapids, Michigan, in August and the theme for the program will be "A Christian Stewardship of Natural Resources," with Clark Pinnock of McMaster Divinity College as theme speaker. Such a programme is indicative of the growing awareness of evangelical intellectuals concerning the vital importance of Christian stewardship in the area of natural resources.

Generally, evangelical Protestants have paid little attention to the value of fasting and abstinence. This neglect, which seems to be at variance with biblical exhortations, probably stems from a reaction to what are perceived as pathetic attempts on the part of superstitious Roman Catholic and Orthodox adherents to earn salvation by acts of pious self-denial. Anglicans, whose official theology warns against attempts to earn salvation through good works, hold in principle a well-balanced view of periodic abstinence and fasting, although it is probably a minority who are conscientious and disciplined in the practice of self-denial in Lent and at other times. At the other end of the theological spectrum, the primitive Anabaptists such as the Amish people and the Hutterites renounce almost totally the contributions of modern technology to the life-styles of their communities.

Interesting parallels could be drawn between the primitive Anabaptist communities and the communes that were established in the last decade by disaffected and disillusioned middle class youth and also by ecologically-minded associations of professionals such as those in "the Ark" of Prince Edward Island. These communities have monastic aspects, some morbidly negative about the hopeless state of the world and some wholesomely positive concerning the values of close-knit communities which live close to the soil in balance with nature. However valuable monastic communities are for their members, there is little impact on the outside world and, in many cases, the members of the communities have little or no concern for outsiders, who are regarded as blind travellers on the road to perdition. In my opinion, these monastic communities cannot serve as models for the lifestyles of most "radical Protestants." Although Mennonite churches have close associations with some primitive Anabaptists, the vast majority of Baptists have very little contact or empathy with such people.

Many people, including Christians, wonder whether there is really a resource crisis or whether it is just a charade orchestrated by the multi-national producers of food and fuel. My own view is that the imminent depletion of resources is a real threat if human beings continue to be irresponsibly greedy, but that it is not the main problem facing the world. It is the gross disparity between the rich and the poor which I see to be a scandal. An economist friend has calculated that if the world's resources of food and consumer goods were distributed equitably, we would all have a standard of living something like that in Greece or Jugoslavia. That doesn't seem to be bad if one is prepared to walk or ride a bicycle, sleep in a room with other members of the family, eat simpler foods and have a small radio instead of a T.V. set. What is frightening and appalling is the juggernaut tendency of North American society to devour resources at an exponentially increasing rate at the expense of the environment and to the detriment of future generations.

As far as energy is concerned, thorium-fuelled modifications of CANDU reactors could produce enough heat and electrical energy for a population of sixteen billion people for several millennia. W.B. Lewis, the "father" of the CANDU reactor, presented this estimate in an address delivered at Orillia, Ontario, last year with the title, "Harnessed Energy Against Starvation." Many concerned citizens are worried about radioactive wastes, but it is my belief that the small volume of dangerous nuclear wastes is a problem that can be solved. For those who don't like the idea of nuclear fission, there is the hope that the deuterium in ordinary water will eventually be a limitless source of fuel. However, the burning of deuterium by fusion processes is at best several decades away. There are enthusiasts for solar and wind energy, but I share the cautious view of Palmer Putnam, which he expressed in his 1953 book, **Energy and the Future**,[8] based on his own extensive research with wind-powered turbines. His estimate was that renewable resources would supply ten per cent at best of the world's energy needs in the century from 1950 to 2050.

One never knows what new reserves of oil and gas will be found. The discoveries of oil and gas in the North Sea have rejuvenated the economies of Britain and Norway. There is new optimism about reserves in Alberta, but these may be mere stopgaps in the next century. However, it is conceivable that hydrogen gas generated by the electrolysis of water could replace natural gas as a fuel, and there are many advocates of the "hydrogen economy" who are trying to find methods of generating, storing and transporting large amounts of hydrogen fuel. One highly speculative idea is that fission or fusion energy could be used to convert the carbon in calcium carbonate (limestone) into organic compounds to be used for food and/or fuel. In my view, there is nothing wrong with attempts to develop alternate sources on a grand scale, provided that society is sufficiently wary of the "technological fix," the blind faith that science and technology can solve any problem in time.

Food resources are a matter of concern in view of the encroachments of deserts and urban civilization on arable land. There are optimists such as Roger Revelle of Harvard and David Hopper of Canada's International Development Research Centre who believe that there are vast untapped land resources for food production such as the upper Nile drainage basin of the Sudan. The September, 1976, issue of **Scientific**

American is devoted to world food production and there is a balance of gloomy and optimistic estimates in the many authoritative articles in that journal. A good Canadian reference on this topic is the proceedings of the Symposium on Canada and World Food held last August in Ottawa under the auspices of the Agricultural Institute and of the Royal Society of Canada. The pessimists, who will undoubtedly call themselves realists on the subject of world food resources, find themselves taking seriously the "Lifeboat Ethics" of Garrett Hardin. A 1976 book, **Lifeboat Ethics: The Moral Dilemmas of World Hunger,**[9] examines this appalling concept from many sides. I really wonder whether Hardin can be expected to take a sufficiently altruistic view of world problems from his vantage point in the lotus-land of Santa Barbara, California. While Joseph Fletcher, the proponent of situational ethics, disparages **ad hominem** attacks on Hardin and other advocates of "lifeboat ethics," I find it hard to believe that there is any other motivation beyond self-preservation that accounts for such a dog-in-the-manger approach to food resources. How a professing Christian can seriously advocate "lifeboat ethics" is beyond me.

Fortunately, there is a new emphasis today upon conservation and stewardship. It can be found in many articles, journals, books and proceedings of conferences. The proposal that Canada become a "conserver society" instead of a "consumer society" has been advocated by the prestigious Science Council of Canada in its September, 1977, report.[10] I find my own thinking to be quite compatible with the central thesis of this report for which much of the research was done by the Gamma Group of Montreal. The report is unduly optimistic about the potential contribution of renewable energy resources, in my estimation, but I have no doubt that there will be a healthy development of these resources in the next decade or so. A "conserver society" is what Christian stewardship demands in a world of unbridled consumption and of uncontrolled exploitation of God-given natural resources. Richard H. Bube, editor of the **Journal of the American Scientific Affiliation**, introduced the September, 1977, issue of the journal with a two-page editorial entitled "A Christian Affirmation on the Stewardship of Natural Resources." His main premise is printed in italics as follows:

> The Christian has specific reasons for responding to the needs of his community and the world in a time of crisis for energy and natural resources. It is essential that Christians be leaders and example-setters in the days ahead, not indiffereent or reluctant followers. Christians in the U.S.A. have been blessed with greater affluence; they have also been given, therefore, greater responsibility.

In Canada, the fraction of society that accepts the idea of a conserver society is probably ten per cent, at most, today. There was a very negative reaction on the part of the press, politicians, business leaders and much of the public to the Prime Minister's 1977 New Year's Day message in which he hinted at major attitudinal changes to the economy of the future. There seemed to be a great reluctance to consider alternatives to the present economic system with its inbuilt dynamics of growth. At the 1976 Assembly of the Baptist Convention of Ontario and Quebec (1975-76 Yearbook, pages 69-70), a resolution on inflation was passed in which the Assembly encouraged the Department of External Affairs to "change its statement of priorities by eliminating the basic aim 'that Canada and all Canadians will enjoy enlarging prosperity in the widest possible sense' in its pamphlet 'Foreign Policy for Canadians'" and urged "all Christian people to resist the popular demand for 'expanding prosperity for all' by simplifying their style of living and consumption." Although the resolution passed by a comfortable majority, there was no ground swell of enthusiasm for its proposals. In the debate over the April, 1978, budget introduced by the federal minister of finance, Jean Chretien, it has become apparent that all parties want more spending, more consumption and less saving on the part of Canadians in order to "stimulate the economy." Prestigious economists have called for substantial tax-cuts and both of the major opposition parties in the House of Commons have demanded major cuts in income tax in order to give more money to consumers to spend. The government for its part has recognized the need for a stimulus but has chosen the method of partial cuts in provincial sales taxes to be financed by federal-provincial sharing of the burden. No one at this time of massive unemployment is advocating conservation and spending in a way that attracts any prominence in the media. What is needed is a conserver ethic which involves sharing of resources and which is sufficiently labour-intensive to generate employment, rather than one which perpetuates the affluence of a small fraction and the poverty of many.

There are those who look to "frontier resources" of energy and minerals as a way out of our present predicament. In the past decade, Canadians have witnessed the undertaking of vast projects in the north and have heard rumours of more to come. Among the sensational hydroelectric projects of the past decade have been the James Bay Project in Quebec, the Churchill River diversion in Manitoba and the harnessing of the Peace River in British Columbia. The quest for oil has led to the Great Canadian Oil Sands and the Syncrude Projects in order to utilize the Athabaska Tar Sands. There has been extensive drilling for oil and gas at sea on the continental shelf, including some very difficult and hazardous explorations in the Beaufort Sea and on the Arctic islands. The discovery of vast resources of oil and gas in the north slope areas of Alaska has led to the planning for trans-continental pipelines from the north and to increased geophysical exploration and drilling in the Yukon and in the Northwest Territories. These undertakings and proposed projects have generated heated debate between developers and environmentalists and conservationists. Christian people from many churches have become involved in the controversy because of a concern for the aboriginal and treaty rights of our native peoples. The

Baptist Convention of Ontario and Quebec has expressed itself in two major resolutions on the topic of northern development and native rights. At the Assembly in Hamilton in June, 1973, (1972-73 Yearbook, pages 54-55), it was resolved that

> this Assembly requests that the Federal, Provincial and Territorial Governments take immediate steps to stop or delay such projects as the James Bay Power Project, the Churchill River diversion, the Mackenzie Valley Highway, etc., until competent impartial studies provide sufficient evidence that completion of the projects will not create unacceptable social, cultural or environmental damage; and asks the Federal Department of Indian Affairs and Northern Development to safeguard the rights of the native peoples in their confrontations with government, big business and multinational corporations.

Again, at the 1976 Assembly in Kingston (1975-76 Yearbook, page 69), a resolution was passed, with only a handful of dissenting votes and hundreds of affirmative votes, to uphold native rights. It was resolved that

> this Assembly express its support to the Native People in their efforts to obtain justice through recognition of treaty, aboriginal and other rights and through a just settlement of their land claims, and request the Federal Government and the appropriate Provincial and Territorial Governments to halt planned development until aboriginal claims are settled and to initiate negotiations on the land claims issues without prior conditions.

This latter resolution was presented to the Ottawa hearings of the Berger Commission in June, 1976, and the results of the vote were communicated to Mr. Justice Berger by the general secretary of the Convention. Despite these resolutions, Baptists have not generally been supportive of the native peoples in their struggle against rapid development in the north. The Baptist Federation did not see fit to participate in Project North, an ecumenical group supported by the major Christian communions in Canada with the aim of upholding native rights has been given by the Committee for Justice and Liberty Project North, then withdrew last year but very recently in April, 1978, renewed their support. Outstanding leadership in the fight to safeguard native rights has been given by the Committee for justice and Liberty Foundation and its executive director Gerald Vandezande. Many of the members of the CJL Foundation, which advocates Christian political involvement, are evangelical Christians from Christian Reformed congregations. One of their number, John Olthius, a lawyer, collaborated with Hugh and Karmel McCallum in the writing of the book, **Moratorium**, as part of the activities of Project North, and the CJL Foundation has made several important presentations to such bodies as the National Energy Board and to the Berger Commission. One wonders if Baptist reluctance to participate in this influential ecumenical witness has been influenced by a desire for the rapid growth of Inuvik where the Baptist Federation of Canada has been promoting its triennium project, a new church for the Arctic.

RESPONSIBILITY FOR WORLD RESOURCES: A RESPONSE

Gerald Vandezande

Our frequent failure to be at peace, rather than at war, with the Lord's "very good" creation may well be because we have not (yet) clearly understood the sweeping significance of John 3: 16, "For God so loved the **world** (the cosmos), that He gave His only begotten Son, that whosoever believes in Him should not perish, but have everlasting life." Rather than reflecting God's love and showing genuine gratitude for the Creator's handiwork, all too often we attack and abuse it in the exploitive ways we live and work, produce and consume, forgetting that scripture teaches: "For God sent not his Son into the world to condemn the world, but that the world through Him might be saved" (John 3: 17). We should always remember that Christ came to save that which He had created (cf. John 1: 2), so that all of life, including the whole of creation, would continue to have its meaning in Him who is the source, guide and goal of all that is (cf. Romans 11: 36). We had better face the truth: dealing with world resources and other environmental issues means dealing deeply with our own selves and the meaning of our salvation.

The Word of God calls creation to life, holds creation in life, and redeems creation to new life.[1] If we would daily live (out of) that biblical confession, we would know how to enjoy life, and how to work, buy, sell and vote meaningfully. We would be God's renewed people, experiencing and conveying the shalom of the gospel as we responsibly develop and preserve all that the Lord gave us to enjoy and to share with His creatures everywhere (cf. Galations 5).

As I understand the inter-relatedness between the biblical teaching of creation and redemption (re-creation), it is not so much a question of "giving the doctrine of creation equal time with the doctrine of redemption," as Professor Klaassen suggests, but to see and acknowledge their integral unity in our triune God "who created all things" (Ephesians 3: 9), in our "one Lord, Jesus Christ, through whom are all things and through whom we exist" (I Corinthians 8: 6). Christ came to "make all things new" (Revelation 21: 5), including creation. Therefore, to be in Christ is to live in the One in whom "all things hold together" (Colossians 1: 16), whose Word of power created, renewed and sustains the universe and who will return to judge everything, even our stewardship, or lack of it, over creation. "So," writes Paul, "whether you eat or drink, or whatever you do, do all to the glory of God" (I Corinthians 10: 31). This is no small task, "but with God all things are possible" (Matthew 19: 26).

When we confess that all things were created by Christ and that He is the Word made flesh, then we really need to acknowledge that there is a Word from God for every human activity and for every area of life. And when, in the power of Christ's liberating Spirit, we honour God's Word for creational living, then a culturally formative way of life develops that brings renewal and healing, peace and goodwill, justice and freedom. Such normative living would be the reward of viewing people in harmony with God's abiding intent for humanity, and using world resources in keeping with His Word of stewardship for the creation. We would treat all resources as **creational** resources, as gifts to be used wisely for the wellbeing of humankind as part of a true way of creational life.

The concrete consequence of such a quality-oriented way of life, concerned with integral human growth and environmental justice, would be tremendously healing both personally and structurally. We would witness the emergence of economies and industries which would be sensitive to the rightful needs and concerns of people, respectful of the unique rights and claims of the creation, and which would do justice to our creaturely task to practice stewardship. Our business enterprises would increasingly feel obliged to manufacture legitimate products and render essential services conducive to the fulfillment of people's cultural mission to be of blessing to their neighbours. Their managers and financers would seek to do so via processes enabling joyful working conditions and conserving creational resources.

A new life of economic service would obviously constitute a principled break with what Mr. Justice Thomas R. Berger has correctly described as "the economic religion of our time, the belief in an ever-expanding cycle of growth and consumption...a faith shared equally by capitalist and communist."[2] We would no longer be seen as "economic animals" whose primary purpose is to produce and consume. We would no longer consider non-renewable resources, such as natural gas, crude oil and coal, as "**natural**" resources, as belonging to nature — unrelated and untouched by redemption. We would no longer look upon them as commodities which may be ruthlessly exploited for the sake of individual greed, corporate profit and political power.

A steward-like resource policy would mean a radical departure from the present development strategies and a new chapter in our industrial history. It would involve a Christian confrontation with the alien ideology of capitalism and a critical examination of its belief that the pursuit of economic growth and material prosperity ensures human happiness and social progress (cf. I Timothy 6: 6-19). It would also require a careful re-assessment of our society's materialistic value system and a rejection of the modern faith in science and technology as the key to all environmental problems.

Admitting that material possessions are not the way to happiness requires a confession as abhorrent to doctrinaire economic-growth advocates as a denial of the virgin birth is to fundamentalist Christians (cf. James 5: 1-8). While Christian believers should make that confession as a matter of principle (Philippians 3:18-21), many are driven more by the pragmatic argument that the realities of our day (increasing energy costs, decreasing supplies of fossil fuels, inadequate social services and insufficient welfare supplements) are forcing a change in values.

An honest appraisal of our economic-growth-oriented society shows we have failed to achieve even a quantity lifestyle for millions of people around the world. It is also becoming apparent that those who have quantity don't necessarily have happiness. In many instances, their quantity has been achieved at the expense of the very basic food, shelter and clothing needs of powerless people both at home and abroad.

In his paper Professor David McLay quite properly reminds us that we should be "wary of the 'technological fix', the blind faith that science and technology can solve any problem in time." However, I would like to assert that unless we look at our society, structured as it is, with its focus on economic gains and accumulation of wealth at virtually all costs, we all too easily fall into the trap of thinking that the problems are essentially of a technological sort and thus, that their solution lies in technological fixes.

Many of the problems we encounter in our society, such as personal and interpersonal distress, national and international tension, labour-management conflict, industrial waste, environmental damage, resource shortages, poverty, malnutrition, disease and starvation, are related to the misdirection and malformation of our socio-economic system. They are the expressions of the basic failure to understand the true nature of people and the creation and thus the type of socio-economic order and production system required to encourage the development and deepening of that nature. Rather than constructing a socio-economic order responsive to a wide range of human needs and to the needs of the ecological system, we have attempted to reconstruct both people and the environment to meet the demands and constraints of the socio-economic system designed to maximize aggregate material wealth. As a result we are fast approaching a critical point where cumulative human and environmental abuse constitutes a real threat to meaningful life for millions of people around the world.

Barry Commoner, Professor of Environmental Science at Washington University in St. Louis, develops the theme that there is a crucial interdependency between the three basic systems — the eco-system, the production system, and the economic system — that, together with the social and political order, govern all human activity. He says that when we understand the nature of the dependencies, namely, that the economic system is dependent on the wealth yielded by the production system, and the production system dependent on the resources provided by the eco-system, it would appear that the economic system ought to be designed to conform to the requirements of the production system, and the production system to conform to the requirements of the eco-system.[3]

Today, because of the basic misunderstanding as to how the creation is structured, an industrial society/world has emerged in which the relationships among these three systems are turned around. The environmental crisis tells us that the eco-system has been disastrously affected by the design of an economic-growth-oriented production system, which has been developed with almost no regard to compatibility with the environment or for the normative purpose of resources. These creational relationships are being turned upside down.

Margaret Mead, Professor of Anthropology at Columbia University, New York, has made this important comment about problems associated with such distorted economic growth situations.

> The amplification of the gross national product, I don't call growth. ...we're beginning to realize that we have built a kind of economy which imprisons us, uses an enormous amount of energy and irreplaceable resources of the world, places a great drain on the rest of the world — and is even making a section of our own population poor, ill-fed and unhappy.... The doctrine that everything could be solved by economic growth, which was preached after World War II, and that disparities between the rich and the poor nations could be corrected by technical assistance are now both proving to be wrong. We have to change them and we have to reorganize our lifestyle.[4]

The doctrine that Margaret Mead refers to is deeply entrenched in us. This popular doctrine is even advanced by Joe Clark, leader of the Conservatives. He claims that the rich in this world owe their "undoubted material and spiritual benefits" to "the industrial transformation" and that our future wellbeing and that of the poor is dependent on the production of more goods. According to Mr. Clark, "We are still not producing enough goods to provide all people with the kind of human liberty we all value...." In his view, "the goal of economic progress is the extension of human liberty" (for liberty is "the original purpose" of "material progress"). "To call a halt now — to freeze the economic status quo — would be the most profoundly immoral act of all." Convinced that "the emerging supereconomy of the advanced countries has been and will continue to be the engine of world progress," Mr. Clark believes that "they must pull the rest of the world in their wake."[5]

Although Mr. Clark's Liberal opponent, Pierre Elliott Trudeau, has on various occasions pointed out that the "Gross National Product is no measurement of social justice, human dignity, or cultural attainment,"[6] the Prime Minister's economic and political decisions such as the sanctioning of the Alcan natural gas pipeline, for the sake of more economic growth, have clearly contradicted these words.

At this point I would like to quote Arnold G. Toynbee, the noted historian.

> ...the Western minority has consecrated greed and has made it into a deliberate objective. This first began when the Americas were discovered. That gave the Western peoples a false impression...of

infinite space and wealth at Western man's disposal. Then,
secondly, at the end of the eighteenth century the mechanization of
industry through the harnessing of steam power again gave us an
impression that we had opened up an infinite source of production.
...but now we have suddenly realized that the biosphere is finite
and that it sets absolutely insuperable limits to material
expansion.... As I see it, the question is: Will the human race as a
whole be able to reverse its attitudes and aims before we run into a
catastrophe?[7]

We Christians need to realize the magnitude of the problem we face
and also the religious depth of the solution which needs to be worked at.

The "emerging super-economy of the advanced countries" has left
rising unemployment and chronic inflation in its wake, the very
problems our economic planners supposedly knew how to fix by
adjusting interest rates and providing tax breaks. This fact, along with
all the human misery which can't be quantified, is forcing people to
become concerned and search for a solution.

Too often, new technologies are seen as the solution to the problems.
Report No. 27 of the Science Council of Canada entitled, **Canada as a
Conserver Society** best illustrates my point. The subtitle "Resource
Uncertainties and the Need for New Technologies" already indicates
the technical focus of its narrow concern. While I in no way wish to
detract from the authors' helpful emphasis on the need to conserve
energy and resources or from their welcome opposition to waste and
pollution, I do think it is crucial to remember that the report basically
views the present capitalist patterns of development as more or less
acceptable, as givens within which "...a conserver approach will lead to
the introduction of new technologies, new opportunities for Canadian
business, and unprecedented challenges to the entrepreneurial spirit."[8]

The authors themselves emphasize that they "are not attempting to
set out a complete blueprint for a new society, nor to specify the exact
modes of transition or how long they may take."[9] "We have tried to stick
to practical matters, with an incremental approach, to identify some of
the technological paths that lead in the right direction, toward
sustainable relationships with material resources and the biosphere."[10]
The concluding paragraph of the "Background of the Study" confirms
the authors' acceptance of our current socio-economic way of life as
well as their rationalistic approach to the future.

It should not be construed, as it sometimes has been, that these
prescriptions for re-directing and modifying Canadian patterns of
growth are aimed at slowing, or freezing in the "status quo," the
productive system in which large numbers of less well-off
Canadians still hope to realize their aspirations. To the contrary,
within finite resources and limited environmental regenerative
capacity, it is only by being more efficient, more intelligent, more
far-sighted, and by changing the style of some technologies, that
we shall all find room for continuing growth and distributive
justice. What applies within Canada applies also to Canada as one
of the more developed countries, in relation to other parts of the

world.[11]

In light of the foregoing, I quite agree with Professor McLay when he states: "What is frightening and appalling is the juggernaut tendency of North American society to devour resources at an exponentially increasing rate at the expense of the environment and to the detriment of future generations." For example, the Canadian government's energy policy appears to be: "Seek ye first energy, then ye shall find wealth, and the good life shall be added unto you." At least, that's how I interpret the following quote:

> The use of energy, in amounts equal to any reasonable demand, is essential to the attainment of a high quality of life in Canada. It is indispensable to generate the wealth that will enable Canadians to improve their social environment, to protect and enhance their natural environment, and to produce the surplus of goods and services, the range of individual choices and actions, the opportunities for education and intellectual development, the leisure time and the bonds within our society that will enable each of us, according to our interests and values, and all of us together, to improve the quality as well as the prosperity of our living. Our energy policy must make this possible.[12]

That Canada's government is caught in the trap of money-settles-everything is illustrated by the Cabinet's decision to allow offshore oil and gas drilling in the ice-infested, environmentally-sensitive Beaufort Sea on the condition that the drilling company post a $50-million bond to cover possible compensation and cleanup liabilities in case of an oil spill or a blow out.

Our Lord clearly did not intend the creation to be a banquet at which we are free to gorge ourselves and He obviously did not create people to eat, drink and merrily exploit creational resources as we see fit. Christ gave His life so that we may enjoy life in all its fullness (cf. John 10: 10). He reminds us that "a man's life does not consist in the abundance of his possessions" (Luke 12: 15) but in the service of Christ's coming kingdom of righteousness (cf. Luke 21: 31). The abundant life in Christ cannot be reduced to, or equated with, contemporary society's definition of the good life which has become synonymous with material abundance which stimulates spending for the sake of consumption and which even encourages waste and obsolescence. ("Planned obsolescence, in my opinion, is another word for progress," says James Roche, a former Chairman of General Motors.) Such environmental violence and economic distortion violates the call to discipleship and stewardship and causes people to suffer and creation to groan (cf. Romans 8: 22,23).

I am deeply concerned that we develop a way of life that would encourage people to realize their God'given potential. This includes an understanding of people's dependent relationship to God, to other people and to the creation which surrounds us and sustains us.

I believe that God gave people an astonishing capacity to develop and express a wide range of feelings such as contentment, joy, despair and anger. He created us to be loving, trusting, just and charitable. He gave us artistic, scientific and other vocational abilities to be used for the benefit of other people, the creation and to His glory. I believe that a meaningful life comes through the dedication of life in all of its dimensions in communal service of neighbours down the street and around the world. The biblical promise is that all who follow such a life of service will in turn receive all the things they require to facilitate that life of service (cf. Matthew 6: 33).

Food, clothing, shelter and the like, are considered but they should not determine the quality of lifestyle. Our values and priorities need to be revised. Whenever we distort our relationship to God, we also distort our relationship to other people and to the creation. This also works the other way — distorted relationships with other people and the creation leads to a distorted relationship with God. Contemporary problems are a result of these distortions.

Walter Klaassen rightly insists that Paul's references to creation's bondage to decay and its groaning in travail "have in our time achieved a frightening reality." Indeed, "the creation waits with eager longing for the revealing of the sons of God." It is clear, as Paul points out, that "the creation itself will be set free from its bondage to decay and obtain the glorious liberty of the children of God" if those "who have the first fruits of the Spirit" show that also in acts of obedience with respect to creational resources (cf. Romans 8: 12-22).

In this connection, I want to refer you to the late E.F. Schumacher.

> The home-comers base themselves upon a different picture of man from that which motivates the people of the forward stampede. It would be very superficial to say that the latter believe in "growth" while the former do not. In a sense, everybody believes in growth, and rightly so, because growth is an essential feature of life. The whole point, however, is to give to the idea of growth a qualitative determination; for there are always many things that ought to be growing and many things that ought to be diminishing.[13]

In conclusion, I would like to quote Bob Goudzwaard.

> Our western societies have not made an irreversible choice for the gods of wealth and technique. Moreover, some still hesitate, some still have a sense of stewardship in the control of the environment. Some of the young reject an economistic and technocratic way of life and seek a possible alternative. And that alternative is a real one, for there still is a bifurcation, a fork in the road. At the crossroads, however, the right direction is only indicated by the signpost of the living Word of God.[14]

Footnotes

ABBREVIATIONS USED:

CB   — Canadian Baptist
CT   — Christianity Today
Fdt.   — Foundations
MQR   — Mennonite Quarterly Review
TDNT   — Theological Dictionary of the New Testament
BQ   — Baptist Quarterly
IDB   — Interpreter's Dictionary of the Bible

PREFACE, J.K. Zeman, p. xi

[1]Max Weber, **The Protestant Ethic and the Spirit of Capitalism**, T. Parsons, tr. (New York: Scribner's, 1958), pp. 144f.

[2]Franklin H. Littell, **The Free Church** (Boston: Star King, 1957), p. 2. Cf. also Ernest A. Payne, **The Free Church Tradition in the Life of England** (London: SCM, 1944) and Gunnar Westin, **The Free Church Through the Ages**, Virgil A. Olson, tr. (Nashville: Broadman, 1958).

[3]J.K. Zeman, **Baptist Roots and Identity** (Toronto: Baptist Convention of Ont. & Que., 1978), p. 13.

[4]George H. Williams, **Wilderness and Paradise in Christian Thought** (New York: Harper, 1962), p. 214.

[5]For a defence of the church as a mixed multitude, see the official statement **Church Membership: Doctrine and Practice in the United Church of Canada** (Toronto: The United Church of Canada, 1963), pp. 16ff. Cf. the Baptist response by Russell F. Aldwinckle, **Of Water and the Spirit: A Baptist View of Church Membership** (Brantford: The Baptist Federation of Canada, 1964).

[6]Cf. a letter to the editor, "The Believers' church — the Pharisees' church?" in which Tom Neufeld condemned the 1978 Winnipeg conference. Published in **Mennonite Reporter** (June 26, 1978), p. 6.

[7]For published papers and reports from the three conferences, see the Appendix.

[8]Distribution by provinces: B.C. - 9, Alberta - 11, Saskatchewan - 11, Manitoba - 54, Ontario - 39, Quebec, 3, the Maritimes - 12; plus 11 from the U.S.A.

[9]Age profile: under 25 years - 7; 25-40 years - 52; 40-55 years - 52; over 55 years - 37.

[10]There were 69 Mennonites and 66 Baptists, including 54 BFC Baptists, 9 from the Baptist General Conference and the North American Baptist Conference, and 3 from the Fellowship of Evangelical Baptist Churches in Canada.

[11]See for example: **The Atlantic Baptist** (July 1, 1978); **Baptist World - North American News** (July-Aug. 1978); **C.B.** (July-Aug. 1978); and **Mennonite Reporter** (May 29, 1978).

GLOBAL PERSPECTIVES, J.H. Yoder, p. 3

[1]H.S. Bender's 1943 lecture may be held to be the foundational document of the modern reappropriation of Believers' Church ecclesiology. First printed in **Church History** (Mar., 1944), then in **M.Q.R.** XVIII (Apr., 1944), and reprinted in

G.F. Hershberger, ed., **The Recovery of the Anabaptist Vision** (Scottdale: Herald, 1957), pp. 29ff.

²G.H. Williams, "A People in Community: Historical Background," James Leo Garrett, ed., **The Concept of the Believers' Church** (Scottdale: Herald, 1969), pp. 102ff.

³Robert K. Greenleaf, **Servant Leadership** (New York: Paulist, 1977).

CANADIAN FOCUS, J.K. Zeman, p. 17

¹Cf. J.K. Zeman, **Baptist Roots and Identity** (Toronto: Baptist Convention of Ont. & Que., 1978).

²Malcolm Muggeridge, "Western Civilization: To Be or Not to Be", **The Reader's Digest** (June 1976), p. 170.

THE PAST IN CANADA, C.J. Dyck, p. 25

¹Douglas J. Wilson, **The Church Grows in Canada** (New York: Friendship, 1966), p. 19.

²Quoted in John S. Moir, **The Church In The British Era** (Toronto: McGraw-Hill Ryerson, 1972), p. 23.

³**Ibid.**, p. 23.

⁴Constant H. Jacquet, Jr., ed., **Yearbook of American & Canadian Churches** (Nashville: Abingdon, 1977).

⁵A good summary of theories concerning the origin of the Baptists is found in Robert S. Torbet, **A History of the Baptists** (Philadelphia: Judson, 1950), pp. 59f. For a different interpretation, see William R. Estep, **The Anabaptist Story** (Grand Rapids: Eerdmans, 1975), pp. 203ff.

⁶John W. Grant, **The Churches and the Canadian Experience** (Toronto: Ryerson, 1963), p. 28.

⁷Moir, **op. cit.**, pp. 17ff.

⁸Maurice W. Armstrong, **The Great Awakening in Nova Scotia, 1776-1809** (Hartford: American Society of Church History, 1948), p. 59.

⁹**Ibid.**, p. 72.

¹⁰**Ibid.**, p. 107.

¹¹Grant, **op. cit.**, pp. 33-34.

¹²**Ibid.**, p. 36.

¹³For historical background see Gordon F. Atter, **The Third Force** (Peterborough: Book Nook, 1962). See also the standard book by Nils Bloch-Hoell, **The Pentecostal Movement** (New York: Humanities, 1964). Also Erna Alma Peters, **The Contribution to Education by the Pentecostal Assemblies of Canada** (Altona: D.W. Friesen, 1970).

¹⁴Information kindly supplied by the staff of Canadian Bible College and Superintendant Robert J. Gould, 3585 Hillsdale St., Regina.

¹⁵See, for example, the intense debate of two decades ago in the following literature: Winthrop S. Hudson, "Who were the Baptists?" **B.Q.** XVI (July, 1956), pp. 303-12; Ernest A. Payne, "Who were the Baptists?" **B.Q.** XVI (Oct., 1956), pp. 339-42; Winthrop S. Hudson, "Who were the Baptists?" **B.Q.** XVII (Apr., 1957),

pp. 53-55; Gunnar Westin, "Who were the Baptists?" **B.Q.** XVII (Apr., 1957), pp. 55-60; James D. Mosteller, "Baptists and Anabaptists," I, **The Chronicle,** XX (Jan., 1957), pp. 1-27; II, **The Chronicle** (July, 1957), pp. 100-114; Norman H. Maring, "Notes from Religious Journals," **Fdt.** I (July, 1958), pp. 91-95; C. Norman Kraus, "Anabaptist Influence on English Separatism as Seen in Robert Browne," **M.Q.R.** XXXIV (Jan., 1960), pp. 1-19.

[16]Stuart Ivison, "Is There a Canadian Baptist Tradition?" in Grant, **op. cit.**, p. 53. CF. J.K. Zeman, **Baptist Roots and Identity** (Brantford: Baptist Convention of Ont. & Que., 1978).

[17]Wilson, **op. cit.**, p. 28.

[18]George E. Levy, "The United Baptist Convention of the Maritime Provinces," in David C. Woolley, ed., **Baptist Advance** (Nashville: Broadman, 1964), p. 141.

[19]**Ibid.**, p. 141.

[20]**Ibid.**, p. 159.

[21]Ivison, in Grant, **op. cit.**, p. 58.

[22]Woolley, **op. cit.**, p. 160.

[23]J.K. Zeman, "Baptists in Canada and Co-operative Christianity," **Fdt.** XV (July-Aug-Sept, 1972), p. 213.

[24]Ivison, in Grant, **op. cit.**, p. 59.

[25]Leslie K. Tarr, **This Dominion His Dominion** (Willowdale: Fellowship of Evangelical Churches, 1968), p. 78.

[26]Woolley, **op. cit.**, p. 178.

[27]**Ibid.**, pp. 178-79.

[28]R. Fred Bullen, "The Baptist Federation of Canada: An Overview," **Report From The Capital** (Sept., 1972), pp. 4,5,7.

[29]Tarr, **op. cit.**, p. 82.

[30]Frank H. Epp, **Mennonites in Canada, 1786-1920** (Toronto: Macmillan, 1974), p. 50.

[31]**Ibid.**, p. 75. The figure given on p. 72 is 5,379. For the Amish story see Orland Gingerich, **The Amish of Canada** (Waterloo: Conrad, 1972).

[32]Cornelius J. Dyck, ed., **An Introduction to Mennonite History** (Scottdale: Herald, 1967), p. 156. Quoted from E.K. Francis, **In Search of Utopia** (Glencoe: Free, 1955), p. 79.

[33]Paul N. Kraybill, ed., **Mennonite World Handbook** (Lombard: Mennonite World Conference, 1978).

[34]For a new history of the Brethren in Christ see Carlton O. Wittlinger, **Quest for Piety and Obedience** (Nappanee: Evangel, 1978).

[35]See Reuben Butchart, **The Disciples of Christ in Canada Since 1830** (Toronto: Canadian Headquarters Publ., 1949).

[36]Woolley, **op. cit.**, pp. 168-73; Tarr, **op. cit.**, pp. 69-75.

[37]**Studies in Church Discipline** (Newton: Mennonite Publ., 1958), p. 212. See also, **Proceedings of the Study Conference on the Believers' Church** (Newton: General Conference Mennonite Church, 1955), pp. 23-39; and Charles W. Deweese, **A Community of Believers** (Valley Forge: Judson, 1978).

[38]J.E. Harris, **The Baptist Union of Western Canada** (St. John: Lingley, 1976), p. 216.

[39]Woolley, **op. cit.**, p. 166.

40Ibid., p. 167.

41Ibid., p. 167.

42Harold U. Trinier, A Century of Service (Toronto: The Baptist Convention of Ont. & Que., 1958), pp. 61f.

43Harris, op. cit., p. 202.

44Ibid., p. 135.

45Zeman, op. cit., p. 233. His article was reprinted in James Leo Garrett, ed., Baptist Relations with other Christians (Valley Forge: Judson, 1974), pp. 105-119.

46Ibid., p. 237. A significant symposium of scholars on "Baptists in Canada 1760-1980" will take place at Acadia Divinity College, Wolfville, in Oct. 1979. Papers from the symposium are scheduled for publication in 1980.

THE FUTURE IN CANADA, R.D. Bell, p. 55

1David Virtue, "Suffer the Little Children to Come Unto Me," The Province (May 6, 1978), p. 7a.

2John Kettle, Hindsight on the Future (Toronto: Macmillan, 1976), p. 43.

3James Leo Garrett, Jr., The Concept of the Believers' Church (Scottdale: Herald, 1969), pp. 314-324. Donald F. Durnbaugh, The Believers' Church (New York: Macmillan, 1968), pp. 32f.

4George H. Williams, ed., Spiritual and Anabaptist Writers (Philadelphia: Library of Christian Classics, XXV, 1957), pp. 43f.

5Carl H. Lundquist, "Journey to Renewal," C.T. (Jan. 13, 1978), p. 13-17.

6Ibid., p. 16.

7Benjamin Zablocki, The Joyful Community (Baltimore: Penguin, 1971). Dave and Nita Jackson, Living Together in a World Falling Apart (Carol Stream: Creation House, 1976).

8Sojourners Magazine, 1029 Bermont Ave., N.W., Washington, D.C. 20005.

9H. Wheeler Robinson, Baptist Principles, 3rd ed. (London: Kingsgate, 1938), pp. 74-75.

10Garrett, op. cit., p. 295.

11Ibid.

BIBLICAL AUTHORITY, C.H. Pinnock, p. 75

1James D. Smart, The Strange Silence of the Bible in the Church (Philadelphia: Westminster, 1970); Brevard S. Childs, Old Testament Books for Pastor and Teacher (Philadelphia: Westminster, 1977), p. 7; Clark H. Pinnock, "Baptists and Biblical Authority," Journal of the Evangelical Theological Society 17 (1974), pp. 193-205.

2For example, I perceive very little evidence of clarity on the final authority of scripture in the conference volume, James Leo Garrett, ed., The Concept of the Believers' Church (Scottdale: Herald, 1969).

3John H. Yoder, "The Hermeneutics of the Anabaptists," M.Q.R. XLI (1967), p. 308.

4Cf. Walter Klaassen, "Anabaptist Hermeneutics: The Letter and the Spirit," M.Q.R. XL (1966), pp. 83-96.

[5]Henry Poettcker, "Menno Simons' Encounter with the Bible," **M.Q.R.** XL (1966), p. 138.

[6]Cf. the excellent discussion in J.R.W. Stott, **Christ the Controversialist** (Downers Grove: Inter Varsity, 1970), pp. 65-89.

[7]W.L. Lumpkin, **Baptist Confession of Faith** (Philadelphia: Judson, 1959), pp. 248, 252.

[8]**Ibid.**, pp. 361f.

[9]**Ibid.**, pp. 411f.

[10]John H. Watson, "Baptists and the Bible as Seen in Three Eminent Baptists," **Fdt.** XVI (1973), pp. 239-254.

[11]Cf. Willis B. Glover, **Evangelical Nonconformity and Higher Criticism in the 19th Century** (London: Independent, 1954).

[12]James T. Burtchaell, **Catholic Theories of Biblical Inspiration Since 1810: A Review and Critique** (Cambridge: Cambridge University, 1969), pp. 1-2.

[13]W. Pannenberg. **Basic Questions in Theology** I (Philadelphia: Fortress, 1970), p. 4.

[14]For the origin and development of this new approach, see Jan Walgrave, **Unfolding Revelation: The Nature of Doctrinal Development** (Philadelphia: Westminster, 1972), pp. 179-277.

[15]Paul G. Schrotenboer, "The Bible in the World Council of Churches," **Calvin Theological Journal** 12 (1977), pp. 144-163.

[16]Norman H. Maring, "Baptists and Changing Views of the Bible (1865-1918)," **Fdt.** I (1958), pp. 52-57 (July); pp. 30-61 (Oct.); James Leo Garrett, "Representative Modern Baptist Understandings of Biblical Inspiration," **Review and Expositor** 71 (1974), pp. 179-195; C. Norman Kraus, "American Mennonites and the Bible, 1750-1950," **M.Q.R.** XLI (1967), pp. 309-329.

[17]William R. Hutchison, **The Modernist Impulse in American Protestantism** (Cambridge: Harvard University, 1976), p. 114.

[18]W.S. Hudson, ed., **Baptist Concepts of the Church** (Philadelphia: Judson, 1959), p. 204.

[19]William N. Clarke, **An Outline of Christian Theology** (New York: Scribner's, 1898), pp. 35,38,46,49,381-85. See also **The Use of the Scriptures in Theology** (New York: Scribner's, 1906), and **Sixty Years with the Bible: A Record of Experience** (New York: Scribner's, 1912).

[20]Kraus, **op. cit.**

[21]Gordon D. Kaufman, **Systematic Theology: A Historicist Perspective** (New York: Scribner's, 1968), pp. 71, 265.

[22]Cited by Harry E. Fosdick, **The Modern Use of the Bible** (New York: Macmillan, 1924), p. 2.

[23]A.H. Strong, **A Tour of the Missions: Observations and Conclusions** (Philadelphia: Griffith & Rowland, 1918), pp. 170-174.

[24]Avery Dulles, **The Resilient Church: The Necessity and Limits of Adaptation** (New York: Doubleday, 1977), p. 94.

[25]Although I believe he is too negative and unappreciative, James Barr has written a devastating critique of conservative shortcomings in his book called simply **Fundamentalism** (London: SCM, 1977).

[26]Peter Stuhlmacher, **Historical Criticism and Theological Interpretation of Scripture** (Philadelphia: Fortress, 1977).

[27]J.D.G. Dunn, **Unity and Diversity in the New Testament: An Inquiry into the Character of Earliest Christianity** (London: SCM, 1977).

A SHORT BIBLIOGRAPHY

Dunn, James D.G., **Unity and Diversity in the New Testament: An Inquiry into the Character of Earliest Christianity** (London: SCM & Philadelphia: Westminster, 1977).

Kelsey, David H., **The Uses of Scripture in Recent Theology** (Philadelphia: Fortress, 1975).

Pinnock, Clark H., **Biblical Revelation: The Foundation of Christian Theology** (Chicago: Moody, 1971).

Rogers, Jack B., ed., **Biblical Authority** (Waco: Word, 1977).

AUTHORITY AND TRADITIONS, D. Schroeder, p. 93

[1]Bibliography by H.D. McDonald, "Authority," **Pictorial Encyclopedia of the Bible** (Grand Rapids: Zondervan, 1975), p. 421.

[2]The deductive argument reminds me of Anaximander (Ps-Plut. **strom** 2) who deduced from the belief that what is perfect must be spherical, the fact that the earth is round (cylindrical) and that people live on its outer side. He was right to a degree but arrived at it apart from empirical data.

[3]The usual way of saying this is to speak of revelation being progressive. That is true, too. But it seems to me that God in every age, and even now, wants to reveal more to us than we are able to hear (Hebrews 5:11f); that God is limited in revealing more to man because of his inability or unwillingness to respond to all that God is revealing to him.

[4]Bibliography by R.L. Harris and D. Guthrie, "Canon of the OT and NT," **Pictorial Encyclopedia of the Bible** I (Grand Rapids: Zondervan, 1975), pp. 731, 745.

[5]Montague Rhodes James, tr., **The New Testament Apocrypha** (Oxford: Clarendon, 1975).

[6]Harry Rimmer, **The Harmony of Science and Scripture** (Grand Rapids: Eerdmans, 1949).

[7]E.J. Carnell, **The Case for Orthodox Theology** (Philadelphia: Westminster, 1959), p. 94.

[8]Bernard Ramm, **The Christian View of Science and Scripture** (Grand Rapids: Eerdmans, 1955), p. 117.

[9]N.H. Ridderbos, **Is There a Conflict between Genesis 1 and Natural Science?** (Grand Rapids: Eerdmans, 1957).

DISCIPLINE AND DISCERNMENT, M. Jeschke, p. 109

BRIEF BIBLIOGRAPHY

Driver, John, **Community and Commitment** (Kitchener: Herald, 1976).

Greenslade, S.L., **Shepherding the Flock** (London: SCM, 1967).

Jeschke, Marlin, **Discipling the Brother** (Scottdale: Herald, 1972).

Klaassen, Walter, "Church Discipline and the Spirit in Pilgram Marpeck" (**De Geest in het Geding**, ed. I.B. Horst, et al., Tjeenk Willink, 1978).

Kraus, C. Norman, **The Community of the Spirit** (Grand Rapids: Eerdmans, 1974).

DISCIPLINE AND DISCERNMENT, J.E. Runions, p. 119

[1]John Knox, "The Book of Discipline," **The History of the Reformation of Religion in Scotland**, C. Lennox, ed. (London: Melrose, 1905), pp. 363-421. The chapter headings are as follows: 1) Of Doctrine; 2) Of Sacraments; 3) Touching the Abolition of Idolatry; 4) Concerning Ministers and Their Lawful Election; 5) Concerning Provisions for the Ministers and for Distribution of the Rents and Processions justly appertaining to the Kirk; 6) Of the Superintendents; 7) Of Schools and Universities; 8) Of the Rents and Patrimony of the Kirk; 9) Of Ecclesiastical Discipline; 10) Touching the Election of Elders and Deacons, etc.; 11) Concerning the Policy of the Church; 12) For Preaching and Interpretation of Scriptures, etc.; 13) Of Marriage; 14) Of Burial; 15) For Reparation of Churches; 16) For Punishment of those that profane the Sacraments and do condemn the Word of God and dare presume to minister them, not being thereto lawfully called.

[2]Goran Forkman, **The Limits of the Religious Community** (Sweden: CWK Gleerup Lund, 1972), p. 32.

[3]**Ibid.**, p. 193.

[4]Kenneth Hein, **Eucharist and Excommunication** (Frankfurt: H.L. Bern, 1973), pp. 75,76.

[5]G.C. Berkouwer, **The Church** (Grand Rapids: Eerdmans, 1976), p. 366.

[6]"In the Synoptic Gospels '**paraggelein**' is used only of Jesus. It denotes his command of authority as the Christ.... In Acts...the verb is relatively common. The reference is always to a directive from an authoritative source.... The word receives its special NT sense...only in virtue of the supreme authority of Jesus as the Christ..., an authority which is imparted to the apostle too.... In the Pauline Epistles the reference is always to the Christian walk.... For Paul, too, the decisive authority is the word of the Lord...in the apostle's saying...the readers have to do with the Lord himself...", Schmitz, **TDNT** V, p. 764.

[7]See O. Cullmann's extended essay, "The Tradition" on the formula in **The Early Church** (London: SCM, 1966), pp. 59-104.

[8]The Schleitheim Confession, art. 2, in Lewis W. Spitz, ed., **The Protestant Reformation** (New Jersey: Prentice-Hall, 1977), p. 91.

[9]E. de W. Burton, **A Critical and Exegetical Commentary on the Epistle to the Galatians** (Edinburgh: Clark, 1975), p. 321.

[10]J. Calvin, **Commentary on I Corinthians, ad loc.**

[11]J. Calvin, **Institutes of the Christian Religion** II (Grand Rapids: Eerdmans, 1953), IV.12.4, p. 455.

[12]Peter Ridemann, **Confession of Faith** (New York: Plough, 1970), p. 44.

[13]Hans Kueng, **The Church** (New York: Image Books, 1976), p. 427.

[14]S.L. Greenslade, **Shepherding the Flock: Problems of Pastoral Discipline in the Early Church and in the Younger Churches Today** (London: SCM, 1967), p. 70.

[15]Buschel, **TDNT** II, pp. 473-4.

[16]F.W. Grosheide, **Commentary on the First Epistle to the Corinthians** (Grand Rapids: Eerdmans, 1953).

[17]Greenslade, **op. cit.**, p. 96.

[18]Frank H. Epp, **Mennonites in Canada, 1786-1920:** The History of a Separate People (Toronto: Macmillan, 1974), pp. 352-4.

[19]David J. Green, "Pioneer Baptist Churches in Upper Canada as Moral Courts," **Canadian Baptist Home Missions Digest,** 6 (1963-4), pp. 238-242.

[20]Greenslade, **op. cit.**, p. 105.

Note. A helpful book on church discipline and membership has appeared since the preparation of this paper: Charles W. Deweese, **A Community of Believers** (Valley Forge: Judson, 1978).

EVANGELISM, E.M. Thompson, p. 127

[1]Gerhard Kittell, ed., **TDNT** VI, W. Bromiley, tr. (Grand Rapids: Eerdmans, 1964-1974), p. 726.

[2]Richard G. Cunningham, "Conversion and Christian Growth in the Baptist Experience," paper presented at the Baptist-Catholic Regional Conference, Menlo Park, Calif. (Oct., 1975), p. 10.

[3]Augustus H. Strong, **Systematic Theology** (Philadelphia: American Baptist Publ., 1886), p. 829.

[4]**Ibid.**, p. 12.

[5]**Ibid.**, p. 11.

[6]Russell F. Aldwinckle, **Of Water and the Spirit** (Brantford: The Baptist Federation of Canada, 1964), p. 21.

[7]C.H. Dodd, **The Apostolic Preaching and Its Developments** (Chicago: Willet, Clark, 1937), pp. 24-29.

[8]Donald Gordon Stewart, **Christian Education and Evangelism** (Philadelphia: Westminster, 1963), p. 47.

[9]J. Stanley Glen, **The Recovery of the Teaching Ministry** (Philadelphia: Westminster, 1960), p. 84.

[10]Quoted by Harry Emerson Fosdick, ed., **Great Voices of the Reformation** (New York: Random House, 1952), pp. 318-319.

[11]Lecture of William Leonard, "Forms of Religious Experience," (Southern Baptist Theological Seminary, Louisville, July 15, 1977).

[12]**Ibid.**

[13]Dennis M. Campbell, **The Authority and the Renewal of American Theology** (Philadelphia: United Church, 1976), p. 12.

[14]Carl J.C. Wolf, ed., **Jonathan Edwards on Evangelism** (Grand Rapids: Eerdmans, 1958), p. 28.

[15]Campbell, **op. cit.**, p. 11.

[16]George A. Rawlyk, "Henry Alline and the Canadian Baptist Tradition," **Theological Bulletin** IV (June, 1977), pp. 4,8.

[17]Horace Bushnell, **Christian Nurture** (New Haven: Yale University, 1960), p. 4.

[18]**Ibid.**, p. 26.

[19]Donald F. Durnbaugh, **The Believers' Church** (New York: Macmillan, 1968), p. 240.

[20]Ibid., p. 241.

[21]David Lyman Hicks, "The Cognitive Significence of Religious Experience — A Whiteadian Perspective" (Unpubl. PhD dissertation, Southern Baptist Theological Seminary, Louisville, 1977).

[22]Keith Yandell, "Religious Experiences and Rational Appraisal," **Religious Studies**, 10 (June, 1974), p. 176.

[23]William James, **The Varieties of Religious Experience** (New York: New American Library, 1958), p. 61.

[24]Rudolph Otto, **The Idea of the Holy**, J.W. Harvey, tr. (New York: University, 1958), p. 11.

[25]Rudolph Bultmann, **This World and Beyond**, H. Knight, tr. (New York: Scribner's, 1960), pp. 21-22.

[26]Emil Brunner, **The Christian Doctrine of the Church, Faith, and Consumation, Dogmatics** III, D. Cairns & T.H.L. Parker, tr. (Philadelphia: Westminster), p. 276.

[27]Wolfhart Pannenberg, **Jesus — God and Man**, L.L. Wilkins & D.A. Priebe, tr. (Philadelphia: Westminster, 1974), p. 27.

[28]Cunningham, **op. cit.**, p. 7.

[29]J.M. Price, James H. Chapman, L.L. Carpenter, W. Forbes Yarmorough, **A Survey of Religious Education** (New York: Ronald, 1959), pp. 12,13.

[30]Arthur C. Archibald, **New Testament Evangelism** (Philadelphia: Judson, 1946), p. 41.

[31]A. Gilmore, ed., **Christian Baptism** (Philadelphia: Judson, 1959), p. 319.

FOR FURTHER READING

Beasley-Murray, George, **Baptism Today and Tomorrow** (New York: St. Martins, 1966).

Hobbs, Herschel H., **The Baptist Faith and Message** (Nashville: Convention, 1971).

Moody, Dale, **Baptism: Foundation for Christian Unity** (Philadelphia: Westminster, 1967).

Stewart, Donald Gordon, **Christian Education and Evangelism** (Philadelphia: Westminster, 1963).

EVANGELISM, H.J. Gerbrandt, p. 137

[1]Gabriel Fackre, **Word in Deed, Theological Themes in Evangelism** (Grand Rapids: Eerdmans, 1975), p. 26.

[2]Lawrence O. Richards, **A Theology of Christian Education** (Grand Rapids: Zondervan, 1975), p. 15.

[3]Myron S. Augsburger, **Invitation to Discipleship** (Scottdale, Herald, 1960), p. 11.

[4]John Howard Yoder, **The Politics of Jesus** (Grand Rapids: Eerdmans, 1972), p. 228.

[5]A.J.F. Zieglschmid, ed., **Die Aelteste Chronik der Hutterischen Brueder** (New York: Cayuga, 1943), pp. 46-47. Quoted in English by H.S. Bender, **Mennonites and Their Heritage** (Akron: Mennonite Central Committee, 1945), p. 22.

[6]J.C. Wenger, **Introduction to Theology** (Scottdale: Herald, 1954), p. 233.

[7]**Ibid.**, p. 338.

[8]E. Stanley Jones, **Conversion** (Nashville: Abingdon, 1959), p. 211.

[9]**Ibid.**, p. 213.

[10]John Howard Yoder, ed. & tr., **The Legacy of Michael Sattler** (Scottdale: Herald, 1973), pp. 55-63.

[11]**Hans Denck, Schriften 2** (Guetersloh: Bertelsmann, 1956), p. 45.

[12]Augsburger, **op. cit.**, p. 46.

[13]John H. Westerhoff III, **Will our Children have Faith?** (New York: Seabury, 1976), pp. 13-16.

[14]J. Russel Hale, **Who are the Unchurched?** Glenburry, Research Centre, 4606, East-West Highway, Washington, D.C.

WORSHIP TODAY, H.L. Mitton, p. 151

[1]Andrew Blackwood, **The Fine Art of Public Worship** (Nashville: Cokesbury, 1939), pp. 45ff.

[2]G. Donald Gilmour, **In The Midst** (Publ. & page unknown).

[3]John Killinger, **Eleven O-clock News** (Nashville: Abingdon, 1975), p. 16.

[4]**Ibid.**, p. 10.

[5]James L. Christensen, **Contemporary Worship Services** (New Jersey: Revell, 1971), p. 9.

[6]James F. White, **New Forms of Worship** (Nashville: Abingdon, 1971), pp. 15ff.

[7]**Ibid.**, p. 48.

[8]Quoted by Henry E. Horn, **Worship In Crisis** (Philadelphia: Fortress, 1970), p. 3.

[9]Jim Wallis, **Agenda For Biblical People** (New York: Harper & Row, 1976), p. 110.

[10]Bernard Schalm, **The Church At Worship** (Grand Rapids: Baker, 1962), p. 10.

[11]**Ibid**.

[12]White, **op. cit.**, pp. 100ff.

[13]James L. Christensen, **New Ways To Worship** (New Jersey: Revell, 1973), p. 20.

[14]White, **op. cit.**, p. 132.

[15]**Ibid.**, p. 133.

[16]**Ibid.**, p. 144.

[17]Christensen, **op. cit.**, p. 28.

[18]Kenneth Hamilton, **To Turn From Idols** (Grand Rapids: Eerdmans, 1973), p. 176.

[19]Stephen Neill, **Jesus Through Many Eyes** (Philadelphia: Fortress, 1976), p. 162.

[20]John R.W. Stott, "'Unhooked' Christians," **C.T.** (Oct. 7, 1977), p. 40.

WORSHIP AND GIFTS, J.D. Rempel, p. 161

[1]Millard Lind, **Biblical Foundations for Christian Worship** (Scottdale: Herald, 1973), p. 18; H.H. Rowley, **Worship in Ancient Israel** (London: SPCK, 1976), pp. 39ff.

[2]Jeremiah 7: 21ff; Micah 6: 8ff.

[3]Rowley, **op. cit.**, pp. 134ff; Matthew 12: 1-8.

[4]Ezekiel 40ff; II Maccabees 3ff.

[5]C.F.D. Moule, **Worship in the New Testament** (Richmond: John Knox, 1967), p. 11.

[6]Gregory Dix, **The Shape of the Liturgy** (London: Daccre, 1975), pp. 50ff.

[7]I Corinthians 11. The Lord's Supper also stands behind passages like John 6: 27ff. Oscar Cullmann, (**Early Christian Worship**, London: SCM, 1966) understands the eucharist as the interpretive key to the Fourth Gospel.

[8]Dix, **op. cit.**, p. 3.

[9]**Ibid.**, pp. 36-102.

[10]Cullmann, **op. cit.**, p. 28.

[11]This decay is acknowledged and lamented by Roman Catholic scholars, as by Protestant ones. See, e.g., Louis Bouyer, **Liturgical Piety** (Notre Dame: Notre Dame, 1957), pp. 1-20.

[12]Cyril Vagaggini, **Theological Dimensions of the Liturgy** (Collegeville: Liturgical, 1959), p. 169. Alvin Beachy, **Worship as Celebration of Covenant and Incarnation** (Newton: Faith & Life, 1968), pp. 16-20, is one of the few Free Church theologians to make the incarnation central to his approach.

[13]This characterizes us more than it does the radical reformers. The Anabaptists know and quote patristic sources, as do the mainline reformers. This limited view has been reinforced by the predominance of Ulrich Zwingli's stark and untypical interpretation of the sacraments as mere symbols and as acts of man alone (not of God). Pilgram Marpeck, e.g., taught the Lord's Supper as a co-witness (**Mitzeugnis**) of Christ's presence, not, however, isolated in the bread and wine but present in the event and the congregation. See especially William Klassen and Walter Klaassen, ed., **The Writings of Pilgram Marpeck** (Scottdale: Herald, 1978), pp. 278-296.

[14]Mennonites, Baptists, Methodists and Pentecostals are all examples of this phenomenon.

[15]This is not to say that the worship life of the Free Churches arose in a vacuum. The differences among Believers' Churches themselves are more than anything because we came to life at different points in history and have been shaped by them. One of the striking evidences of the historical conditioning of our churches is the Protestant, especially Reformed, concept that God is to be worshipped in spirit, i.e., with the mind, as individuals. To oversimplify, we have mistaken the western religious mind of late Medieval and Reformation times for that of the New Testament era.

[16]The examples are many. One of them is the use of entertainment in the form of musicians, ventriloquists, etc. Another, at the other end of the spectrum, is the indiscriminate importing of "impressive" details from the worship of liturgical churches without understanding their theological or historical meaning. For an example of the latter see T.W. Coleman, **The Free Church Sacrament and Catholic Ideals** (London: J.M. Dent, 1930), esp. pp. 67-77.

[17]The movement from plural to one man ministry shows how, in confessions with an unclear understanding of tradition, practices entrench themselves on pragmatic grounds but without theological or traditional warrant.

[18]William Nichols, **Jacob's Ladder: The Meaning of Worship** (Richmond: John Knox, 1958), p. 31.

[19]Robert Friedmann, **Mennonite Piety Through the Centuries** (Scottdale: Mennonite Publ. House, 1949), p. 88.

[20]This danger is equally present in the "high" churches with their emphasis on correct ceremony and in the "low" churches with their craving for intense religious experience in and of itself.

[21]This term, as it is coming to be used in free churches, is historically incaccurate, in any case. In "high" churches it refers only to that part of the building in which the altar stands. The meeting room (where the congregation sits) is called the nave.

[22]G.R. Beasley-Murray, **Baptism in the New Testament** (London: Macmillan, 1962), is one of the few Believers' Church theologians who has embarked on this task. Paul's understanding of baptism in Romans 6 is that "we are baptized in his death." The modern notion of symbol can make no sense of that. The ancient notion of that word is that a symbol partakes in what it represents. Arthur Crabtree's "The Eucharist in Baptist Life and Thought" in W. Baum, ed., **The Eucharist in Ecumenical Dialogue** (New York: Paulist, 1976), pp. 106-115, tries to recapture sacraments as actions of God's grace. Elmer Arndt's treatment is similarly stimulating (**The Font and the Table**, Richmond: John Knox, 1967).

[23]Walter Klaassen, **Biblical and Theological Bases for Worship in the Believers' Church** (Newton: Faith & Life, 1978), p. 15.

WORSHIP/SPIRITUAL GIFTS, A.G. Patzia, p. 171

[1]Ralph P. Martin, **Worship in the Early Church** (Grand Rapids: Eerdmans, 1964), pp. 130ff.

[2]**Ibid.**, p. 131.

[3]Ferdinand Hahn, **The Worship of the Early Church** (Philadelphia: Fortress, 1973), p. 67, n. 9.

[4]Scholars have shown that there is much that we do know about worship in the first century. However, most of these authors are quick to stress the development, change and diversity of worship. See, among others, G. Delling, **Worship in the New Testament** (London: Darton, Longman & Todd, 1962); L. Goppelt, **Apostolic and Post-Apostolic Times** (New York: Harper Torchbook, 1962); F. Hahn, **op. cit.**; C.F.D. Moule, **Worship in the New Testament** (London: Lutterworth, 1961); E. Schweizer, **Church Order in the New Testament** (London: SCM, 1961) and "The Service of Worship: An Exposition of I Corinthians 14" in his book **Neotestamentica** (Zurich-Stuttgart: Zwingli Verlag, 1963), pp. 333-343.

[5]Cf. Goppelt, **op. cit.**; Schweizer, **op. cit.**

[6]Cf. Hahn, **op. cit.**, Table of Contents.

[7]Cf. Richardson, "Worship," **I.D.B.**, IV, pp. 883-894.

[8]Cf. Arnold Bittlinger, "The Charismatic Worship Service in the New Testament and Today," **Studia Liturgica** 9 (4, 1973), pp. 215-229.

[9]Hahn, **op. cit.**, p. 107.

CHURCH GROWTH, P. Collins, p. 177

[1]Peter Wagner, "Confused about Church Growth?" **Canadian Conference on Church Growth** (Winter, 1975), p. 1.

[2]Constant H. Jacquet, Jr., ed., **Yearbook of American and Canadian Churches** (New York, Abingdon); and **His Dominion** (Regina: Canadian Church Growth Centre, 4:3, Summer, 1977), pp. 18-19.

[3]Robert C. Berry, promotional secretary, Baptist Overseas Mission Board, personal conversation (Mar., 1978).

[4]Donald McGavran, **Understanding Church Growth** (Grand Rapids: Eerdmans, 1970), pp. 198ff.

[5]"Nations" could be substituted for "cultures" referring to ethnic groupings. There can be many "nations" (ethnic groups) within Canada.

[6]Rene Padilla, "Evangelism and the World," **Let the Earth Hear His Voice**, J.D. Douglas, ed. (Minneapolis: World Wide Publ., 1975), 2:6, pp. 125ff.

[7]Peter Wagner (unpubl. class notes, Fuller Theological Seminary, 1975), p. 7.

[8]A Peter Wagner reference during Advanced Church Growth Seminar, Pasadena, Jan., 1975.

[9]Suggestion by John Keith, general secretary, Canadian Baptist Overseas Mission Board.

[10]This quality-quantity dichotomy is referred to in a number of articles, e.g., Ralph D. Winter, "Quality or Quantity," D. McGavran, ed., **Crucial Issues in Missions Tomorrow** (Chicago: Moody, 1971), pp. 175-187.

[11]The word is used to negatively describe church growth interest in statistics.

[12]Peter Wagner, **op. cit.**, and other of his published articles including "Intensity of Belief: A Pragmatic Concern for Church Growth," Wagner and Arthur Johnson, **C.T.** (Jan. 7, 1977), pp. 10ff.

[13]Peter Wagner, "Fierce Pragmatism in Missions — Carnal or Consecrated?" **C.T.** (Dec., 1972), pp. 13ff; Alan R. Tippett, "Pragmatic Strategy for Tomorrow's Mission," **God, Man and Church Growth** (Grand Rapids: Eerdmans, 1973), pp. 164-169.

[14]E.P. News Service, "Missionary Calls 'Lausanne Covenant' Too Weak on Practical Evangelism" (Aug., 11, 1974), p. 11.

[15]"To Evangelize," editorial, **Presbyterian Journal** (Aug. 14, 1974).

[16]In fairness, since then Stott has either enlarged or qualified his definition of evangelism by stating, "We have no liberty to conceal the cost of discipleship...the results of evangelism include obedience to Christ, incorporation into His Church and responsible service in the world" (Lausanne Covenant, 4: The Nature of Evangelism).

[17]J.I. Packer, **Evangelism and the Sovereignty of God** (Downer's Grove: Inter-Varsity, 1961).

[18]Billy Graham, "Why the Berlin Congress?" C. Henry & W.S. Mooneyham, eds., **One Race, One Gospel, One Task** I (Minneapolis: World Wide, 1967), pp. 22-34.

[19]Wagner, Advanced Growth Seminar cited.

[20]J.K. Zeman, "The Believers' Church," Syllabus of Course, Section E, p. 17 (Acadia Divinity College, Wolfville, 1976; mimeographed).

[21]Winter, **op. cit.**

[22]McGavran, **op. cit.**, pp. 90-93.

[23]Should the Believers' Church movement espouse one mode, or allow all modes and paedobaptism? See Zeman, **op. cit.**, p. E 19.

[24]**Ibid.**, p. C 14.

[25]**Ibid.**, p. F 20f.

[26]**Ibid.**, p. H 23: "The Evangelical Anabaptists were the only people within the Continental Reformation who recaptured the early Christian missionary zeal and mission. To become a Christian meant to be a **witness** and missionary, usually at the risk of death. In many areas, the majority of the Brethren sealed their witness with martyrdom." Cf. Donald F. Durnbaugh, **The Believers' Church** (New York: Macmillan, 1970), pp. 226-238.

[27]J.E. Runions, and N.L. Hersom, "Church and Ministry," unpublished educational program objectives paper, upon which the Baptist Union of Western Canada based its current educational ministry (Edmonton: University of Alberta, 1975).

[28]Norman H. Pell, "Church Growth Principle Applied to Local Situation," undated mimeographed article, Vancouver Reachout (1976?).

FOR FURTHER READING

Roland, Allen, **The Spontaneous Expansion of the World Church** (Grand Rapids: Eerdmans, 1962).

Conn, Harvie M., ed., **Theological Perspectives on Church Growth** (Nutley: Presbyterian & Reformed Publ., 1976).

Stott, John R., **Christian Mission in the Modern World** (Downer's Grove: Inter-Varsity, 1975).

CHURCH GROWTH, D.M. Oliver, p. 185

[1]As Wolfgang Schaufele has demonstrated, "Anabaptism would not have been able to spread so rapidly and to take such firm roots if the missionary activity of the leaders had not been vigorously supported by the missionary activity of the ordinary members...[who] spread the message in the framework of their own contacts with their environment." "The Missionary Vision and Activity of the Anabaptist Laity," **M.Q.R.** XXXVI (Jan., 1962), p. 99.

[2]The common Believers' Church emphasis on baptism most often implies a clear commitment to, and enfolding into, the local church.

[3]Jo-Ann Badley, "Latest Survey: Decline Continues for Big Churches," **His Dominion**, 4:3 (Summer, 1977), pp. 18-19. Pentecostal Assemblies of Canada have no national statistics officially reported, but estimates are given of 120,000 adult members.

[4]Reginald W. Bibby & Merlin B. Brinkerhoff, "The Circulation of the Saints," S. Crysdale & L. Wheatcroft, ed., **Religion in Canadian Society** (Toronto: Macmillan, 1976), pp. 346-358; Ken Little **et al.**, "Are the Conservative Churches Reaching Canada?" **His Dominion**, 4:2 (Spring, 1977), pp. 12-13. The present writer's independent survey of many Canadian congregations confirms the conclusions of the above studies.

[5]Dean M. Kelley in **Why Conservative Churches Are Growing** (New York: Harper & Row, 1972) has spotlighted the fact of mainline decline, but interpreted it with a misconception which can lead Believers' Church "conservatives" into a mistaken satisfaction with the **status quo**.

[6]Dennis M. Oliver, "Checklist for Church Growth," **Mennonite Brethren Herald** (Mar. 31, 1978), pp. 6-8.

[7]Many of these bulletins have a continental focus, dominated by American data. Others, such as **Intercom** (Fellowship of Evangelical Baptist Churches of Canada) and the now discontinued **Church Growth Leadership Letter** (Pentecostal Assoc. of Canada) are more indigenously Canadian.

[8]The 1971 census indicates 9,974,895 nominal Roman Catholics — more than all of Canada's nominal Protestants combined. Some recent research indicates that by and large Catholics are **less nominal** than Protestants. See Hans Mol, "Major Correlates of Churchgoing in Canada," in Crysdale & Wheatcroft, **op. cit.**, pp. 241-254.

[9]See Harry H. Hiller, "Alberta and the Bible Belt Stereotype," in Crysdale & Wheatcroft, **op. cit.**, pp. 372-383.

[10]H.J. Gerbrandt, " Church in Crisis: Can the Opportunities be Grasped?" **His Dominion**, 4:3 (Summer, 1977), p. 9.

FOR FURTHER READING

Church Growth: Canada and His Dominion (Regina: The Canadian Church Growth Centre, 1974ff).

Jacquet, Constance J., ed., **The Yearbook of American and Canadian Churches** (New York: Abingdon, 1973ff).

Mann, William E., **Sect, Cult and Church in Alberta** (Toronto: University of Toronto, 1955).

Slater, Peter, ed., **Religion and Culture in Canada** (n. l.: Canadian Corporation for Studies in Religion, 1977).

CHURCH AND STATE, J.H. Redekop, p. 191

[1]**Church-State Study Conference Papers** (Akron: Mennonite Central Committee Peace Section, 1965), p. 8.

[2]E.K. Francis, **In Search of Utopia: The Mennonites in Manitoba** (Altona: D.W. Friesen, 1955), p. 9.

[3]R.J. Smithson, **The Anabaptists: Their Contribution to Our Protestant Heritage** (London, 1935), p. 217.

[4]Thomas G. Sanders, **Protestant Concepts of Church and State** (New York: Holt, Rinehard & Winston, 1964), p. 75.

[5]**Ibid.**, p. 81.

[6]For the text of the Schleitheim Confession see Harry Fosdick, **Great Voices of the Reformation** (New York: Random House, 1952), pp. 288f.

[7]Sanders, **op. cit.**, p. 86.

[8]John C. Wenger, ed., **The Complete Writings of Menno Simons** (Scottdale: Herald, 1956), p. 200.

[9]**Ibid.**, p. 922.

[10]**Ibid.**, p. 549.

[11]Sanders, **op. cit.**, p. 88.

[12]"Theology, Anabaptist-Mennonite," **Mennonite Encyclopedia** IV (Scottdale: Mennonite Publ. House, 1959), p. 706.

[13]Harvey Plett, "The Church and the State," B. Hoeppner & D. Schellenberg, ed., **Know Your Beliefs** (Winnipeg: EMMC and EMC Board of Education & Publ., 1972), pp. 47-49).

[14]"The Christian Witness to the State," editorial, **Gospel Herald** (Oct. 17, 1961), p. 912.

[15]J.C. Wenger, ed., **The Mennonite Church in America** (Scottdale: Herald, 1966), p. 341.

[16]Paul Erb, **We Believe: An Interpretation of the 1963 Mennonite Confession of Faith for the Younger Generation** (Scottdale: Herald, 1969), p. 83.

[17]**Confession of Faith of the General Conference of Mennonite Brethren Churches** (Winnipeg: Mennonite Brethren Board of Christian Literature, 1976), pp. 20-21.

[18]Apparently 47 Anabaptists went to Nova Scotia as United Empire Loyalists in 1783. Frank H. Epp, **Mennonites in Canada, 1786-1920** (Toronto: Macmillan, 1974), p. 50.

[19]D.J. Wilson, **The Church Grows in Canada** (Toronto: Ryerson, 1966), p. 78.

[20]Epp, **op. cit.**, p. 56.

[21]Quoted in Epp, **Ibid.**, p. 71.

[22]**Ibid.**, p. 77.

[23]Wilson, **op. cit.**, p. 106.

[24]Francis, **ob. cit.**, pp. 44-45.

[25]**Ibid.**, p. 47.

[26]Epp, **op. cit.**, p. 192.

[27]**Ibid.**, pp. 346f.

[28]**Ibid.**, pp. 345-347.

[29]**Ibid.**, p. 349.

[30]Frank H. Epp. **Mennonite Exodus** (Altona: D.W. Friesen, 1962), p. 97.

[31]**Ibid.**, p. 94.

[32]Francis, **op. cit.**, p. 203.

[33]Epp, **Mennonite Exodus**, pp. 246-250.

[34]**Ibid.**, p. 319.

[35]**Ibid.**, p. 319.

[36]**Ibid.**, pp. 392f.

[37]Epp, **Mennonites in Canada**, pp. 99-101.

[38]**Ibid.**, p. 101.

[39]**Ibid.**, p. 103.

[40]**Ibid.**, p. 366.

[41]**Ibid.**, p. 367.

[42]**Ibid.**, p. 371.

[43]**Ibid.**, p. 393.

[44]**Ibid.**, pp. 406-407.

[45]Epp, **Mennonite Exodus**, p. 325.

[46]**Ibid.**, pp. 325-326.

[47]**Ibid.**, p. 327.

[48]**Ibid.**, pp. 328f.

[49]**Ibid.**, p. 331.

[50]Nov. 4, 1944; quoted in Epp, **Ibid.**, p. 331.

[51]Ibid., p. 331.

[52]Wilson, op. cit., p. 103.

[53]Epp, Mennonites in Canada, p. 108.

[54]Ibid., pp. 223f.

[55]Quoted in John A. Toews, A History of the Mennonite Brethren Church (Fresno: Mennonite Brethren Board of Christian Literature, 1975), pp. 199-200.

[56]Epp, Mennonites in Canada, p. 327.

[57]J.H. Kauffman and Leland Harder, Anabaptists Four Centuries Later (Scottdale: Herald, 1975), p. 157.

[58]Ibid., p. 161.

[59]Ibid., pp. 162-163.

[60]Ibid., p. 158.

[61]For an elaboration of this view see John H. Redekop, "The State and the Free Church," J.R. Burkholder & C. Redekop, eds., Kingdom, Cross, and Community (Scottdale: Herald, 1976), pp. 179-195.

[62]Sanders, op. cit., p. 110.

[63]Ibid., p. 111.

[64]Epp, Mennonites in Canada, p. 367.

[65]T.M. Parker, Christianity and the State in the Light of History (London: A. & C. Black, 1953), as quoted in Stephen Neill, The Unfinished Task (London: Edinburgh House, 1957), p. 70.

CHURCH AND STATE, H.A. Renfree, p. 207

[1]Matthew 22:21.

[2]Romans 13:1.

[3]Acts 5:29.

[4]Philip Schaff, History of the Christian Church, III (New York: Scribner's, 1903), pp. 30-31.

[5]Robert G. Torbet, A History of the Baptists (Valley Forge: Judson, 1963), p. 489.

[6]Ibid.

[7]John S. Moir, ed., The Cross in Canada (Toronto: Ryerson, 1966), p. 1.

[8]John S. Moir, Church and State in Canada, The Carleton Library, 33 (Toronto: McClelland & Stewart, 1967), p. 1.

[9]Ibid., p. 2.

[10]Ibid., p. 73.

[11]Moir, The Cross in Canada, pp. 65-66.

[12]Watson Kirkconnell, The Baptists of Canada (Toronto: The Historical Committee of the Baptist Federation of Canada, 1958), p. 3.

[13]George Edward Levy, The Baptists of the Maritime Provinces (Saint John: Barnes-Hopkins, 1946), p. 18.

[14]Moir, Church and State in Canada, p. 33.

[15]Levy, op. cit., p. 20.

[16]Moir, **The Cross in Canada**, pp. 87-88.

[17]Torbet, **op. cit.**, p. 137.

[18]Levy, **op. cit.**, p. 43.

[19]**Ibid.**, pp. 55-56.

[20]Moir, **Church and State in Canada**, p. 51.

[21]**Ibid.**, p. 52.

[22]**Ibid.**

[23]I.E. Bill, **Fifty Years with the Baptists** (Saint John: Barnes, 1880), p. 110.

[24]**Ibid.**, p. 111.

[25]Levy, **op. cit.**, p. 118.

[26]Bill, **op. cit.**, p. 116.

[27]G. Gerald Harrop, "The Baptist Convention of Ontario and Quebec," **Baptist Advance** (Nashville: Broadman, 1964), pp. 165,166.

[28]Alan Wilson, **The Clergy Reserves of Upper Canada** (Ottawa: The Canadian Historical Assoc. Booklets, No. 23, 1969), p. 3.

[29]**Ibid.**, p. 6.

[30]Moir, **Church and State in Canada**, pp. 164,165.

[31]**Ibid.**, p. 169.

[32]Edward M. Checkland, **Religious Liberty in Canada** (unpubl. thesis, McMaster University, 1946), p. 79.

[33]Moir, **Church and State in Canada**, p. 195.

[34]**Ibid.**

[35]Harold U. Trinier, **A Century of Service** (Toronto: Baptist Convention of Ont. & Que., 1958), p. 7.

[36]Harrop, **op. cit.**, p. 166.

[37]**Ibid.**, p. 167.

[38]Moir, **Church and State in Canada**, p. 213.

[39]**Ibid.**

[40]**Ibid.**

[41]**Ibid.**, p. 243.

[42]Harrop, **op. cit.**, p. 166.

[43]Moir, **The Cross in Canada**, p. 149.

[44]Arthur R. Lower, **This Most Famous Stream** (Toronto: Ryerson, 1954), pp. 151,152.

[45]Trinier, **op. cit.**, pp. 138,139.

[46]Senate Report, Ottawa, Dec. 13, 1966.

[47]James E. Wood, Jr., "Religion and Public Education in Historical Perspective," **Journal of Church and State**, IV:3 (1972), p. 406.

[48]R. MacGregor Dawson, **The Government of Canada** (Toronto: University of Toronto, 1969), p. 567.

[49]Neil G. Price, **Education — Religion — Politics in Ontario** (North Bay: Northland, 1966).

[50]Year Book of the United Baptist Convention of the Atlantic Provinces (Saint John: Lingley, 1964), pp. 16, 49.

[51]Year Book of the United Baptist Convention of the Atlantic Provinces (Saint John: Lingley, 1965), pp. 19, 207.

[52]Bill No. 49 of the Legislature of the Province of Nova Scotia, "An Act Respecting Acadia University," Halifax, 1966.

[53]Alan Battye, quoting the Bishops' Letter, The Calgary Herald (Jan. 28, 1978), p. E9.

[54]Maurice C. Boillat, Creed in the Canadian Crisis (Moncton: Baptist Federation of Canada, 1964).

[55]William Sturhahn, They Came from East and West (Winnipeg: The North American Baptist Immigration and Colonization Society, 1976), p. 289.

[56]M. James Penton, Jehovah's Witnesses in Canada (Toronto: MacMillan, 1976), p. 223.

DIVISIVE/UNITIVE FORCES, W.E. Ellis, p. 221

[1]Donald F. Durnbaugh, The Believers' Church: The History and Character of Radical Protestantism (New York: Macmillan, 1968), p. 283.

[2]Bryan R. Wilson, ed., Patterns of Sectarianism: Organization and Ideology in Social and Religious movements (London: Heinemann, 1967), p. 4.

[3]Ibid., p. 2.

[4]S.L. Greenslade, Schism in the Early Church (New York: Harper, 1949), pp. 21-9.

[5]Durnbaugh, op. cit., pp. 32-3.

[6]Robert S. Paul, The Church in Search of Its Self (Grand Rapids: Eerdmans, 1972), pp. 47-57.

[7]Balthasar Hubmaier, Eighteen Dissertations, in William L. Lumpkin, Baptist Confessions of Faith (Valley Forge: Judson, 1969), p. 19, 21.

[8]London Confession, 1644, in Lumpkin, op. cit., p. 158. The Second London Confession, 1667, Ch. I, 6, set out a clear restorationist agenda, stating: "The whole Council of God concerning all things necessary for his own Glory, Man's Salvation, Faith and Life, is either expressely set down or necessrily contained in the Holy Scripture; ..."

[9]Paul, op. cit., p. 86, views restorationism as normative for all reforming movements, "even when biblical authority gives way to a more charismatic principle, or when one aspect of New Testament Christianity...appears to take precedence over the rest."

[10]"The Right of Private Judgment," editorial, Montreal Register (May 23, 1844), pp. 1-2.

[11]Paul, op. cit., pp. 104-5.

[12]Harry E. Fosdick, "Christianity and Progress," B. Gatewood, ed., Controversy in the Twenties: Fundamentalism, Modernism and Evolution (Nashville: Vanderbilt University, 1969), pp. 62-3. Fosdick attacked the concept of authority stating, "The marvel is that the idea of authority, which is one of the historic curses of religion, should be regarded by so many as one of the vital necessities of faith...they believe what they do believe because a divine church or a divine book or a divine man told them." He then proceded to enthrone "personal experience" in place of church and book.

[13]Reply of the Churches in Membership with the Baptist Union to the "Appeal to all Christian People" issued by the Lambeth Conference of 1920, in Ernest A. Payne, **The Baptist Union** (London: Carey Kingsgate, 1958), p. 280; see also, **The Baptist Doctrine of the Church, 1948**, pp. 283-7.

[14]**The Orthodox Creed**, 1678, XXIX,XXX; in Lumpkin, **op. cit.**, pp. 318-19. The marks of the church were three: "And the marks by which she is known to be the true spouse of Christ are these, viz. Where the word of God is rightly preached, and the sacraments truly administered, according to Christ's institution, ...having discipline and government."

[15]**London Confession, 1644, Address**, in Lumpkin, **op. cit.**, p. 155; also XLVII, pp. 168-9. "And although the particular Congregations be distinct and severall Bodies, every one a compact and knit Citie in itselfe; yet are they all to walk by one and the same Rule, and by all meanes convenient to have the counsell and help one of another **in all needfull affaires of the Church**, as members of one body in the common faith under Christ their onely head."

[16]Paul, **op. cit.**, p. 106; see my note on the pragmatic trend in Baptist polity. For detailed treatment, W.S. Hudson, ed., **Baptist Concepts of the Church** (Chicago: Judson, 1959).

[17]Paul M. Harrison, **Authority and Power in the Free Church Tradition** (Princeton: University, 1953), p. 7.

[18]William B. Riley, "Divinely Ordered Divisions," address prepared and delivered before the Constitutional Convention of Chicago called for the purpose of creating an Orthodox Baptist Foreign Mission Society, Oct. 29, 1943, in, **Riley Papers**, Northwest Schools, Minneapolis, pp. 8-9.

[19]**The Montreal Register**, July 11, 1844; Mar. 14, 1844.

[20]S. Ivison, "Is there a Baptist Tradition?" in Douglas J. Wilson, **The Church Grows in Canada** (Toronto: Ryerson, 1966), p. 126.

[21]**The Orthodox Creed**, in Lumpkin, **op. cit.**, p. 327.

[22]British Baptist Union, **Baptists and Unity, op. cit.**, p. 21.

[23]**Ibid.**, p. 25.

[24]Durnbaugh, **op. cit.**, pp. 210-11.

[25]**The Second London Confession, 1677**, XXVI, iii; in Lumpkin, **op. cit.**, p. 285.

[26]Edward T. Hiscox, **The Hiscox Guide for Baptist Churches** (Valley Forge: Judson, 1968), pp. 132-6.

[27]Cited in Greenslade, **Schism in the Early Church, op. cit.**, p. 19.

[28]**Canadian Baptist Magazine and Missionary Register**, III,5 (Nov., 1839).

[29]Greenslade, **op. cit.**, p. 33.

[30]Willard L. Sperry, **Religion in America** (Cambridge: Cambridge University, 1945), pp. 76, 94; Greenslade, **op. cit.**, p. 191.

[31]Franklin H. Littell, **The Free Church** (Boston: Starr King, 1957), p. 131.

[32]Walter E. Ellis, "Gilboa to Ichabod: Social and Religious Factors in the Fundamentalist-Modernist Schism Among Canadian Baptists, 1895-1934," **Fdt.**, XX,2, pp. 109-126.

[33]Paul, **op. cit.**, pp. 115-6.

IDENTITY AND UNITY, R.J. Sawatsky, p. 233

[1]The literature on this union is quite extensive. Some valuable interpretations include the following: C.E. Silcox, **Church Union in Canada: Its Causes and Consequences** (New York: Institute of Social and Religious Research, 1933); E. Lloyd Morrow, **Church Union in Canada: Its History, Motives, Doctrine and Government** (Toronto: Thomas Allen, 1923); Edgar F. File, "A Sociological Analysis of Church Union in Canada" (Ph.D. dissertation, Boston University, 1961); and John W. Grant, **The Canadian Experience of Church Union** (Richmond: John Knox, 1967). On the recent discussion with the Anglicans see: **Plan of Union** (Toronto: General Commission on Church Union, 1973).

[2]Morrow, **op. cit.**, documents the reasons these groups declined the invitation.

[3]The definition of the Believers' Church accepted here is the one developed by Donald F. Durnbaugh, **The Believers' Church: The History and Character of Radical Protestantism** (Toronto: Collier-Macmillan, 1968).

[4]Toronto: University of Toronto, 1948. For one critique among others see: H.H. Walsh, "Canada and the Church: A Job for Historians," **Queen's Quarterly** LXI (1954), pp. 78ff.

[5]"The Sectarian Tradition in Canada," in John W. Grant, ed., **The Churches and the Canadian Experience** (Toronto: Ryerson, 1963), p. 132. See also his **Church and State in Canada West** (Toronto: University of Toronto, 1959); and **Church and State in Canada, 1827-1867** (Toronto: McClelland & Stewart, 1967).

[6]An excellent compilation of interpretations of denominationalism is Russel E. Richey, ed., **Denominationalism** (Nashville: Abingdon, 1977).

[7]H.H. Walsh, "The Challenge of Canadian Church History to its Historians," **Canadian Journal of Theology** V (1959), p. 168. See also: John W. Grant, "Asking Questions of the Canadian Past," **Canadian Journal of Theology** I (July, 1955), pp. 98-105.

[8]**Census of Canada 1971**, Vol. I, Part 3, Section 9-1.

[9]Constant H. Jacquet, Jr., ed., **Yearbook of American and Canadian Churches 1977** (Nashville: Abingdon, 1977), pp. 233-243.

[10]Harry H. Hiller, "Continentalism and the Third Force in Religion," (Unpublished paper available from the author, Department of Sociology, University of Alberta, Calgary).

[11]For a brief history see Stuart Ivison, "Is there a Canadian Baptist Tradition?" in John W. Grant, ed., **The Churches and the Canadian Experience** (Toronto: Ryerson, 1963) pp. 53-68.

[12]This is a partial summation of an article which is essentially identical in thesis to this present essay. Jarold K. Zeman, "Canada," in James L. Garrett, ed., **Baptist Relations with Other Christians** (Valley Forge: Judson, 1974), pp. 105-120. A longer version appeared earlier in **Fdt.** XV (1972), pp. 211-240.

[13]The relation of the fundamentalist-liberal debate in Canada to the American story can be noted in Leslie K. Tarr, **This Dominion, His Dominion** (Willowdale: Fellowship of Evangelical Baptist Churches, 1968).

[14]H.H. Walsh, "A Canadian Christian Tradition," in Grant, ed., **op. cit.**, pp. 157-158.

[15]E. Lloyd Morrow, **Church Union in Canada**, p. 35.

[16]See John E. Smylie, "National Ethos and the Church," **Theology Today** XX (October, 1963), pp. 313-321; and Sidney E. Mead, **The Nation with the Soul of a Church** (New York: Harper & Row, 1975).

[17]Quote from S.E. Mead, **The Lively Experiment: The Shaping of Christianity in America** (New York: Harper & Row, 1943).

[18]For valuable summaries and extensive bibliographic resources on this Protestant culture religion, see R.T. Handy, **A Christian America: Protestant Hopes and Historical Realities** (New York: Oxford University, 1971) and M.E. Marty, **Righteous Empire: The Protestant Experience in America** (New York: Dial, 1970). For the important role of millenialism, see J.F. Maclear, "The Republic and the Millenium," in E.H. Smith, ed., **The Religion of the Republic** (Philadelphia: Fortress, 1971), pp. 183-216.

[19]"A Sermon on the Vocation of the French Race in America," in Ramsay Cook, ed., **French-Canadian Nationalism: An Anthology** (Toronto: Macmillan, 1969), p. 154.

[20]For primary and interpretive esays of French-Canadian nationalism see: Ramsay Cook, **op. cit.**, and his **Canada and the French-Canadian Question** (Toronto: Macmillan, 1966).

[21]Everett C. Hughes, **French Canada in Transition** (Chicago: University of Chicago, 1967 ed.), pp. 143-159.

[22]S.F. Wise, "God's Peculiar Peoples," in W.L. Morton, ed., **The Shield of Achilles** (Toronto: McClelland & Stewart, 1968), p. 59.

[23]Goldwin French, "The Impact of Christianity on Canadian Culture and Society Before 1867," p. 34. See also his: "The Evangelical Creed in Canada," in W.L. Morton, ed., **The Shield of Achilles**, pp. 15-35.

[24]William Kilbourn, ed., **Canada: A Guide to the Peaceable Kingdom** (Toronto: Macmillan, 1970), p. xvi.

[25]N. Keith Clifford, "His Dominion: A Vision in Crisis," in Peter Slater, ed., **Religion and Culture in Canada** (Waterloo: Canadian Corporation for the Study of Religion, 1978), p. 38, notes this trend in the work of Leslue K. Tarr, **This Dominion, His Dominion: The story of Evangelical Baptist Endeavour in Canada** (Toronto: Fellowship of Evangelical Baptist Churches, 1965), p. 172; and in T. Johnstone, "Our Spiritual Heritage," in E.W.O. Kulbeck, ed., **Canada's Centennial** (Toronto: Pentecostal Assemblies, 1967), pp. 10-11.

[26]For a summary statement see: Guy F. Hershberger, **The Recovery of the Anabaptist Vision** (Scottdale: Herald, 1957).

[27]Harold S. Bender, **These Are My People: The New Testament Church** (Scottdale: Herald, 1963).

[28]C. Norman Kraus, **The Community of the Spirit** (Grand Rapids: Eerdmans, 1974).

[29]Franklin H. Littell, **The Origin of Sectarian Protestantism** (New York: Macmillan, 1964).

[30]Walter Klaassen, **Anabaptism: Neither Catholic nor Protestant** (Waterloo: Conrad, 1973).

[31]See Richard Quebedeux, **The Young Evangelicals: The Story of the Emergence of a New Generation of Evangelicals** (New York: Harper & Row, 1974), and Jim Wallis, **Agenda for a Biblical People** (New York: Harper & Row, 1977).

[32]Dean M. Kelley, **Why Conservative Churches are Growing** (New York: Harper & Row, 1972).

PUBLIC EDUCATION, K.R. Davis, p. 243

[1]In 20 pages and about 400 items of bibliography in R.G. Torbet's **A History of Baptists**, rev. ed., (Valley Forge: Judson, 1969), only three or four items refer to education and even in the text there are only passing references to Baptists' attitudes to the development of public education.

[2]H.J. Hillerbrand, ed., **The Protestant Reformation** (New York: Harper Torch, 1968), p. 127 (Conrad Grebel's "Letter to T. Muntzer"); p. 148 (Elizabeth's "Letter").

[3]K.R. Davis, "The Way of the Cross: The Foundation for a 16th Century Counter-Culture," **Northwest Journal of Theology** (July, 1976), p. 27.

[4]J.C. Wenger, "The Schleitheim Confession of Faith," **M.Q.R.** XIX (1945), pp. 243ff (cf. article 4).

[5]Cf., B. Hubmaier, "On Fraternal Punishment" and "On Christian Excommunication" in Hubmaier's **Writings**, G. Davidson, tr. (Wm. Jewell College, 1939); D. Phillip, **Handbook**, A. Kolb, tr. (LaGrange: Pathway Publ., 1966), pp. 390-1 ("The Church of God"); "Answer of Some Who Are Called Anabaptists Why They Do Not Attend the Churches," S. Peachy & P. Peachy, tr. **M.Q.R.** XLV (Jan., 1971), p. 19.

[6]R. Friedmann, **The Theology of Anabaptism** (Scottdale: Herald, 1973), pp. 36-46; and "The Schleitheim Confession," article 4.

[7]**Ibid.**, p. 41.

[8]**Taeufer Akten: Bayern** I (Leipzig: Schornbaum, 1934), p. 254.

[9]Davis, **op. cit.**, p. 41.

[10]Friedmann, **op. cit.**, p. 45.

[11]E.H. Harbison, **The Christian Scholar in the Age of the Reformation** (New York: Scribner's, 1956), p. 1, from Tertullian's, **De Praescriptione Haereticorum**.

[12]"The Schleitheim Confession" (article 6), and P. Marpeck, **Writings**, Wm. Klassen & W. Klaassen, tr., unpubl. manuscript (Waterloo: Conrad Grebel College, 1972), pp. 119, 82. (The Strasburg Confession, 1531-1532.)

[13]For more details cf. K. Davis, C.M. Hynds, M. Pipe, **Essays on Education** (Toronto: Fellowship of Evangelical Baptists, 1974), pp. 11-13.

[14]H. Marrou, **A History of Education in Antiquity** (New York: New American Library, 1964), p. 426f.

[15]Davis, **Essays in Education**, p. 13.

[16]**Mennonite Encyclopedia** II, p. 154.

[17]**Ibid.**

[18]Torbet, **op. cit.**, p. 306; cf. also J. Wickersham, **A History of Education in Pennsylvania** (Lancaster: Inquirer Publ., 1886), p. 101.

[19]Among some 19th century Baptists in the U.S.A., some uneasiness and some sense of need for separate Christian schools to combat the secularism which was beginning to appear in the state colleges emerged, and was openly expressed by the Wisconsin Convention in the 1870's. Cf. A.E. Wickman, "The Story of Baptist Education in Wisconsin," **The Chronicle** XI, 2 (Apr., 1918), pp. 66-76.

[20]Torbet, **op. cit.**, p. 308 — some of the same attitude may have been transferred to Canada by the extensive activity there in the early 19th century by U.S. Baptist Missionary Societies.

[21]T. Smith, **Revivalism & Reform** (New York: Abingdon, 1957), p. 40.

[22]L. Cremin, **The Colonial Experience** (New York: Harper & Row, 1970), pp. x, xi.

[23]Smith, **op. cit.**, p. 34.

[24]**Ibid.**, pp. 34,35.

[25]Torbet, **op. cit.**, p. 144.

[26]W.T. Gunn, **His Dominion** (The Canadian Council of the Missionary Education Movement, 1917), p. 86.

[27]**Ibid.**, p. 86.

[28]D.J. Wilson, **The Church Grows in Canada** (Toronto: Ryerson, 1966), p. 60. By 1875, however, "the subject of Christian morals was dropped from the curriculum by unanimous vote of Upper Canadian teachers in their annual convention (cf. The Ecumenical Study Commission, "Religious Education in Ontario Before the Keiller Mackay Report").

[29]Gunn, **op. cit.**, p. 85.

[30]Cremin, **op. cit.**, pp. x, xi. Cf. also N.K. Clifford, "His Dominion: A Vision in Crisis" (A paper read at the Canadian Society for Church History).

[31]Cf., R.T. Handy, **A Christian America: Protestant Hopes and Historical Realities** (New York: Oxford, 1971).

[32]**Ibid.**, p. 271.

[33]H.A. Snyder, "A World Come Full Circle," **C.T.** (Jan. 7, 1972), p. 9 (from **The Year 2000**).

[34]E. Lund, M. Pike & J. Slok, **A History of European Ideas** (Reading: Addison-Wesley, 1962), p. 306. For additional documentation of the nature and extent of the change both in society and public education, see also Davis, **Essays in Education**, pp. 14-26.

[35]Many reasons can be given to account for the change in Canadian and American society, including (a) the alliance of secularism and revolution against oppressive church-state regimes in 19th century Europe, (b) religious and philosophical liberalism which in part evolved into secular theology and religious humanism, (c) the industrialization and urbanization of society with resultant dislocation, isolation and collapse of community and family life, (d) the moral trauma of World Wars I and II, (e) subsequent affluency with the enhancement of materialism, eroticism and self-indulgence.

[36]M.B. McMahon, "Religion, Scientific Naturalism and the Myth of Neutrality," **Intellect** (Apr., 1974), p. 431.

[37]K. Campbell, **Tempest in a Teapot** (Cambridge: Coronation, 1975), pp. 270-5.

[38]Cf., J. Ellul, **The Technological Society** (New York: Knopf, 1964), pp. 344ff.

[39]E.S.C., **Religion In Our Schools**, p. 12. The Commission refers to "the increasingly secular character of the public schools."

[40]**Ibid.**

[41]**Mennonite Encyclopedia II**, p. 153. Some recent and limited studies in B. Hunsberger, "A Reconsideration of Parochial Schools," **MQR LI** (Apr., 1977), and D. Kraybill, "Religious and Ethnic Socialization in a Mennonite High School," **MQR LI** (Oct., 1977), challenge the effectiveness of private schools; but their data base may not take adequately into consideration recent changes in public education.

[42]Ontario District Conferences of the Pentecostal Assoc. of Canada, "Brief to Hon. T.L. Wells, June 1973."

[43]K.R. Davis, C.M. Hynds, M.A. Pipe, **Essays on Education** (Toronto: Fellowship of Evangelical Baptists, 1974).

[44]K.R. Davis, "Education in Ontario: New Problems and Changing Perspectives." A brief presented to the Ministry of Education by **Renaissance** (Oct., 1976).

[45]In the past five years private schools have increased in Ontario from 270 and 43,000 students to 355 and 59,000 students. Cf., "Man Searches Province for Private School Support," **Kitchener-Waterloo Record** (Apr. 19, 1978).

[46]Julianne Labreche, "Education," **MacLeans** (Sept. 5, 1977), p. 50.

[47]J. McQuilkin, "Public Schools: Equal Time for Evangelicals," **C.T.** (Dec. 30, 1977), p. 8.

[48]R. Gregory, L. Mackey, "B.C. offers aid to private schools," **Faith Today** (Nov., 1977), pp. 15,16.

[49]This is not saying quite the same thing as the E.S.C.'s statement in **Religion in Our Schools**, p. 9, that "the Commission recognizes that it has no right or desire to ask for a position of privilege for the Christian Faith in the curriculum." Rather, as the religion of the majority and as part of our roots, Christianity should rightfully command dominance, but no longer an exclusiveness. Actually the E.S.C. report seems somewhat contradictory since later (p. 23) it grants that the Judeo/Christian tradition should have an "eminent place" in any curriculum in Religion — but the only reason given is because it is more culturally relevant.

[50]K. Mackay, **Religious Information and Moral Development: The Report of the Committee on Religious Education in the Public Schools in Ontario** (Toronto: Queen's Printer, 1969).

[51]E.S.C., **Moral and Religious Education** (Toronto: np, 1974), p. 19.

[52]L. Kohlberg, "Education for Justice: A Modern Statement of the Platonic View", **Moral Education**, N.E. & T.R. Sizer, ed. (Cambridge: Harvard University, 1970), pp. 57-83. He totally separates the study of religion and morality; C. Beck, **Moral Education in the Schools** (Toronto: Ont. Institute of Studies in Education, 1971), follows the same viewpoint.

[53]K.R. Davis, "Education in Ontario: New Problems and Changing Perspectives." A brief presented to the Ministry of Education by **Renaissance** (Oct., 1976).

[54]J.R. McQuilken, in "Public Schools: Equal Time For Evangelicals," **C.T.** (Dec. 30, 1977), p. 10, has advocated granting any group of parents authorization "to provide a teacher for an elective course in religion and morals. This approach recognizes that value and neutral instruction is a fiction and that true freedom in the area of religion and morals exists only if parents and students have a choice of instructors" [and curriculum]...I am urging not the Christianization of all education, but rather concerted effort to provide true freedom" — a position fully consistent with the historic convictions of most Believers' Churches. The Ontario Ministry of Education expressed some sympathy for this position in response to another **Renaissance** brief, presented in Apr., 1978, and critical of the secular "values education" courses presently being fostered by the Ministry in Ontario.

PUBLIC SCHOOLS IN CANADA, P.H. Peters, p. 257

[1]D.C. Masters, **Protestant Church Colleges in Canada** (Toronto: University of Toronto, 1966), p. 32.

[2]Ibid., p. 33.

[3]C.E. Phillips, **The Development of Education in Canada** (Toronto: W.J. Gage, 1957), p. 225.

[4]Ibid., p. 226.

[5]Frank H. Epp, **Mennonites in Canada, 1786-1920** (Toronto: Macmillan, 1974), p. 85.

[6]Leo Driedger, "Developments in Higher Education Among Mennonites in Manitoba," **Proceedings of the Sixteenth Conference of Mennonite Educational and Cultural Problems** (Goshen: Goshen College, 1967), p. 65.

[7]E.K. Francis, **In Search of Utopia: The Mennonites in Manitoba** (Altona: D.W. Friesen, 1955), p. 172.

[8]Ibid., p. 174.

[9]Frank H. Epp, **Education With A Plus: The Story of Rosthern Junior College** (Waterloo: Conrad, 1975), p. 16.

[10]These two terms were Mennonite identifications, respectively, for the 1874 and 1923 immigrants.

[11]Margaret Loewen Reimer, "Enrolments Stable in Private Schools," **Mennonite Reporter** (Oct. 31, 1977).

[12]Epp, **op. cit.**, p. 396.

[13]Ibid., p. 397.

[14]Margaret Loewen Reimer, "Enrolments Stable in Private Schools," **Mennonite Reporter** (Oct. 31, 1977).

[15]Epp, **Mennonites in Canada**, p. 38.

[16]Donald F. Durnbaugh, **The Believers' Church The History and Character of Radical Protestantism** (Toronto: Collier-Macmillian, 1968), p. 104.

[17]S.D. Clark, **Church and Sect in Canada** (Toronto: University of Toronto, 1948), Introduction.

[18]Ibid., p. 250.

[19]Masters, **op. cit.**, p. 77.

[20]Ronald Stewart Longley, **Acadia University, 1838-1938** (Kentville: Kentville Publ., 1939), p. 140.

[21]Ibid., p. 119.

[22]Masters, **op. cit.**, p. 64.

[23]Margaret E. Thompson, **The Baptist Story in Western Canada** (Calgary: The Baptist Union of Western Canada, 1974), p. 118.

[24]Ibid., p. 11.

[25]Ibid., p. 13.

[26]Donald B. Kraybill, **Mennonite Education Issues, Facts and Changes** (Kitchener: Herald, 1978), pp. 68-69.

GLOBAL MISSION, N.L. Gingrich, p. 273

[1]Peter J. Dyck, "A Theology of Service," **MQR**, XLIV (July, 1970), p. 272.

[2]W.A. Visser't Hooft, "The Church's Mission and Service in the Lord," **National Christian Council Review** (Mar., 1964), pp. 110-111.

[3]Ronald J. Sider, **Evangelism, Salvation and Social Justice** (Bramcotte Notts: Grove, 1977), p. 20.

[4]Visser't Hooft, **op. cit.**, p. 111.

[5]John K. Stoner, **A Theology of Development: Beyond Relief and a Theology for Witness to the State** (unpubl. speech), 1977, p. 1.

[6]Hendrikus Berkhof, "The Church's Calling to Witness and to Serve," **The Christian Century** (Oct. 16, 1957), p. 1225.

[7]Visser't Hooft, **op. cit.**, p. 107.

[8]Sider, **op. cit.**, p. 4.

[9]**Ibid.**, pp. 3-6.

[10]Dyck, **op. cit.**, p. 273.

[11]Berkhof, **op. cit.**, p. 1225.

[12]Jacob J. Enz, "The Biblical Imperative for Mission," **Focus** V,2 (1976).

[13]Stoner, **op. cit.**, p. 7.

[14]Sider, **op. cit.**, p. 7.

[15]Jacob J. Enz, "The Biblical Imperative for Discipleship," **Mennonite Life,** XIII (Jan. 1958), pp. 3ff.

[16]E. Yamauchi, "How the Early Church Responded to Social Problems," **CT** (Nov. 1972), pp. 6ff.

[17]Stoner, **op. cit.**, p. 2.

[18]Berkhof, **op. cit.**, p. 1226.

[19]Stoner, **op. cit.**, p. 3.

[20]Visser't Hooft, **op. cit.**, p. 108.

[21]Leighton Ford, **The Church and Evangelism in a Day of Revolution** (U.S. Congress on Evangelism, 1968).

[22]Enz, **op. cit.**, p. 11.

[23]H.S. Bender, quoted by Dyck, **op. cit.**, p. 272.

[24]J. Newbigin, quoted by Dyck, **Ibid.**

[25]Quoted by Dyck, **op. cit.**, p. 272.

[26]Visser't Hooft, **op. cit.**, pp. 110-111.

[27]Quoted by Dyck, **op. cit.**, p. 268.

[28]**Ibid.**, p. 271.

[29]Frank C. Peters, "The Faith that Works," **Mennonite Central Committee News Service** (May, 1966).

[30]Robert Kreider from a personal letter, Nov. 29, 1977.

[31]Ford, **op. cit.**, p. 7.

CHRISTIAN LIFE-STYLE, E. Wiens, p. 303

[1]Quoted in E. F. Schumacher, **Small is Beautiful: Economics as if People Mattered** (London: Abacus, 1974), p. 19.

[2]Donella Meadows, **The Limits of Growth: A Report for the Club of Rome's Project on the Predicament of Mankind** (New York: Universe, 1972).

[3]Quotations are from **The New English Bible** (Oxford and Cambridge: Oxford and Cambridge University, 1961).

[4]Ronald J. Sider, **Rich Christians in an Age of Hunger: A Biblical Study** (Downers Grove: Inter-Varsity, 1977).

[5]Calvin Redekop, **The Free Church and Seductive Culture** (Scottdale: Herald, 1970), p. 114.

[6]Dave and Neta Jackson, **Living Together in a World Falling Apart** (Carol Stream: Creation House, 1974).

FOR FURTHER READING:

Gish, Arthur G., **Beyond the Rat Race** (Scottdale: Herald, 1973).

Heilbroner, Robert L., **An Inquiry into the Human Prospect** (New York: Norton, 1974).

Hostetler, John A., **Amish Society**, rev. ed. (Baltimore: John Hopkins University, 1968).

Huntington, Gertrude E., **The Hutterites in North America** (New York: Holt, Rinehart & Winston, 1967).

THE PROBLEM OF JUSTICE, C.G. Brunk, p. 313

[1]For a good summary of the record of the Believers' Churches in social service, see Donald Durnbaugh, **The Believers' Church: The History and Character of Radical Protestantism** (Toronto: Collier-Macmillan, 1968), Chpt. xi.

[2]Ernst Troeltsch, **The Social Teaching of the Christian Gospel**, I (New York: Harper, 1960), pp. 331ff.; Vol. II, pp. 993ff.

[3]As the early Anabaptists held; see the Schleitheim Confession in J.H. Yoder, ed., **The Legacy of Michael Sattler** (Scottdale: Herald, 1973), p. 39.

[4]Richard Shaull, "President Carter as Baptist Leader," **Sojourners**, 7 (Jan., 1978), p. 12.

[5]Ibid., p. 14.

[6]These are some of the elements of peacemaking identified and articulated by Adam Curle in his book **Making Peace** (London: Tavistock, 1971). The model of peacemaking as involving research, education, confrontation, conciliation, bargaining and development activities was clearly influential in the formulation of the MCS proposal.

[7]This is the difficulty I see in the recent attempts of the Mennonite theologian John Howard Yoder to reinterpret the political implications of the gospel. In his book **The Politics of Jesus** (Grand Rapids: Eerdmans, 1972) Yoder has made a significant contribution towards the understanding of the political relevance of agape which calls into serious question traditional sectarian views. However, this book, as well as an earlier one entitled **The Christian Witness to the State** (Newton: Faith & Life, 1964), still basically holds to the negative definition of justice espoused by Niebuhr. As the earlier book especially shows, Yoder believes that the agape witness acts as a negative constraint on the ideal of justice which tends always towards too easy compromise with evil. The implication of this view is that love makes justice unnecessary. The view I am espousing is that love requires the highest conformity with the demands of justice.

BAPTISTS AND PEACE, P.R. Dekar, p. 325

[1]Miriam Therese Winter, "Peace upon Earth," **Gold, Incense and Myrrh, Twelve Contemporary Christmas Carols**; John XXIII, **Pacem in Terris**, Encyclical Letter (Apr. 11, 1963).

[2]C.F. Evans, "Peace," **A Theological Word Book of the Bible**; E.M. Good, "Peace in the O.T." **IDB**; C.L. Mitton, "Peace in the N.T." **IDB**.

[3]Dale W. Brown, "Peace and the Peace Churches," **Christian Century** (Mar. 15, 1978), pp. 266-270.

[4]Donald F. Durnbaugh, **The Believers' Church: The History and Character of Radical Protestantism** (London: Collier-Macmillan, 1968), p. 254.

[5]Gerald O. Pederson, ed., **Peace—On Not Leaving it to the Pacifists** (Philadelphia: Fortress, 1975); for an excellent theological introduction, John Macquarrie, **The Concept of Peace: The Firth Lectures, 1972** (London: SCM, 1973).

[6]Winthrop S. Hudson, "Baptists Were Not Anabaptists," **Chronicle** 16 (Oct., 1953), pp. 171-179; Ernest A. Payne, "Contacts Between Mennonites and Baptists," **Fdt.** IV (Jan., 1961), pp. 38-55.

[7]William L. Lumpkin, **Baptist Confessions of Faith**, rev. ed. (Valley Forge: Judson, 1969), p. 140.

[8]Ibid.

[9]Thomas Helwys, **A Short Declaration of the Mistery of Iniquity** (1612; facsimile ed., London: Kingsgate, 1935). A convenient discussion is in Robert G. Torbet, **A History of the Baptists**, rev. ed., seventh printing (Valley Forge: Judson, 1969), pp. 33-57. Also, Robert Barclay, **The Inner Life of the Religious Societies of the Commonwealth**, 3rd ed. (London: Hodder & Stoughton, 1879), p. 73.

[10]Lumpkin, **op. cit.**, p. 233.

[11]Barclay, **op. cit.**, pp. 254-55, 295 et passim, notes that while George Fox preached at some Baptist gatherings in the early 1640s, and that Baptists were "tender then," Fox could not join them. When they became, in Barclay's words, "Baptists and Independent priests" and the rift deepened, Fox felt a sharp sense of betrayal, as several references in his **Journal** attest. For a background see B.S. Capp, **The Fifth Monarchy Men** (London: Faber, 1972); Craig W. Horle, "Quakers and Baptists 1647-1660," **B.Q.** XXVI (Oct., 1976), pp. 344-362; W. Stanford Reid, "The Battle Hymns of the Lord: Calvinist Psalmody of the Sixteenth Century," Carl S. Meyer, ed., **Sixteenth Century Essays and Studies**, II (Saint Louis: Foundation for Reformation Research, 1971); Peter Toon, ed., **Puritans, The Millennium and the Future of Israel** (Cambridge: James Clarke, 1970); B.R. White, "John Pendarves, the Calvinistic Baptists and the Fifth Monarchy," **B.Q.** XXV (Apr., 1974), pp. 251-271.

[12]John Bunyan, **The Holy War Made by Shaddai upon Diabolus for the Regaining of the Metropolis of the World, or, the Losing and Taking again of the Town of Mansoul**, James F. Forrest, ed. (n. p.: Copp Clark, 1967), pp. 284-85.

[13]Edmund S. Morgan, **Roger Williams: The Church and the State** (New York: Harcourt, Brace & World, 1967), esp. pp. 120-26.

[14]Bryant R. Nobles, Jr., "John Clarke's Political Theory," **Fdt.** XIII (1970), pp. 221-36; George Selement, "John Clarke and the Struggle for Separation of Church and State," **Fdt.** XV (1972), pp. 111-25.

[15]**Maritime Baptist**, Feb. 18, 1942, p. 4; cf. Torbet, p. 500.

[16]A. H. Newman, "Sketch of the Baptists of Ontario and Quebec to 1851," 45th **Baptist Yearbook**, 1900, p. 73; Gordon Stewart and George Rawlyk, **A People Highly Favoured of God: The Nova Scotia Yankees and the American Revolution** (Toronto: Macmillan, 1972), p. 187.

[17]"Peace and War," **CB**, Feb. 13, 1893, p. 104.

[18]"The End of the War," **CB**, June 5, 1902, p. 294.

[19]"The Peace Congress," **CB**, May 11, 1899, p. 8.

[20]Richard Allen, **The Social Passion: Religion and Social Reform in Canada 1914-28** (Toronto: University of Toronto, 1973), p. 1. See also his **The Social Gospel in Canada: Papers of the Interdisciplinary Conference on the Social Gospel in Canada, Mar. 21-24, 1973 at the University of Regina** (Ottawa: National Museums, 1975; Murray Meldrum, "An Examination of the Emergence of a Social Consciousness within the Baptist Denomination from 1890 to 1914," (Honours Thesis, York University, 1973).

[21]Walter E. Ellis, "Gilboa to Ichabod. Social and Religious Factors in the Fundamentalist-Modernist Schisms among Canadian Baptists, 1895-1934," **Fdt.** XX (1977), p. 109; cf. F.W. Waters, "Memorial Institute," Baptist Archives, McMaster Divinity College (1962).

[22]Charles M. Johnston, **McMaster University, I: The Toronto Years** (Toronto: University of Toronto, 1976), p. 129.

[23]**CB** (Aug. 13, 1908), p. 1; **CB** (May 29, 1913), p. 1.

[24]Meldrum, **op. cit.**, p. 61.

[25]Steven R. Ramlochan, "The Baptists of Ontario and World War I," (Graduate Paper, McMaster University, 1973), p. 12. For this and subsequent discussion a number of sources have been consulted, including periodicals, the yearbooks of the Atlantic, Ontario-Quebec and Western conventions, biographical files and correspondence available at the Baptist Archives, McMaster Divinity College, including a letter from J.G. Brown to Acting Minister of Militia A.E. Kemp, Apr. 4, 1916. Also, Allen, pp. 35-62; Carl Berger, **The Sense of Power: Studies in the Ideas of Canadian Imperialism 1867-1914** (Toronto: University of Toronto, 1970); J.M. Bliss, "The Methodist Church and World War I," **Canadian Historical Review 49** (Sept., 1968), pp. 213-33; Johnston, **op. cit.**, 128-49.

[26]Charles Thompson Sinclair Faulkner, "For Christian Civilization: The Churches and Canada's War Effort, 1939-1942," (Ph.D. dissertation, University of Chicago, 1975), p. 143; I am indebted to Sinclair-Faulkner for making this study available to me along with his seminar paper, "Uncertain Trumpets: The United Church of Canada and the Second World War."

[27]"Conscience vs. Citizenship," **CB** (July 9, 1931), p. 7; Anson Phelps Stokes and Leo Pfeffer, **Church and State in the United States**, rev. ed. (New York: Harper & Row, 1964), pp. 117-18, 475-76. See especially his **God in a World at War** (London: George Allen & Unwin, 1918) and **Social Religion** (New York: Scribner's, 1939).

[28]Faulkner, "For Christian Civilization," pp. 42-44, 156.

SOCIAL CONCERNS, T.R. Hobbs, p. 333

[1]Quoted in W.L. Lumpkin, **Baptist Confessions of Faith** (Valley Forge: Judson, 1969), p. 21.

[2]The quotation is from the English Baptist "Propositions and Conclusions" (1612), article 84. See Lumpkin, **op. cit.**, p. 139. This attitude to the civil authorities tends to persist throughout these early confessions.

[3]"Confessions of the Thirty Congregations," Lumpkin, **op. cit.**, p. 185.

[4]**Ibid.**, pp. 97ff.

[5]**Ibid.**, pp. 114ff.

[6]**Ibid.**, p. 139. See also J.D. Hughey, "Baptists and Religious Freedom," **B.Q.** XVII (1957-1958), pp. 249-255. A recent Baptist position on the subject is found in T.W. Lorenzen, "Die theologische Basis der Religionsfreiheit," **Theologische Zeitschrift 33** (1977), pp. 226-242. For a very general survey cf. D.F. Durnbaugh, **The Believers' Church** (New York: Macmillan, 1968), pp. 249ff.

[7]Thomas Helwys, **The Mistery of Iniquity** [1612] (London: Baptist Historical Society — Kingsgate, 1935), p. 46.

[8]A most helpful summary of the position of the Baptist World Alliance (representing almost 30,000,000 Baptists) on the issue of religious liberty is found in E. Ruden, "A Written Review of the Commission on Religious Liberty and Human Rights" (Paper distributed by the Baptist World Alliance July 1973).

[9]On what follows cf. W.G. Pitman, "Baptist Triumph in Nineteenth Century Canada," **Fdt.** III (1960), pp. 157-165; "The Baptists and Public Affairs in the Province of Canada, 1840-1867" (Unpublished MA Thesis University of Toronto 1956).

[10]Pitman, "Baptists and Public Affairs," p. 58.

[11]Pitman, "Baptism Triumph in Nineteenth Century Canada," p. 161.

[12]**Ibid.**, p. 163.

[13]Cf. K.R.M. Short, "English Baptists and American Slavery," **B.Q.** XX (1963-1964), pp. 243-262.

[14]Cf. P. Wright, **Knibb the Notorious Missionary** (London: Sidgwick & Jackson, 1973), p. 31.

[15]Knibb was sent to Jamaica as a teacher and a replacement for his deceased brother. Although he lacked formal training, he was for a time the pastor of the Falmouth Baptist congregation.

[16]Following the abolition of slavery in 1833, Knibb fought the "apprenticeship" system by which blacks were hired as labour for minimal wages. He later campaigned for the rights of the white immigrants to the island.

[17]From an early letter home, quoted in Wright, **Knibb**, p. 42.

[18]A revealing testimony from Rauschenbusch dealing with his transition into the "social gospel" was published in the **Rochester Democrat and Chronicle** (Jan. 25, 1913), and is repeated in the introduction to **The Righteousness of the Kingdom** (Nashville: Abingdon, 1968), pp. 16-17.

[19]Cf. Durnbaugh, **op. cit.**, pp. 13f. However, see M. Stackhouse, "The Continuing Importance of Walter Rauschenbusch," in **The Righteousness of the Kingdom**, pp. 13-59; especially pp. 21ff., who argues for both the catholic and sectarian influence on Rauschenbusch.

[20]Cf. "The Practice of Religion," in **The Righteousness of the Kingdom**, pp. 264ff.

[21]How much Rauschenbusch was consciously dependent upon the works of Wellhausen on the religion and history of Israel is not documented. However, the similarities between the high regard of both for the primitive stage of religion, their love of the prophets and their denigration of certain characteristics of Judaism, are striking. The sources of Wellhausen's thought can be traced in part to the ideals of the Romantic movement. See L. Perlitt, **Vatke und Wellhausen** (Berlin: W. de Gruyter, 1968). **The Righteousness of the Kingdom** was an early manuscript of Rauschenbusch, although only recently published. In his **Theology for a Social Gospel** (New York: Macmillan, 1917), pp. 118ff., he favours an alternative to what he calls the "exaggerated individualism" of the Reformation.

[22]John Roach Straton, one-time pastor of Calvary Baptist Church, Brooklyn, is better known for his championing of fundamentalist issues during the theologically active days of the 1920s. However, he was also an astute social critic, whose statements on the reconstruction of society by the Gospel were hardly characteristic of his contemporaries. See H.H. Straton, "John Roach Straton, Prophet of Social Righteousness: Three Decades of Protestant Activism," **Fdt.** V (1962), pp. 16-38. See also J.R. Straton, **The Salvation of Society** (Baltimore: Fleet-McGinley, 1908). It was Straton's firm belief that the Kingdom

of God was to be established upon earth, and was not to be relegated to some uncertain, eschatological time.

[23]Lumpkin, **op. cit.**, p. 397.

[24]**Ibid.**, p. 406.

[25]J. Bright, **The Kingdom of God** (Nashville: Abingdon, 1955).

[26]N. Perrin, **The Kingdom of God in the Teaching of Jesus** (London: S.C.M., 1963).

[27]For a preliminary statement see T.R. Hobbs, "Theology and Social Ethics," **C.B.** (Dec., 1977), pp. 372-373.

CREATION AND DOMINION, W. Klaassen, p. 339

[1]Harold K. Schilling, "The Whole Earth is the Lord's," **Earth Might be Fair,** I.G. Barbour, ed. (Englewood Cliffs: Prentice-Hall, 1972), p. 102.

[2]Karl Barth, **Die Kirchliche Dogmatik, III Band, Die Lehre von der Schoepfung** I (Zurich: Evangelischer Verlag, 1945), Vorwort.

[3]De Chardin wrote a great deal and much of it has been translated into English and published posthumously. His major works are **The Phenomenon of Man, Le Milieu Divin, Man's Place in Nature, The Future of Man.**

[4]Schilling, **op. cit.**

[5]Loren Eiseley, **The Firmament of Time** (New York: Athenaeum, 1974), p. 11.

[6]William G. Pollard, "The Uniqueness of the Earth," in Barbour, **op. cit.**, p. 96.

[7]Lynn White, Jr., "The Historical Roots of Our Ecologic Crisis," P. Shepard & D. McKinley, ed., **The Subversive Science: Essays Towards an Ecology of Man** (Boston: Houghton Mifflin, 1969).

[8]See also Isaiah 33:7-9.

[9]Teilhard de Chardin, **Hymn of the Universe** (New York: Collins Fontana, 1971), p. 23.

RESOURCE EXPLOITATION, D.B. McLay, p. 349

[1]Rachel Carson, **Silent Spring** (New York: Houghton Mifflin, 1962).

[2]Francis A. Schaeffer, **Pollution and the Death of Man: The Christian View of Ecology** (Wheaton: Tyndale, 1970).

[3]Hugh Montefiore, **Can Man Survive?** (London: Collins, 1970).

[4]David R. McLay & D. McCormack Smyth, "Christians and the Ecological Crisis," **C.B.** (Jan., 1975), pp. 10,11,29.

[5]Donella H. Meadows, **The Limits of Growth** (Washington: Potomac Assoc., 1972).

[6]David R. McLay, "Christians in a Technological Society," **C.B.** (Apr., 1970), pp. 17,18,31.

[7]Schaeffer, **op. cit.**

[8]Palmer C. Putnam, **Energy in the Future** (New York: Van Nostrand, 1953).

[9]George B. Lucas, Jr. & Thomas W. Ogletree, ed., **Lifeboat Ethics** (New York: Harper & Row, 1976).

[10]Science Council of Canada, Report No. 27, **Canada as a Conserver Society** (Ottawa: Science Council, 1977).

RESOURCE EXPLOITATION, G. Vandezande, p. 357

[1]James H. Olthuis, "The Word of God and Creation," Institute for Christian Studies, 229 College St., Toronto, Ontario, M5T 1R4.

[2]Thomas R. Berger, **Northern Frontier, Northern Homeland**, Report of the MacKenzie Valley Pipeline Inquiry I (Ottawa: Printing and Publ., 1977), p. 199.

[3]Barry Commoner, **The Poverty of Power, Energy and the Economic Crisis** (New York: Knopf, 1976).

[4]John Oltmans, ed., **On Growth: The Crisis of Exploding Population and Resource Depletion** (New York: Capricorn, 1974), p. 27.

[5]Notes from a speech given by Joe Clark, M.P., Leader of the Opposition, to the Canada-U.K. Chamber of Commerce (London, England, Sept. 21, 1976), as issued by his House of Commons office.

[6]Notes from a speech given by Pierre Elliott Trudeau, M.P., Prime Minister, at Duke University (Durham, North Carolina, May 12, 1974), as issued by his House of Commons office.

[7]Oltmans, **op. cit.**, p. 27. It is noteworthy that Harvey Wheeler, Senior Fellow at the Center for the Study of Democratic Institutions in Santa Barbara, believes that capitalism developed in the United States "in its most decisive and qualified form." According to this American liberal, capitalism has "stamped its image and ideals on almost every American institution," has "indulged in an unconscionable waste of resources" and has "turned America into a cultural wasteland characterized by profanation of almost everything that might ennoble human existence." Harvey Wheeler, **The Politics of Revolution** (Berkeley: Glendessary, 1971), p. 13ff. Interestingly enough, the Canadian socialist, Charles Taylor, Professor of Political Science at McGill University in Montreal, has pointed out that "if we are to build a society with radically different priorities, one which will not be driven by this mania of consumption, then we will have to evolve a different foundation for technological society, a quite different self-definition to serve as the basis of its cohesion." Laurier La Pierre, et al., **Essays on the Left: Essays in Honour of T.C. Douglas** (Toronto: McClelland & Stewart, 1971), p. 232ff.

[8]**Canada as a Conserver Society**, Science Council of Canada, Report No. 27, p. 55.

[9]**Ibid.**, p. 15.

[10]**Ibid.**, p. 14.

[11]**Ibid.**, p. 15.

[12]**An Energy Policy for Canada**, Phase 1, 1973, available from Minister of Energy, Mines and Resources, Commons, p. 29.

[13]Schumacher, E.F., **Small is Beautiful, A Study of Economics as if People Mattered** (New York: Harper & Row, 1973), p. 148.

[14]Bob Goudzwaard, **Aid for the Overdeveloped West** (Toronto: Wedge, 1975), p. 20ff.

Appendices

APPENDIX I

A MESSAGE TO CHRISTIANS AND CHURCHES IN CANADA

Assembled in Winnipeg in the Study Conference on the Believers' Church in Canada, May 15-18, 1978, we affirm our common Free Church heritage:

1. The Lordship of Christ to be expressed in personal and congregational Christian life, and to be witnessed to as God's sovereign claim upon societies and nations.

2. The authority of the Word of God as revealed in the scriptures of the Old and New Testaments, over all church traditions and individual interpretations.

3. The concept of the gathered church as a voluntary fellowship of baptized believers, as a community committed to a life of sharing, mutual support and discipline.

4. The calling of all church members to their respective ministries in the church and in the world.

5. The right of religious liberty and dissent for all.

6. Equal human rights for all persons as creatures of the one God, Maker of the universe.

7. The freedom of the church and its members to bear unhindered witness by word and deed to the gospel of Jesus Christ at home and abroad.

We confess that in our generation, our respective churches and we ourselves have not always followed Christ in clear witness, consistent life-style and sacrificial service. We repent of our disobedience.

Conscious of the urgent needs in Canada and in the whole world, we call upon fellow Christians to join with us in commitment:

1. To seek together a clearer understanding of God's truth;

2. To obey His will more fully;

3. To pray for the renewal of our churches by the power of His Holy Spirit;

4. To share more effectively in His mission, to the greater glory of Jesus Christ, the only Saviour and Lord.

APPENDIX II

RESOLUTION OF APPRECIATION

As participants in the Study Conference on the Believers' Church in Canada, we express our appreciation to the Mennonite Central Committee (Daniel Zehr and his staff), to the Baptist Federation of

Canada (R.F. Bullen and his staff), and the steering committee chaired by J.K. Zeman for the efficient preparation and administration of the conference; to the Canadian Mennonite Bible College and the Mennonite Brethren Bible College, and to their respective presidents, faculties and staff for serving as hosts for the conference; to the congregation of the Portage Avenue Mennonite Brethren Church, the Mennonite Children's Choir and the choir of Broadway First Baptist Church for joining the conference fellowship at the public rallies; to the many speakers; to Lydia Penner, Larry Kehler, C. Alvin Armstrong and George E. Simpson for their services in the conference press room, and to all persons who have shared in the planning and programme of the conference.

APPENDIX III

CANADIAN TASK FORCE
ON BELIEVERS' CHURCH WITNESS

As participants in the Study Conference on the Believers' Church in Canada, meeting in Winnipeg, May 15-18, 1978, we record our hope and desire for further opportunities for fellowship and discussion among representatives of the various Believers' Church traditions in Canada. With no intent of furthering new inter-church structures, we endorse the appointment of a Task Force on Believers' Church Witness in Canada to continue the interest which has been engendered at this study conference. It is recommended that the Task Force be composed of a representative named by each of the following: the Mennonites, the Pentecostal Assemblies of Canada and the Baptist Federation of Canada, with power to add.

APPENDIX IV

SEMINAR TOPICS

Two papers and two prepared responses were presented in each of the twelve seminars.

A. SEMINARS ON THE BELIEVERS' CHURCH IN
   CONGREGATIONAL CONTEXT

1. Biblical authority and denominational traditions
   Papers: Clark H. Pinnock
                 David Schroeder
   Responses: William Klassen
                 Stuart E. Murray

2. Discipline and discernment
   Papers: Marlin Jeschke
               J. Ernest Runions
   Responses: Donald W. Bastian
               Glenn Brubacher

3. Evangelism: Christian initiation and nurture
   Papers: H.J. Gerbrandt
               Eugene M. Thompson
   Responses: Henry Brucks
               Archibald R. Goldie

4. Worship and spiritual gifts
   Papers: Harold L. Mitton
               John Rempel
   Responses: J. Harry Faught
               Arthur G. Patzia

B. SEMINARS ON THE BELIEVERS' CHURCH IN THE
   CANADIAN CONTEXT

5. Church growth in the Believers' Church perspective
   Papers: Phillip Collins
               Dennis M. Oliver
   Responses: Vern G. Middleton
               Robert Orr

6. Church and state in Canada: Co-operation and confrontation
   Papers: John H. Redekop
               Harry A. Renfree
   Responses: Walter Dinsdale
               Alvin Gamble

7. Divisive and unitive forces in the Believers' Church tradition
   in Canada
   Papers: Walter E. Ellis
               Rodney J. Sawatsky
   Responses: William R. Eichhorst
               William R. Wood

8. The Believers' Church and public schools in Canada
   Papers: Kenneth R. Davis
               Peter H. Peters
   Responses: Neil G. Price
               Robert Wilson

C. SEMINARS ON THE BELIEVERS' CHURCH IN THE
   GLOBAL CONTEXT

9. Global mission: Word and deed
   Papers: Newton L. Gingrich
               John F. Keith

Responses: R.J. Graham
                     Russell D. Legge

10. Christian lifestyle in an affluent society
    Papers: Bruce W. Neal
                     Erwin Wiens
    Responses: Henry Poettcker
                     William A. Sturgess

11. Peace and social concerns
    Papers: Conrad G. Brunk
                     Paul M. Dekar & T. Raymond Hobbs
    Responses: Alfred C. Bell
                     Larry Kehler

12. Responsibility for world resources: Creation
    and ecology
    Papers: Walter Klaassen
                     David B. McLay
    Responses: Gerald Vandezande
                     William Ward

APPENDIX V

PROGRAMME LEADERS

BASTIAN, DONALD W., Bishop, Free Methodist Church in Canada, 3
    Harrowby Ct., Islington, Ont. M9B 3H3
BELL, ALFRED G., Chaplain, Stony Mountain Penitentiary, Box 169,
    Stony Mountain, Man. R0C 3A0
BELL, ROY D., Pastor, First Baptist Church, 969 Burrard St.,
    Vancouver, B.C. V6Z 1Y1; President, The Baptist Federation of
    Canada
BRUBACHER, GLENN, Pastor, First Mennonite Church, 96
    Homewood Ave., Kitchener, Ont.
BRUCKS, HENRY, Executive Secretary of the Board of Evangelism of
    the Canadian Conference of the Mennonite Brethren Churches, 75
    Carmen St., Winnipeg, Man.
BRUNK, CONRAD G., Professor, Conrad Grebel College, Waterloo,
    Ont. N2L 3G6
BULLEN, R. FRED, General Secretary, The Baptist Federation of
    Canada, Box 1298, Brantford, Ont. N3T 5T6
COLLINS, PHILIP, Area Minister for B.C., The Baptist Union of
    Western Canada, 8411 Rosebank Cres., Richmond, B.C. V7A 2K8
DAVIS, KENNETH R., Professor, Dept. of History, University of
    Waterloo, Waterloo, Ont. N2L 3G1
DEKAR, PAUL M., Professor, McMaster Divinity College, Hamilton,
    Ont. L8S 4K1

*DINSDALE, WALTER, The Hon., M.P. (Brandon), The House of Commons, Ottawa

DYCK, CORNELIUS J., Professor, Mennonite Biblical Seminary, 3003 Benham Ave., Elkhart, IN 46514

EICHHORST, WILLIAM R., Professor, Winnipeg Bible College and Theological Seminary, Otterburne, Man. R0A 1G0

ELLIS, WALTER E., Pastor, First Baptist Church, 902 Market St., Tacoma, WA 98402

EWERT, DAVID, Professor, Mennonite Brethren Biblical Seminary, 4824 South Butler, Fresno, CA 93727

*FAUGHT, J. HARRY, Pastor, Capitol Hill Pentecostal Church, 1706-20 Ave. N.W., Calgary, Alta. T2M 1H1

GAMBLE, ALVIN, 1097 Bronson Ave., Ottawa, Ont. K1S 4H2

GERBRANDT, H.J., General Secretary of the Conference of Mennonites in Canada, 600 Shaftesbury Blvd., Winnipeg, Man. R3P 0M4

GINGRICH, NEWTON L., Pastor, Chairman, Mennonite Central Committee, 21 Henry Vogt Ave., Tavistock, Ont. N0B 2R0

GOLDIE, ARCHIBALD R., Secretary, Dept. of Canadian Missions, Baptist Convention of Ontario and Quebec, 217 St. George St., Toronto, Ont. M5R 2M2

*GRAHAM, R.J., Professor, Northwest Baptist Theological College and Seminary, 3358 S.E. Marine Dr., Vancouver, B.C. V5S 2H6

HOBBS, T. RAYMOND, Professor, McMaster Divinity College, Hamilton, Ont. L8S 4K1

JESCHKE, MARLIN, Professor, Goshen College, Goshen, IN 46526

KEHLER, LARRY, Pastor, Charleswood Mennonite Church, 699 Haney Ave., Winnipeg R3R 0Y7

KEITH, JOHN F., General Secretary, Canadian Baptist Overseas Mission Board, 217 St. George St., Toronto, Ont. M5R 2M2

KLAASSEN, WALTER, Professor, Conrad Grebel College, Waterloo, Ont. N2L 3G6

KLASSEN, WILLIAM, Professor, Dept. of Religion, The University of Manitoba, Winnipeg, Man. R3T 2N2

KRAHN, HENRY G., President, Mennonite Brethren Bible College, 77 Henderson Hwy., Winnipeg, Man. R2L 1L1

LEGGE, RUSSELL D., Professor, Dept. of Religious Studies, University of Waterloo, Waterloo, Ont. N2L 3G1

LITTELL, FRANKLIN H., Professor, Dept. of Religion, Temple University, Philadelphia, PA 19122

McLAY, DAVID B., Professor, Queen's University, 97 Beverley St., Kingston, Ont. K7L 3Y7

MIDDLETON, VERN G., Professor, Northwest Baptist Theological College and Seminary, 3358 S.E. Marine Dr., Vancouver, B.C. V5S 2H6

MIKOLASKI, SAMUEL J., Professor, 1112 S. First Ave., Sioux Falls, SD 57105; formerly President, Columbia Bible Institute, Clearbrook, B.C.

MITTON, HAROLD L., Principal, Acadia Divinity College, Wolfville, N.S. B0P 1X0

MURRAY, STUART E., President, Atlantic Baptist College, P.O. Box 1004, Moncton, N.B. E1C 8P4

NEAL, BRUCE W., Pastor, Walmer Road Baptist Church, 188 Lowther Ave., Toronto, Ont. M5R 1E8

OLIVER, DENNIS M., Director, The Canadian Church Growth Centre, Canadian Theological College, 4404-4th Ave., Regina, Sask. S4T 0H8

ORR, ROBERT, Pastor, Ness Ave. Baptist Church, 2700 Ness Ave., Winnipeg, Man. R3J 1A7

PATZIA, ARTHUR G., Pastor, Ebenezer Baptist Church, 6858 Fraser St., Vancouver, B.C. V5X 3V1; formerly Professor, North American Baptist Seminary, Sioux Falls, SD

PETERS, FRANK C., President, Wilfrid Laurier University, Waterloo, Ont. N2L 3C5

PETERS, PETER H., Principal, Mennonite Brethren Collegiate Institute, 173 Talbot Ave., Winnipeg, Man. R2L 0P6

PINNOCK, CLARK H., Professor, McMaster Divinity College, Hamilton, Ont. L8S 4K1

POETTCKER, HENRY, President, Canadian Mennonite Bible College, 600 Shaftesbury Blvd., Winnipeg, Man. R3P 0M4; President-Elect, Mennonite Biblical Seminary, Elkhart, IN

PRICE, NEIL G., Pastor, Wolfville Baptist Church, Wolfville, N.S. B0P 1X0

REDEKOP, JOHN H., Professor, Dept. of Political Science, Wilfrid Laurier University, Waterloo, Ont. N2L 3C5

REMPEL, JOHN, Chaplain and Lecturer, Conrad Grebel College, Waterloo, Ont. N2L 3G6

RENFREE, HARRY A., Executive Minister, The Baptist Union of Western Canada, 4404-16th St. S.W., Calgary, Alta. T2T 4H9

RUNIONS, J. ERNEST, Principal, Carey Hall, 5920 Iona Dr., Vancouver, B.C. V6T 1J6

SAWATSKY, RODNEY J., Professor, Conrad Grebel College, Waterloo, Ont. N2L 3G6

SCHROEDER, DAVID, Professor, Canadian Mennonite Bible College, 600 Shaftesbury Blvd., Winnipeg, Man. R3P 0M4

STURGESS, WILLIAM A., Pastor, Broadway-First Baptist Church, 790 Honeyman Ave., Winnipeg, Man. R3G 0Y1

THOMPSON, EUGENE M., Area Minister for Western Nova Scotia, United Baptist Convention of the Atlantic Provinces, Box 1152, Middleton, N.S. B0S 1P0

VANDEZANDE, GERALD, Executive Director, Committee for Justice and Liberty Foundation, 229 College St., Toronto, Ont. M5T 1R4

WARD, WILLIAM, Director, Environmental Management Division, Province of Manitoba, 149 River Oaks Dr., Winnipeg, Man. R3J 1R2

WIENS, ERWIN, Executive Director, Mennonite Central Committee (Ontario), 50 Kent Ave., Kitchener, Ont. N2G 3R1

WILSON, ROBERT, Professor, Atlantic Baptist College, P.O. Box 1004, Moncton, N.B. E1C 8P4

WOOD, WILLIAM R., Pastor, First Baptist Church, 401-4th Ave. N., Saskatoon, Sask. S7K 2M4

YODER, JOHN HOWARD, Professor, Goshen Biblical Seminary, 3003 Benham Ave., Elkhart, IN 46514

ZEHR, DANIEL, Director of Peace and Social Concerns, Mennonite Central Committee (Canada), 1483 Pembina Hwy., Winnipeg, Man. R3T 2C8

ZEMAN, JAROLD K., Professor, Acadia Divinity College, Wolfville, N.S. B0P 1X0

* unable to attend in person

NOTE: The names of seminar chairmen and secretaries, and of the respondents in plenary sessions are not included.

APPENDIX VI

FOR FURTHER READING

1. Believers' Church Conferences

Proceedings of the Study Conference on Believers' Church held at Mennonite Biblical Seminary, Chicago, August 23-25, 1955 (Newton: General Conference Mennonite Church, 1955).

The Concept of the Believers' Church: Addresses from the 1967 Louisville Conference. ed. James Leo Garrett, Jr. (Scottdale: Herald, 1969).

The Chicago Theological Seminary Register, LX, No. 6, September 1970. Five papers and the Findings Committee Report from the Believers' Church Conference held at the Chicago Theological Seminary, June 29 - July 2, 1970.

Journal of the American Academy of Religion, XLIV, No. 1, March 1976. Eight papers presented at the Conference on Restitution, Dissent and Renewal held at Pepperdine University, Malibu, California, June 5-8, 1975.

2. Other Publications on Related Topics

Bender, Ross Thomas. **The People of God: A Mennonite Interpretation of the Free Church Tradition** (Scottdale: Herald, 1971).

Durnbaugh, Donald F. **The Believers' Church** (New York: Macmillan, 1968). [the basic book on the subject]

Dyck, Cornelius J., ed. An Introduction to Mennonite History (Scottdale: Herald, 1967).

Epp, Frank H. Mennonites in Canada, 1786-1920: The History of a Separate People (Toronto: Macmillan, 1974).

Estep, William R. The Anabaptist Story (Grand Rapids: Eerdmans, 1975).

Klaassen, Walter. Anabaptism: Neither Catholic nor Protestant (Waterloo: Conrad, 1973).

Littell, Franklin H. The Origins of Sectarian Protestantism (New York: Macmillan, 1964).

Olson, Arnold T. Believers Only (Minneapolis: Free Church Publications, 1964).

Payne, Ernest A. The Free Church Tradition in the Life of England (London: SCM, 1944).

Redekop, Calvin. The Free Church and Seductive Culture (Scottdale: Herald, 1970).

Tarr, Leslie K. This Dominion - His Dominion (Toronto: Fellowship of Evangelical Baptist Churches, 1968).

Watt, J.H. The Fellowship Story (Toronto: Fellowship of Evangelical Baptist Churches, 1978).

Westin, Gunnar. The Free Church Through the Ages. tr. Virgil A. Olson (Nashville: Broadman, 1958).

White, B.R. The English Separatist Tradition (London: Oxford University, 1971).

Williams, George H. The Radical Reformation (Philadelphia: Westminster, 1962).

Woolley, David Collier, ed. Baptist Advance: The Achievements of the Baptists of North America for a Century and a Half (Nashville: Broadman, 1964).

Yoder, John Howard. The Politics of Jesus (Grand Rapids: Eerdmans, 1972).

Zeman, J.K. Baptist Roots and Identity (Toronto: Baptist Convention of Ontario and Quebec, 1978).

Zeman, J.K., ed. Baptists in Canada, 1760-1980 (Papers from a symposium, to be published in 1980).

NOTE. See also the bibliography in Garrett's book listed in section (1) above.